THE UNIVERSITY ...
W...

With Nature

D1556693

With Nature
Nature Philosophy as Poetics through Schelling, Heidegger, Benjamin and Nancy

Warwick Mules

intellect Bristol, UK / Chicago, USA

First published in the UK in 2014 by
Intellect, The Mill, Parnall Road, Fishponds, Bristol, BS16 3JG, UK

First published in the USA in 2014 by
Intellect, The University of Chicago Press, 1427 E. 60th Street,
Chicago, IL 60637, USA

A catalogue record for this book is available from the
British Library.

Cover designer: Stephanie Sarlos
Cover image photograph: Warwick Mules
Production manager: Tim Mitchell
Copy-editing: MPS Technologies
Typesetting: Contentra Technologies

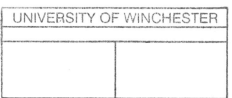

Print ISBN: 978-1-84150-573-2
ePDF ISBN: 978-1-78320-291-1
ePub ISBN: 978-1-78320-292-8

Printed and bound by Hobbs, UK

To Helen

Contents

Preface

The fundamental threat facing humans today is our inability to live in a non-exploitative relation to the natural world. Our environments are currently unsustainable and nature has become absorbed into a simulated world of technological process. But the threat conceals a profound difficulty: the inability to think about our relation to nature other than in terms of technologically produced 'nature' already present to us as something self-evident; something waiting there for us to exploit, enjoy, manage and protect. Nature 'for us' is our nature, the nature we possess according to subjective needs, wants and desires. However, the technologies employed to conquer the earth are now so thoroughly entwined in our way of life, we risk becoming enslaved by them. In seeking to find a more sustainable, less exploitative way of living with nature, we risk becoming further entwined in our own *techne* – our 'way of being' through making and producing things – unable to think outside it. One answer is to find a counter-*techne* that leads us out of our current relation with technologically produced nature such that we can think otherwise. This book is a response to the challenge to think of the human-nature relation 'otherwise', to set us on another path, another way of being with nature.

The book undertakes this task by opening up a line of critical thinking beginning with the Enlightenment philosopher Immanuel Kant's critique of reason, exposing a gap in reason subsequently addressed by post-Kantian philosophy as a means of grounding thought in the movement of nature itself (*poiesis*). In particular, I examine the work of the German Idealist philosopher Friedrich Schelling whose nature philosophy sets the scene for thinking with nature within the limits of critique. By following Schelling's insights through to more recent attempts to ground thought in *poiesis* (Heidegger, Benjamin, Nancy), my aim is to think with nature without surrendering the rigour of critique.

Thinking with nature exposes technology to its own limits and reveals a counter-*techne* turning otherwise within it. A name for this counter-*techne* is art. The work of the artwork is to open technology to possibilities unthinkable from the technology itself. Thinking with nature is to think from the stance taken by the artwork both with and against technology so that it is turned otherwise, leading to the uncertain ground of a radical openness. Standing on this uncertain ground allows us to rethink the human-nature relation in the hope of another way of being with nature. By following the turning of art out of technology, we may be able to see another, more just, non-exploitative way of being with nature.

Acknowledgements

I would like to acknowledge a number of people who have helped and encouraged me in my endeavours with this book. In particular I would like to express my gratitude to Helen Miller for her constant support, ideas and suggestions throughout the writing of the book. I would also like to thank Rod Giblett for his encouragement as well as the challenge his own work set for me in developing the argument of this book, and Tony Thwaites for helping me gain a better grasp of how to think the 'that' of things. Others who have helped in my journey with this book include David Baker in our conversations about the philosophy of science, Grayson Cooke and Phil Roe for many discussions related to theory and visual arts, Nick Mansfield and Nicole Anderson for our lively discussions on Derrida and Heidegger. I would also like to thank Colin Shingleton who generously shared his thoughts on Heidegger and Schelling with me. I am also grateful for the support and collegiality of many others, including Emily Potter, Stuart Cooke, Joseph Carew, Gene Flenady, Jane Stadler, Gabriella Blasi, Martin Rice, George Petelin, Elizabeth Stephens, Greg Hainge, John Ryan, Juha Tolonen and Carole Mules.

Sections of Chapter 7 of this book were published in 'Heidegger, Nature Philosophy and Art as Poietic Event' in *Transformations*, no. 21, 2012.

Introduction

Wanted – A Nature Philosophy

I

The title of this book *With Nature* signifies a hope that critical thinking in the humanities and arts can retain its long-forgotten connection with nature. Today, speaking and writing about nature requires a detour through the subject who speaks, so that nature is pushed to the background as something other, while the speaking itself takes centre stage as the outward sign of a reflection designed to gain knowledge of nature: to gaze upon it, control it and live in it, or even to say that it does not exist. Nature becomes 'other' to its rationalization in the saying. This book confronts the limits of this saying, and opens it to other ways in which nature might be said. My aim is to retrace a way of saying the 'being with' of nature buried in the writings on nature by the German Idealist philosopher Friedrich Schelling and following through to the philosophy of Martin Heidegger, Walter Benjamin and Jean-Luc Nancy. Schelling's long-neglected nature philosophy (*Naturphilosophie*) provides a way of thinking that promises to think with nature, not against it. A critique that sets out to think with nature suspends the detour through the subject and draws nature back into the critique. The task of critique is then shifted from defining and defending the subject's right to speak about nature, towards thinking with nature as a possibility and what it might bring forth and enable.

The book counters a tendency in ecocritical writing to forget nature.[1] For instance, in his book *Ecology without Nature: Rethinking Environmental Aesthetics*, Timothy Morton argues that ecocritics should stop using the word 'nature': 'The main theme of the book is [...] that the very idea of "nature" which so many hold dear will have to wither away in an "ecological" state of human society. Strange as it may sound, the idea of nature is getting in the way of properly ecological forms of culture, philosophy, politics, and art' (Morton 2007, p. 1). What is Morton's point? He is saying that by invoking nature as an all-encompassing 'Thing over There that surrounds and sustains us' (p. 1), we are inventing an elusive phantom that always 'gives us the slip' (p. 2). This elusiveness of nature is something that happens in the literary writings about nature itself, which he then proposes to explore: '*Ecology without Nature* takes nature out of the equation by exploring the ways in which literary writing tries to conjure it up. We discover how nature always slips out of reach in the very act of grasping it' (p. 19). Nature is not an untouched domain 'in itself', but the other of nature writing itself. Morton's mode of critique is thus negative.[2] It produces nature as the negation of writing and the thinking subject in whose name such writing takes place. On this score, Morton's position falls in line with a conventional position in both the humanities and the sciences that, since Kant, limits critique to what it can know about what it critiques, and consequently negates what it critiques in coming to know about it.

In the humanities and science disciplines, nature is understood as the negation of the human. Nature is that which the human is not. As such, human thinking cannot be said to access nature directly, but only indirectly, either through representations or through special kinds of aesthetic experiences or apodictic intuitions. The consequences of this kind of saying of nature have been especially limiting for the arts and humanities, as it places them at a disadvantage with respect to the sciences in articulating accounts of nature. While the sciences develop positive representations of nature through the facility of apodictic truth supported by mathematical certainty, the arts and humanities confine themselves to self-reflections on nature forever running up against their own limits.

For the humanities, nature can only be addressed as a subjective construct or inner experience, and not as an objectively verifiable thing or event. Unlike the sciences, which secure knowledge of nature and natural things through methods of objectification and verification, the humanities employ ad hoc approaches and scholarly interpretations applied in localized sites and texts, producing speculative knowledge about the things of nature with no grip in the world of objective facts. Unlike scientific knowledge that universalizes from the particular, approaches of the arts and humanities tend to stay with the particular, revealing complexity and deep or thick meaning in specific works and practices. The positive side is that the arts and humanities are well capable of producing knowledge enriched by singular encounters with things. However, the negative side is that this enriched knowledge does not easily convert into positive facts in the way scientific knowledge does; it is not highly valued by institutions and bureaucracies who seek the certainty of scientific method, technical fact and economic validity. As a consequence, the humanities and arts tend to play a supplementary role to science and economics in producing facts about nature and the human relation to it. The arts and humanities are reduced to supporting scientific enquiry with knowledge gained indirectly, especially through the critique of nature in terms of subjectively defined aesthetic experience.[3]

It is not difficult to see that the reluctance of the humanities to engage with nature in any kind of positive way comes from the humanities disciplines themselves. The humanities place limits on themselves to secure critical and speculative knowledge about nature within the rigours of self-reflection. But the price paid is to disable any capacity to engage with nature positively. Nature is negated – pushed to the background or made to disappear behind a mirror of representation that reflects thought back onto itself in the quest to know. Critical enquiry becomes engrossed in analysing the frameworks of representation and the finite modes of subjectivity that produce nature as a meaningful construct or environment for the living subject. Positive knowledge of nature can only be had by way of the negative route of self-reflection; nature is never fully present to the knowing self but always receding or fading away. In its quest to know about nature and natural things, the knowing self constantly runs up against the limits of its own self-reflection. As Timothy Morton has said, nature always 'gives us the slip'.

Two questions immediately come to mind in response to this self-limitation. First, is it possible to think of nature positively within the western philosophical tradition without first having to go via this negative route? And, second, is it possible to think of this positivity without surrendering the rigours of critique? Is it possible to think of nature neither 'in itself' nor 'for us' but as a necessity of critique in its very *praxis*? This book is a response to these two questions. What, then, is a positive philosophy of nature? Instead of thinking of nature as the negation of the human, a positive philosophy begins with the fact that nature and the human are part of the same being. This being is neither nature nor human as they are currently understood, but something common to both yet exceeding them at the same time. In positive philosophy, nature and the human must be thought together as part of the same being, and not as two beings separated by an unbridgeable gap. Although separate beings, they nevertheless share something in common: the fact that they *are*. This fact is other to both nature and the human, constituting what Schelling calls the 'third potency' – the power to begin (Schelling 2000, p. 19).[4] Otherness is not assigned to nature as separate from human being, but to possibilities opened up in-between the human-nature relation itself, in the contingency of finite existence. I argue in this book that by adopting a positive philosophy of nature, the arts and humanities can encounter and challenge their own self-limitations, opening themselves to possibly new human-nature relations, and seizing back some of the ground ceded to the sciences in a renewed capacity to make positive claims about nature and the human relation to it.

In returning to Morton's suggestion that ecocriticism should stop using the word 'nature', I suggest that placing such a limit on critique simply makes nature come back into the critique in all sorts of unaccounted ways, and indeed, Morton's own book is a good example of this 'return of the repressed'; its pages contain numerous instances of the word 'nature', as well as lengthy arguments about nature as a construct of human discourse, thus smuggling nature back, in order to banish it yet again in repeated gestures of disavowal. This negative approach to nature, which reduces nature to nothing while elevating its constructedness by and for the human subject to a central place, reaffirms the anthropocentric view of nature – that nature is nothing but a projection of human meaning and value – and remains powerless to change the human relation to nature as such. Instead, my aim is to seek an *ecological* account of the human-nature relation that places the relation itself *en abyme*, at the very edge of critique. Here, nature can be encountered in its already negated state as the beginning of another possibility, another way of being with nature.

II

The book begins with the problem of things. Things are possibilities of being. Part I of the book consists of two chapters addressing the 'things of nature' from the position of critique. In Chapter 1, I begin by asking: what is an encounter with the things of nature?

How does this encounter enable us to *be* in relation to nature itself? This beginning begins with a refusal. The refusal is to say 'no' to thinking of things as objects standing opposed to a subject; to let them be as things. But in saying this, we find that the refusal is itself embedded in this very subject-object relation. The things of nature are already objects of our thought. The book thus begins with a critique of the objectification of the things of nature into knowable objects. My aim is to uncover a set of problems, issues and concepts concerning how we have already come to know nature as an objective domain, and how this knowledge limits our encounter with the things of nature by steering it into specific ways of seeing and experiencing them in systems of applied reason and technical control. My aim is to draw out of this critique a set of positive concepts (postulates), to explore and address the human-nature relation and our place in it. In particular I examine how a critique of nature always begins with 'things' so that its thinking carries things with it in what it says and does, opening up possibilities and lines of enquiry.

In the work that it does, critique employs postulates: concepts invoked by the critique as it responds to the questions put to it in its encounter with things. In the chapter I propose the concept of *poiesis* as one of these necessary postulates. *Poiesis* refers to emergent transitivity: the activity of shifting and shaping evident in the way the things of nature come forth and show themselves. The chapter examines how *poiesis* can be used to identify resistivity within system environments. A system can only operate by overcoming the things under its control. For instance, an ecosystem will have already reduced nature to a *techne* (its means of technical control), so that the things of nature can only appear there in terms of the *autopoiesis* of the system itself (its mode of self-regulation). However, in their finite singularity, things resist the control of the system, opening it otherwise. The chapter suggests ways in which critique can switch position, to think with things in their *poietic* line of flight, opening the system otherwise, against its own *autopoiesis*.

To clarify how this switching of position might take place, the chapter examines ways in which nature has been understood as an organic system in the writings of Karl Marx, showing how his dialectical theory of nature (drawn from Hegel) proposes an anthropocentric projection of human desire onto nature. However, buried in Marx's writings is a positive concept of the human-nature relation, defined as 'the self-mediated being of nature and of man' (Marx 1975, p. 356). This concept of a self-mediated relation between man and nature offers a possibility for ecological thinking to think with the human-nature relation in terms of its own self-mediation. The human-nature relation itself is something positive: a mediation with its own being, its own possibilities, its own 'life'. This possible life can be understood in terms of the renaturing of 'denatured' nature (Nancy 2007, pp. 87–88). For Jean-Luc Nancy, denatured nature does not mean pristine nature stripped of its nature by technology, but nature produced as the 'event' of technology itself (p. 87). Technology is precisely this event of 'denaturing nature' – of producing nature as already denatured. To live in a world of denatured nature is to live 'naturally' as a product of technology. In such a world nature in its 'naturalness' is turned into a technical fact. By renaturing I mean the restoration of the human-nature relation to the power of *poiesis*. To renature nature is to turn the human-nature relation away from its denatured state in technical facts and systems, and to open it to *poietic* possibility. To follow this line of enquiry I propose the nature philosophy of Schelling. Schelling's *Naturphilosophie* moves past anthropocentric dialectics and towards an ecological account of the human-nature relation, where things can be encountered in their singular 'thatness', other than as categorical objects of critique (Schelling 2007, p. 147). From this position, we encounter things in their turning otherwise – following their *poietic* line of flight, carrying the human relation with it.

In Chapter 2 my critique asks: in what way can things be 'said'? In saying things, we bring them into being, making them meaningful in certain ways. Saying is transitive in its action: it shifts meaning from the saying to that which is said. My concern is to show how the things of nature can be said *poietically* with the creative shaping of nature, from within systems of meaning and production. We encounter them there as part of nature withdrawing from us. In this withdrawing, they retain a relation with us, a forgotten connectivity reinvigorated in the encounter that leads us out of ourselves, into the in-between of nature as a withdrawing ground and the possibilities it enacts. By staying in this in-between we can 'say' nature otherwise; we can carry it elsewhere in a *poietic* act of saying. To develop this line of enquiry I draw on Ernesto Laclau's concept of the 'empty signifier' (Laclau 1996, p. 37), showing how nature can be understood as an empty signifier, excluded from the system yet returning and interrupting it at the same time. Nature withdraws from the system, yet returns to haunt it with an irreducible otherness. I draw on Nietzsche's writings on art and nihilism to suggest ways in which the returning of nature can be perceived as a releasing of the human being from enclosure in nihilistic subjectivity. Part I concludes by proposing that critique should become transitively located in what it critiques. To recover a sense of what this might entail, I indicate a return to the seminal moment of modern critique in Kant's critical philosophy and Schelling's response to it.

Part II of the book undertakes a reading of Schelling's nature philosophy as a response to Kant's critical philosophy. Chapter 3 examines the gap in reason exposed by Kant in the *Critique of Pure Reason* (Kant 1929), and the question of being it raises. The gap in reason is the nothing in-between subject and object, exposing a pre-subjective self to the abyss of absolute freedom. The gap is precisely that which relates subject to object, marking the place of their impossible connection. Kant recoiled from the abyssal gap, warning that it placed a limit on reason and could not constitute a beginning for critical thought, which must always begin from its own auto-reflection. I then examine the response to Kant's exposure of the gap in reason by Schelling, whose nature philosophy begins not by recoiling into subjective self-affirmation as others had done, but by moving into the gap itself as a place to rethink the human relation with nature. By inhabiting the gap, Schelling restores nature as a positive moment in critique.

Post-Kantian philosophy is dominated by Schelling and Hegel, the two major figures of German Idealism whose work sets the tone for modern philosophical and theoretical critique. Hegel's response to Kant's exposure of the gap in reason is in many respects similar to Schelling's, but differs in one crucial aspect. While Hegel develops a dialectical critique that continues to negate nature as other, Schelling begins with the otherness of nature and turns this into a positive moment in the critique itself. For Hegel, thought moves dialectically to overcome nature, whereas for Schelling, nature always retains itself as an 'indivisible remainder' (Schelling 2006, p. 29) in thought's dialectical relation with it. Hegel criticized Schelling's concept of the indivisible remainder as the 'night in which [...] all cows are black' (Hegel 1977, p. 9), a vacuous non-place without any enabling capacity. For Schelling, the indivisible remainder is a positive moment in the negativity of thought: a place that enables beginnings.

Schelling and Hegel take critique on diverging paths. Hegel takes the path of negative critique where, in Timothy Morton's terms, nature is always giving us the slip, while Schelling takes the path of positive critique where nature is always beginning, always possible. Hegelian critique occludes nature in thought's self-becoming, while Schellingian critique opens itself to nature as an indifference in thought itself – as thought's possibility. We can delineate two strands of critique out of these diverging paths: one strand continues to see nature as the other to human thought and action, while the other strand begins in nature's 'event', as the absolute possibility of human thought and action. A nature philosophy must decide which path it wants to take: the negative path that sees nature as other, thereby consolidating thought in its own self-limiting, or the positive path that sees itself as already with nature in its otherness, as an open possibility. One secures knowledge of nature in thought's categories and the consistencies of the system, while the other opens these categories and systems to the possibility that things can always be otherwise. In what follows in this book I take the latter, Schellingian path.

In Chapters 4–6, I explore Schelling's philosophy as positive critique, and draw from it a number of key concepts, including the unground, *partage*, positive freedom and virtual nature, to be employed throughout the book. My aim in these chapters is to uncover a conceptual terrain in Schelling's philosophy that I call 'factical ontology', or critique addressing the fact of things as irreducibly and contingently *there*, and encountered as such. Facticity is present throughout Schelling's philosophy as a subtended necessity 'that nature be', and, as such, philosophizing about nature must begin from this fact. By uncovering this factical-ontological terrain in Schelling's philosophy I counter two tendencies in Schellingian scholarship – to see his philosophy as either failed Hegelianism, or as a materialist alternative to Hegel's idealist philosophy. Instead, I propose that Schelling's philosophy is specifically placed to set us on the path of positive critique.

Chapter 4 engages with Schelling's philosophy of freedom, in particular his key idea of the 'indivisible remainder' found in *Philosophical Investigations into the Essence of Human Freedom* (Schelling 2006) as the absolute indifference separating things in a common being. The indivisible remainder becomes the unground: the contraction of being into 'nothing', enabling things to relate to one another while withdrawing from them. Schelling's argument sets up a positive mode of critique that thinks with things in terms of the remainder, opening them to free possibility. Schelling's nature philosophy can be read in terms of the things of nature as singularly resistive to objectification in the causal-mechanistic determinations of the system of nature, as established by Newton and confirmed in Kant's critiques. In this resistive mode, things are eternally free in the sense that they partake of the free being of nature as the indifferent withdrawing ground opening otherwise.

Chapter 5 continues this pursuit of the indivisible remainder in terms of the fact of freedom – the fact that humans exist freely in relation to the withdrawing ground. In its positive mode, nature is neither good nor evil but indifferent to both – a free living ground opened to possibility and otherness. Schelling's task is to recover this living ground as it withdraws from us. The freedom Schelling recovers is not the negative freedom that negates nature in affirming itself, but the positive freedom of being with nature opened to possibility in the eternal beginning of the decisive act of freedom, yet blocked from taking place by the determinations of the system. Positive critique releases the blocked living ground by thinking with nature, not against it. The paradigm case for this kind of freedom is the artist's stroke; in making a stroke the artist resists the *techne* that determines how an artwork should look through generic conventions, while entering further into the deed of art as a matter of being free with the artwork itself. The gesture of freedom is exemplified by the artist's stroke.

Chapter 6 recovers a sense of virtual nature from Schelling's middle-period writings, especially in *The Ages of the World* (2000). In Schelling's terms, virtual nature is the nature to come: an age of providence beginning to emerge in the current age. Schelling historicizes his dialectical philosophy of nature as the evolution of reason seeking to free itself from the determinations of the current age, in rotations of the 'wheel of nature' (Schelling 2000, p. 46) as time realizing itself in phases of tensed being (the past, the present, the future). The future age (providence) is already pre-figuring itself in the present age, but is blocked from coming forth by the present age keeping itself present to itself and determining itself to be. The chapter examines this dialectical movement of possible historical ages coming forth in turn by considering Schelling's philosophy of art.

In *The Philosophy of Art* (Schelling 1989), Schelling argues that art is founded in myth. Myth reconciles the finite with the infinite thereby providing the world with meaning. For Schelling, myth begins in the Greek beginning (the age of Homer) where human thought and action were immediately connected with nature. The world suffers a fall with the advent of reason, triggering a dialectical movement within reason itself into distinct ages. These ages are analysed by Schelling in terms of interactions between symbol, schemata and allegory. Art works through the symbol to reconcile the other two modes, thereby restoring human being to mythic unity with nature. For Schelling, the aim of critique is to unblock the '*inhibition* of the *formation*' (Schelling 2004, p. 6) of the current age to allow a 'new mythology […] to arise' (Schelling 1978, pp. 232–33). However, Schelling's analysis runs up against its own limits. The current age will never get beyond its own allegorizing of the mythic beginning. Any new beginning will always repeat the old myths in a new guise, closing the new age in a regression to myth. To counter this return to myth, we need to 'demythify' the existing myths blocking the beginning from coming to pass. In its allegorical mode, art demythifies the mythic union of the human and nature, carrying the human-nature relation with it in open possibility. By demythifying myth we keep the current age in perpetual 'beginningness', always open and connected in free possibility. Art can point us in this direction.

In the third part of the book (Chapters 7–8) I reopen the question of being put to critique by the exposure of Kant's gap, in terms of the event of nature. In Schelling's nature philosophy, the things of nature are not dealt with sufficiently as things, but as momentary possibilities that disappear into the activity of eternal becoming. To counter this insufficiency, the book begins again with things. This second beginning begins with Heidegger's questioning of the being of things in his seminal work *Being and Time* (Heidegger 1962), and returns critique to the things themselves as already disposed in the world.[5] For Heidegger the modern world has formed in such a way that the things of nature are already given over to the ordering and controlling that makes this world what it is. Thought already finds itself thrown into this world of predisposed things as products of *techne*: equipment ready-to-hand for human use (Heidegger 1962, p. 98).[6] The challenge to think positively with the things of nature therefore requires a resistance to the *techne* already turning them into objects or items of 'standing reserve' (Heidegger 1977, p. 17).

In Chapter 7 I examine Heidegger's later writings on art and technology in terms of the things of nature as things that 'thing', or gather other things to them in an event of Being.[7] In the modern world, things are already given over to technology, so that a thing can only 'thing' from within its already technologically enframed position. Thus, the opening of the event of Being requires a turn out of technology. Heidegger identifies this capacity to turn out of technology with art, and more specifically with the work that the artwork does. Art enables a beginning by turning out of technology, a beginning-in-resistance that opens into absolute indifference, preparing the way for a world to come. The artwork's turning is thus an event of Being (*Ereignis*): a special moment of openness (the Open) that must be kept open if the event of Being is to be encountered. Heidegger's insight is that the openness of Being must be kept open and not closed in some historical or natural way of being. Heidegger's later writings on technology and nature have been used in ecocriticism – the critical-cultural study of the human-nature relation – to argue for a return to pre-technological nature (e.g. Foltz 1995).[8] I will show how this reading of Heidegger overlooks crucial issues of the turning out of technology, a turning that does not leave technology behind, but stays within it 'otherwise' in an absolutely open sense. Turning awaits the event of Being, it does not move into it.

In Chapter 8, my aim is to develop a *poetics* that avoids the trap of mythifying nature. In this chapter I employ the concept of 'poetizing' used by both Heidegger and Benjamin in their readings of Hölderlin's poetry. Why poetics and not aesthetics? Aesthetics reduces nature to subjective states, feelings or affects, thereby keeping nature at bay while it attends to the subject's responses to it. By way of contrast, poetics concerns itself with the 'saying' of nature as a stance in the world that carries nature with it. Poetics reads the poem or the work of art in terms of the stand it takes with respect to what it says about the world it calls into being. Poetizing is this carrying of nature as part of the artwork as well as the reading of it. Heidegger's poetizing makes Hölderlin's poetry stand with respect to a world already mythified in a special moment of predestined being (Being), thus undermining his insight that the openness of Being be kept open and not re-enclosed in myth. I show how Benjamin poetizes the same poetic work (although not the same poem) in the opposite way: as a demythification of Being. The poem does not stand steadfast awaiting the event of Being, but is unravelled by it in a disseminating movement of *poietic* openness. Benjamin's poetizing of Hölderlin's poems demythifies their mythic foundations, sending them into an openness called forth by the poems themselves.

A similar demythification of myth can be found in Celan's poetry, in particular his poem 'Todtnauberg', written on the occasion of his visit to Heidegger in his mountain hut in 1967. In the chapter, I read this poem in terms of the stand it takes with respect to the voice that speaks through it, a voice that comes from an absolute nowhere. This voice bears witness not only to the meeting between the poet and the philosopher, but also to the death event of the Holocaust, and hence to the death of Meaning as such. The voice is empty: it is not Celan speaking as subject of his own thoughts, but the voice of the other opened in possibility. The poem thus calls forth others to inhabit this empty space, to bear witness to the bearing witness, thereby keeping the space open for repeated witnessing. In its own enactment, in its poetic stance, the poem opens itself to future readings always to come. My aim in these readings is to counter the argument made by Alain Badiou that the age of the poets is over (Badiou 1999, p. 71); poetry and art can no longer carry the meaning of the world, a responsibility now carried by science and logical calculation. My counter argument is that poetizing cannot afford not to continue; it must continue to keep the Open open, thereby fending off the closure of Being in the *matheme* and its tendency towards system and controlling *techne*.

In the fourth part of the book (Chapters 9–10) I extend the poetics established in Chapter 8 into the question of technology and the human-nature relation embedded in it. Chapter 9 examines Benjamin's concept of mythic connectedness as an aura produced in technological mediation. My aim is to counter Jonathan Bate's proposal for an ecopoetics based on a pre-technological, pre-political re-mythologizing of the human relation to nature. For Bate, industrialized things cannot 'thing' because they lack *poietic* openness. I challenge this view, and propose that industrialized things are capable of thinging when experienced as auratically charged fallen objects – things having fallen from objectification into obsolescence, yet flashing with residual mythic connectedness in the 'in-between' of new and old technologies.

Benjamin's essays on technologically produced things such as photographs, films and mechanical devices, can be read in terms of his broad concern to 'form a pure and systematic continuum of experience' (Benjamin 1996, p. 105) – a connectedness between things irreducible to objectification in categorical thought. My aim is to open the human-nature relation by drawing from Benjamin's analyses of finite experience and encounters with things in industrialized technology. Unlike Heidegger's analysis of technology that stands in readiness for the event of Being, Benjamin's analysis is already part of the event of Being in dissipating technologically produced things. We do not await the nature to come; we are already part of its unstable, chaotic dispersal. I propose an ecopoetical stance situated on the unstable ground of experience in-between fading and emerging technologies, where another nature is beginning to form. This other nature is neither nature 'in itself' nor nature 'for us', but the *poietic* openness of a nature not yet formed and always unknown. Following Benjamin, the politics of ecopoetics shifts from seeking out experiences with things in pre-technological myth, to the critical-analytical task of demythifying the already mythified objects of industrialized technology, to allow them to 'thing' in residual mythic connectivity. The politics of ecopoetics concerns a *poietic* release of things from the totalizing tendencies of technology and a defence of their connectedness to other things. For Benjamin, connectedness through poetizing is the 'supreme sovereignty of relationship' (Benjamin 1996, p. 34) that must be defended at all costs. By defending the relation of things to themselves we also defend our own free being with nature, insofar as things are already opened to us *poietically*. I argue that an ecopoetics needs to defend the commonality of the relation itself by keeping the openness of the relation open (keeping the Open open); by following the *poietic* movement of things otherwise.

Chapter 10, the final chapter of the book, employs Jean-Luc Nancy's concept of denaturing to develop a critique of the current way of saying nature in terms of biotechnologically produced life. In *The Creation of the World, or Globalization* (Nancy 2007), Nancy argues that the world is now subject to a process of infinite globalization that denatures the world by stripping it of its existing nature in order to recreate it with globalized *techne*. I call this 'derenaturing'. A derenatured world produces the illusion of natural plenitude hiding behind technical facts. The chapter examines contemporary bio life as the life produced in biotechnologically engineered environments, seeking to expose the *techne* hidden in the facts such that it might be turned otherwise. The chapter critiques the artwork of Eduardo Kac, whose living bio art creations parody the production of genetically engineered life. In the chapter I also examine the work of bio artists Oron Catts and Ionat Zurr, whose living tissue bio art creations question the ethics of biotechnologically engineered life through ironized and parodic play. However, I argue that the work of bio art reaches a limit in that its parodic creations cannot break free from the *techne* they aim to subvert. Bio art requires another turn to do this. I show how the artwork of Patricia Piccinini undertakes a double turn out of the *techne* of biotechnological engineering. By locating her creations in-between the current technology and its anticipated obsolescence, her works stand against the progressivist *techne* of biotechnology, and speak to us otherwise. While Kac's and Catts and Zurr's work remains within the denatured nature of biotechnological engineering, Piccinini's work renatures it such that it opens against itself, releasing another nature, earthed in another beginning.

My aim in this book is to recover the possibility of thinking with nature. Thinking with nature means thinking with nature in its negated state as the other of human existence. To think with nature is to think with the things of nature in their resistive otherness, opening a *way*, neither forward nor backward, but staying where we already are turned otherwise. In this being turned otherwise, we find ourselves on the uncertain ground of another beginning. This other beginning begins with the human-nature relation open and exposed to an absolute sense of what might be. It is up to us to decide just what this relation might become.

Part I

The Things of Nature

Chapter 1

Nature Otherwise

Encountering things

To know nature is to set up a distinction between a subject who knows about nature and nature as the object of this knowing. Nature as something given, something close at hand, disappears in the playing out of what nature signifies for the knowing subject and its objectification into systems of knowledge.[1] To speak of nature as an object of knowledge is to enter a self-reflection where nature becomes mirrored between subjective and objective modes of knowledge production.[2] Nature loses all sense of being this nature, and becomes instead an appearance for the subject whose interests determine what nature is and could be.[3] In its aesthetic mode, knowledge of nature passes through the subject in terms of internal states and affects; while in its scientific mode, knowledge passes through the same subject but in terms of the apodictic certainty of concepts held in the mind. In both cases, the subject acts as a conduit for the knowledge of nature. Speaking about nature becomes speaking on behalf of the subject who already knows about and experiences nature through self-reflection.

In this subjective mode of knowledge, the mirroring of nature is mistaken for nature itself reflecting the subject's own thought, while encounters with the things of nature – whatever is at hand to think with – are blocked by the knowledge applied to them.[4] A thinking that thinks with the subject in seeking to know nature overlooks the fact that the things of nature remain where they are, close at hand and accessible in a certain way. There, they can be encountered otherwise. Such an encounter is not a matter of sensory contact or observation, but takes the form of a questioning of the fact that such things are, requiring an account of their mode of being.

To encounter nature otherwise is to see nature for what it can be, other than as a mirror image of our own thought. In such encounters, we free up thinking for another way of relating to nature. Thinking about nature is no longer determined by a self-reflecting subject producing nature as an object of its thought, but occurs right at the place where nature is encountered. Why do we need to do this? For reasons related to industrialized production and consumption on a vast globalized scale, we are now faced with a critical issue of how to live on the earth; how to live well without exploiting nature for our own ends. To see nature otherwise is to be already with nature in its possibilities, as the beginning of something else, some other human-nature relation. In this book I develop a line of enquiry to see and to think nature otherwise – to think with nature rather than against it.[5]

My aim is to engage in critique. By critique I mean thinking about nature in its possibilities, for what it can be, as distinct from what it already is. Possibility here refers to enablement, as proposed by Martin Heidegger in his 'Letter on "Humanism"' (Heidegger 1998, p. 242). Something is possible in this enabling sense, not because it is calculable, inevitably or necessarily so, but because it can happen within finite, contingent circumstances – it is enabled by the situation. Enabled possibility is not a matter of choosing between possibilities set up in advance, but *is* the very fact that something could be otherwise, a fact built into what something is. Possibility is its exigent otherness.[6]

Insofar as nature is something and not nothing, then it must be something encountered in a particular way, at a finite place, for somebody. It must already be there even as it disappears into the mirror play of the subject/object set-up. I call this already being there of nature, nature 'as such'. Nature 'as such' is the being there of nature – the irreducible 'this' of the 'things of nature' as we encounter them and think about them.[7] Nature 'as such' – the things of nature – *are*, not as outwardly perceived objects nor as inner subjective states, but as positive remainders of that which thought is not: a residue that partakes of, yet remains irreducible to, this thinking. We always experience the things of nature as such 'otherwise', in the residual sense that thought leaves behind. I argue that to get out of the mirror play of subject and object that locks thinking about nature into fulfilling our own desires we need to encounter the things of nature 'as such' – as affirmations of the 'not' of thought.[8]

By encountering the things of nature as the 'not' of thought, they take on an enabling capacity. They call for thought and beckon us to action. Rather than projecting our desires onto them as mute objects of our thought, we let them be in their possibilities as such. To do this, I argue, requires another way of thinking, neither subjective nor objective, but a thinking 'in-between'. Thinking in-between the subject/object set-up requires that we begin our thinking with the 'there is' of what is, insofar as this *there* leads us not back to our already-known self, but to somewhere else in this thinking otherwise, an always remaining possibility.

Nancy's cat

To think right at nature is the task before us. Jean-Luc Nancy describes this kind of thinking as follows:

> It is an impossible thought, a thinking that does not hold itself back from the circulation it thinks, a thinking of meaning right at [à même] meaning, where its eternity occurs as the truth of its passing. (For instance, at the moment at which I am writing, a brown-and-white cat is crossing the garden, slipping mockingly away, taking my thoughts with it.)
> (Nancy 2000, p. 4)

Here Nancy describes a way of thinking that follows what disturbs it in thinking about something. This 'impossible thought [...] does not hold itself back'; that is, it does not hold itself back into a self-reflection, but lets itself go, and in so doing, finds itself right at meaning in its connection with things.

Nancy describes this being right at meaning as a moment of distraction where a cat crosses the garden right there where he is thinking, taking his thoughts away into an endless circulation – an intimation of Nietzsche's "'eternal return'" (p. 4). The cat comes to interrupt the thinker's thinking, thereby bringing it to a threshold. Nancy describes this threshold as the 'eternity' of thought occurring as the 'truth of its passing'. That is, the thought, suddenly reduced to its finite occurrence, is 'eternal', in that it has no temporality to ground itself except for the 'moment' of its thinking. At this moment thought is placed *en abyme*, in an open or 'absolute' possibility. However, in this momentary state of being *en abyme*, it still remains attached to the 'outside' – it latches on to a 'something' already in the vicinity, no matter how insignificant (a cat slinking away will do). Thought's eternity – its 'truth' in the singular moment of its happening – is revealed as a 'passing' and 'slipping away' with some thing. Here, the thing is grasped not in itself, but in its contingency. As a contingent thing, it withdraws, and in so doing takes thought away with it. The subject gives itself up to the uncertainty of an irrecoverable otherness in the way it encounters things in their withdrawing from thought.

Finite thinking is thought interrupted by the transitive movement of the thing in its slipping away. This slipping away has no destination, no aim, no goal, but is simply the transitivity of the thing itself, in its restless yearning to be elsewhere other than where it already is. Thinking right at nature is a finite thinking that leads away from itself into an abyss of not knowing. Yet in this movement a freedom to be otherwise is affirmed.

Schelling – Heidegger – Benjamin – Nancy

To develop the critical and conceptual terrain to think right at nature I will initially engage with the philosophy of the German Idealist philosopher Friedrich Schelling (Chapters 3–6). Schelling's nature philosophy (*Naturphilosophie*), written in the late eighteenth and early nineteenth centuries, thinks the 'in-between' of thought and nature as an emergent, differentiating movement of free becoming.[9] Schelling's *Naturphilosophie* provides a positive account of the human relation to nature, which I will propose as an alternative to the negative account that Kant provides in his critique of reason.

Schelling's philosophy of nature presents ideas about nature and singularity, *partage* (the being-together-apart of singular things) and free-being that can be deployed to develop a nature philosophy today. Schelling argues that critique needs to begin not with the Kantian subject who only knows the things of nature as objects of thought, but with the 'thatness' of things – the fact that they *are*. For Schelling, Kantian critique proposes only 'the concept of a thing [...] but nothing of its *thatness* [*Daß*], of its existence' (Schelling 2007, p. 147). Schelling overcomes the subject/object opposition separating mind and nature in Kant's critique by beginning with things in their 'thatness', as possibilities opened up in encountering them. A nature philosophy following Schelling's insights would be a philosophy that thinks with the things of nature, not against them.

Although providing a beginning, Schelling's *Naturphilosophie* cannot provide all of the conceptual material needed for a nature philosophy today. It remains steeped in idealist assumptions about higher nature and mythic fulfilment, as well as '*the will to System*' in the aftermath of Kant (Lacoue-Labarthe & Nancy 1988, p. 33).[10] To assume such providential ideas about higher nature and mythical renewal is to overlook the situation today, where nature disappears into nothingness within systems of meaning and production. A nature philosophy must first respond to this nothingness (*nihil*) and think nature otherwise from this place.

To think from the nothing that nature has become in today's technologically ordered world, I will turn to the philosophy of Heidegger (Chapter 7), in particular his writing on technology and art (Heidegger 1971, 1977), and on the event of Being as *Ereignis* or finite openness (Heidegger 1999). Heidegger relates the things of nature to art and technology, and his argument that art constitutes a turn in technology as epochal opening (Heidegger 1977, p. 35, pp. 41–43) indicates a role for art in nature philosophy that picks up on Schelling's own ideas of art and epochal history (Schelling 1978, Parts 5 and 6; 1989, Part 1). Heidegger's later philosophy provides insight into the kind of thinking about the nature-art-technology nexus needed to respond to this coming epoch, a thinking that says 'yes' and 'no' to technology at the same time (Heidegger 1966, p. 54). My aim here is to work with Heidegger's philosophy to draw out the complex issues of art, technology and *poietic* becoming (*poiesis*) in the modern epoch, and to show how a nature philosophy can engage with this nexus to begin the kind of otherwise thinking adequate for an age of technology. However, there are limitations to Heidegger's position. His central insight – that the event of Being opens to an otherness that 'must be *held open* and free for the current factical possibility' (Heidegger 1962, p. 355)[11] – is undermined when he turns his own critique back into myth. Heidegger's critique is not critical enough to break away from an underlying mythification that haunts it throughout.[12]

To counter Heidegger's lapse into mythical thinking, I will propose the idea of a transitional poetics that remains within the 'in-between' of the nature-art-technology nexus as a way of keeping openness open. To do this I will draw on Walter Benjamin's concept of the 'poetized' as the shaping force (of nature) enacted in artworks as singular events of absolute 'truth' (Benjamin 1996, pp. 18–19), as well as the poetics of Paul Celan who, in his poems and essays, proposes a post-mythic mode of poetic 'speaking' (Celan 2005). By doing this, I will retain the *poietical* opening of nature (its transitivity) carried by the artwork and the poem, but in terms of a critical demythification of the place of nature in the contemporary world of industrialized objects, systems and technical procedures. A transitional poetics, I will argue, allows us to think nature otherwise without turning this otherwise into a new mythology of nature awaiting human being. Rather, it indicates a critical interruption of the systems of meaning that perpetuate the mythic terrain of the human-nature relation in its current configuration as technical fact. Through its singular activities, a transitional poetics continues the essentially political task of pursuing freedom and justice not just for human beings but for the things of nature as well, as part of an expanded sense of human responsibility towards 'free being' with nature.[13]

Broadly speaking, I will propose an ontological critique of nature 'as such' by drawing from Schelling, Heidegger and Benjamin, employing concepts derived from their thinking about nature as *poietic* becoming, while also recognizing their shortcomings. From Schelling I will draw on the concept of nature as the beginning of possibility in the ungrounding of nature (*Unground*) as positive freedom; from Heidegger, I will draw on the concept of nature as an event of Being – an epochal opening into otherness (*Ereignis*); from Benjamin and Celan I will draw on the poetic act as one of enabling-transition. I will also draw on the work of Jean-Luc Nancy, in particular his idea of world-forming (*mondialisation*) as the reclamation of the finite place of a renewed possibility of being with nature within denatured globalizing worlds (Nancy 2007, pp. 27–28). These concepts will help me to develop a critical approach to nature 'as such' right at the place where it happens, in the breaching of technological order by thought thinking 'otherwise'.

Poiesis

Poiesis will be a key concept in this book. I take *poiesis* to be a postulate of critique. A postulate is a principle demanded by critique in its *praxis*:

> [I]t indicates the inseparability of theoretical from practical philosophy by grounding all theoretical knowledge in the activity of a positing self. In contrast to an axiom, which has the strange form of a product not recognized as having been produced by anything, a postulate is always the product of a postulating *activity*.
>
> (Lauer 2012, p. 47)

Axioms are *fiats*; they announce projects as 'things to be done'. Postulates, however, are part of the *praxis* of the announcing; they 'do' the very thing that they announce as needing to be done. Postulates are not *fiats* but speculations in open possibility; they pose questions and open up lines of enquiry.

Poiesis is postulated in this present work as the *transitivity* of nature. To define *poietic* transitivity we can turn to classical Greek philosophy, where *poiesis* means 'making' or 'producing', as distinct from *praxis*, meaning 'doing' or 'acting' (Taminiaux 1987, p. 137). *Poiesis* is neither an independent force (e.g. an *élan vital*, the 'power of nature') that acts on things, nor a vital materialism (hylozoism) acting in things. Rather *poiesis* is that which is required by critique to account for the fact that things have their being in a 'bringing forth' (Heidegger 1977, p. 10). *Poiesis* is 'a change of place or of situation' (Weber 1996, p. 64), a transition that carries the thing to where we can say 'it is'. In Benjamin's terms *poiesis* is the 'shaping principle' (Benjamin 1996, p. 23): an ontological openness in poetic and art works, extending to all the things of nature and the material world, as 'the underlying foundation of all relations' (p. 25). *Physis* – the becoming of material nature – is also *poietical*, in the sense that the development of organisms or the transformation of geological and cosmological strata demonstrates creative, shaping tendencies and possibilities. Because human being is itself part of nature, then every aspect of human production (technical, artistic, manufacturing) is also part of *poietic* making and becoming. *Poiesis is*, as part of each thing, yet exceeds each thing at the same time. In its potential to be other – in its possibilities of some altered or changeable state of being – a thing *is* the *poiesis* that it exhibits. *Poiesis* is an ontological concept and not an empirical fact. It identifies the being of things in their becoming other: in their creative, shaped and connected possibilities.

There is no separate *poiesis* of trees, rivers, stones, human beings, microchips or ecosystems. Rather trees, rivers, stones, human beings, microchips and ecosystems are all part of *poietic* becoming, evident in the possibilities opened up in their specific dispositions, dispersals and ideations at particular junctures. For instance, an artist painting a tree partakes of *poiesis* that is also part of the tree's becoming.[14] Although two distinct things (*a* tree, *an* artwork), they nevertheless share, at their point of juncture, a possibility of a co-becoming other. In being-together-there, the artwork and the tree share a common being: an art-tree matrix. *Poiesis* happens as the tree-becoming-art, or art-becoming-tree, at the particular place wherever this matrix is and has its being. Thinking about *poiesis* requires us to think of the relation between things in terms of their finite juncture, and how this juncture enables released creative potential as part of a renewed sense of shared being.

Capital and nature

In his writings on the human-nature relation, Karl Marx sets in train a way of thinking of nature as a kind of work, where 'economic development must be conceived as something natural' (Ryan 1984, p. 82). Nature's *poiesis* is replaced by 'man made' practices of turning nature into a product, so that 'nature appears as *his* work and his reality [...] and he can therefore contemplate himself in a world he himself has created' (Marx 1975, p. 329). Human *praxis* substitutes its own activity for the 'work' of nature (its *poietic* becoming) thereby setting in motion attempts to exploit nature for a humankind representing to itself its own 'natural' needs and desires. Marx's insight here is powerful, as it suggests a profound illusion that forms within human self-consciousness in modern industrialized societies, that nature is simply there for human self-fulfilment which is itself a completion of the ends of nature.

Marx employed this insight in his early work to propose a theory of human labour as the struggle for human emancipation in 'free being' (Marx 1975, p. 327), blocked in its present stage by capital and its demands on the worker. The idea that nature should be subordinated to human will and freedom is not confined to Marx's early writings, but is present in his mature work as well. For instance, in *Capital Vol. III*, Marx asserts that 'The true realm of freedom, the development of human powers *as an end in itself*, begins beyond [nature's blind power], though it can only flourish with this realm of necessity as its basis' (Marx 1981, p. 959, emphasis added). Throughout his writings, Marx's views on nature are consistently anthropocentric; they place human emancipation on centre stage, where nature's part is to lend a hand in helping humans towards achieving their own freedom as an 'end in itself'.

However, within Marx's writing there appears another possibility. In the 'Economic and Philosophical Manuscripts', Marx describes the possibility of a 'self-mediated being of nature and of man' that eludes the consciousness of those who labour for others. Here is the passage in full:

> A *being* sees himself as independent only when he stands on his own feet, and he only stands on his own feet when he owes his *existence* to himself. A man who lives by the grace of another regards himself as a dependent being. But I live completely by the grace of another if I owe him not only the maintenance of my life but also its *creation*, if he is the *source* of my life. My life is necessarily grounded outside itself if it is not my own creation. The *creation* is therefore an idea which is very hard to exorcize from the popular consciousness. This consciousness is *incapable of comprehending* the self-mediated being [*Durchsichselbstsein*] of nature and of man, since such a being contradicts all the *palpable evidence* of practical life.
>
> (Marx 1975, p. 356)

The 'self-mediated being of nature and of man' Marx mentions here is something incomprehensible to those who believe that their being is indebted to the 'grace of another' – to another being who *creates* them (e.g. a god). In Kantian terms, such a being has no dignity.[15] He does not stand freely and independently on his own feet but is dependent on another. Marx suggests here that a truly free being is one who stands upright on his own, but not alone; rather, as part of a self-mediated relation with nature. Man's freedom is tied up with the freedom of nature that he shares as part of 'free being' (p. 327).[16] The self-mediated being of nature and of man offers a possibility for an ecological thinking that Marx himself introduces here but does not pursue. That is, the human-nature relation itself can be understood as something positive: a mediation with its own being, its own possibilities, its own life. I will return to this idea shortly.

Debates about Marx's ecological credentials often focus on the proposal that 'Nature is man's *inorganic body*' (Marx 1975, p. 328).[17] In his essay 'Marx's Inorganic Body', John Clark has argued that Marx's position on nature as the inorganic body of the human is thoroughly anthropocentric and, on those terms, cannot be used in the cause of ecological theory (Clark 1989). John Bellamy Foster and Paul Burkett reject Clark's argument, maintaining that Marx develops a non-anthropocentric concept of nature in which 'human beings, as objective, organic creatures, are also dependent on inorganic nature as part of their own species being' (Foster & Burkett 2000, p. 411). The difference between the two positions relates to whether the human-nature relation in Marx is based on an ontological break or an interconnectivity between human beings and nature. Foster and Burkett argue for the latter: 'Rather than postulating a sharp ontological break between human beings and nature [...] Marx thus attempted to describe the material interconnections and dialectical interchanges associated with the fact that human species-being, similar to species being in general, finds its objective, natural basis outside of itself, in the conditioned, objective nature of its existence' (p. 411). However, we need to question these assumptions.

In the section of the 'Economic and Philosophical Manuscripts' from which Foster and Burkett draw their argument, Marx does not say that human species-being is similar to species being in general, but that 'man is a species-being [...] because [...] he looks upon himself as a *universal* and therefore free being' (Marx 1975, p. 327). For Marx, human being is not the same as species being in general as Foster and Burkett claim, but different from other beings insofar as it recognizes its 'free being' to be universal for it alone. Foster and Burkett do not address the issue of freedom as an essential part of Marx's argument, as this would mean having to accept the fact that there is an ontological difference between human being (free) and nature (determined) in Marx's argument, ultimately leading to an overcoming of inorganic nature in free human being as 'the personal property for man' (Marx 1975, p. 320). On this score, Marx's position is thoroughly anthropocentric. Consequently, we cannot follow Foster and Burkett in seeking an ontological connectivity between human being and nature in Marx's writings. However, we can if we follow Clark.

Although rejecting Marx's anthropocentrism, Clark nevertheless identifies an opening in Marx's thought towards an 'ecological dialectic' where the human-nature relation is understood in terms of 'unity in diversity':

> [T]he way is opened for the development of a truly ecological dialectic that avoids what Marx aptly diagnoses as 'the antithesis of nature and history'. In such a dialectic, the entire course of natural history, including the emergence of life, consciousness, and self-consciousness (with all its modes of rationality and symbolization) are seen as aspects of the development of a complex whole. Central to such an analysis is an elaboration of the mutual determination of all forms of life within the biosphere as a *unity in diversity*.
>
> (Clark 1989, p. 250, emphasis added)

The concept of 'unity in diversity' presented in the above passage can be employed to rethink the human-nature relation in ecological rather than anthropocentric terms. A unity in diversity can be postulated in terms of how things *are* in their being as such, as different from other things to which they are connected. The unified thing is both singularly itself (i.e. unified in being the thing that it is) and connected to a diversity of other things. Take for instance an ecosystem. An ecosystem is unified in its singularity (its *autopoietic* consistency) while at the same time connected to other things both within and outside it as part of a 'complex whole' (Clark 1989, p. 250). The complex whole is the connectedness between things: an open, dynamic becoming (*poiesis*) running through the ecosystem and opening it to other possibilities and ways of relating. Unified things such as ecosystems are always opened to otherness in relation to the complex whole that runs through them. (See Figure 1).

If, as Marx argues, the human and nature are locked in a dialectical struggle in which labouring man prevails over nature by overcoming his current stage of subordination to

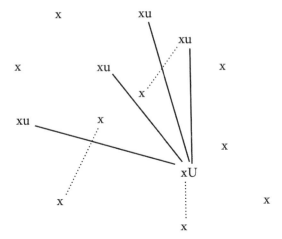

x : a thing
U : a unity
u: an element making up the unity
xu: the thing as an element of the unity
xU: the unity as thing

The lines from u to U represent the gathering of things into a Unity (a consistency of value).

The dotted lines represent the connecting vectors between things (not all possibilities shown).

Connecting vectors cut across the coordinates of the unity.

In xu, the thing resists its coordination with the Unity through its connectivity to other things.

In xU, the unity is transformed by its interconnectivity with things.

Figure: a Unity in Diversity
Figure 1.

capital, thereby releasing natural productivity and realizing his free being as mastery of the earth, then hidden within this struggle is a mediating moment of otherness in the singularity of things. Previously I suggested that Marx's idea of a 'self-mediated being of nature and of man' could be used in terms of the sharing of free being – the human shares free being with nature as a self-mediating relation. This idea can be applied to the 'moment' of singularities in their openness to the free being of otherness. This moment is a moment of the in-between – a self-mediated being of the singularity that comes between man and nature, holding them together while keeping them apart in *poietic* becoming.

This in-between of the human and nature cannot be reduced to either the human or nature, but is *that* which comes between – the mere possibility of something else, of another way or direction in which things might be – a being not yet able to be thought in the dialectical becoming of 'man' and his triumph over nature. This in-between is not nothing; rather it is the merest sense of what binds the human and nature together, but released from its bondage to either term. An ecological thinking of the human-nature relation can begin from 'the self-mediated being of nature and of man' as Marx suggests, in terms of the being-free of the relation itself. By taking a turn that interrupts dialectics in its very operation in pursuit of the 'self-mediated being of nature and of man', ecological thinking can uncover the activity of *partage* – the difference in-between the human and nature – in encounters with the things of nature in their singular being: neither affective objects, nor subjective perceptions, but as bearers of sense. *Partage* – the essential keeping apart of being together – is always at work in any given event of the human-nature relation as such. In releasing the being-free of the singular relation, the interruption counters not only the exploitation of human labour in working for capital, but the exploitation of nature itself.

Myth

Marx's insight that the work of humans (*praxis*) substitutes for the labour of nature (*poiesis*) leads inevitably to the question of myth. We can turn to Roland Barthes for clarification. For Barthes, myth 'transforms history into nature' (Barthes 1973, p. 129) so that nature appears to be speaking to itself. That is, myth naturalizes human *praxis* (history) as if it were the *poietic* speech of nature. The illusion produced by myth is through a double turn, where nature is denatured and simultaneously renatured by the mythic self-representation of humans in systems of cultural meaning – an imposition of a closed mythic system on the open becoming of nature. The human relation to nature becomes one of renatured-denatured-nature.[18] Nature is denatured and simultaneously renatured (derenatured) as the mythic enactment of human life. In this case, the exploitation of nature by humans is no longer a matter of human self-aggrandizement, where, in Marx's words, for man 'nature appears as *his* work and his reality' (Marx 1975, p. 329), but becomes part of nature itself. Human work and the work of nature become part of the same natural being, thereby compounding the appropriation of nature by humans into ever greater entwinements of system control.

Derenaturing mythifies the human body into a quasi-*autopoietic* self-production entwined in systems of control, where human work is made to look like natural labour.[19] Individuals are *steered* towards their own free being with nature by the feedback mechanisms of the system itself, continuing the derenaturing of nature underway since industrialization. The question this derenaturing of nature poses for nature philosophy is as follows: how can critique enable us to see other possibilities in these *autopoietic* entwinements, thereby releasing a resistive thought to follow the *poietic* line of flight?[20] An answer lies in demythification. In his book *Against Nature*, Stephen Vogel proposes what he calls a 'quasi-Hegelian argument' (Vogel 1996, p. 6), where nature is understood to be socially constructed. In this case, nature is reified into social systems so that the 'socially situated subject [...] sees the static and putatively "natural" as standing for those aspects of the world whose social character has been hidden and forgotten and have thus become "reified"' (p. 5). Adopting this line of thinking against 'naturalist' arguments that tend to see nature as a positive yet insubstantial 'otherness',[21] Vogel proposes a 'liberatory critique [...] to dereify or "uncongeal" – to dissolve false immediacies, to reveal to human subjects that what they think of as "natural" is actually the product of their own socially organized activity' (p. 5). Here we have the possibility of a liberating, demythifying critique in which human subjects are released from 'false immediacies'. However, Vogel has not gone far enough. The mythic immediacy of nature conceals not just the social character of the world, but the work of the system itself, so that the system appears there as if it were part of nature. Thus the dereification of the 'false immediacies' of nature needs to take another turn – to demythify the system itself, to expose it to otherness such that it turns against its own self-enclosure. In this case, the human subject is confronted not simply with the knowledge of the social constructedness of nature as Vogel suggests, but with an irrevocable gap in its own reasoning about this constructedness. Demythification exposes the subject to this gap, opening up a resistive line of thinking that thinks the system otherwise.

Connectivity

Further into his book *Against Nature*, Stephen Vogel proposes Habermas's theory of rational communication to avoid reducing nature to a subject/object opposition: 'Habermas means that rather than taking the model of an *individual subject confronting an object* in the world as theoretically central, philosophy should concentrate instead on the *linguistically mediated relations among subjects*' (Vogel 1996, p. 145). Communicative rationality avoids turning nature into an object for the cognizing subject, and instead establishes 'validity and consensus' (p. 145) between rational subjects aligned in intersubjective relations with one another. Intersubjectivity enables a way of gaining knowledge of nature irreducible to the self-interest of the subject, guided by common interests and a sense of a common good. However, if, as Habermas argues, 'the phenomena in need of explication are no longer, in and of themselves, the knowledge and mastery of an objective nature, but the intersubjectivity of possible understanding and agreement' (Habermas, qtd. in Vogel 1996, p. 145), then there is nothing to stop this 'understanding and agreement' from taking on a subjective form at another level of discourse, which simply continues the objectification of nature by those subjects already in the intersubjective arrangement, acting as a coalition of like minds bent on further exploitation and domination.

In countering this turn to intersubjectivity, Eric Nelson has argued that 'Habermas's discourse replicates the levelling of the "natural" to the instrumental. It reproduces the anthropocentric blindness that divides the human from the natural material world, which remains unrecognized as something other than and in excess of human rationality and communication, and reinforces the misuse and destruction of animals and environments' (Nelson 2011, p. 106). Nelson argues that intersubjectivism remains entirely within the subjective mode of the subject/object dialectic, but deludes itself in thinking that it has got around it. Appeals to intersubjectivity to initiate a more sympathetic attitude to nature need to be mindful that intersubjectivity remains within the bounds of subjectivity and are at best 'constructivist' accounts of nature.

Appeals to subjectivity and intersubjectivity as a means of ordering the human relation to nature are versions of what Friedrich Nietzsche calls 'nihilism' (Nietzsche 1967, p. 9): the replacement of essential meaning with values projected and circulated by humans in their systems of production and consumption.[22] Truth becomes a matter of agreements reached and alliances formed through intersubjective communication, further entrenching the separation of the human and nature, and encouraging anthropocentrism, contractual ethics and a constructivist view of nature based on the will to power played out in terms of human self-interest.

If we cannot get around nihilism by appealing to intersubjectivity, then what strategies remain? Nelson provides an answer with his idea of 'inappropriable connectedness' (Nelson 2008, p. 139). Drawing on Heidegger's analysis of *Dasein* (there being), Nelson describes inappropriable connectedness as a relation to the nonrelational: 'In this relationality, including its "relation" to the nonrelational, *Dasein* is both dependent and free in its relations to things, others, and the world' (p. 139). *Dasein* is always turned and connected to things in their 'otherness' as possibilities of co-becoming. Inappropriable connectedness is the connectedness of the relation itself in what it makes possible, what it enables.

Nihilism can be countered, I suggest, by employing a concept of connectedness facing the otherness that nature has already become and by realigning our relation to this otherness in terms of what it enables, what connections it makes possible. Drawing on the idea of singular being as *partage* – the keeping apart while being together of things – found primarily in Schelling's nature philosophy, but also in the work of Heidegger, Benjamin and Nancy, and following Nelson's idea of inappropriable connectedness, I will propose a concept of 'ontological connectivity' in pursuit of a human-nature relation that does not appropriate nature for the human, but keeps it there in open connectivity. [23]

Ontological critique

In the first section of this chapter, I suggested that a nature philosophy needs to engage in critique. To critique something is to *think with it* in such a way that opens up new possibilities and ways of thinking and being. The seminal statement of modern critique is to be found in Kant's transcendental critique of reason, a groundbreaking statement of Enlightenment thinking that elevates reason above superstition, dogmatism and mere opinion.[24] Kantian critique *systematizes* thought and grounds it in acts regulated by reason.

Critique is always a critique of something. This something is that which is presented to thought in its critical self-reflection. Kantian critique involves a moment in which thought makes contact with some thing. Crucially, Kant refuses to allow this moment of contact to have any part to play in self-reflective thought, and reduces it to a mere nothingness, inconsequential for the self-constitution of the subject. But if critique cannot avoid being a critique of something, then this something must at some point be part of the critique itself. Here critique becomes ontologically grounded in its own *praxis*. Ontological critique begins in an encounter with some thing, and opens this relation to what it makes possible; what it allows thinking to think. Ontological critique can thus be renamed 'factical-ontological critique' insofar as it takes account of the fact that critique is itself involved in what it is that is being critiqued – in the fact that this thing is and has possibility.[25]

Ontological critique opens thought to possibilities in its encounter with things. Iain Mackenzie has argued that ontological (immanent) critique

> is, therefore, conceptual innovation as the construction of whole-scale alternatives to that which is being criticized from a position that is nonetheless immanent to the criticized by virtue of being the actualization of differences 'within' the domain of the criticized itself.
>
> (Mackenzie 2004, p. 77)

Immanent (ontological) critique exposes the 'differences' discovered in an encounter with the thing, thereby releasing them in the name of 'conceptual innovation' of alternatives (possibilities) within the finite terrain of the encounter itself. These differences are differences opened up in the thing's resistive relation to the system of reason in which the thing is found to be already embedded as an 'object' of thought, which, I will argue, are differences in fact (and not purely differences of negation), or differences that affirm the thing-as-other in the system itself. Ontological critique affirms the thing as already there, a disclosure of its truth as other to the system, opening up 'alternatives' or possible ways of relating to things that the system cannot allow, yet allows nevertheless because of this very fact.

In factical-ontological critique possibility is understood strictly from the finite encounter with something, as distinct from the possibilities of a system. Ontological possibility is limited to the pathways opened up in singular occurrences of being-with something that enable localized beginnings in temporal and spatial events resistive to the system, and takes account of the limitations, threats and resistances at work in the situation. Ontological possibility is thus fraught with existential issues of the being for whom the possibility befalls (Nelson 2008, p. 130). Ontological critique begins in the 'homeless' (*unheimlich*) state of the self, exposed and opened to absolute possibility, and stays within the finite terrain of the moment of contact with the thing rendered immanent to the critique itself.

I will argue in this book that ontological critique has a special relation to art as *praxis*, as a creative act that opens itself to otherness. Art is the exemplary thing that is both allowed and not allowed by the system. Like Nancy's cat, art interrupts our everyday thought in a positive way, taking it somewhere else. To encounter art in this way is to be opened to otherness that is not elsewhere but already 'here' and 'there' at the same time. To encounter art like this is to 'unwill' thinking; to let thinking be carried away; to free thought up for otherness. Nietzsche also placed a special emphasis on artists who have a certain capacity for involuntary or non-willing freedom:

> They [artists] know only too well that it is precisely when they cease to act 'voluntarily' and do everything of necessity that their feeling of freedom, subtlety, fullness of power, creative placing, disposing, shaping reaches its height – in short, that necessity and 'freedom of will' are then one in them.
>
> (Nietzsche 1973, p. 126)

By letting go of striving and projecting, and instead, confronting the necessity of having to be, artists find themselves possessed by a certain kind of involuntary freedom that grants them powers of shaping and creating – powers that release their works into open possibility. This kind of 'weak' power overturns the strong will to power that seeks endlessly for the same, and leads to an awakening of the senses in creative expression (Nietzsche 1997, p. 135). As a weak counter-power, art interrupts the stronger will to power, taking it elsewhere to some other place. Art is thus a transitive act or 'deed' that undoes what it says in the saying, opening itself out to otherness as absolute possibility. In Chapter 5, I will show how Schelling's concept of the artistic deed resolves the differences between freedom and necessity that Nietzsche invokes here, suggesting the possibility of a creative experience in the *praxis* of art as a transitive act of freedom, and in its relation to nature as such.

Beginning with things

My use of Schelling's work is not to develop a critical philosophy of material nature as Grant and others have done (Grant 2006)[26] but to provide a position for critique to think freely in terms of finite possibilities opened up in encounters with things. In the *First Outline of a System of the Philosophy of Nature*, Schelling makes the following comment about things in relation to the 'unconditioned' of nature:

> The unconditioned cannot be sought in any individual 'thing' nor in anything of which one can say that it 'is'. For what 'is' only partakes of being, and is only an individual form or kind of being. – Conversely, one can never say of the unconditioned that it 'is'.

For it is BEING ITSELF and as such, it does not exhibit itself entirely in any finite product, and every individual is, as it were, a particular expression of it.

(Schelling 2004, p. 13)

The unconditioned (nature as absolute) is not 'in' things; rather things partake of the unconditioned as a 'particular expression of it'. Schelling postulates that being a thing is both finitely singular and part of unconditioned being ('BEING ITSELF'). This is not a rejection of things, but a beginning with them in order to think the absolute as the unconditioned of nature. Consequently, I argue that Schelling's *Naturphilosophie* can be understood as a work of factical-ontological critique, moving from finite things towards possibilities guided by the 'question of being' – the question posed to critique by the thing as to its 'thatness': the fact that it *is* and hence partakes of being. Although Schelling rejects the analysis of things as individual products of nature, he nevertheless begins the thinking of nature from the finite encounter with things in their 'inhibited' activity (p. 5) as 'self-canceling singularities (p. 6), or '*simple actants*' (p. 21).

It is perhaps a fault of Schelling's that he moves at times too far away from things, losing track of the requirement that nature philosophy be guided by what things call for, what they enable thinking to think in a finite sense. Heidegger criticized Schelling's philosophy for driving a wedge between beings and Being (between things and the unconditioned) such that they lose contact with one another (Heidegger 1985, p. 161). Factical-ontological critique needs to remain with things and not move too quickly away from them. Thus, the 'dynamics from which all ground, and all bodies, issue' (Grant 2006, p. 8) as the movement of unconditioned nature must be thought as something that happens with things and not separately from them.

Schelling's *Naturphilosophie* can be understood as a factical-ontological critique of the Kantian (and Newtonian) mechanistic reduction of nature to bodies as mechanical objects, thereby releasing thought to think with the things of nature otherwise in terms of what they enable, what they make possible other than as mechanisms of a system of nature. My argument seeks to find an opening in the human-nature relation itself, a beginning with nature as enabling possibility. I reread Schelling's *Naturphilosophie* not so much for what it can tell me about material nature, but for the critical position it draws from Kantian critique, and how, by adopting this position, we might rethink our relation with nature's 'free being' (*poiesis*) through our encounter with things as such.

The will to system

Knowledge is secured *systematically* through the application of reason to things, converting them into objects positioned within a system of interrelating values.[27] In the broadest sense, a system is an abstraction of 'what is' into a set of values sustained by the system itself. The singular life of a tree, for instance, counts for nothing unless it contributes to the totality of a system (e.g. a system of tree farming, an ecosystem, an economic system, the tree itself as an organic system) defined as a set of interrelating, self-correcting exchange processes abstracted from the tree as such.

In his seminal work on cybernetic systems, *Steps to an Ecology of Mind*, Gregory Bateson describes how a system works. A system, he argues, has its own mentality, its own mind: '*the mental characteristics of the system are immanent, not in some part, but in the system as a whole*' (Bateson 1972, p. 316). The thinking self is not outside the system, but part of it. In system environments, human agents do not think outside the system, but within it, as a function of the thinking of the system itself: 'if we desire to explain or understand the mental aspect of any biological event, we must take into account the system – that is, the network of *closed* circuits, within which that biological event is determined' (p. 317).[28] Bateson provides an example: 'Consider a man felling a tree with an axe. Each stroke of the axe is modified or corrected, according to the shape of the cut face of the tree left by the previous stroke. This self-corrective (*i.e.* mental) process is brought about by a total system, trees-eyes-brain-muscles-axe-stroke-tree; and it is this total system that has the characteristics of immanent mind' (p. 317).

Bateson's description presents the basics of a systems theory approach to nature. In the way he describes it, the tree has no independent existence but is given over entirely to the system. It partakes of the system of tree felling, directed by a self-correcting feedback loop of successive cuts; each cut into the tree is positioned for the next stroke that adjusts according to an *eidos* (a foreseeable plan or calculation) that requires that the tree be chopped down for the 'good' of the system – the efficient felling of the tree by an expert woodcutter adjusting his actions according to the 'mind' of the system itself. In this case, the tree's 'being' is entirely given over to its felling and being turned into a material product. However, if we were to think of this 'being for the system' not in terms of the efficiency of the system but according to power relations between productive and resistive forces, a different set of operators becomes apparent, where the active force of production (the wilful act of cutting down the tree) is met by the passive force of resistance (the tree's refusal to give itself up readily to the axe). The very fact that the axe needs to be applied violently to the tree indicates the work of a resistive force at the heart of the system: a silent 'no' uttered by the tree as it presents itself to the axe. Resistance is not something added, but already part of the tree's being-for-the-system.

As Michel Foucault has argued, in any system of power relations, 'resistance comes first, and resistance remains superior to forces of the process; power relations are obliged to change with the resistance' (Foucault 1997, p. 167). Without resistance, force could not come to be the force it is (force without resistance is abstract force, detached from what it affects and makes happen). Thus resistivity must already *be* if force is to occur. As a process of production, the system of tree felling must already be inhabited by a resistivity as part of the tree's being: a First Force resistivity that says 'no' to the system's 'yes'. The links between 'trees-eyes-brain-muscles-axe-stroke-tree' that constitute the system of tree felling are thus forged by a First Force resistivity specific to each element. For instance, when a sore muscle sends a signal to the brain to stop using it, the muscle 'is' first and foremost before being part of a signal relay. Its signalling to the brain affirms the fact of its existence, interrupting the smooth running of the system that threatens to break down at any moment. The system's actions are given over to overcoming the muscle's (and the tree's) resistance; the system requires resistance to be the system it already is. Thus, the mentality of the system is formed not simply on the needs of the efficient coordination of its elements, but on the will to overcome the resistance of the things within it; the will to order and control their refusal to act in accordance with the system's mentality – its *eidos* or planned outcome. Resistance is a positive force acting both with and against the system. As First Force, resistance affirms the tree's being otherwise.

From the perspective of critique, a system is an artefact of the human subject thinking transcendentally, according to the principles of *a priori* reason (i.e. thinking scientifically).[29] By assigning reason to an ecosystem as if it stood independently of human thought is to risk naturalizing the system, mistaking the system for nature itself. It places human thought in a transcendent position – a position of theoretical dominance over the system and the elements within it. To get around this problem we need to ensure that the human self remaining within the system does so in some kind of free and active state.[30]

It is possible to think both for and against the system at the same time; both for what the system 'wills' for its own good order, while retaining a sense of how things resist, in their being there just as they are. The deficiency in a systems theory approach is that it provides no room for a resistive thinking capable of thinking otherwise. As a consequence, contingency is obscured by the will to system that seeks only to fulfil itself at the expense of the things of nature found there, in their being as such. The things that a system controls and orders cannot be seen in any other way than as already given over to the system; they cannot be seen as singular things, as resistances to the system itself. In their being there, things are as resistances to the will to system, without which the system could not function. By that very fact, in their singular resistive thatness, they open up possibility of an otherness that goes elsewhere, to some place not yet known. To see the tree in its resistive being – in its saying no – is to see it otherwise, to see it *poietically*, as open possibility. *Poietic* seeing is a non-possessive seeing that releases the things seen from the control of *eidos*, enabling an 'inappropriable connectedness' with otherness (Nelson 2008, p. 139).

Ontological connectivity

Previously I suggested that the concept of ontological connectivity could be employed in critique as a counter to nihilism (the reduction of meaning to subjective will). Ontological connectivity is the opening of human being otherwise, exposing it to an absolute possibility, and enabling other ways of being. In absolutely open connectivity, the human no longer sees itself reflected in the mirror of nature, but encounters nature otherwise, in the possibilities of being with things as they lead us away from where we are. In encountering these things of nature there, in this openness, they pose questions to us, making us account for their mode of being and our relation to them. In this way, we are turned into an abyss. By turning into the abyss of nature as the 'not' of thought, we see there a possibility that something else might come about, a new relation starting to figure itself out as *poietic* becoming. In ontologically open connectivity, we think with things in their flight from being – in their becoming other.

Chapter 2

Saying Nature

Nature is

To begin an ontological critique of nature, we need to suspend any specific predications associated with the word 'nature' by subtracting the prediction, so that we are left with the assertion: *nature is*. We need to shift from:

> *Nature is x*
> to
> *Nature is*

An ontological critique of nature is concerned with the substantive assertion 'nature is', and asks, 'how can this assertion be said?' In other words, an ontological critique is not concerned with what nature is or could be, but with the fact that it can be said that it is. That nature 'is' then becomes the issue for critique. The *that* of nature (the fact that it is) is seen to be bound up in the 'saying' that marks it in its thatness – as some thing.

What is saying? Saying something is not the same as knowing what one says. One 'says' something not in terms of what one knows about what one says, but simply to say it with regard to something, to announce one's relation to whatever the saying is about. Saying is a *deixis*: it marks the act of saying in a specific place in relation to the thing spoken about. Saying is thus transitive: it shifts meaning from the saying to the thing.[1] A person who says something does not need to know the language she speaks in a technical sense. To know language as language, one needs to study its structure, its *langue*, whereas to say something is to make this something meaningful; to bring it into being; to enable something to take place.[2] Saying concerns sense in relation to the world of things and events, whereas knowing concerns significance: a relation to a system of meaning.[3] By saying something you are orienting yourself within a world of things and events, and not to a system of signification.

Ontological critique is a critique of the saying of nature. It asks: in what ways can nature be said? It thus invokes a certain kind of facticity concerning things. The fact that it can be said that 'nature is' invokes a 'that' about which this saying is concerned, and so requires an attentive gaze on things – the things of nature – not as already formed objects, but as contingently placed singularities invoked by the critique itself. These things of nature must be dealt with according to the requirements of critique in exploring their phenomenal limits, and what it is to say such things – to bring them into being in the saying itself. [4]

The ontological critique I will be invoking in this book concerns *poiesis*, or the *poietic* saying of being as a creative making attuned with nature.[5] The early Greeks understood *poiesis* to be the shaping force of nature that runs through all things, including human beings who are both shaped by and employ *poiesis* in their way of being (Taminiaux 1987). *Poietic* saying is a saying that partakes of *poiesis*, as the shaping of the relation between human being and nature itself. Drawing from the nature philosophy of Friedrich Schelling and the phenomenological-ontological philosophy of Martin Heidegger, I will outline an ontological critique of the things of nature in terms of how these things can be said as *poietic* becoming. A *poietic* approach to nature philosophy is situated in the finite place where critique occurs, in its unfolding complexity as a saying of nature. *Poietic* critique is concerned with the saying of the things of nature, and their capacity to open up modes of being other than those currently in force. Why? Because without critique, the saying of nature can only be said in one way – the way it is currently said – thus obscuring alternative ways of saying nature, or making it difficult for humans to say any relation with nature at all and simply 'talk' it.[6] By obscuring or concealing *poiesis*, the dominant mode of being – the mode by which we live out an already normalised way of being – blocks openness and possibility of nature's becoming, leading to an inability to think through our current relation to nature other than in terms of what we already say about it.[7]

Poietic critique is not the same as aesthetics. Since Kant, aesthetic critique reduces encounters with the things of nature to inner subjective states of being, effectively pushing the things away, whereas *poietic* critique begins with the things of nature, responding to what they say and how they enable other ways of being.[8]

Is nature an empty signifier?

In the previous section I indicated that an ontological critique of nature needs to account for the *that* of nature. That nature is, is what is at issue. This thatness of nature is tied up in the way nature is said: by saying nature in a certain way, the things of nature become meaningful and are brought into being. Thus we come to the following question: how is nature said today? In our knowledge-driven discourse, nature can only be said according to a system that determines its meaning in advance. But in being determined in advance nature must necessarily withdraw. Why? Because, as Ernesto Laclau has argued, a system cannot contain the thing it determines without simultaneously breaching its own limits. The thing must be missing from the system, otherwise the system would be the thing. Thus all systems contain a void or 'empty place' (Laclau 1996, p. 40) filling in for the missing thing: 'we are not dealing with an impossibility without location, as in the case of a logical contradiction, but with a *positive* impossibility' (p. 40). The aim of all systems is to produce this void as if it were the thing itself. This is the condition of the 'empty signifier':

An empty signifier can, consequently, only emerge if there is a structural impossibility in signification as such, and only if this impossibility can signify itself as an interruption (subversion, distortion, etcetera) of the structure of the sign. That is, the limits of signification can only announce themselves as the impossibility of realizing what is within those limits – if the limits could be signified in a direct way, they would be internal to signification and, *ergo*, would not be limits at all.

(Laclau 1996, p. 37)

As the place of the void, the empty signifier announces both the possibility of the thing's presence to the system and its exclusion, triggering a return of difference in fulfilment of the system's claim over the thing's being as a never-ending, self-defeating task. This is the negative condition described by Timothy Morton in his book *Ecology Without Nature*, where nature is affirmed negatively, as always 'giv[ing] us the slip' (Morton 2007, p. 2; see Introduction).

But what if the void were itself an enablement, that, in announcing the absence of thing's being, caused the system to open up against itself? Such an enablement would itself be part of the being announced; it would affirm this being but otherwise, other than in terms of the system itself.[9] The empty signifier would become the site of an opening into otherness that does not immediately close into the 'desire' of the system to complete itself, but rather, would be the beginning of otherness the system has admitted against itself. To see the empty signifier in this way is to switch critical modes, from negative to positive critique: from a critique of the system in its failure to deliver on its promises, to an affirmation of possibility from within but against the system itself. Rather than beginning from the system of meaning as negation of the thing, a positive mode begins from the thing itself, as already there, already placed in the system but not of it.

As an empty signifier, nature is the 'thatness' that interrupts the system. Whatever the system might designate the meaning of nature to be, it also says something else, in the in-between marked by the interruption itself. This saying opens the system out to an otherness required for the system to work, yet sufficiently resistive to it to trigger a turn in the system itself. I will contend that the name of this turning otherwise is art. Art is the saying-turning of nature otherwise. This saying-turning otherwise is not simply an other saying – an alternative story about nature not told by the system, but the system itself saying itself otherwise such that it turns against itself in a real, historical sense of becoming other.

Nature as the place of non-place

Is a return to a more secure and original sense of place adequate for a nature philosophy today? Ecocriticism often proposes a naturalistic concept of place, adjacent to, yet separate from, the industrialized world, as an alternative means of 'inhabiting the earth' (Foltz 1995).[10] However, in a thoroughly globalized world, such places are themselves products of a derenaturing by technological systems so that inhabiting them risks falling in with the will of the system itself.[11] Ecocriticism also invokes past places as 'the locus of the holy', leading to a 'romantic reanimation of nature [as] resacralization' (Rigby 2004, p. 45). There are difficulties here too. A romantic return to sacred places enters a hermeneutic circle where the lost place is projected dialectically into some future state of being, only to be seen there as a reflection of its own obsolescence. Romantic yearning for a return to nature is itself a symptom of the modernity it tries to surpass and cannot get beyond its own desire.[12]

Attempts to retrieve a natural or sacred place to counter the unnatural, secularized placelessness of the modern world tend to overlook the power of the system to determine place as already natural, already sacred, already 'at home' (*heimlich*). Nature is already the ideal place sought for in critique. An ontological critique should therefore begin not by imagining an alternative place of nature, but from the place where nature currently is, in the placelessness assigned to it in the modern world. It can do this, I suggest, by retrieving a sense of the place of nature as void; a sense of nature as already placed in placelessness. The issue then is not to identify certain places of nature as natural or sacred, but to see nature as everywhere both placed and unplaced. To do this is to remember nature as *poiesis*.

Disappearing nature

An ontological critique of nature needs to begin with the fact that nature is already a 'privileged expression of an ontology' (Vallier 2003, p. xvii), described by Merleau-Ponty in the following way:

> Nature is the primordial – that is, the nonconstructed, the noninstituted; hence the idea of an eternity of nature (the eternal return), of a solidity. Nature is an enigmatic object, an object that is not an object at all; it is not really set out in front of us. It is our soil [*sol*] – not what is in front of us, facing us, but rather, *that which carries us*.
> (Merleau-Ponty 2003, p. 4, emphasis added)

From early Greek thinking to the present, nature bears an ontological truth: nature as being itself – as the 'primordial' All, its essential movement and transformation of matter into timeless eternity. We (human beings) are not separate from nature, but carried along by it: nature is 'that which carries us'. In our possibility we are already carried by nature as *poietic* becoming.

The western tradition remains captive to an ontology of nature as dynamic being. However, the modern epoch institutes a decisive break (the Cartesian moment) where the 'solidity' or substance of nature becomes subject to a calculation in thought itself. Nature is now presented as either knowable or unknowable to a thinking subject. In effect, nature is reduced in its power and authority, and in its place the capacity of the thinking subject is elevated to a decisive position to determine nature's meaning through the subject's access to reason. The crucial shift in the modern epoch is not simply that nature is submitted to the calculations of reason, but in order for this to happen, nature in itself, in its absolute or primordial state, must be banished from subjective thought. In the modern epoch, nature must be thought either as the knowable product of calculative reason, or as the unknowable other against which calculative reason takes measure of itself. There are thus two natures in modernity: an unknowable First Nature indifferent to human being and a knowable Second Nature, the nature of science and calculative reason.

Nature as originary being is retained in the modern epoch, but as the other to nature as a product of calculative reason. In what sense is this retention understood? According to the temporal logic of modernity, a logic that privileges the punctual now as the ground of infinite calculation, nature as being is retained as a fading or withdrawing from the present. Nature can only appear by disappearing at the same time. Nature is here with us, but in the mode of being elsewhere, at some place other than the present moment; in a distant past or a fleeting moment escaping from one's perception; a place remaining forever elsewhere as an idealized vision; a place of divine inspiration or unified bodily fulfilment, countering the fragmented, alienated state of the contemporary world. This retention of nature as other – as a withdrawn, elusive presence – constitutes the 'privileged' ontological condition of nature from which we must begin our critique. This does not mean that critique should begin from the places assigned to nature by the modern epoch (which always remain as ideals and hence beyond existence), but that it should begin from the movement of the retention itself, in the way the modern epoch holds nature to itself by disavowing it at the same time. The aim should be to show how nature is retained disjunctively, as 'that which carries us' – that which bears us away into open becoming, but from within the movement of retaining-withdrawing itself.

Remembering nature

In the previous chapter I introduced Nietzsche's idea of nihilism in terms of the negation of the things of nature in relations between subjects (intersubjectivity). Nihilism sets up a seemingly insurmountable gap between subjective states of being and the otherness of nature that, as we have seen in the previous section, withdraws from us the more we try to reach it. But Nietzsche does not simply diagnose the condition of nihilism, he also offers a way out by suggesting that we engage with things in their *poietic* withdrawal from us by switching positions.

In *The Will to Power*, Nietzsche diagnoses the nihilism of the modern epoch as 'faith in the categories of reason' (Nietzsche 1967, p. 13). He says:

We have measured the value of the world according to categories *that refer to a purely fictional world.*

Final conclusion: All the values by means of which we have tried so far to render the world estimable for ourselves and which then proved inapplicable and therefore devaluated the world – all these values are, psychologically considered, the results of certain perspectives of utility, designed to maintain and increase human constructs of domination – and they have been falsely *projected* into the essence of things. What we find here is still the *hyperbolic naiveté* of man: positing himself as the meaning and measure of the value of things.

(pp. 13–14)

Here Nietzsche diagnoses nihilism as a false projection of values into 'the essence of things', an objectifying of things according to utility and domination. Things lose their anchorage in being-as-becoming, and become placed in 'a purely fictional world' of calculative reason, as objects of human thought, will and desire. What solution does Nietzsche offer? He suggests we should steer clear of subjective truths (the truths of calculative reason and the aestheticization of the senses as internal to human being) and instead value being-as-becoming, or the force of nature that carries us outside the system: 'one should value more than truth the force that forms, simplifies, shapes, invents' (p. 326). Nature (being-as-becoming) is already operating in the system, already available to take us elsewhere, if only we have the vision to see it there. In Aphorism 44 of *Daybreak* he says:

Why is it that this thought comes back to me again and again and in ever more varied colours? – that *formerly*, when investigators of knowledge sought out the origin of things they always believed they would discover something of incalculable significance for all later action and judgment, that they always *presupposed*, indeed, that the *salvation* of man must depend on *insight into the origin of things*: but that now, on the contrary, the more we advance towards origins, the more our interest diminishes; indeed, that all the evaluations and 'interestedness' we have implanted into things begin to lose their meaning the further we go back and the closer we approach the things themselves. *The more insight we possess into an origin the less significant does the origin appear*: while *what is nearest to us*, what is around us and in us, gradually begins to display colours and beauties and enigmas and riches of significance of which earlier mankind had not an inkling. Formerly, thinkers prowled around angrily like captive animals, watching the bars of their cages and leaping against them in order to smash them down: and *happy* seemed he who through a gap in them believed he saw something of what was outside, of what was distant and beyond.

(Nietzsche 1997, pp. 30–31)

Here, speaking with a voice from the future, Nietzsche diagnoses the nihilism of the modern age as due to an unbridgeable gap between the human subject and the 'origin of things'. In the pre-modern age (and here, Nietzsche has pre-Socratic Greek culture in mind), it was possible to think of the origin of things in terms of 'incalculable significance', that is, in terms of their meaning as something already given, something that was simply there without any need to calculate or value them. However, to seek knowledge of the origin of things in the modern age is to project values into them, so their original meaning withdraws: '*the more insight we possess into an origin the less significant does the origin appear*'. Nihilism is this withdrawal of the meaning of the origin, leaving us with nothing but our own values projected into things, and leaving the knowledge seekers trapped like wild animals in a cage of reason. Nihilism is not simply the reduction of meaning to the subjective will, but indicates a disjuncture in the originary moment of being, setting in motion an advancing/withdrawing movement that leaves human existence alone and abandoned by the flight of the gods, yet strangely enabled with a power to see '*what is nearest us*, what is around us and in us […] colours and beauties and enigmas and riches of significance'.

In this alienated yet enabled existence, Nietzsche offers a way out. For those who can see, what is nearest to us begins to flash colours in rich complexities that open us to the dawning of a new era.[13] Importantly for Nietzsche, this experience of wondrous openness could not be had by 'earlier mankind', that is, by pre-modern humans; because for them, things are already open in wonder. Rather for modern humans the shining of things (*Schein*) occurs as a disruption within rational modern systems and not outside them.[14] Nietzsche proposes a postmodern experience of otherness by thinking of a kind of prescient seeing that takes place in the disjuncture (the 'gap' in the bars of the prison house of reason), opening to the unknown outside as something 'distant and beyond' yet experienced very near to us ('what is around us and in us'). To see in this way requires a turning in the seeing itself: Nietzsche has to reverse the withdrawing of nature by overturning our relation to it, thus making it come back to us in its withdrawal. Such an experience is one of art, as 'an excess and overflow […] through the images and desires of intensified life' (Nietzsche 1967, p. 422).

Nietzsche's aphorism suggests we can turn within the modern epoch to overcome nihilism. Turning involves an encounter with nature as it withdraws from us so that we see it coming back to us in a chromatic display of overflowing colours that 'intensifies life'. At this stage I want to suggest that this encounter with nature in turning to it in its withdrawing is a remembering of nature. This is a remembering that comes not by looking directly at nature, but by dwelling in the in-between of nature as withdrawn ground and the possibilities it enacts. This is both a joyous and melancholic way of being: joyous insofar as we are able to think with nature as becoming, as open possibility, and melancholy in that we are constantly reminded of the finitude of our existence and of all living things in the face of nature's indifference – its non-concern for human affairs and the destiny of individual living things. Remembering nature is thus about an absolute forgetting in which the relation between the present and the past is collapsed in the turning, thereby making way for another space from which to build a future. Withdrawing nature enacts forgetting, not as the loss of the past, but in terms of an affirmation of the collapsed present as prefigured future. This forgetfulness takes place as a remembering of nature's void – its grounding in the dynamic stillness of *poietic* capacity. Remembering of nature is both joyous and melancholic insofar as to remember nature is to be open to absolute possibility, but, at the same time, to be reminded of one's finitude in mortal existence, alienated from the fulfilment of the very possibility one remembers. *Poietic* capacity is thus a capacity to be held in this state of joyous-melancholic openness, neither fully joyous in the embrace of the absolute, nor fully melancholic and locked into one's subjective state of being.

The thought of an absolute remembering invokes nature as a void or abyss. We can find this idea of the void of nature in the writings of Walter Benjamin, whose concept of the dialectical image as a flashing insight into absolute futurity causes the present to show itself as ruin.[15] Benjamin thinks the absolute from the ruins of the present as it withdraws from us. Heidegger's reading of pre-Socratic Greek philosophy allows him to develop a concept of the *Augenblick*: the 'blink of an eye, a momentary look at what is momentarily concrete, which as such can always be otherwise' (Heidegger 1997, pp. 112–13). Both Benjamin and Heidegger draw their ideas from post-Kantian philosophers and their responses to Kant's separation of the subject from the thing-in-itself. The challenge here is to try to think the thing-in-itself not as something we disavow or push away as essentially unknowable, but as that which opens us to absolute possibility. To do this, we need to encounter some thing.

Carrying nature

An ontological critique is not concerned with what nature is, but with the way it is said. Here are two ways nature can be said:

1. Nature can be said in discourse
2. The saying of nature as *poiesis*

Through a self-limitation the humanities disciplines accept point 1 but not 2. Humanities accept that nature is said discursively, as a construct of human thought, imagination and categorization, but cannot bring itself to think of nature itself as saying anything at all. Nature as *poiesis* – as a shaping force acting through all things – is often described and commented upon, but quickly turned into a backdrop or stage on which to play out the problem of human subjectivity locked into its own categories of thought.

Ontological critique will need to counter this limitation by responding to the following challenge: how can critique say nature (1) as its own saying (2), while remaining within the limits of critique? To say nature as its own saying is to carry nature in the critique itself. Critique needs to become transitively located with respect to what it critiques. This is the challenge I have set myself in this book.

To develop a transitive critique of nature I turn to the philosophy of Schelling.

Part II

Nature Philosophy

Chapter 3

Schelling after Kant

Beginning with Schelling's nature philosophy

The nature philosophy of Friedrich Schelling has been overlooked as a way of rethinking the human-nature relation. By returning to Schelling I begin again the task of this rethinking. The aim of this chapter is to situate Schelling's *Naturphilosophie* in relation to Kant's neglect of nature in his critique of reason, showing how the question of nature can be reposed in terms of being with nature and not against it.

For Schelling, philosophizing about nature is not empirical investigation, but partaking of nature as a creative act: 'to philosophize about Nature means *to create* Nature [...] in other words to tear *yourself* away from the common view which discerns in nature only what "happens" – and which, at most, views the act as a *factum, not the action itself* in its acting' (Schelling 2004, pp. 14–15). By 'tear[ing] [ourselves] away from the common view' we encounter things as part of the activity itself. The *fact* that things are is not the end result of a prior activity 'extinguished in its product' (p. 14), but part of the creative productivity in our encounter with the thing itself. Our philosophizing not only points to this activity but partakes of it creatively.

To partake of nature creatively is to be free with nature; to partake of nature's freedom. Nature's freedom is its capacity to be otherwise, in the possibility of a tear in nature itself; in the eternal cision that splits things into the heterogeneous multiplicity that nature is always becoming (pp. 5–19). The things of nature are not isolated atoms, closed off from the outside, but 'apparent products' (p. 16), poised on the verge of becoming other. Things are kept in place by the 'inhibiting' or blocking of the thing's yearning to move away from itself by a 'limitation of its [Nature's] own activity' (p. 17). To be free with nature is to unblock the blocked thing: 'to quicken it with freedom and set it on its own free development' (p. 14).

Schelling's *Naturphilosophie* has been described as a '"realist" metaphysics' (Kojevè 1969, p. 152) or alternatively, as a philosophy of matter (Grant 2006). Neither of these terms is suitable. The term 'realist' carries metaphysical assumptions about knowledge as a dimension of the real, while a philosophy of matter reduces things to independent components of the physical universe. Schelling would refute both these terms. A more suitable term for Schelling's philosophy is 'factical ontology'.[1] A factical ontology encounters the things of nature as things that *are*, posing questions about what being 'this thing' means. My aim in this and the following three chapters is to retrieve from Schelling's philosophy certain key ideas – *Unground, partage*, positive freedom, virtual nature – in developing a factical ontology of the 'things of nature'.

The possibility of being free with nature counters objections by deep ecologists who argue that the crisis of the environment is caused by humans having too much freedom (Zimmerman 2004, p. 209). In this argument, the freedom associated with human being negates nature, allowing humans to exploit and control it in pursuit of their own ends. The solution of deep ecology is to surrender freedom in order to return human being to nature, to 'let things be', thereby aligning human ends with the ends of nature in a common determinacy.[2] But can we dispense with human freedom all that easily? To do so would be to deny the very fact that humans already *are* free to think about and reflect on nature (e.g. as wilderness, environment, force, organism, ecosystem, symbol, representation). To surrender this freedom would be to deny the very basis of human thought and action. The solution is not to deny human freedom, but to think about freedom in a different way.

Following Schelling, I propose to develop a critique that retains freedom in its positive mode aligned with nature. By seeing human being as already part of the 'free being' of nature, critique can retain the freedom to think freely with nature while acknowledging the restraints and responsibilities that our relation to nature places on us.

Kant's gap

The philosophical problem that Schelling and his contemporaries were confronted with was a fatal flaw in Kant's critique of reason (the seminal philosophical system in modern thought at that time), which meant that knowledge remained trapped in subjective self-reflection, thereby perpetuating the gap between the inner domain of reason and the outer domain of the senses.[3] This gap exposed human knowledge to sheer contingency, a fact that Kant accepted as a necessity of existence, but which he then elided in favour of transcendence in *a priori* reason. Kant's gap exposes the possibility of a thinking and seeing otherwise from the contingency of human knowledge – an exposure that can only occur in the critique itself.[4]

For Kant, knowledge of things is limited to their appearances as objects of thought, as distinct from things in themselves to which there is no direct access: 'What the things-in-themselves may be I do not know, nor do I need to know, since a thing can never come before me except in appearance' (Kant 1929, p. 286). Our contingency as finite beings will not allow us the God-like view of things in themselves. However, we are, ourselves, different from the things that appear to us insofar as we have access to ideas (the ideas of reason, e.g. unity, causality) that enable us to make sense of these appearances, and so we can be guided by these ideas in pursuit of knowledge of the objects of thought. Kant's critical philosophy recognizes the ineluctable contingency of human existence in relation to the things that we experience in the world and offers a way of dealing with this by showing how knowledge transcends this contingency according to *a priori* principles of reason.

To do this, Kantian critique gives up any preconceived dogmas proposing a substrate of being – a substance – that underlies things.[5] This means that for Kant, being a thing is limited to mere things, or things just as they appear to the thinking subject. Mere things – the things presented to thought – are stripped of their connectedness to other things and reduced to the status of 'actualities' related to the perception of the subject guided by transcendental principles of reason.[6] Things are thus atomized[7] into discreet entities with their own particularity in relation to the systems of reason that make them objectively meaningful to a thinking subject in categorical ways (Kant 1929, pp. 24–25).[8]

Atomized things are mechanistic in that they occupy positions in abstract mathematical space governed by laws of physical causality and inertia.[9] We can see here a seminal procedure for the classical-modern scientific outlook on nature as an aggregate of particular things organized according to procedures of object formation. The ground of such objects – the necessary conditions of their existence – is not to be found in some underlying substrate or material process, but in subjective thinking itself, insofar as it conforms to the guidance of universal reason enacted in a *praxis* situated exclusively in rational space and time. The things of nature are reduced to discrete objects of thought, the efficacy of which is discovered in the rational principles reflected in, and practiced by, the thinking subject.[10]

Kant's reduction of the things of nature to objects of thought means that thought must reflect on what it perceives in a process of 'coming-to-know'. It does this through the necessity of the 'I think' (Kant 1929, p. 153), operating as a pre-subjective 'apperception' or intuition accompanying any given act of thinking that enables the systematic application of the 'faculties' or 'powers' (judgement, understanding, reason) to things as they appear as such (Kant 1987, p. 37). This process of coming-to-know is not the coming-to-know of an already knowing subject, but the coming-to-know that is necessary for a subject to 'be' as a rationally thinking being. Rational systems thus depend on the possibility of something outside the system – a potential for a subject to be in the 'I think' of absolute thought.[11] This self-potential exists indeterminately as the very possibility of subjectivity.[12] Without such a self, reason would have to lift itself up by its own bootstraps in order to bring things into being, a possibility that denies the grounding of reason in specific subjective acts. And since Kant's critical philosophy is precisely an attempt to show how reason is necessarily grounded in specific subjective acts, then reason must be accompanied by a self-potential irreducible to the system itself.

The ground of system-objects must therefore always be an open possibility, a free space that opens into new potentials through finite acts of reason of the subject's coming-to-know. The self exists freely in the open ground as a potential for being – something not yet subject to reason, and, as such, could always be otherwise. In any given subject formation or system of reason, a possibility of being otherwise can be brought about through critical reflection on the self's free existence as a possible other to the system itself. Kant's grounding of reason in subjective acts solves the problem of universal reason reflecting on itself, but opens up further issues of a self existing in the open ground of finite freedom, offering ways of being unaccounted by the systems of reason themselves. Kant will be obliged to develop further critique to account for this freedom, through a regulative principle of reason in moral action accessed through a special intuition of apperception (i.e. consciousness of self-consciousness). Those who followed Kant (post-Kantian philosophy) needed to posit a positive element, a moment of revelation (*Schein*), to compensate for the lack of any ground for reason to take grip in real, historical existence.[13]

The subject, as the self's realization in systems of reason, must be both free and constrained by reason, constituting a 'paradox of freedom' that nevertheless calls for a resolution.[14] Why? The subject must be free from the determinations of reason, otherwise it will have already been determined and hence no longer be a possibility as such. Thus, as we have already seen, Kantian critique implies the existence of something not yet subject to reason – a self existing in relation to the things of nature other than as subject; a self existing in the possibility of what a subject could be.[15] This self is not yet a subject, but a possibility to come. To confuse this free self with the subject is to make a fundamental error against Kantian critique – to assign freedom to the subject that it has no right to have.

This not-yet-subject cannot be determined by the necessity of the laws of reason, otherwise it would lose its contingent status and no longer be free. Rather the self must be that which acts absolutely on possibilities in a free relation to nature. The self must, in essence, be an absolutely free self – a self deciding absolutely (and not in terms of different kinds of selfhood) on what it could be, which, for Kant, must be in accordance with the laws of reason transcendent in reflective thinking. To think of the paradox of freedom adequately, we need to abandon temporal sequence (i.e. where the free self is said to exist prior to the rational subject), and think of the free self and the rational subject at the same time. The subject is thus doubled by its own possibility. The decision to 'be oneself' cannot be made by the subject as the subject *is* 'not yet'; rather, the self is its own decisiveness, its own 'deed' of being-decisive.

For Kant, the deciding self (as the subject *in potentia*) should be guided by the regulative ideas of reason in which it should willingly participate as a means of achieving rational ends.[16] The crucial issue here is that Kant's critique opens up an ontological gap between the free self and the regulative idea – an unruliness in subjective being that, for Kant, must be overcome by the 'categorical imperative' – where the will of the subject accords with universal reason. The point to keep in mind, however, is that the ontological condition of the self – the condition of the self's being – is that it be free to exist separately from its subjectification to reason. This freedom is based not on the autonomous will of the subject willing itself into existence, but on possibilities of being, a distinction I will take up in terms of enablement in the following chapters of this book.[17]

'All support here fails us'

In an illuminating passage of the *Critique of Pure Reason* Kant outlines the basic issues related to the possibility of a free self:

> Unconditioned necessity, which we so indispensably require as the last bearer of all things, is for human reason the veritable abyss. Eternity itself, in all its terrible sublimity […] is far from making the same overwhelming impression on the mind; for it only *measures* the

duration of things, it does not *support* them. We cannot put aside, and yet also cannot endure the thought, that a being, which we represent to ourselves as supreme amongst all possible beings, should, as it were, say to itself: 'I am from eternity to eternity, and outside me there is nothing save what is through my will, *but whence then am I?*' All support here fails us.

(Kant 1929, p. 513)

Here Kant tries to 'think' absolute being (unconditioned necessity), only to find that such thinking leads to an abyss. He tries to put into words what such an absolute being (an absolute 'I') might say about itself in order to 'ground' itself in the human subject as 'indispensably require[d]', and finds in doing so that he has to posit a further 'I' and so on *ad infinitum*: "'I am from eternity to eternity, and outside me there is nothing save what is through my will, *but whence then am I?*" *All support here fails us*' (final emphasis added). In this passage Kant exposes the supplementary logic of self-positing where the 'I' can only posit itself by invoking the possibility of another 'I' outside it, in the abyss of reason 'where all support here fails', but he does this in order to demonstrate its danger. We entertain this thought of the abyssal free self, Kant says, at pain of losing our groundedness in reason. In the very attempt to ground absolute being in a finite act of philosophical reason (in the very words that Kant uses in his critique), the supplementary logic of self-positing sets in train an opening in reason itself.

The self-positing of the subject that here tries to will itself into existence must by necessity be accompanied by an 'I' separate from the will. This 'I' is not something that posits itself wilfully in a single stroke of self-presence, but marks itself as a possibility about which Kant conjectures, invoking an abyssal supplementary logic where the saying of a single 'I' summons up another and another, all necessary for the thought to go on. In being the mark that it is, the 'I' always escapes its conditions of self-regulation to the point where Kant is forced to conclude that 'all support here fails'. The 'I' is exposed to a radical contingency in the very fact that it can be said, a contingency that is always in the mode of having yet to find its ground; it exists in the groundlessness of pure possibility or absolute contingency.[18]

But in being the mark that it is, the I nevertheless grounds itself in what it does, what it enacts and sets going. That is, the I's 'is-ness' (its singularity) is to be an ungrounded mark, something already grounded in ungroundedness. The I is positive precisely in the sense that its free being is affirmed in the mark of what it announces, what it makes possible, without this possibility ever coming into actuality in the announcement itself. The I says what it wants to be: another just like me; someone 'we represent to ourselves as supreme among all possible beings' – the proxy-god of the *cogito* reflecting itself into existence. But in saying this, the I holds itself back, marking itself there in the free space of absolute possibility. This means that the speaking of self-presence cannot be reduced to the *logos* (the regulation of reason in self-identity) where what is said is said solely on behalf of the subject who speaks, but is also a saying of an openness in being itself. Self-presence carries a necessity inimical to its own operation; in breaking with the *logos* the I speaks otherwise, interrupting self-presence in the immediacy of its own act, opening it out to an absolute possibility. In this openness, the other, already excluded from the reason of self-presence (from its self-identification in the *logos*), is suddenly able to speak back. As the excluded other, things can speak back to us when we communicate with them in their otherness from within the systems of reason themselves.[19]

The positive moment

In considering the unruly logic of the I-self (the not yet subject), we need to keep in mind Kant's important transcendental move, which is to bracket out knowledge of things in themselves in order to establish a secure ground in reason for reflecting on how we come to know things as objects of thought. The problem here is that Kant's transcendental move, where the groundless self leaves its abyssal existence for the security of rational grounds in reflective thought, elides free existence as open possibility. However, free existence can never be erased because to do so would be to shut down the very possibility of the transcendental gesture itself. Free existence as open possibility must always remain in order to retain the freedom necessary to initiate reflective thought in the first instance. This positive element must already be marked in the transcendental gesture itself. In Schelling's words,

> [in Kant's transcendental critique] the *concept* of a thing contains only pure *whatness* [*Was*] of the concept, but nothing of its [the thing's] *thatness* [*Daß*], of its existence. Kant shows in general how futile it is for reason to attempt through inferences to reach beyond itself to existence [...] The question, therefore, had to arise whether after the breakdown of the old metaphysics [by Kantian critique] the *other* positive element is completely destroyed or whether – on the contrary – after the negative philosophy had been beaten down into pure rationalism the positive philosophy, now free and independent from the negative, must configure itself into its own science.
>
> (Schelling 2007, p. 147)

For Schelling the 'thatness' of the thing – its 'existence' as a positivity in open possibility – is unaccounted in Kant's 'negative' philosophy. This unaccountability is not an unfortunate lapse by Kant, but a necessary moment in the way negative philosophy seeks to transcend its own enactment. The positive moment of free existence of the thing is a product of, yet elided in, negative philosophy itself. Schelling suggests that negative critique harbours a moment of positive critique, configuring itself into a science of things in open possibility. Another name for this science is deconstruction.

Kantian critique reproduces an elision of free existence within its own operations. That is, the ground on which Kant establishes his transcendental gesture into pure reason always harbours within it a groundlessness that destines the gesture to fail in the *praxis* of its own procedure.[20] However, this groundlessness is not negative (it is not simply the gaping abyss of reason) but a positive element of critique itself, offering an opening to otherness elided by the negativity of critique. This built-in failure of Kantian critique with its implicit possibility of positive critique becomes a crucial issue for any attempt to address nature because it means that there can be no royal road to nature through negative reason; no science or philosophy capable of addressing nature in itself in such a way that would rid itself of this flaw or gap in reason. To counter this problem, we need to think of the gap between subject and object not simply in terms of the failure of reason to overcome it, but as something positive: a positive disjuncture in ground itself from which the human-nature relation might be rethought and rebuilt.

By thinking of the groundlessness of the free self as a disjuncture and not an abyss, we collapse Kant's atomization of things into singular potentials through the action of the disjunctive ground operating in and between them. As ontological facts, singular things are not subject to reason's transcendental laws, but open possibilities yet to be thought in the 'being-together' with other singular things, in a plurality of the things of nature. This being-together needs to be thought not as a function of categorical reason, but as a possibility resistive to the rational ordering of the world of things and the human subject's already constituted relation to them.

Kant's negative critique can only say 'no' to nature. And yet negative critique harbours a positive moment in which the things of nature are affirmed in their other possibilities. They say 'yes' to us when we hear them otherwise.

Responding to Kant's gap

My concern is to examine some of the conceptual terrain presented in Schelling's *Naturphilosophie* as it works itself out in relation to the challenges of Kantian critique in terms of Kant's gap. Kant's transcendental philosophy proposes that the subject can know the natural world through causal-mechanistic laws enacted in specific mental operations (intellectual intuitions of the idea of space and time) following *a priori* reason. Its real aim is to refute dogmatic assertions about the relation between reason and nature; that is, to refute assertions imposed and not tested by critique. The problem is not that Kant severs reason from nature; rather, in attempting to solve this problem of severance, Kant discovers a gap in reason itself.

This discovery does not lead him to abandon the causal-mechanistic laws of nature in favour of some other kind of determining principle. Rather, it simply means that the system of nature based on causal-mechanistic laws is seen to be inhabited by an indeterminable something – an excess (x) – that cannot be accounted for in the critique itself: an absolute possibility that critique fails to grasp in its determining powers. Critique will, henceforth, need to account not only for the causal-mechanistic laws of nature, but also for this excess inhabiting them.[21] That is, when confronted with the excess of nature, it is not a matter of abandoning the system in seeking the indefinable principle of nature, but of showing how the system is itself exceeded by a possibility not yet thinkable in the system itself – a possibility that happens in contingent encounters with exceptional (i.e. non-systemic) things.[22] In the following chapters, I will emphasize this not-yet-thinkable aspect of nature – nature as such. I will trace the efforts of Schelling's *Naturphilosophie* to develop concepts adequate to this unthought aspect of nature.

Chapter 4

Unground

In the previous chapter I outlined some basic features of Schelling's *Naturphilosophie* in terms of Kant's gap: the gap discovered in transcendental critique between the thing-in-itself and the subject's knowledge of it. Schelling's aim is to resolve this gap by revealing a common ground of nature 'in itself' and nature 'for us' in the critique itself. To do this, he shifts from Kant's predictive-universalist mode of critique to a critically speculative mode based on the contingency of the things of nature as finite possibilities. In this chapter I show how these ideas are taken up by Schelling into a more complete philosophy of nature that takes account of the fact that humans exist in a material universe indifferent to human being, yet accommodating the 'free being' of humans at the same time. To do this, Schelling develops ideas about chemical-organic nature set forth in *Ideas for a Philosophy of Nature* (first published in 1797) into a speculative metaphysics through a series of publications, including *On the World-Soul* (1789) and *First Outline of a System of the Philosophy of Nature* (1799) in the early *Naturphilosophie* stage, aiming to test the limits of Kantian critique, and to produce a critical philosophy of nature that recognizes its own freedom to think, while remaining compatible with the science of the day.

These nature philosophy publications can be read in tandem with the important essays of the middle period: the *Philosophical Investigations into the Essence of Human Freedom* (first published 1809) and *The Ages of the World* (1813–15), where Schelling tries to think the being-free of philosophical speculation compatible with the freedom of nature understood in terms of material-ideational becoming, as 'the *material* proof of idealism' (Fichte & Schelling 2012, p. 44).[1] To arrive at this position, Schelling has to counter a major impediment in the form of Fichte's ego philosophy – a radicalization of Kantian subjectivism – which proposed an absolutely free subject based on the will ('I *will* be') positing itself at the expense of nature.[2]

The unaccounted x

In *Philosophical Investigations into the Essence of Human Freedom* (the Freedom essay), Schelling identifies the philosophy of Fichte as deficient in that it banishes nature to dead, inert matter that 'lacks a living ground' (Schelling 2006, p. 26).[3] Here Schelling continues his critique of Fichte begun earlier in correspondence between the two philosophers,[4] and connects with his *Naturphilosophie* more generally as an ongoing attempt to recover the 'living ground' of nature reduced by Fichte to 'empty froth' (Schelling 1988, p. 54). To recover this ground, Schelling develops a factical ontology of nature as a living dynamic principle. In the opening pages of *First Outline of a System of Philosophy of Nature*, he calls this principle the 'unconditioned of nature':

> The unconditioned of Nature *as such* cannot be sought in any individual natural object; rather a *principle* of being, that itself 'is' not, manifests itself in each natural object.
>
> (Schelling 2004, p. 13)

Here Schelling pursues the *is-not* of nature: the affirmation of nature (*natura naturans*) as part-of-yet-not the produced things of nature (*natura naturata*).[5] Unconditioned nature is not a property of things, nor is it something added to the things themselves, but a transimmanence that partakes of all things.[6]

Schelling's argument relates to the Platonic-Aristotelian principle of negation that works on the basis that 'things which *are not* nevertheless are' (Horn 1989, p. 5; see also Agamben 1991). This principle requires that the copula (the verb 'to be') both separates and preserves the difference between subject and predicate (Wirth 2003, p. 69). In the Freedom essay Schelling provides an explanation:

> the proposition, 'this body is blue', does not have the meaning that the body is, in and through that in and through which it is a body, also blue, *but rather only the meaning that the same thing which is this body is also blue, although not in the same respect.*
>
> (Schelling 2006, p. 13, emphasis added)

'Being this body' and 'being blue' are not two separate beings with nothing in-between; rather, their separate existences share a common ground (the 'same thing') that remains indifferent to either of them. Thus Schelling introduces a *tertium quid* (a 'third') as the 'in-between' of nature.[7] The third is the withdrawing immanence of 'nothing', which draws the other two together. Without a withdrawing third there would only be the annihilating self-sameness of the two passing into one another.

We can give this further consideration with Schelling's proposal in *Ideas for a Philosophy of Nature* that 'Nature should be Mind made visible, Mind the invisible Nature' (Schelling 1988, p. 42). The proposition: nature should be mind (A = B) depends on something else, an unaccounted x, that brings mind and nature together, yet escapes the logical closure required for the proposition to count as valid.[8] In *The Ages of the World*, Schelling clarifies:

> The true meaning of every judgment, for instance, A is B, can only be this: *that which* is A is *that which* is B, or *that which* is A and *that which* is B are one and the same. Therefore, a doubling already lies at the bottom of the simple concept: A in this judgment is not A, but 'something = x, that A is'. Likewise, B is not B, but 'something = x, that B is', and not this (not A and B for themselves) but the 'x that is A' and 'the x that is B' is one and the same, that is, the same x.
>
> (Schelling 2000, p. 8)

A is B only insofar as there is an x that they share in common – an 'absolute identity' (Schelling 1988, p. 42) that withdraws from the proposition. The concept A is doubled in that it is both equal to itself (A = A) in being that which it is in x, yet not itself (A = B) at the same time. Schelling's concern here is to recover the facticity of being (the elusive x as the 'there is' of the thing) through the copula.[9] A concern to recover the facticity of being runs throughout Schelling's philosophy, and can be seen for instance in Schelling's dispute with Fichte over the status of the absolute in their correspondence (Fichte & Schelling 2012, p. 60). In response to Fichte's positing of the absolute as a pure or spontaneous activity, Schelling writes: 'one can only say that it *is*, never that it is active' (p. 60). In this case, what counts is the fact that something *is* 'not other', as distinct from Fichte's position, which is to say that something (here the absolute) is first of all such and such (e.g. an agility or activity), which then accounts for what it is not (dead matter).

In Schelling's terms, a proposition implies a withdrawn ground, an archaic origin doubled into it, such that its truth depends on an act of forgetting – a remembering (A = A) that forgets the very ground of its own constitution.[10] If this archaic origin is invoked through the proposition in order to bring it back to memory, it will immediately be forgotten again. This is because to remember the forgotten origin is to double the proposition yet again in a further act of forgetting the withdrawn ground that supports it. The x must necessarily remain as the withdrawn unknown, as the absolute condition that enables the truth of the proposition to assert itself as such. Despite its archaic origins, x is ineluctably future-oriented in that it opens up being to what it can become, but only by doubling back on itself, in a recapitulation to a perpetually re-forgotten past. To think with the x is to awaken thought to the 'other beginning', right at the place where this otherness shows itself.[11] These beginnings can be seen as flashes of possibility, opened up in singular acts of remembering the forgetting of being.

The copula retains its position as the site of an irreducible facticity (x), the indifferent ground of both subject and predicate. Ground is thus a void – a virtuality that partakes of finite things in their possibilities of being other. As the ground of things, nature is an immanent void inhering in things as other: 'a *principle* of being, that itself "is" not, [and which] manifests itself in each natural object' (Schelling 2004, p. 13). Schelling's *Naturphilosophie* is an attempt to describe this indifferent ground as a movement of free being releasing itself from the determinations of materiality in the perpetual beginning of an absolutely ideal act (eternal decisiveness).

The eternal beginning

In the Freedom essay Schelling describes nature in general as unconditioned becoming where 'there is no first and last because all things mutually presuppose each other [and where] no thing is another thing, and yet no thing is not without another thing' (Schelling 2006, p. 28).[12] The concept of unconditioned becoming is, according to Schelling, 'the only one appropriate to the nature of things' (p. 28) and requires us to think of nature as heterogeneous potential operating at singular sites, and happening as such.[13] Schelling coins the term 'dynamic atomism' (Schelling 2004, p. 21) to define the being of nature as unconditioned becoming that 'manifests itself in each natural object'.[14] This 'manifestation' is an immanence in each single instance of being, 'like light that requires no higher light in order to be visible' (p. 13). Light is the immanence that makes possible relations between seers as 'being seen'.[15] Things are not discrete entities acted upon by forces outside them as they are in Kant's mechanistic model, but part of a transitive field of forces shared with other things. Things relate to other things transimmanently, constituting a multiplicity of things as *partage* – as part of 'being-together'.[16]

The wholeness of the multiplicity does not precede each thing. Rather, each thing is a beginning for the possibilities of what it is capable of being, together with other things, as 'an ever-*becoming* product' of things in general (Schelling 2004, p. 28). The idea of the eternal beginning is taken up in *The Ages of the World*, where each thing partakes of an 'eternal beginning' (Schelling 2000, p. 19): a beginning that begins everywhere, all the time; a beginning '… that does not happen once and for all, but in a moment that is eternally, always, and still happening' (p. 29). Such a beginning is always true to itself. It stays where it is in its own 'beginningness', forever opening into free possibility without leaving for some end.

The whole of nature is itself the dynamic potential of each of its parts as co-existing things in perpetual beginningness. Schelling describes such things as '*simple actants* of indeterminate [or] infinite multiplicity in matter, as *ideal* ground of explanation' (Schelling 2004, p. 21). As '*simple actants*', things do not exist in isolation from other things, but are bound together by an 'indivisible remainder' (Schelling 2006, p. 29) – a transimmanence that is neither in things nor outside them, but part of each thing's being with other things.[17] Each thing is a beginning, together with other things, in an 'eternal act of self-revelation' (p. 29) occurring in all things but which is singular to each thing. Furthermore, each thing is already charged with the 'potency' of nature in its possibilities, in its 'highest' power. Each thing 'yearns' for its full self-expression of that which it is capable of being. This yearning is not for some state of being outside itself, but the already happening beginning – the 'force of the beginning' (Schelling 2000, p. 30) – of what it is, in open possibility, in 'eternal freedom'.

The indivisible remainder

Schelling describes the dynamism between the eternal act and the things enacted as an unsettling movement of *ground* experienced by the human self retroactively as an anarchic force of becoming:

> After the eternal act of self-revelation, everything in the world is, as we see it now, rule, order and form; but anarchy still lies in the ground, as if it could break through once again, and nowhere does it appear as if order and form were what is original but rather as

if initial anarchy had been brought to order. This is the incomprehensible base of reality in things, the *indivisible remainder*, that which with the greatest exertion cannot be resolved in understanding but rather remains eternally in the ground. The understanding is born in the genuine sense from that which is without understanding. Without this preceding darkness creatures have no reality; darkness is their necessary inheritance.

(Schelling 2006, p. 29, emphasis added)

For Schelling, the self finds itself not in an originating act of its own auto-reflection as it does with Kant, but in *medias res* with the world of things: a world of formal order threatened by unconditioned nature as 'unruly' or 'anarchic' becoming. This situation parallels that proposed in the resistive concept of nature in *Ideas for a Philosophy of Nature* where thinking thinks in-between the determinate order of universal laws and the free contingency of nature as 'an *endeavour* of matter to escape from the equilibrium and yield to the free play of its forces' (Schelling 1988, p. 148). In a move that anticipates Heidegger's concept of the 'thrownness' of *Dasein* in the world (Heidegger 1962, p. 174), Schelling proposes that we think of the free self in terms of a releasing encounter with the 'free play of [...] forces' (i.e *poiesis*) figuring themselves out on originary anarchic ground. This ground, which, as we have seen previously, is a void of possibility, cannot be separated from human existence and thus takes the form of a historical movement of being-as-becoming, which Schelling will identify in other publications as having an epochal character.[18]

How, then, does Schelling describe the void of nature (unconditioned nature) in its relation to human existence? Unconditioned nature is not an inert mass of dark matter waiting to be activated by an enlightened act of self-revelation, but an 'indivisible remainder' that inheres in things by withdrawing from them. The self is 'born in the genuine sense' not from internal self-reflection as it is with Kant, but out of the indivisible remainder as an originary *ecstasis* – a movement of being out of itself – producing the knowable out of the unknowable, the intelligible out of the sensible, the idea out of the material, light out of dark, in a vibrant pulsing rhythm of universal forces rotating ceaselessly between expansion and contraction at any given place and time. In *The Ages of the World*, Schelling describes this pulsing movement in terms of the rotating wheel of nature: 'There is only an unremitting wheel, a rotatory movement that never comes to a standstill and in which there is no differentiation' (Schelling 2000, p. 20). The self is an original experience or primary revelation of the absolute in open possibility brought about by primary 'longing' in a chaotic becoming that *turns* (rotates) according to the expansions and contractions of primordial being.[19] The turning movement of being-as-becoming can be understood in terms of the epochs through which being comes into its own freedom through successive periods, which Schelling defines in *System of Transcendental Idealism* as a movement from destiny (a 'wholly blind force'), to nature ('*natural law*' and '*natural plan*'), to '*providence*' that is 'imperfectly revealing itself' in the previous two periods (Schelling 1978, pp. 211–12). Providence is thus the 'third', or unaccounted x, that promises freedom while remaining indifferently withdrawn from the other two.

Remembering that what is at stake here is not simply the 'things of nature' but how the self comes to be, freely, in relation to the things of nature, then the indivisible remainder cannot be something that determines and hence constrains the self. Rather the indivisible remainder is the withdrawn void of the materially real of absolute possibility, withheld (remaining 'eternally in ground') yet nevertheless experienced as an anarchic becoming (anarchic or unruly because not yet subject to the rule of reason in self-reflection). The ground of nature is thus pure potential – forever withdrawn from the self yet affectively real in that it makes the free self possible; it enables this possibility as a specific state or way of being – of being free. The self's free existence – its separation from the causality of nature – is not something that it has by virtue of its own autonomous will (its capacity for self-positing), but is itself part of the will of the forever becoming-withdrawing ground that makes freedom possible as absolute openness – the 'will that wills nothing' (Schelling 2000, p. 24). The self's freedom is not, therefore, drawn uniquely from within itself, because this inner being is already part of the outside, as absolute possibility opened up by the giving-withdrawing of the indivisible remainder that eternally runs through it.

To access free possibility (the way of being free) the self cannot simply draw from within itself in an act of *sui generis*; rather it must give itself up to the absolute through 'releasement' (*Gelassenheit*) (Schelling 2000, p. 63): an act that affirms the task of life and education (*Bildung*) to 'free oneself from oneself'[20] by releasing the self from aggrandizement in ideals and 'supreme concepts' (p. 63).[21] Schelling asks: what is it about lowly 'corporeality' or material nature that offends those seeking higher spirituality and ideals? He answers that if we engage with 'lowly' material nature through 'releasement' (the free act of being part of yet separate from nature) we will see something there running through all things: 'that releasement [*Gelassenheit*] shows that something of the qualities of that primordial stuff still dwells within them ['lowly' things of nature], of the stuff that is passive on the outside but on the inside is spirit and life' (p. 63). Here Schelling radicalizes Kant's exposure of the unruliness of free existence (the abyss of reason discussed in Chapter 3). This unruliness is not something to be controlled by the regulation of reason as Kant proposes, but actively encountered and loved,[22] as the beginning of the possibilities of being; a beginning that always begins in the finite moment of stilled chaos, in a never-ending production of being-as-becoming. In a retroactive releasement, the self catches sight of its own archaic origin ('something of the qualities of that primordial stuff'), not by transcending its finite existence in grand ideas and concepts, but in encounters with humble things all around it. By experiencing this archaic origin that irrupts in the contingency of present experience (*Ursprung*), the self can begin again, toward a 'new mythology' drawn out of the archaic yet active origin that is everywhere at work (Schelling 1978, pp. 232–33).

Schelling's solution to the problem of 'being free' in the finitude of already determined existence is to turn to myth – to await the arrival of new myths, whose creation releases human being into another phase of being 'to come', which, for Schelling, can only be a stage closer to the absolute ideal working itself out in materiality. However, *contra* Schelling, a releasement that leads to proposals for a new mythology is no releasement at all, as it requires a willing with nature as already willed. That is, it requires an already willed sense of the ideal as something already here, thus negating the self's freedom to be in open possibility. Schelling's version of releasement has an insufficient sense of the resistivity necessary for the self to retain its free being, and gives itself over too easily to mythic self-renewal. A releasement is indeed necessary in order to let the self be in its relation to nature, but this cannot be a releasement that simply awaits new mythologies; rather it can only be a movement of resistance within the already willed mythologies of nature, constituting a demythification of nature as such. Schelling's appeal to myth needs to be countered by its demythification (I undertake this task in Chapter 6).

The unground

From the point of view of the free self, the void of nature occurs as an irruption of ground (its anarchic force) after the act of self-revelation (the act that inaugurates the self's free capacity to know itself), in terms of the way the world appears 'as if' the ground were ready to break through what has already been ordered: 'as if it could break through once again' (Schelling 2006, p. 29). As a necessary condition, ground exceeds the self insofar as the self experiences it retrospectively as an anarchic, irruptive force that had hitherto been brought to order. Ground is thus retroactively originary – its origins lie not in an original event that precedes and is separated from all the subsequent events that it causes, but in eternal eventness as a chaos of potential beginnings. The becoming of ground is thus an ungrounding of what it grounds, constituting a chiasm or crossed movement of primary being that disseminates being in all directions at once as absolute potential.

The ungrounding of ground is the movement of nature in its unconditioned becoming, as 'pure facticity' (Gabriel 2009, p. 59) or nature as such. Schelling calls this unconditioned movement of being-as-becoming the *Unground*:

> there must be a being *before* all ground and before all that exists, thus generally before any duality – how can we call it anything other than the original ground or the *non-ground* [*Unground*]? Since it precedes all opposites, these cannot be distinguishable in it nor can they be present in any way. Therefore, it cannot be described as the identity of opposites; it can only be described as the absolute *indifference* [*Indifferenz*] of both.
> (Schelling 2006, p. 68)

Ground as unground (*Unground*) exceeds the self in a dynamic movement of becoming.[23] The unground is not 'for' the self in its act of 'self-revelation' but 'indifferent' to it. Furthermore this indifference is absolute. It cannot be reduced to the 'identity of opposites' but remains as an unassimilable otherness (the 'darkness' of the indivisible remainder; the unaccounted x) that is nevertheless present as the possibility that something is. Absolute indifference is the original unity from which difference emerges – an originariness perpetually affirming itself in the indifference of ineluctable becoming.

For Schelling the unground affirms ground but in such a way that exceeds the unreleased self at the same time (its 'indifference' to the self). The self is thus constituted by a forgetfulness of the fact that its existence is grounded in ungrounding:

> Most people forget, when they come to that point of examination where they must recognize a disappearance of all opposites, that these have now really disappeared, and they once again predicate the opposites as such as arising from the indifference which had emerged precisely due to their total cessation.
>
> (Schelling 2006, p. 68)

What people 'forget' is that the withdrawal of ground is an irreversibly real withdrawal – a nullification of opposites in irreducible indifference that necessarily exceeds self-positing. This cessation or nullity of ground as such is forgotten ('people forget'), thereby invoking the self's predication of opposites ('they once again predicate the opposites') in repeated attempts to reclaim existence 'for us'.

Paradoxically, the withdrawing ground affirms the self in its possibilities for being. It does this by ungrounding the self in a chiasmic movement – a movement that moves back and forth at the same time – constituting a disjunctive openness at the heart of the 'free self'. The self's self-positing is thus affirmed but not according to an 'inner' principle of necessity (a law unto itself, an *arche*); rather, the self's affirmation comes from the ground of nature itself, in its chiasmic 'becoming' as unground. Schelling's concept of unground provides us with an affirmation of nature.[24] Nature is not inert matter (negated self) awaiting the self to make it meaningful. Rather, as absolute indifference, nature exceeds the self's capacity to take command over it as a system of things arrayed before it in terms of subject-object relations, and in so doing, ungrounds the self in the self's enacting of that very capacity (i.e. in its attempts to *be* the subject of nature). By ungrounding the self against its 'will-to-be-subject', nature as unground releases the self into free possibility. Nature is not the irrational other of the reasoning self, but the self's very possibility of being free, seen in the obscure clarity of a lightning flash: 'one can think that everything occurred just as if in a lightning flash' (Schelling 2000, p. 77).[25] The flash (*Augenblick*) comes to the self in systems of reason as the other way opened in the instance of flashing, but not yet taken.

The unground recedes from the self into dark incomprehension, which is also a proliferation of the 'indivisible remainder' as indifferent excess that ruins all oppositions: 'indifference is its own being separate from all opposition, a being against which all opposites ruin themselves' (Schelling 2006, p. 69). Unlike Hegel's negative philosophy in which nature is the absolute other of the self reflecting its own becoming, Schelling's positive philosophy proposes nature as a becoming that ungrounds and thus ruins the oppositions of self-reflection in its indifference to them.[26] The self is affirmed not in terms of self-identity, but as part of the ungrounding of the ground of the self in a productive potential that opens into the 'agelessness' of the absolute past as a remembering of lost connectivity with nature.

Preserving nature

Nature 'as such' is the necessity of nature as absolute, in the possibilities of what can and cannot be. Nature as such is the fact of nature in itself, as it is for us, and hence something more – an excess or 'indivisible remainder'. In this case, nature as such is originary in the sense that it begins from wherever we already are, in a forward movement that cannot be taken fully back into itself (a beginning can only ever be singular; it cannot begin again or turn back on itself without destroying its singularity). The *autopoietic* capacity of nature to bring itself forward out of itself must therefore be thought in terms of something even more original yet close at hand: a pre-originary beginning that begins everywhere and all at once, all the time, and always at *this* place where specific acts of thinking occur.[27] Nature 'as such' does not occur at the very beginning, in a 'first time' before which there is no other time, but in a first time that happens all the time, in an absolute origin or *ursprung* of the *hic et nunc* of existence. Nature as such is an upsurge of originariness, which is always beginning everywhere and all at once. Schelling calls this withdrawing-advancing of nature *Unground* (unground): the ungrounding of ground in the very act of self-grounding. In grounding itself, the self is differentiated from ground that withdraws from it, and in so doing the withdrawing ground advances, thereby exceeding the self in an upsurge that ungrounds it at the same time. The unground is the origin of both ground and existence.

The issue here concerns the violence involved in self-becoming – the eternal break or rupture (*ursprung*) between ground and existence, allowing something singular to come into being. *Ursprung* makes new being possible through epochal rupture or 'ages' in human history.[28] Without such violence nothing could come to pass, and all would be the same forever. Rupture occurs not as an all-consuming abyss, but as a disjuncture in being itself (between ground and existence), where the self 'begins with a *dissonance*' (Schelling, qtd. in Bowie 1993, p. 157). By beginning with the 'dissonance' of disjuncture, the self is made capable of being (as being-free with nature), without having to negate its ground. In this way, the self conserves ground instead of destroying it: 'instead of abolishing this distinction [between ground and existence] once again, as was thought, the non-ground rather posits and confirms it' (Schelling 2006, p. 69). Here we have a self-affirmation that preserves rather than destroys nature. This is achieved not in the self's self-positing (*sui genesis*), but through a resistive-creative-affirmation where a self comes into being. The self is not sublated (absorbed and lifted into a higher state of being), but enabled in the sense of finding itself in a disjunctive 'free being' with nature as 'indifferent' otherness.

The idea of disjuncture allows us to think of nature not as the negated other of the self that the self must master in order to fully be, but as the self's very possibility of being. In this case the self is called to make itself anew in the ruined grounds of what it is. To renew itself, the self cannot seek inwardly in a Kantian act of self-creation, but, in being called upon, the self must decide to 'be itself', by withdrawing from what it is already committed to be by the system of sense/meaning in which it currently exists. This is not a matter of choice, as if the self had arrayed before it so many possibilities from which to choose. Rather the decision must be a decision *to be*. To decide in this way is to decide for the self in its 'could-be-ness', in resistance to what it finds itself as already subject to, without knowing what this 'could-be' is in advance; that is, to decide absolutely in free and opened possibility.

Partage

Schelling's *Naturphilosophie* asks that we think of nature not as a substrate of being but in terms of the singular beings of nature. There is no underlying Nature to natural things; rather, natural things are themselves both the production and product of an immanent activity: '*Nature is absolutely active if the drive to an infinite development lies in each of its products*' (Schelling 2004, p. 18). The things of nature are thus part of an incessant productivity that exceeds them in an infinite process of differentiation and dissemination. By extension then, all things are things of nature, since natural productivity is their ground of being, their possibility as such. The early Greeks called natural productivity *ousia* or original being. To think of things in terms of *ousia* is to think of them as singularities: bare facts of nature without conceptual determinacy. They are not particulars in relation to a whole (part/whole), but singular 'actants' disseminated 'indifferently' in a pluralization of singular being (single/plural). The productivity of nature inheres in each thing, rendering them singularly indeterminate with respect to other things, but in such a way that frees them up for future being-together.

Schelling's ideas open the way for a genetic theory of nature as non-linear interconnectivity (see Delanda 2002, p. 119) prefiguring contemporary ideas in quantum physics and biogenetic theory, as well as more recent nature philosophy, for instance in the work of Deleuze and Guattari (Deleuze & Guattari 1987, see especially Chapter 3).[29] Iain Grant suggests that Schelling's *Naturphilosophie* can be understood as a radical theory of evolution based on recapitulation or what Schelling calls "'the continuous self-construction of matter'" (qtd. in Grant 2006, p. 13), through a movement of involution that folds back on itself. Grant highlights certain materialist ideas embedded in Schelling's *Naturphilosophie*; ideas that lead to an understanding of evolution as a non-linear recapitulation of "'unrestricted being'" (p. 13). They suggest the far-reaching idea that material becoming is based on singular elements moving in unrestricted ways toward unknown ends. Schelling's exceptional thought is to think this movement of unrestricted becoming from the elements themselves, as inescapable facts from which both organic and inorganic life perpetually begins. From Schelling's materialist-idealist perspective, there is no ideal mentality that unifies the facts of nature in advance of materiality. Rather, the ideation of nature is entirely immanent to material becoming in its potential for infinite dissemination and self-differentiation. Any unity of nature, any idealized organization or formal structure, must be grasped from the elements themselves (and not from primary causes or predetermining ideal states), which are always perceived by finite humans retroactively as facts of stilled chaos in an infinite potential of eternal beginningness.

Following these insights, the key issue for Schelling is not what unifies the things of nature, but what keeps them apart, what makes them singular and hence different from each other:

that spirit [mind] does not have an intuition of itself in any individual product – that it has no intuition of itself in unity, but rather in the infinite *keeping apart* of its opposed activity *from one another* (which are only unified at all by virtue of this holding apart).

(Schelling 2004, p. 19)

To account for this ontological fact (that things *are* by being separate from other things) Schelling proposes that original being is a creative 'dissonance' or cision that keeps things apart in the decisive act of self-creation. Things relate to other things not by virtue of something in them that they receive from a primary cause or predetermining ideal state, but by virtue of the very fact that *they are* as things apart, and hence, in their 'being-together' are singularly already on their way to somewhere else, some other time and place. Things relate to other things in a transitive sense, so that their identity is always possibly 'other'.

To grasp things in a transitive sense is to grasp them as singularities in a contraction of being – a negation that withdraws in order to overcome itself and begin again: '[a beginning] must be expressly posited as that which does not have being. A ground is thereby given for it to be. No beginning point (*terminus a quo*) of a movement is an empty, inactive point of departure. Rather, it is a negation of the starting point and the actual emerging movement is an overcoming of this negation' (Schelling 2000, p. 16). In this contraction of being, things relate to other things in the splitting of the two, an eternally decisive act that runs through all things, keeping them apart: 'As such, it always remains that if one of them has being, then the other cannot have the *same* being […] eternity opens up into time in this decision' (p. 76). *Partage* is this keeping apart by 'eternal decisiveness' that maintains the difference between the two without allowing them to pass into one another as part of the same being. Singularities are thus poised in indecisiveness between ground and existence; a disjunctive dissonance that resists resolution into oppositional logic and the order of the same (the order of identity).

A critique that follows the principle of *partage* requires the deconstruction of systems of identity formation in order to free things in their singularity for an otherness they could possibly become, without this possibility being known in advance. A deconstruction is not negative in the sense that it negates the system that produces and maintains a state of being, but positive in that it affirms the power of systems, but otherwise, by catalysing the dissonance that both sustains them in their self-differentiation and exceeds them at the same time, opening them to unassimilable otherness.

The void

The unground does not disappear into an abyss, but remains as the place of the void. The void is placed in a certain way, as ground that remains by being voided or crossed out (i.e. made 'null and void') in such a way that its remaining becomes visible as the obsolete mark of renewed possibility, in the ruins of what is, as such, exposed to an absolute condition of being.[30] The void is thus the mark of the withdrawn ground appearing as meaningless residue or *signifiance* – the originating nothing that ungrounds the something in the possibility of past and future life.[31]

This 'indivisible remainder' that Schelling equates with original unity therefore contains within it a destructive principle that perpetually interrupts the continuity of being, creating new life, new beginnings and possibilities.[32] To account for this destructive/creative principle (*poiesis*), we need to rethink the void not as a nullity, but as a place of beginnings that opens up possibility as such. If we can do this, then we will have set ourselves on a path to recover something of the possibilities of nature as such.

Chapter 5

Positive Freedom

Nature and freedom

In Schelling's *Naturphilosophie* nature is something more than the residual material of a dialectical movement between nature 'in itself' (*naturans*) and nature 'for us' (*naturata*). Rather, nature is primary ground in the sense of a necessity with respect to human existence (self-consciousness). Ground comes prior to existence and not the other way around. But given the fact of existence – the fact that self-consciousness *is* and *that* we exist – the priority of ground over existence has to be thought in the immediacy of the self's being what it is. In this case, the self finds itself apart from ground (a-part; that is, apart from a being part of), so that ground is experienced retroactively as a withdrawal from existence.[1] Ground withdraws and in so doing differentiates itself from the existing self. The self exists as part of ground, but sees itself as separate, as independently free.

The issue of freedom is set forth most prominently in *Philosophical Investigations into the Essence of Human Freedom* (Schelling 2006). In this work, Schelling argues that the self's autonomy with respect to the necessity of nature as ground is a retrospective illusion. However, the experience of freedom is nonetheless real in the fact that the self exists freely in relation to the withdrawing ground of nature.[2] Schelling's task is to recover this experience of the withdrawing ground as it happens, in the free contingent world of what we are now as existing beings.[3] That is, Schelling sets himself the task of recovering the 'living ground' (p. 26) of existence from the place where existence happens without losing sight of it as ground, or without allowing ground to disappear into the abyssal negation of the self-positing subject, and, instead, by thinking of this withdrawal of nature 'against itself' as the very fact of freedom; the very possibility of being *this* self as distinct from any other kind of self. As John Sallis puts it: 'Schelling ventures to recover such a living ground, to differentiate secluded [i.e. withdrawn] nature from the self-positing subject to which otherwise – and indeed throughout modern philosophy – it is assimilated' (Sallis 1999a, p. 73). Thus Schellingian nature, or nature as such, needs to be understood as something (the unaccounted x) that grounds the oscillation between nature 'in itself' and 'for us' without becoming assimilated to either of them, thereby affirming the self's freedom at the place of disjuncture between ground and existence understood as transimmanent sense – sense that releases the self for otherness.[4] Freedom is not internal to the self but part of the self's relation to nature. Freedom is an attribute of nature itself.[5]

Good and evil

In a significant shift from Spinoza's mechanistic system of nature and with repercussions for future philosophy, Schelling extends freedom to things (Schelling 2006, p. 22).[6] The things of nature such as parts of an organism are free in that their singular being is affirmed through a capacity to become detached from the organism: 'An individual body part, like the eye, is only possible within the whole of an organism; nonetheless, it has its own life for itself, indeed its own kind of freedom, which it obviously proves through the disease of which it is capable' (p. 18). The eye has a positive freedom – it affirms 'its own life for itself' – with respect to the whole of which it is part. The diseased eye does not negate the whole; rather its being part of the whole entails a necessary freedom in its capacity for singularization (in this case, by becoming diseased). This positive freedom of the diseased eye is however evil in that by becoming diseased, it corrupts and inverts the whole. From this perspective, evil is not the negation of the good, but bound up with good itself in the health of the body.[7]

In Schelling's conceptualization of good and evil, there can be no such thing as a good (i.e. fully healthy) body against which ill health is measured. Rather, bodies such as organisms are susceptible to both 'good' and 'evil', so that a healthy body is one that constantly enacts the 'deed' of health in an endlessly dialectical process of deciding for the good of health rather than the evil of disease: 'the transition from disease to health can in fact only occur through its opposite, namely through restoration of the separate and individual life into the being's inner glimpse of light, from which restoration division (*Krisis*) once again proceeds' (Schelling 2006, pp. 34–35). Evil (disease) is an ever-present fact in the life of an organism, and is thus part of its free contingency: its capacity to 'be itself' as a possibly healthy thing.[8] Things are free insofar as they have a 'capacity for good and evil' (Schelling 2006, p. 23). Thus, in any finite situation, an organism will be possessed by both good and evil elements in what Jason Wirth calls an 'ataxia of sickness' (Wirth 2003, p. 174): a categorically unstable constitution of undecidable health (is it healthy? is it sick?), forever repairing itself under threat of death. The good is not initially posited as an ideal state subsequently compromised or destroyed by evil, but a possibility intimated by the undecidability of the finite situation (the healthy eye can only *be* healthy so long as its possibility is continually enabled by the blocking of the 'evil' of ill-health). Thus any given 'whole' is always in a state of incompletion, turning either towards good health or evil disease such that both good and evil (health and disease) are configured in its possible ways of being.

From a Schellingian perspective, we cannot posit a normative 'good' of nature, for example, the homeostasis of an ecosystem or the balanced harmony of natural cycles, subsequently disrupted by an 'evil' outside. Rather everything must begin from the 'there is' of nature 'as such', in the possibilities presented there for both good and evil, health and disease. Disruptions are potential to the system's capacity for good or evil understood as a part of the freedom of the system itself, its capacity to be 'otherwise'.

Schelling's concept of freedom calls upon Aristotle's theory of causality that accounts for the fact of something in terms of immanent causes. The cause is not proof of a thing's existence; rather, *that* the thing exists is proof of its cause: 'It is not because we think truly that you are pale, that you *are* pale, but because you are pale we who say this have the truth' (Aristotle 1941, p. 833). This reversal of the conventional idea of causality resonates with contemporary ideas in the philosophy of organic biology.[9] A singular element of organic life is not the effect of prior causes but 'an open question' (Moss 2009, p. 104): an affirmation of life in the possibilities of what it can be. Schelling's philosophy is positive in that it begins with the 'that' of what is, as a fact of existence opened to possibility.

Positive freedom

Schelling's idea of positivity can be understood in terms of the difference between negative and positive freedom.[10] In negative freedom, the self assumes its freedom by negating otherness. I am the free being that I take myself to be in the act of negating what I am not. Negative freedom is thus intransitive in that it chooses what it wants to be (the 'I-will'). Negative freedom is reversible: I can always choose another way of being, since I am always free to do so. Indeed, in negative freedom, I can always calculate the options available to me to maximise my chances at attaining whatever I want (infinite freedom). However, in positive freedom, the self is free not in terms of its own self-relation, but on the ground of being with others. My freedom is dependent on my being on this ground in a way that makes me free with others. Positive freedom is not, therefore, a matter of choice, but the affirmation of singular being: the being-free grasped decisively by me as *this* possibility at *this* place and time.

Positive freedom posits what I can be, not in terms of my autonomy as a free being, but in the being-free that makes me what I am. Positive freedom is thus an irreversible fact, opened up to finite possibility in the contingency of what is. Given my finite existence, I am affirmed in freedom to be the self that I can possibly be ('I-can'). By affirming that I am, I resist the determination of ground and am opened into freedom. This freedom is not infinite, but limited by the exigencies of the finite event.[11] Jean-Luc Nancy calls this 'finite freedom': '[finite] freedom is not a sense conferred on existence (like the senseless sense of the self-constitution of a subject or freedom as an essence). Rather, it is the very *fact* of existence as open to existing itself' (Nancy 2003, p. 13). Positive freedom is transitive – it does what it frees: 'its positive concept is to be the being which *can* be' (Schelling, qtd. in Bowie 1993, p. 153). The task for a positive philosophy[12] is to 'free oneself from oneself' (Schelling, qtd. in Matthews 2007, p. 5) – a releasement that takes place by resisting what one already is (unfree, determined by identity) for possibilities to come.[13]

The being-free of the self is a being free with otherness in what is achievable, what can be.[14] Thinking this 'being-free-with' in terms of nature can be achieved, I propose, through the transitive formation of human-nature relations in creative acts of resistive affirmation, as acts of positive freedom.[15] The aim of such acts is to unblock the determinations that limit the human-nature relation to specific meanings and values centred on the human self (anthropocentrism), thereby releasing the relation for an otherness that retains positive freedom as part of being with nature.

Žižek on Schelling

In his two books on Schelling (Žižek 1996, 1997), Slavoj Žižek consistently reads Schelling through Hegel, making it appear that Schelling proposes a negative concept of nature as other in relation to self-reflection.[16] These readings, however, run counter to Schelling's proposal for a positive concept of nature as the ground of primary excess (*Unground*), as established in the previous chapter.[17] Wherein lies this confusion? It lies in the particular way Žižek represents Schelling's concept of freedom. In his reading of Schelling's *The Ages of the World* (second version), Žižek argues that Schelling's solution to the Kantian paradox of freedom[18] is to posit freedom itself as a primary fact:

> For Schelling, then, the primordial, radically contingent fact, a fact which can in no way be accounted for, is freedom itself, a freedom bound by nothing, a freedom which, in a sense, *is* Nothing; and the problem is, rather, how this Nothing of the abyss of primordial freedom becomes entangled in the causal chains of Reason.
>
> (Žižek 1996, p. 16)

Žižek suggests here that Schelling overcomes the paradox of freedom (how can a self be free yet constrained by the necessities of causal reason) by positing freedom as a 'radically contingent fact', which is indeed what Schelling proposes in the opening sentences of the *Philosophical Investigations into the Essence of Human Freedom*.[19] However, a price must be paid for making this move, which is to surrender any reference to an *autonomously* free self (i.e. a self whose first relation is with itself). If a self were autonomous in its freedom, then any act of freedom would not be free in an absolute sense, since it would already be determined by the necessity of having to enact its freedom autonomously. But this is what Žižek goes on to say:

> Following in Kant's footsteps, he [Schelling] explains the paradox of freedom by invoking *a noumenal, extra-temporal act of self-positing by means of which a man creates himself, chooses his eternal character.*
>
> (1996, p. 17)

Schelling's self, according to Žižek, is one that chooses its 'eternal character' in a 'noumenal, extra-temporal act' in order to separate itself from its entanglement in causality.[20] Now, here is what we read in the passage of *The Ages of the World* (second version) to which Žižek is referring:

> Nevertheless, it is a well known fact that nobody can be given character, and that nobody has chosen for himself the particular character he bears. There is neither deliberation

nor choice here, and yet everyone recognizes and judges character as an eternal (never-ceasing, constant) deed and attributes to a man both it as well as the action that follows from it. Universal moral judgment thus acknowledges that every man has a freedom in which there is neither (explicit) deliberation nor choice, a freedom that is itself fate and necessity.

(Schelling 1997, p. 175)

Here Schelling specifically rules out a self who is either subject to a predetermined character or knowingly chooses its character ('there is neither deliberation nor choice here'), but admits that people are held to account for their choices retroactively as part of an 'eternal (never-ceasing constant) deed'. Everyone recognizes that doing and acting entails a decision, but this is not the kind of decision made by an autonomous self choosing what it wants to be. Rather, the decision is an act of freedom by virtue of the fact that the human is free by 'fate and necessity'. The decision is thus pre-subjective – a pure act of being free; a *fall* into an absolutely free openness rather than a standing on the knowledge of certain ground.[21] In this case, a decision is not a decision to be a certain kind of self from the standpoint of already secured and projected possibilities, but a releasement into the free space of not being. A decision is an act of freedom in an absolute sense, in which 'eternity opens up into time' (Schelling 2000, p. 76).[22] A decision is not a matter of the self choosing its 'eternal character' as if it were choosing from a set of possible character types, but the enactment (the 'deed') of freedom as eternal freedom: 'the subject is itself *nothing other than eternal freedom*' (Schelling, qtd. in Bowie, 1993, p. 131).[23] The question this raises is not 'how can I be free' but, as Andrew Bowie puts it, 'how this "freedom" has taken on the determinate forms of the existing world, including ourselves' (p. 131).[24]

In his discussion of the self in *The Parallax View* (Žižek 2006), Žižek provides a description of how the free self comes into being: the self is

the elementary form of escaping the 'control of solid earth' through self-relating. As such, it underlies all other forms: the self relating of the agent of perception/awareness, as it were, creates (opens up) the scene on which 'conscious content' can appear; it provides the universal *form* of this content, the stage on which the preprocessing work of mediation can collapse into the immediate 'raw' givenness of its product.

(p. 213)

Here Žižek describes the self in terms of a release from material origins, constituting itself in transcendent self-relation. From this transcendent position, the self, in its self-relating, opens up the scene of consciousness with universal form and content. However, if the self is a release into transcendent self-relation that 'underlies all other forms', then these forms cannot help but be products of an idealization already abstracted from the materiality of 'solid earth'. In this case, the 'work of mediation' cannot 'collapse' the forms into raw materiality as Žižek proposes, but rather substitutes for it, constituting a second nature mirroring the one left behind in the releasing.[25] Material becoming is mirrored by an idealization of the self in its transcendence of first nature materiality. In other words, the possibility of self-consciousness as self-relating must always be something posited prior to any real material experience of first nature. Yet threaded throughout Žižek's argument is a description of self-consciousness as if it were part of first nature, for instance in terms of neurobiological processes (p. 212). There is thus potential for confusion between first and second nature. In what way does this confusion manifest itself in Žižek's argument?

After a lengthy discussion of scientific descriptions of brain activity interspersed with his own Hegelian insights, Žižek has this to say about neurobiological science and freedom:

> This is how the brain sciences open up the space for freedom: far from being opposed to genetic programming, and violating it, the space for freedom is itself 'programmed'. We now know, for instance, that the neurons specialized in language atrophy if they are not stimulated by the maternal [sic] voice: genes lay the ground for the unpredictable intersubjective interaction.
>
> (pp. 213–14)

Having set up the 'space for freedom' earlier in this section in terms of a transcendent self that 'underlies all other forms', Žižek now attributes this very same space to the material processes of the brain opened up by neurobiological science. Yet these material processes are in fact second nature descriptions of science mirroring a hypothetical first nature. This second nature *determines* the self's freedom to be a function of first nature material processes. Thus Žižek is obliged to say that the 'space for freedom' in brain activity discovered by science is 'programmed', a determination confirmed by him with the following words: 'We now know', as if what counted was an enlightenment about the self's freedom based entirely on the truth-saying of science.

In opting for scientific explanation, Žižek goes along with the saying of science, accepting its truth as setting us on the right path to understand how the free self comes to be ('we now know'). Žižek makes freedom out to be determined by science. However, if freedom is determined, then it cannot be free. It can only *be* free by enacting itself as a free act. Schelling calls this an 'eternal deed' (Schelling 1997, p. 175) or eternal act of freedom. A free act cannot emerge out of a material process; rather it is something that *befalls* materiality as an eternal act in the 'in-between' – a decisive splitting between first and second nature. The in-between of the decisive act of freedom remains as the very possibility that nature could always be otherwise, other than its determinations in the current saying. That is, the free self can only be free by being right at the in-between, neither ideal nor material, but singularly *there*. If it is to be free, the self cannot be a form of transcendent self-relating as Žižek proposes, but a relating without relation, by suspending relations in the in-between opened to otherness.

A self cannot be explained in terms of material processes as the coming of freedom; rather the self is itself the site of freedom. From this place materiality must then be explained, and not the other way around. Schelling's idea of a postulate of critique gets around this problem in that it is not presented in order to explain a material process 'in itself', but in response to the requirement of critique. For Schelling the self is not something that has to be explained in terms of material process – the self does not 'become' out of some primary matter – but is itself something necessarily posited in any 'free' thinking of the material world (that is, thinking that does not appeal to an already existing theory of the self as 'consciousness' emerging in material process). In any theory of a material self, there will always be another theory, another way of thinking the self, so long as there is the freedom necessary to think in terms of possibility. This freedom cannot itself be reduced to an element in whatever theory is being presented, but must always be a possibility within it leading 'otherwise', in keeping the very fact of possibility open.

Decisiveness is not a characteristic of the subject exercising free choice, but freedom itself as absolute, affirming itself in the subject while remaining irreducible to what the subject decides upon.[26] Decisiveness is neither a conscious act of the subject, nor part of an unconscious reserve of possibilities brought to consciousness by the subject in choice-like decisions.[27] Rather, decisiveness is an a-conscious potential retroactivated in the possibilities of what a subject can be in absolute exposure to otherness. Schelling calls this potential 'God', which is another name for absolute-being-possible as chance: the singular act of making something come about in its 'being possible'.[28] Marcia Schuback describes Schelling's thinking about the decision as 'the cision between subject and object, the de-cisional character of consciousness [...] a moment in which the life of life exposes itself in its negativity as nothingness' (Schuback 2005, p. 69). As pure chance, the decision enables being as other.

The artist's stroke

A paradigm case for the a-conscious retroactive decision can be found in the artist's stroke. An artist-painter usually works within the confines of a system of art – a genre or style accorded with a training and competence that enables her to produce particular objects recognizable as art to a community of experts. However, built into this work is a certain resistance that makes the art object stand out in its singularity as different from other objects. An artwork is, above all else, *this* artwork, not any other. In making each brush stroke, the artist is not simply executing a plan according to a style or genre (according to an *eidos*); rather, she is always aware of the possibilities that open up in the singular stroke of each brush on canvas.[29] Each stroke carries a risk that the whole of the art work could be irremediably altered. Art risks collapsing into a chaos of possibilities:

There is no painter who has not had this experience of the chaos-germ, where he or she no longer sees anything and risks foundering: the collapse of visual coordinates. This is not a psychological experience, but a properly pictorial experience, although it can have an immense influence on the psychic life of the painter. Painters here confront the greatest of dangers both for their work and for themselves.

(Deleuze 2003, p. 83)[30]

In Schelling's words, 'all artists [...] are involuntarily driven to create their works, and that in producing them they merely satisfy an irresistible urge of their own nature; [so that] free activity becomes involuntary' (Schelling 1978, p. 222).[31] The risk taken by the artist in the decision to make the stroke is art-in-practice – the *praxis* of art. In making the stroke, the artist decides (i.e. partakes of the decisiveness of the 'event'), but this decision is not conscious in the sense that she is choosing to paint one way rather than another according to the rules of technique or form (in accordance with a system of art).[32] Rather, in making the stroke, the artist risks the integrity of the whole of what she makes in the possibilities opened up in creative effort. The artist is not projecting her schema onto the art work, but allowing the art work to address her in terms of the whole of which they both partake. The art work 'calls for' the artist to respond in the decisiveness of an artistic stroke, risking *what is* in the chance of something else. In Schelling's terms such 'aesthetic intuition simply is the intellectual intuition become objective' (Schelling 1978, p. 229). The event of art 'happens' in the in-between of the artist and the artwork – in the *Ursprung* of creative beginning that that 'deed' of art makes manifest.[33]

Such decisions come to the decider in the momentary glance or 'blink of the eye' (*Augenblick*) of prescient sight: a seeing that sees absolutely in the possibilities of the yet-to-come.[34] This kind of seeing is not an enactment of the schema (the plan or calculation), but a retroactive traversal of the whole of the artwork in both its actual and virtual modes of being. The *Augenblick* traverses the artwork by working against pre-planned outcomes of technique or design (*eidos*), triggering a 'fall' into open possibility. This release from *eidos* is the deed of the artistic stroke, registered retroactively in self-consciousness. The artist 'knows' retrospectively that artwork is taking/has taken place – a knowing that carries the artist further and further into the deed of art, thus affirming the artist's being-as-artist in the freedom of artistic creativity.[35] The artist both partakes of the system of art and resists it at the same time, thereby opening herself and the artwork to possibility as such.[36] The artist's relation to the artwork – her concern to ensure its happening as a creative act – is characterized by care: the careful attentiveness that comes from a fundamental being-together in absolute possibility, the sharing of a common risk and fatality. In the introductory chapter of this book I proposed that art could be used to counter the closed anthropocentric thinking of nature. In this proposal, I suggested that art, understood as a disjunctive counter-movement within technology, could be aligned with *poiesis* (the shaping principle of nature in its 'coming forth') to open up thinking 'otherwise'. In Schelling's account of artistic *praxis* as free involuntary decisiveness, we begin to get a sense of what such an alignment might entail.

By resisting the *eidos* of the schema or system, artistic practice initiates possibilities of seeing excluded from the *eidos*; possibilities already built into the system but otherwise, in the affirmation that the art decision *is*. The *praxis* of art allows us to think these possibilities as a glimmering of nature as other: 'through the world of sense there glimmers [...] the land of fantasy, of which we are in search' (Schelling 1978, p. 232). In its 'deed' as the decisive act of free resistance, art opens a space of possibility as a glimmering or *Augenblick*: a 'seeing' that frees us from ourselves in order to lead us 'to the very point where we ourselves were standing when we began to philosophize' (p. 232). Art allows us to philosophize in a way that philosophy (and science) cannot, by affirming free being resistively in the very act of what it is, thereby aligning itself with the *poiesis* of nature. Unlike Hegel's philosophy of art that declares the 'death of art' in its capacity to carry essential being (Hegel 1993, p. 13),[37] Schelling's philosophy of art allows us to think with the artwork positively, as enabling openings in nature as an event of being.

The good of nature

For Schelling, the good is simply itself: 'the good is its Being *per se*' (Schelling 2000, p. 25).[38] The good cannot itself be good, but can only be. In what way, then, can we speak of the good of nature without turning this good into something other than nature itself, thereby compromising the very good we seek to define? To turn nature into a good is to deny its goodness as such; to relate what it is to some other thing taken to be its good. For instance, to equate nature with sustainability (i.e. a sustainable human-nature relation) is to treat the good of nature as something other than itself – to see nature as lacking in some way, requiring efforts on the part of humans and their technologies to ensure its goodness is 'sustained'. However, the good of nature simply is, and, as such, any attempt to define it in other terms does a kind of violence to it, destroys its integrity, and supplants it with something other than the good itself. As such, nature-as-good stands against the system of predications (the knowledge system) where it becomes the good for something other than itself. This raises the problem of evil. If the good of nature is the fact that it is, then wherein lies evil?

An evil condition is one in which the good is blocked from coming to pass. In Schellingian terms, this condition occurs when 'evil [as subject] tries to obliterate its relationship to the ground upon which it is dependent' (Bowie 1993, p. 93). In this case, nature cannot be experienced as a 'living ground' (Schelling 2006, p. 26) of possibility but one deadened by necessity and determination. Evil contracts being back to the earth in a deathly return to the same. The task of ontological critique is to unblock this deathly contraction, by enlivening being with possibility. It can do this, I suggest, by situating itself in the 'in-between' of ground and existence, to see possibility opening up in critical activity when the critical self affirms itself otherwise catalysed by creative work. By resisting the determinations of the system that grounds itself in its own being, the critical self is turned towards openness in a momentary conjunction of the human and nature (*poiesis*); in the lightning flash of an intuition or absolute perception that is the eternal decision striking through it. Such moments, I argue, are not reserved for special individuals bestowed with superior powers; rather, they are an existence-element of all living things, in their co-partaking of the eternal decision to *be* as free singulars, distinct from, and resistive to their function as particulars in a system of organized things. Iain Grant suggests that 'Natural freedom consists in the unlimited actions of the naturesubject' (Grant 2006, p. 205), in the beginnings that become possible through decisive breaks with the system: 'the freedom at issue [in Schelling's *Naturphilosophie*] is not that which eludes physical causation, but rather, that which eludes regularity, or which breaks from the system' (p. 205). By grasping Schelling's idea of '*Nature as subject*' (Schelling 2004, p. 202) in transitive critical-creative activity that breaks with the system, we see the possibility of a *poietically* enabled ecoself shifted onto a living ground, working with nature in an open creative *praxis*.

Chapter 6

Virtual Nature

The virtual

In the previous chapter I looked at the way Schelling philosophized the possibility of a dialectical 'overcoming' of the difference between human being and nature by invoking an existing self in a free relation with nature. The self does not autonomously choose its freedom, but is finitely free with regard to its relation to nature as withdrawn yet excessive ground, as the 'indivisible remainder' or absolute being that keeps things together in their being apart. Schelling understands this being-together-apart (*partage*) as an ontological fact that something is, and as such, can always be otherwise, a fact that must be accounted for in the philosophizing itself. Thus Schelling's philosophy, throughout its various phases, can be regarded as critique at the level of ontological facticity, where it cannot be assumed that a 'free self' already has autonomous powers to be free, but must receive such power from its relation to the indivisible remainder: absolute or indifferent nature as part of the self's 'free being'. In other words, freedom is, in Schelling's terms, something given to the self (in the sense of giving way or ceding ground), manifesting as an awareness of the 'fact of freedom' (Schelling 2006, p. 9) and not a self-evident property of the self positing its own freedom. Freedom is part of the indivisible remainder: the withdrawing ground giving itself as the 'gift of nature', its providence in providing the potential for any thing to *be* in its freely existing state, singularly there in its difference from other things. To grasp this ontological fact is to understand that nature 'is' in terms of its capacity to 'give itself freely' in becoming whatever it is for whomever experiences it as such (i.e. singular human beings insofar as they are beings capable of such awareness).

Nature's becoming enacts a decisiveness 'to be', enabling things to have their own being distinct from other things. Without such decisiveness, nature would be 'in harmony with itself [...] [and] [...] never become Two' (Schelling 2000, p. 12). The movement of nature is thus fissured by a cisional splitting without which 'there would be no movement, no life, no progress. There would only be eternal stoppage, a deathly slumber of all of the forces' (p. 12).[1] Nature's decisiveness is thus attributable to its own freedom as a perpetually happening-beginning that opens up possibility in the de-*cision* between ground and existence, as the perpetual act of an 'eternal beginning'.

In this chapter I examine Schelling's *Naturphilosophie* and concepts of freedom and epochality in his subsequent writings, in terms of what can be called 'virtual nature', or nature understood as a possibility that remains as part of the 'whole' of what is. Virtual nature is not set apart from real nature as one of its possibilities, but is itself part of real nature insofar as it enables actual things of nature to be what they are, as singular beings, separable from other beings. I argue that Schelling's philosophy of nature and his philosophizing of the ontological status of human being as part of the being of nature is an inaugurating philosophizing of the 'virtual' and, despite its Neo-Platonic language, contains sufficient critical development of key concepts of nature, freedom, contingency and becoming to counter the recent turn to Spinoza as a means of theorizing the virtual in contemporary culture and ecocriticism, thereby retaining a specifically critical stance with respect to thinking about nature in the spirit of post-Kantian philosophy and critique.[2]

Schelling replaces Spinoza's determinist-mechanistic model of nature as a mathematical-mechanical system of interacting bodies, with a speculative-organicist model based on nature as active force (Beiser 2003, p. 182).[3] Schelling's philosophy of nature shifts the concept of the whole from a universalism in which the whole remains the same when various of its parts alter in their relation to one another, to a globalism where the whole and the parts alter together as part of the same being-whole.[4] In this case, the whole 'is' as part of the parts such that an alteration of the parts alters the whole at the same time. The whole is thus never fully whole but always incomplete – a 'partial whole' or 'insufficiency' to itself, perpetually becoming whole. It forever lacks the wholeness it yearns to be.[5]

Time

In his *Philosophy of Nature* Hegel argues that it is a mistake to understand things as arising and passing away *in* time; rather 'time itself is this *becoming*' (Hegel 1970, p. 230). Hegel makes the further comment that in becoming, time is the '*Cronos* which engenders all and destroys that to which it gives birth'. Thus, Hegel's concept of time involves an *Aufhebung* that destroys what it leaves behind, which ultimately leads to time realizing itself in its full 'reason' through the destruction of everything contributing to its becoming; that is, through the destruction of nature 'as it has been'. Nature today owes its being to what it negates: its past way of being, which no longer exists 'in itself' but only as a sublation into another level of being. By way of contrast, in *The Ages of the World* and in other writings, Schelling proposes time as eternally present in the cision of difference, such that the *Aufhebung* both differs *and conserves* at the same time. Beginning with the same insight that Hegel has: that nothing comes into being 'in' time, he argues the following:

> The mistake of Kantism [i.e. the mechanistic concept] (with respect to time) is that nothing comes into being in time. Rather that in each thing time comes into being immediately from eternity into the new [...] The beginning of time is in each thing, and indeed, each thing is the same as the eternal beginning. Each particular comes into being through this cision through which the world comes into being.
> (Schelling, qtd. in Wirth 2003, p. 218)

In Schelling's concept of the temporal becoming of nature (as time realizing itself in the movement of things), nature-as-time is always already realized in its ideal 'reason' (its past, present and future tenses); however, in each instance, this realization is not fully present to experience, but inhibited by the particular constellation of its elements at finite moments of its event. Thus any given moment in time presupposes all of time's possibilities of which only one is exhibited. A particular thing is not 'in' time but carries time in it such that at any given moment it exhibits all of its tensed modalities as possibilities of being: 'Out of the "before" and "after," out of the excluding relationship, emerges an "at this same point in time," a *joint and intertwined continuing*' (Schelling 2000, p. 37, emphasis added). As bearers of time, things are stretched across their temporal dimensions in a virtual-actual connectivity, which Schelling calls here 'a joint and intertwined continuing'. This stretching of the thing is the thing's plasticity – a mutable transfiguration of ideational-material becoming, folding back onto itself through recapitulated stages of the realization of nature's temporal possibilities: 'Indeed (what is not to be overlooked), what in the movement was the beginning or the first now becomes the lowest; what was the middle becomes here the intermediary; what was the end and the third becomes the highest' (pp. 37–38). Here Schelling describes the revolving nature of time, where any 'point' in time is experienced out of a continuum given all at once in an eternal present realizing itself in a tensed sequencing of 'before' and 'after'. All of time is immanent in the event of this cision in time in such a way that it remains open to possibilities in eternal beginningness. Thus any given event of nature's becoming is not evidence of a destruction, but of a possibility not yet realized.[6]

Schelling's philosophy operates with a virtual concept of nature, as the 'becoming' of freedom in human self-awareness through time. The whole as the 'indivisible remainder' is situated virtually with respect to 'what is', such that actual things can only be thought of in terms of their possibilities described as tensed expressions of time. These expressions of time work themselves out dialectically as the coming of freedom, as actual temporal experiences of the human self. As 'withdrawn ground' the indivisible remainder does not disappear into an annihilating abyss, but remains as active force in an oscillating back-and-forth movement that turns on itself, a turning described by Schelling as 'the wheel of nature' (Schelling 2000, p. 46). This oscillating movement is not independent of the human self; rather the human self, in its coming to self-awareness, is enacted through it, so that, at any given juncture between ground and existence, the self will be able to see itself as both separate from what went before as well as from what could be in a future being. This self-awareness in historical becoming requires a cision within itself, where the self tears itself loose from what it is, in order to see itself 'freely' as having historical self-awareness, as being destined for 'otherness' and hence as having an enabled relation to nature as historical becoming:

Only the person who has the power to tear themselves loose from themselves (from what is subordinate in their essence) is capable of creating a past for themselves. This is also the only person who enjoys a true present and who anticipates an actual future. Even these customary reflections would bring to light that no present is possible that is not founded on a decisive past and that no past is possible that is not based on the present as something overcome.

(p. 42)

The cision or 'tear' in the self is its coming to awareness of the tensed modality of temporal existence, differentiated into the past, present and future. Each mode is differentiated from the others, leading to an epochal idea of history or the coming to consciousness of free being as a 'distinction of times' (p. 45).

An epochal idea of nature as historical becoming needs to be distinguished from the paleontological-scientific concept of ages of natural evolution (the Anthropocene age etc.). The scientific concept of ages of nature objectifies nature and elides the specific moment when this kind of thinking about nature could be thought.[7] For science to 'say' that there *are* ages of nature requires an initial thought that nature can have 'being' – a reflex that comes to humans at a specific historical time in the 'evolution' of human thinking.[8] Thus, the ability of science to propose various evolutionary eras is made possible by an initial revelation or 'discovery' that the world *is*, and in being so, poses questions to the humans who think about what it is, its properties and potentials, as well as questions about who those who think this thought (human beings to whom 'the question of being' has been posed) are and what kind of capacity is constituted in this thought. The epochs or 'ages' outlined by Schelling are not equivalent to paleontological ages; rather they indicate ontological categories of the I-think, the originating reflex of thinking that turns in accordance with a movement of reason, from inchoate materiality to ideational spirit – a turning in thought itself. For Schelling, the 'ages' of world-forming are not paleontological ages, but epochal moments of the I-think that is 'telling its own history, but is not thereby becoming that history' (Lauer 2010, p. 63).

The wheel of nature

For Schelling, the self is enabled to be free in three successive stages of coming to self-awareness of free being (the fact 'that I am free'), corresponding to the past, present and future.[9] These three aspects of 'eternal consciousness' or free being evolve through the 'eternal beneficence' (Schelling 2000, p. 46) of nature as the indifferent absolute that, in its indifference, nevertheless gives being (by withdrawing or giving way, allowing or 'letting be'). Schelling's argument is not a scientific observation or historical interpretation of the past, but the necessary working through of the mind's 'free' relation with nature as absolute in terms of a dialectical movement between the past, present and future understood as part of eternal being (which Schelling calls the Godhead). These three modalities are played out in terms of the following triad: body, soul and spirit (p. 46), equivalent to the potencies of matter, ideation and reason.[10] The coming to consciousness of free being can be understood as the turning of the three modalities – body-past, soul-present and spirit-future – that are recapitulated into one another in the turning of the 'wheel of nature':

> Then these three are linked to one another and, in their unfree, undivided state, together constitute that wheel of nature that in the person is what is authentically interior. But the spirit of eternity is not bound to nature, but abides in eternal freedom in relationship to nature, although spirit cannot separate itself from nature. For spirit can only become tangible in its relationship to nature as the eternal healing, reconciling potency, as eternal beneficence itself.
>
> (p. 46)

Spirit as future being is 'not bound to nature' and so moves towards the ideal, but at the same time spirit 'cannot separate itself from nature', thus returning to the already 'past' material body of nature in a recapitulation of ideality and materiality into one another.[11] Thus Schelling proposes a model of nature's becoming that retains both ideation and materiality as 'eternal beneficence itself'. This triadic concept takes the whole of time as temporal becoming, which collapses temporality onto its own openness in perpetual beginningness. Unlike Hegel's *Aufhebung* that separates its modalities through a sublation that cancels the negated other, Schelling's *Aufhebung* retains all the separated modalities in an affirmation of the perpetual moment of the eternal beginning.

In proposing these triads, Schelling is effectively providing a way of philosophizing about time and temporal becoming as a movement of tense within thought itself, as a transition in modes of being. Where Kant had established the transcendental necessity of the 'I think' as the absolute condition of thought, Schelling ontologizes this 'I think' into a mode of becoming acted out dialectically in tensed phases or epochs of nature as historical becoming. That is, the mind becomes free in the philosophizing act itself when it thinks according to the dialectical rotation of the triadic movement thinking-temporality itself as distinct 'ages' of the world; as distinct epochs in which the world reveals itself as *a* world whose self-presence is 'conscious of itself' as distinct from unconscious nature. Furthermore, this coming to presence of free being as a distinct kind of world formation is thanks to the 'eternal beneficence' of nature (p. 46).[12] However, given that what is at stake here for Schelling is not real historical evolution but the 'content' of the 'I think' necessary for critique to occur, then these 'ages' are not simply real historical periods but possibilities of world-forming inherent in human thinking and self-consciousness. Thus Schelling, like Heidegger who followed him, thinks the coming-to-being of human self-consciousness backwards, so that the most recent 'age' is not to be understood as coming at the end of a long evolutionary process, but is itself the departure point for any thinking of the past.[13] Schelling's historical philosophizing is cast in a speculative mode in which the possibilities of the ages are played out according to the 'logic' of the turn, or the rotating turns of nature, whereby the domination of one is to the exclusion of the others in turn, according to successive rotations of the 'wheel' of nature.[14]

Blockages

Schelling's philosophy of ages of nature is a model for mapping possible modal distinctions in the evolution of nature as material-ideational becoming. Any given age will be composed of the different elements such that one comes to dominate the others. The others are blocked from coming-to-be by the dominance of the element that characterizes the particular age, for instance in inorganic nature, the organic and the universal are mixed in such a way that they are potential yet not actualized.[15] Schelling's concept of 'ages of the world' provides an organic-dynamic-dialectical model of historical becoming tied to human consciousness that accounts for becoming as quantitative rather than qualitative change. The change is not a qualitative change whereby an earlier age is absorbed and surpassed by the following age, but a division within the 'absolute indifference' of reason itself (Lauer 2010, p. 85, p. 187, n. 4). Quantitative difference does not lead to a transformation of reason in smooth transitions from one age to the next, but a diremption (separating, dividing, tearing apart) of the unity of reason in absolute indifference. Reason progresses by leaps, disjunctures and discontinuities within contingently located sites acting as beginnings of the possible. The problem Schelling sets for critique is not how difference evolves in temporal succession, but how difference occurs in the splitting of indifference by reason acting as a decisive event in nature's becoming.

For Schelling reason affirms itself all at once in its various modalities, or not at all: 'reason is absolutely *one*, because it does not admit of degrees, and because it is the *absolute itself*' (Schelling 2004, p. 132). Any given age will exhibit all of reason but according to a constellation of 'potencies' (Lauer 2010, p. 86).[16] These powers of reason (as absolute identity) are not to be thought of as acting in succession, but as hierarchically ordered potentials such that, in any given age, one power blocks the others from coming to be (pp. 86–87). For instance, an age of technology would not emerge through successive technological advances but would need to appear all at once as a *coup*, in localized moments of rupture, breaking decisively from the previous age. These moments would not necessarily happen at the same time, but at different times that, in retrospection, can be seen as part of the same emerging age. Through the agency of its rationality that offers 'adequate' explanations of all the natural phenomena presented to it, the age of technology would necessarily block the previous age from continuing to be the age that it can be, while also blocking any future age from coming about.

Reason does not evolve from a state of unreason, since, by necessity, it is eternal. Rather, reason tries to make sense of, and control the blind destructive force, the 'swathing' of unreason that threatens it, enacting the 'deed' of reason that separates the contracting and expanding forces of nature, 'soothing' them into stasis, where a 'product must come forth that, like matter, stands between total restriction and complete expansion, stopped, so to speak, in the middle' (Schelling 2000, p. 33).[17] Reason orders and stills material chaos, so that something can *be*. Different constellations of reason will thus produce different ways of being within contingently located sites, by fending off 'otherness' as unreason or chaotic nothingness.

By acting at a single stroke in order to separate itself from unreason, reason inaugurates an absolute beginning (the 'absolute itself'), but this beginning is always in the midst of things in their unruliness such that its absoluteness can only be claimed retrospectively as something that 'had to be'. The decisiveness of reason inaugurating a new beginning, a new world formation, is thus founded on myth, and in particular, the myth of an absolute beginning in the 'nothing' that 'had to be', a nothing out of which reason arises 'naturally'. Epochs are necessarily founded on myth as retrospective projections of reason – as the sacrosanct 'other' of reason itself. Myth not only separates reason from unreason, but, through its power of resolution, tames the unruliness of nature, its chaotic destructive force, thereby pacifying things as 'products' of nature ruled by reason enacted in finite acts of self-consciousness. As Roland Barthes argues in his essays on myth, through science and reason, myth 'reconciles the infinite power of man over nature with the "fatality" of the sacrosanct, which man cannot yet do without' (Barthes 1973, p. 70).

Schelling's philosophy is a-teleological in that it does not advance in a direct line from lower to higher forms of life (e.g. from inorganic matter to ideal spirit, although it may seem this way to modern human beings looking at it from their finite perspective of self-consciousness); rather, at any given age both lower and higher forms of life are mixed together in particular ways, according to contingent factors concerning the natural and historical circumstances of their coming together. Any given age is not the culmination of forces gathered up and transformed from previous ages, but a stasis in becoming where forces are stilled into an illusionary stability. Any system of nature devised by humans is necessarily part of the age in which it is devised, thereby blocking nature from becoming otherwise. The current age, which Schelling defined as the age of 'natural law' (the age of natural philosophy and scientific empiricism), is thus blocking the foreseen age (the age of providence) from coming to pass.[18] The task of critique becomes one of unblocking the prevailing system of nature in order to await the age to come, where the material and the ideal are unified in the revelation of the absolute itself.

However, a significant problem emerges here. How might one think of this new age, if the alternative is the chaos of unreason? Surely critique does not set about dismantling the institutions and discourses of the current age on the basis that they are blocking the possibilities of the future, only to collapse these possibilities into chaotic unreason? Schelling's answer is to propose an ultimate unity in absolute indifference split between an 'unconscious' ground and a 'conscious' existence already active in the ground of being. Here we encounter the idea of the Thing (*das Ding*). For Schelling, the Thing is a 'higher' ideality located in the indifferent ground between subject and object:

Now if this higher thing be nothing else but the ground of identity between the absolutely subjective and the absolutely objective, the conscious and the unconscious, which part company precisely in order to appear in the free act, then this higher thing itself can be neither subject nor object, nor both at once, but only the *absolute identity*, in which is no duality at all, and which, precisely because duality is the condition of all consciousness, can never attain thereto.

(Schelling 1978, pp. 208–09)

This 'higher thing' or Thing is neither object nor subject, but resides in the indifferent ground in-between subjective and objective polarities. The Thing enables the 'free act' of the self, without which there would be no duality and hence no self-consciousness at all. The Thing is thus the splitting between the stilled object in the stasis of the potencies in the current age and its possibilities 'to come'. Or to put this another way, the Thing is the virtualization of the object in its possibilities for being in indeterminate otherness. The Thing is an image detached from its object, floating in the 'in-between', without a proper place and not yet secured in a subjective perception.[19]

Keeping in mind that what we are seeking here is the way in which a future age announces itself, then these possibilities of the Thing cannot be from the future, as the new age has not yet arrived. Rather, they can only be possibilities of the new age already announcing themselves from within the withdrawn ground of being itself, as residual archaic marks blocked from coming to view by the current constellation of powers. In order to think of the Thing in its absolute possibilities, we need to think of something caught between an advancing and retreating movement of being-as-becoming; something held back from coming forward. To think of this held back possibility, critique needs to 'tarry' in the splitting of indifference; in the in-between of ground and existence, right at where it happens, in order to see such possibilities as an openness in being itself, where the archaic marks can be seen glimmering as the flash of possibility. In Chapter 9, I will turn to Walter Benjamin's concept of the mark as archaic material potential to show how the thing-as-mark can be released from its objectification by technology into nature as such.

Partage

Schelling's doctrine of ages of the world set out in *The Ages of the World*, which we have been following so far, requires a concept of nature as actual-virtual that must be thought together as part of the same being: being-as-becoming. The whole, as actual-virtual, cannot be thought 'in itself' as something standing over and against that which is, but is 'in' actual things: 'There is a silent, exclusively passive [i.e. virtual] Whole, not an actual Whole that could be articulated as such. Hence, it is certainly always full of life with respect to the particular parts, but considered from the outside or as Whole, it is utterly without effect' (Schelling 2000, p. 55). The whole is 'full of life with respect to particular parts [i.e. singularities]', but this 'life' does not gain its meaning from any overriding sense of the whole acting outside the parts that 'could be articulated as such' (for example, the life of the parts could not be attributed to a system of nature acting outside the parts as the preordained whole); rather, the life of each singularity 'yearns' for ideational fulfilment in a whole that is always emergent and ever beginning. That is, the whole never fulfils itself in some idealized location outside its parts, but is perpetually beginning itself anew insofar as parts 'part' or partake in the whole as the parting of the parts themselves. The whole is a 'sufficiency' to itself in that it retains itself contingently in its parts.[20] In holding to such a concept of the whole as self-parting (*partage*), one must accept the fact that the whole is already in the beginnings that happen, and is seeking ideation in the 'parting of the parts', and not at a 'higher' level of completion.

The historical 'evolution' of ages is not towards a completion of nature in an ideation beyond its parts (which would be to deny nature as such; to deny the very fact of the singularity of the things of nature as already 'carrying' the whole), but remains as the 'eternal' restless 'turning' of the material-ideational becoming of everything, in which nature, as the beneficial element, advances in a chiasmic movement that simultaneously withdraws (as the 'indivisible remainder'). As withdrawn being, nature is already ahead of its 'parts' yet still with the parts as that which 'remains'. This suggests that Schelling's doctrine of epochal becoming of 'free being' does not require a teleological understanding of historical unfolding towards higher and freer states of being, but rather calls for an ever-present moment of actual-virtual openness in specific instances (singular acts) of becoming in which what is at stake each time is an idealization or a 'becoming free' of what is otherwise blocked in its present historical being. Schelling's doctrine of ages enables a *praxis* in which 'free being' is at stake. For Schelling this *praxis* is art.

Art

In *System of Transcendental Idealism*, Schelling describes how art enables the coming of free being. By being the artwork that it is, it 'proceeds from freedom' (Schelling 1978, p. 231) and thus testifies to the fact of freedom in resistance to the blind necessity of material becoming (its entropic force). By holding itself together against the tendency of things to fly apart, the artwork presents the absolute as 'eternal and original unity':

> Art is paramount to the philosopher, precisely because it opens to him, as it were, the holy of holies, where burns eternal and original unity, as if in a single flame, that which in nature and history is rent asunder, and in life and action, no less than in thought, must forever fly apart.
>
> (p. 231)

Schelling thinks that in its 'original unity', its factical thereness, art opens access to the 'holy of holies' – the 'glimmer[ing]' of the absolute itself: 'there glimmers, as if through words the meaning, as if through dissolving mists the land of fantasy, of which we are in search' (p. 232). The absolute is not located in some realm outside the artwork, but glimmers through it as part of the artwork itself. The glimmering of the absolute that Schelling describes here is the sense of openness one encounters in an artwork, in its presentation as art.[21] For Kant, the singular presentation of a natural thing invokes an indeterminacy of reason associated with a sense of beauty (Kant 1987, p. 62). The feeling of pleasure one gains when looking at a thing of nature is indeterminable with respect to categories of reason, leading to a reflection in search of a principle of unity that, for Kant, resides in the formal harmony of reason discovered in thought itself. However, for Schelling, the ideal unity is not reflected in thought but intuited in nature (Schelling 1978, pp. 217–18).[22] Aesthetic experience belongs not to the self reflecting on nature, but in the self's seeking for it in nature ('the land of fantasy') as a sense of glimmering or *Schein*. In German Idealist philosophy *Schein* refers to the appearance of the thing, as distinct from the thing 'in itself', and is associated with semblance or illusion. However, for Schelling, it is precisely and only through *Schein* that we have access to the absolute as the ultimate ground of things.[23] As the shining of things, *Schein* can be understood in a virtual sense, in terms of how the thing glimmers in its possibilities, how it opens itself to otherness.

For Schelling what matters is not what an artwork is but *that it is*. By emphasizing this factical-ontological aspect of Schelling's philosophizing on art and nature, we uncover a powerful theory of singularity in which things are understood in terms of *partage*, in relation to their dynamic possibilities. As a singular thing, the artwork 'refuses' to give ground; in being there, it stays where it is, thereby testifying to the *poietic* force that moves things in their difference from other things. The problem of thinking of unity-in-difference as parts in relation to a whole is resolved so long as we take the movement of difference from the thing 'as such', in the in-between of virtual and actual modes of being, and not posit this movement as emanating from the thing 'in itself'. The movement itself is always the beginning of what can be – an enabling without knowing what this enabling is leading to – without knowing its destination in advance.

As a singular thing, the artwork remains as it is, a 'whole' or 'unity' as such, and not something that signifies something else, or something reducible to a set of properties or qualities. In this case, we need to revise Schelling's characterization of the work of art as providing access to the 'holy of holies'. The artwork is not holy or holistic, but singularly 'whole'. To see the artwork in this way is to let it be in its singularity. By letting the artwork be, we do not see it for what it signifies; rather, given the fact that it is, we ask what it enables, what it 'calls forth'. Art enables otherness, and, as such, it calls forth a beginning. Art's task is to begin. However, the beginning cannot be for a destination already known, as this would mean that the beginning has already begun (by knowing your destination, you are already on your way, already moving forward and hence already past the beginning). Rather, the beginning must itself *be* a beginning, and therefore be wrested from already known destinations and pathways. Art's task is to resist the already known modes of being that determine things as subject to thought, and to *be there* as the artwork that it is, to enable beginnings to be. With his doctrine of the epochal evolution of reason, Schelling takes us some way towards this ontological task for art as the beginning of being-enabling.

Myth

How does art begin, and in what way does it relate to the absolute? In *The Philosophy of Art*, Schelling argues that art begins in myth: '*Mythology is the necessary condition and first content of all art*' (Schelling 1989, p. 45). By myth, Schelling means the stance to the world taken by the ancient Greeks in their poetry and drama, in which speech and action are directly linked to the absolute. The gods of ancient Greek poetry 'act with freedom, since it is their nature to act thus and they know no other law than their own nature' (p. 39). As absolutely free beings, the gods are the absolute in the sense that they unify the particular and the universal by their very deeds. The poetic presentation of these deeds mediates between the universal and the particular thereby founding human being in 'free' nature. By identifying these aspects of myth in Greek poetry and drama, Schelling is able to posit a principle of unity in art based on historical precedents (the Greek beginning) yet in accordance with the postulates of critique. Critique requires a mediating presentation of the universal and the particular, which Schelling finds in ancient Greek myth.

In unifying human being and nature, myth carries the absolute, and is, for Schelling, the initial point of reference for the coming of 'free being', which, as we have seen, evolves in thought as the 'turning' of reason's elements, manifesting in particular configurations identified as specific 'ages' of the world. Drawing from Schelling's philosophy of myth, Jean-Luc Nancy has noted that 'In myth the world makes itself known, and makes itself known through declaration or through a complete and decisive revelation. The greatness of the Greeks – according to the modern age of mythology – is to have lived in intimacy with such speech and to have founded their *logos* in it: they are the ones for whom *muthos* and *logos* are "the same"' (Nancy 1991, pp. 48–49). Myth founds *logos* in nature in a 'tautegorical' sense: myth 'says nothing other than itself and is produced in consciousness by the same process that, in nature, produces the forces that myth represents' (p. 49). Myth does not refer to some other world beyond what it says, but brings a world into existence through the very enactment of this saying. In reconciling the *logos* (the discursive authority of reason) with nature, myth founds human being in absolute meaning, and justifies human existence as being fit for a particular world.

For Schelling, elements of the heroic age of the ancient Greeks are carried into our current thinking, enabling us to think of art as part of the absolute, as the coming of free being. Thus, in his philosophy of art, Schelling begins with myth as a unifying presentation of the absolute, which he understands in symbolic terms.[24] In a particularly dense proposition, Schelling presents his concept of the symbolic:

> *Representation of the absolute with absolute indifference of the universal and the particular* **within the particular** *is possible only symbolically.*
>
> (Schelling 1989, p. 45)

The absolute can only be presented as such – as an absolute indifference between the universal and the particular – through the symbolic in the particular. That is, the symbolic works 'within the particular' by maintaining the absolute indifference between the particular and the universal. As we saw in Chapter 4, Schelling analyses the proposition in terms of the copula as 'indifferent' to both the subject and the predicate, where indifference means the capacity to hold the subject and predicate together while remaining irreducible to either of them. Indifference is assigned to the absolute as its capacity to be itself and to retain itself in itself while enabling difference to take place. The symbol is thus equivalent to the copula in the sense I have just described.

In a key passage a few pages on, and with the problem of unity-in-difference in mind, Schelling sets out a concept of the artwork as symbol through the following set of propositions:

> That representation in which the universal means the particular or in which the particular is intuited through the universal is *schematism*.
>
> That representation, however, in which the particular means the universal or in which the universal is intuited through the particular is *allegory*.
>
> The synthesis of these two, where neither the universal means the particular nor the particular the universal, but rather where both are absolutely one, is the *symbolic*.
>
> (p. 46)

Here Schelling identifies three elements of a system of absolute reason: schematism, allegory and the symbolic. The symbolic is the 'higher' element in that it synthesizes the other two. Schematism (following Kant) is the application of a schema of universal concepts to the particular object, while allegory is schematism in reverse, in that the particular object acts as a sign for the universal. Both schematism and allegory maintain the separation between the universal and the particular, and are thus 'an indifference of the universal and the particular' (p. 47), while the symbolic dissolves this separation in a synthesis of the other two. The symbolic founds both schematism and allegory in mythic union with nature, synthesizing them in 'absolute indifference' so that art can begin. The absolute can only *be* in the symbolic, which, to make itself known, requires a dissolution of the indifference between the universal and the particular set up by the other two modes. The synthesizing power of the symbol enacts the mythic union of the universal and the particular, which, as we have seen, is to be found in ancient Greek poetry and art.[25] Consequently, Schelling finds a solution to the Kantian gap (see Chapter 3) in poetry and art as the enactment of mythic union between human being and nature in the symbolic mode of representation. This solution remains faithful to the postulate of absolute indifference that requires a concept of unity-in-difference in which a whole must be complete in itself and hence indifferent to its parts while being part of the parts at the same time. In order to do this, Schelling proposes a triadic-dialectical relation between elements of absolute reason, such that one dissolves the other two, which nevertheless retain their separate existences.

Having set up the formal system of mythic representation, Schelling now shows how this system works itself out historically. Art begins in the symbolic mode in the Greek beginning, as an immediate presentation of the absolute in a full living poetic spirit, but then proceeds to separate itself out into its other modes through time. Thus the allegorical mode comes in a later age: 'The separation of the allegorical element in [Greek myth] was only something that occurred to a later period, something possible only after all poetic spirit was extinguished' (p. 48). Allegory comes after the symbolic in another age, in order to make the symbolic live again. This is where we see Schelling's system start to turn against itself. The symbolic affirms the mythic beginning, but only if this beginning is presented allegorically in the current age. Schelling identifies this allegorical presentation with Christianity as a 'Subordination of the finite to the infinite' (p. 62). In signifying the infinite, allegory wipes out finitude, which 'counts only to the extent that it means or signifies the infinite' (pp. 61–62). However Schelling does not recognize that allegorizing is itself a finite event – an event that must also count in the presentation. In its presentation as allegory, allegorizing is doubled on itself insofar as it simultaneously presents and withdraws the infinite. It thus opens up an in-between, neither finite nor infinite, from which something emerges.

In proposing the symbol as the unifying power, Schelling did not go far enough in his thinking of the counter-power of allegory. As the founding moment of myth that reawakens the dead poetic spirit, the symbol cannot simply be, but must allegorize itself in finite events of art. This means that the symbol must already be its own allegory and hence must deconstitute its own beginning. Myth is already inhabited by a countering demythication occurring as an allegorizing of its own founding moment in the symbolic domain. Thus, a mythic beginning cannot occur through the symbol acting on its own behalf, but only through the demythification of already operating myths that continually lay claim to such founding moments in the current age. The event of art is not myth-founding, but precisely the reverse: the demythification of its own mythic foundations as the work that the artwork does in its happening 'as such'. Art enables a mythic beginning, but paradoxically, this beginning does not lead to myth. Rather, the beginning-enablement suspends the artwork in-between myth and its demythification. In Chapter 8, I show how Walter Benjamin's reading of Hölderlin's poetry offers a demythification of myth along the lines I have outlined here.

Demythification

In *System of Transcendental Idealism*, Schelling identifies three possible ages in the evolution of reason as free being: the age of destiny ruled by a 'wholly blind force' that destroys everything that it builds (the 'tragic' age of the Greek beginning, of which hardly anything survives); the age of natural law 'compelling freedom and wholly unbridled choice to subserve a *natural plan*' (Schelling 1978, pp. 211–12), based on mechanistic principles (the principles of causality); and the age of providence 'wherein the force which appeared in the earlier stages as destiny or nature has evolved itself as *providence*' (p. 212). These three ages correspond with Schelling's dynamic model of nature as absolute time revealing itself through a historical evolution of human thought. It also corresponds to the three temporal modes of past (destiny), present (natural law) and future (providence), such that the future (the 'yet to come' age of providence) is virtually located within the other two.

Schelling locates his own age on the cusp of the age of providence wherein 'it will become apparent that even what seemed to be simply the work of destiny or nature was already the beginning of a providence imperfectly revealing itself' (p. 212). The age of providence has not yet arrived and 'When this period will begin, we are unable to tell' (p. 212). This new age 'imperfectly revealing itself' in the other two ages is thinkable but yet to come; it has already begun but not yet arrived. From this in-between position Schelling seeks out a medium whereby this new age might come about. He finds this medium in myth:

> for in mythology such a medium existed, before the occurrence of a breach now seemingly beyond repair. But how a new mythology is itself to arise, which shall be the creation, not of some individual author, but of a new race, personifying, as it were, one single poet – that is the problem whose solution can be looked for only in the future destinies of the world, and in the course of history to come.
>
> (pp. 232–33)

Here Schelling posits myth as a solution to the problem of mediating the coming of the new age. This 'problem' occurs because of the 'breach' of the unity of the ages by the diremption of reason (the tear in reason itself), opening a void in-between past and present modes of being. As we have already seen, Schelling proposes to fill this void with the symbol as the unification of the infinite in the finite thing. The providential age comes into being through a 'new mythology' already beginning in the current age, and opening up a new world formation founded on the eternal beneficence of the absolute (which Schelling calls God). In saying this, Schelling suggests a solution to the 'fall' of human being into the rationality of science and technology and the perversion of nature in human ends and desires. This solution requires that we wait on the coming of a new mythology already preparing to emerge in the current age. But this 'new mythology' would not be entirely new, as it already existed in the Greek beginning before the fall of reason into historical self-consciousness, a time when *logos* was united with *muthos* and humans were at one with the gods in absolute freedom. Such a myth would have to be projected backward as a reason for the current age to justify its way of being to itself. If myth rises out of the void to found human being in nature, this nature cannot be a nature 'in itself', but a nature already tamed by reason.

Myth does not begin of its own accord. As noted earlier, the rationality of a historical epoch requires a mythic enactment of its own beginning. Myth is thus a retrospective projection of reason to justify itself *ex nihilo* in an absolute beginning. Myth cannot simply enact itself, but must do so through reason. For Schelling, this takes the form of a symbolic presentation, which, as we have already seen, is also an enactment of its own deconstitution if it is to live on in historical consciousness and partake in the world-forming to which historical consciousness gives rise. This suggests that Schelling's call for a new mythology needs to be reversed. Rather than seeking a new mythology to begin a new age of natural providence so that nature might be saved from the human fall into reason, we need to recognize that the mythic nature of the current age is already blocking access to any such beginning whatsoever. The myth of nature inhibits the emergence of any kind of new human-nature relation and keeps the current age enclosed in its own mythic self-consciousness.

The emergence of natural providence 'already revealing itself' cannot be the coming of a new age, but the same age repeating itself in a new guise. To enable an absolutely new age to begin, there must first be a demythification of the existing myths blocking our encounter with nature 'as such'. By demythifying myth we do not abandon the mythic encounter, but keep the current age open in 'mythic possibility'. In doing this, we rediscover pre-mythic openness (the nothing or void out of which myth arises), in the disjuncture between the symbolic presentation of the human and nature as united in absolute being (the universal), and its allegorization circulating in the current age (the particular). This pre-mythic openness appears as a flash occurring in-between singular things of nature and their disjunctive connection to objects of the current age. Things flash in the void of nature, in the in-between opened up as providence or the promise of being to come. This possibility is not the possibility of the same but the other possibility brought on by the allegorization of the symbol that initiates the fall into historical being, but which also opens up finite possibility right at the juncture between ground and existence, the place of the void occupied by things as such.

There are no new myths, only the same myth repeated endlessly – the enactment of the unity of meaning and being in the single beginning. In the current age myths already lay claim to nature as given over to human being, as already destined for human freedom. These myths, which are really the same myth repeating itself in a new guise, block nature from becoming other, condemning human being to repeat the same error of confusing human *praxis* with the *poietic* saying of nature (as proposed in Chapter 1). A nature philosophy, I argue, should therefore reject the call to re-enchant the world with new myths and instead seek out openings in current mythic formations through the disjuncture between ground and existence, enabling otherness to shine forth as absolute possibility.

Art as counter-image

Schelling's system of mythic presentation contains three elements: the schemata, its allegorical reversal, and their synthesis in the symbol. But Schelling identifies another element in this system, which he calls the image. The image 'is always concrete, purely particular, and is determined from all sides such that only the definite factor of the space occupied by the original object prevents it from being identical with the object itself' (Schelling 1989, p. 46). The image comes between the particular object and the universal concept (the schemata) that gives it form and meaning, and is prevented from coinciding with the object by the fact that the object takes up a definite space. The image is real ('concrete' and 'particular') but not actual (it occupies no specific place). It thus virtualizes the object by extending it into its possibilities, according to either a schemata or its reversed allegorical mode of presentation. But the image is ultimately a product of the synthesizing power of the symbol – the power necessary for myth to actualize itself in a sensuous recuperation of the object into full meaningfulness: 'A necessary *corollary* issuing from this entire discussion is then the following: Mythology as such and every poetic rendering of it in particular are to be comprehended neither schematically nor allegorically, but rather *symbolically*' (p. 48). Thus, an image can only be sensuously meaningful (*Sinnbild*) if it coincides with the symbol in its capacity to dissolve the difference between the universal and the particular, thereby actualizing myth in an absolute beginning. An image makes the object shimmer in mythic aura. However, this coincidence of image and symbol can never be the case in any current mythic representation because, as noted earlier, the symbolic must already be allegorical and hence have already deconstituted itself in its founding gesture.[26] The aura of the image is more like a glimmer or fading light, the trace of a possible mythic fullness disseminated from the archaic past, offering something of the power of myth in its absence. The image offers the possibility of mythic connectivity in the absence of the full power of myth itself: a chiasm of distance and proximity in mediated experience, described for instance by Nietzsche as the flashing beyond already near us (see Chapter 3) and by Benjamin as aura in a technologically mediated age (Benjamin 2002, pp. 104–05) (see Chapter 9).

From these lines of enquiry I will make some preliminary conclusions with respect to the image, art and the founding gesture of myth. First, the image does not coincide with its object but slips away from it into indefinable possibilities; second, the art image does not gather the universal and the particular into a consolidated symbolic presentation, but disperses them through demythification; and third, art can only happen in the current age if it demythifies its objects such that they are released from symbolic representation, and opened into an absolute indifference in the 'in-between' of the universal and the particular. Through demythification, art becomes the counter-image of myth, turning myth into its other, thereby releasing sense into absolute possibility as a singular beginning.

The Thing

In *The Encyclopaedia Logic*, Hegel argues that the absolute does not lie 'far beyond, but [...] is precisely what is wholly present, what we, as thinkers, always carry with us and employ, even though we have no express consciousness of it' (Hegel 1991, p. 59). The absolute is a limit on thought in thought itself, which, in Hegel's logical philosophy, concerns how the objective world comes to be in relation to a subject who thinks it. The absolute is itself the passing of subject into object in a reflexive *Aufhebung*. As 'wholly present' to thinking, the absolute is thus reduced to the subject/object dialectic, so that there can be no absolute outside (Žižek 1999, p. 95).[27] Being is also limited by the absolute in the movement of the dialectic so that there can be no outside Being: 'Thus, *Being*, for example, is a pure thought-determination' (Hegel 1991, p. 59). The problem with this position is that it projects an anthropomorphic idea of the absolute as subject, reducing everything to the human right to exist.[28] This anthropomorphic projection is also antagonistic to what it encounters, in that its highest good is the subject's own self-preservation set against a contesting other: 'this is the notion of the individual which must constantly assert and affirm himself in order to be real [...] so that he can exist only by incessantly winning and testing his existence against something or some-one which contests it' (Marcuse, qtd. in Wilden 1980, p. 128).[29] Any thing outside the dialectic gets drawn into the dialectical process in order to feed the desire of the subject in its self-preservation. The dialectic imposes subjectivity on things, demanding that they too partake in the subject's quest for self-certainty. The remainder (x) revealed in Kant's transcendental critique becomes an insignificant residue, a 'hardly-anything-at-all', incapable of bearing meaning or sense, and hence grist for the mill of the dialectic. Here we encounter an offence to nature, where the things of nature lack the dignity afforded to human subjects. Their lack of dignity (their lack of their own self-sustaining being) consigns them to objectification in the subject's own struggle to be – its own dignity.[30]

At the theoretical and critical level, what can be done to counter this subjectification of nature to human will and self-perpetuation? The way to counter this is to think of things first, as obstacles or barriers to the subject's quest for self-knowing, and then to switch positions by thinking with the thing in its resistivity to thought. In this way, we can retain the initial post-Kantian insight that identifies the gap in reason as an irreducible remainder (x), but instead of then making this remainder subject to reason's dialectical movement, we allow it to retain its resistivity, such that the dialectical movement includes this resistivity without absorbing it. That is, the dialectical movement becomes inhabited by an absolute interruption that outlives the reason applied in trying to limit and contain it. In this case the thing becomes both included and excluded in the dialectic, an *Erscheinung* or apparition of otherness, always *there* but never objectively present.[31]

In Seminar VII of his seminars on the ethics of psychoanalysis, Jacques Lacan develops an analysis of the Thing (*das Ding*) (Lacan 1992), which is 'sharply distinguished' from the Hegelianism that takes no account of the irreducible remainder (p. 134).[32] Previously in this chapter I showed how Schelling's own analysis of the Thing can be understood as a demythified image, where the mythic union between the universal and the particular in the symbolic is allegorized in the current age. The Thing allegorizes the mythic union by repeating it retroactively so that it flashes as an archaic origin awaiting restoration to full mythic presence. The Thing marks the place of the lost origin returning as demythified possibility. In Lacan's psychoanalytical version, the Thing becomes a 'sublimation' of the lost object: 'sublimation [...] raises an object [...] to the dignity of the Thing' (p. 112), triggering an uncanny sense of mythic fulfilment (*Erscheinung*).

To exemplify what he means by sublimation, Lacan presents the reader with a 'little fable' about a collection of empty match boxes he once encountered at a friend's house some years earlier. Lacan describes how he 'saw there a collection of match boxes. Why the image has suddenly resurfaced in my memory, I cannot tell' (p. 114). An image of the match boxes suddenly comes to him from nowhere in particular, triggering an uncanny yet pleasurable feeling of shock, novelty and excess that makes him think about its meaning. What was so special about the matchboxes to have triggered such a response? This is how Lacan describes their appearance: 'they were all the same and laid out in an extremely agreeable way that involved each one being so close to the one next to it that the little draw was slightly displaced. As a result they were all threaded together so as to form a continuous ribbon that ran along the mantlepiece, climbed the wall, extended to the molding, and climbed down again next to a door' (p. 114). This 'continuous ribbon' of intertwined match boxes with each draw inserted in the adjacent box, suggests for Lacan a 'mutant form of something', not random, but 'liberated' from the boxes, something 'that subsists in a match box', as a 'revelation of the Thing beyond the object'. Lacan describes this liberated Thing as something presenting itself with a 'copulatory force' suggested by the displaced image of the sexual act, but also (I propose) as an image of the body restored to nature as an original continuum of life. The continuous ribbon of copulating boxes winds its way across the room without aim or purpose, pointing to the 'thingness' of the match box itself: 'The wholly gratuitous, proliferating, superfluous, and quasi absurd character of this collection pointed to its thingness as match box' (p. 114). The match boxes' lack of purpose, their sheer excessiveness, shifts them from being a common consumer item to a thing. What is at stake here?

In Lacan's fable, we are presented with a case of sublimation where a common object (a match box) is raised to the 'dignity' of a Thing. In this reworking of Kant's analysis of the 'beautiful object' in the *Critique of Judgment*, Lacan shows how an aesthetics does not reflect back on the subject in search for a harmony of reason to makes sense of indeterminate experience, but is thrown into an already existing terrain of taken-for-granted things requiring repeated confirmation that they are indeed similar things, and ensuring that the alienated self exists in a continuous world ruled by the Same. However, the continuity of this world of sameness, of familiar items and objects of use, can be interrupted by an event that defamiliarizes the self, triggering an *Erscheinung*: here described in terms of an uncanny yet pleasant experience that Lacan identifies with the Thing. In specific terms, Lacan describes the *Erscheinung* as a resurfacing image: 'why the image has suddenly resurfaced'. In the unusual display, the match box as an 'object of use' is sublimated into a thing by turning it into an uncanny image. The match box can still be seen there as an object, but its objectivity is de-objectified and turned into something else: a 'mutant form'. The image thus has two modes of presentation: an affirmative or 'yes' mode in which the object holds its place as a particular object, as part of the 'idea' of a match box, and a disavowing or 'no' mode that refuses to allow the match box its particularity as a match box. In the simultaneity of these modes the match box is singularized, turned into an undecidable 'thing'.

By singularizing the linked matchboxes into a thing, the image deconstitutes their objectivity, triggering an *Erscheinung* that 'points' to an indefinable sense of the mythic restitution the body to nature. The myth is allegorized by Lacan's fable – brought to our attention as an example of the work of sublimation in repairing the self's alienation from nature. But the reparation is short-circuited by the very act of sublimation itself. How does this take place and why? The fable repeats the original moment of restitution in the *Erscheinung*, and thus affirms the myth as having affective force. But in presenting it in the full force of its original plenitude *as a recollected image* recounted in the fable, the myth is simultaneously disavowed. The self's restitution thus fails to come about, but what emerges is the Thing, a proxy image of full restitution that enables the self to 'live on'. The fable thus presents the Thing revealed as simultaneously saying 'yes' and 'no' to mythic union with nature. The Thing is both an image of mythic union *and* its impossibility.

Lacan's fable gives some indication of the role that art might play in a nature philosophy in an age of technology. I have argued in this chapter, following Schelling's philosophy of art, that the function of art is to *be* the artwork that it is, to enable a beginning in open possibility as resistance to already known ways of being. As an artwork, the match box installation is resistant to the mode of being of the match boxes as technologically produced objects such that they are turned against themselves, becoming a 'mutant form' (Lacan 1992, p. 114) that says otherwise to what the objects are usually saying. This turning of the technological object happens not in an initial encounter with the artwork, but 'after the fact', in this case, in Lacan's fable that repeats the encounter as an *Erscheinung* or retroactive image. In repeating it, the fable turns the artwork another time, carrying it into a future possibility. My own reading of it, here in this book that you are currently reading, turns it yet again, and one can imagine any number of turnings through many readings, proliferating the artwork into a general openness constrained only by the contingencies of time and space. The Thing that the artwork triggers – the empty void of possibility – is thus carried along by the *work* that turns the art*work* (the work of the installation itself, but also the critical writings, the viewings, discussions and artworks of a similar kind), releasing consumer objects into demythified openness that carries a mythic charge.

While resisting myth, the artwork remains mythically enabled, staying in the 'in-between' of the past as original plenitude and an empty but possible future, maintaining a sense of openness such that things can go on without reproducing the myth of nature 'in itself'.[33] Rather, myth is challenged by the artwork to reveal itself as myth, thereby demythifying the objects that it commands, releasing them to be otherwise. In this way, technologically produced objects can be released from their mythic function and returned to the openness of possibility.

Part III

Poetics

Chapter 7

Heidegger's Thing

Hidden nature

A nature philosophy begins with things. This concern for things stems from Kant's critique that posits the 'thing-in-itself' as the absolute limit of thought in its endeavours to think itself into an existing 'I', a self capable of knowing the world of things as objects of thought. From the Kantian position, the finite world of human experience can only know the thing as an appearance and never as the thing-in-itself: 'What the things-in-themselves may be I do not know, nor do I need to know, since a thing can never come before me except in appearance' (Kant 1929, p. 286). By postulating the thing-in-itself as the absolute limit of thought, Kant is able to develop a critique that reflects back on itself, securing itself in the categories of reason in order to make sense of what it perceives as an object in relation to the thinking subject. But Kant's critique reveals a gap in reason, the gap in which the self exists in-between subjective and objective polarities. This gap becomes the site of an absolute openness, a place of free being, leading into indeterminate possibility.

As we saw in Chapter 3, Kantian critique elides free being in seeking a ground in reason. This leads to the diminution of the things of nature. They become 'mere things', nothing more than preparatory stuff for the production of objects into a system of reason. As Schelling argued, the thing's 'thatness' – its factical being – is effaced (Schelling 2007, p. 147), replaced by an appearance for the subject. In this way Kantian critique isolates things from their surroundings, 'atomising' them into a categorical-mechanistic system, which is then projected back onto nature as a transcendent space of objects, subject to *a priori* laws and principles. Nature as such is thus elided by the will to system in the rational ordering of the world. This elision of nature can be seen everywhere today in technological formats designed to gain control over nature as an 'environment' of ordered things and technical processes. To counter this projection of an ordered environment back onto nature and the closure on nature that it causes to happen, a way needs to be found to rethink critique from the things themselves.

The elision of nature as something given, something close at hand, is a foremost theme in Martin Heidegger's *Being and Time* (Heidegger 1962). In Section 70, Heidegger develops an analysis of the 'things of nature' in terms of the way their mode of being is hidden by our everyday way of using things:

> 'Nature' is not to be understood as that which is just present-at-hand, nor as the *power of Nature*. The wood is a forest of timber, the mountain a quarry of rock; the river is water-power, the wind is wind 'in the sails'. As the 'environment' is discovered, the 'Nature'

thus discovered is encountered too. If its kind of Being as ready-to-hand is disregarded, this 'Nature' itself can be discovered and define simply in its pure presence-at-hand. But when this happens, the Nature which 'stirs and strives', which assails us and enthralls us as landscape, remains hidden.

(p. 100)

'Nature' is not 'present-at-hand' as an object to be examined and investigated, nor is it the 'power of Nature' that acts on things. Nature is already something else, for instance a forest of timber, a quarry of rock, wind for propelling a sailboat – something bound up in technologies of production and the harnessing of power for human purposes. When we think about nature as forest, quarry or useful wind power, we are only thinking of nature as projected by technology and consequently we miss a 'hidden' nature. This nature – the nature that 'stirs and strives' – is nature 'as such', the very possibility of a natural way of being other than the way already technologized. However, this 'hidden nature' is not out there in the forests, rocks and breezes but 'discovered' within technologized nature itself, as part of the way we deal with the ordinary things or 'equipment' used in everyday life: 'In equipment that is used, "Nature" is discovered along with it by that use – the "Nature" we find in natural products' (p. 100). What is discovered is not simply the nature of the thing now turned into a product or item of equipment, but an unaccounted openness in our use of such products that harbours hidden possibility.

For Heidegger, the things of nature are not initially things *of* nature subsequently taken up by humans for their own purposes, but things *already* used in human dealings and concerns. That is, things are already items of equipment (ready-to-hand or present-at-hand) as part of a world (a 'workshop') made meaningful by 'circumspection' (*Umsicht*): an attentive awareness of things grasped practically in their usefulness.[1] However, circumspective looking cannot see this world of things *as* a world since its attention is all for the things seen in the context of references and significations in which these things gain their meaning as useful equipment. The fact that 'a world is' can only be discovered when something in it breaks down or goes missing, making this world stand out in its 'worldly character' (p. 103). The broken or missing thing 'enters into the mode of *obtrusiveness* [...] and "stands in the way" of our concern' (p. 103) as obstinate stuff (*Zeug*). As an obtrusion, the broken thing resists the mode of being to which it belongs. In this resistant mode, the thing is 'lit up' as *that* thing:

this makes a *break* in those referential contexts which circumspection discovers. Our circumspection comes up against *emptiness* [emphasis added] and now sees for the first time *what* the missing article was ready-to-hand *with*, and *what* it was ready-to-hand *for*. The environment announces itself afresh. What is thus lit up is not itself just one thing ready-to-hand amongst others; still less something *present-at-hand* upon which equipment ready-to-hand is somehow founded: it is in the 'there' before anyone has observed or ascertained it. It is itself inaccessible to circumspection, so far as circumspection is always directed towards entities; but in each case it has already been disclosed for circumspection.

(p. 105)

That which is 'lit up' in the break or deficiency is not the thing as ready-to-hand or present-at-hand, but in the 'there': in the fact that the thing *is*. This 'thereness' of the thing, lit up when things break down or go missing, is 'inaccessible to circumspection', but nevertheless already disclosed for circumspection as what can be termed the 'that-of-the-there' of circumspection opening otherwise. This that-of-the-there is what Heidegger draws attention to when he says that 'In equipment that is used, "Nature" is discovered along with it by that use – the "nature" we find in natural products' (p. 100). Nature is an 'emptiness' that 'lights up' when things break down or go missing, opening up the possibility of another way of being. *There*, right at the broken or missing thing, an open possibility announces itself. The 'hidden' nature that 'stirs and strives' is now revealed to be the stirring and striving of things to be other: an immanent *poietic* movement that resists their current way of being.

Heidegger's analysis of things as equipment in *Being and Time* provides a preliminary account of nature as otherness to technology and technological ordering. However, it does not go far enough in describing things themselves as announcements of open possibility. That is, *Being and Time* is concerned not so much with things but with *Dasein*: the possibility of 'there being' announced by the thing's challenge to everyday circumspective looking. *Dasein's* concerns occlude the thing's openness in its own activities. Thus the possibility of a Heideggerian nature philosophy is short-circuited by a limitation placed on Being itself, insofar as it is always understood as Being-for-*Dasein*, and not Being as such. This possibility can only be realized once Heidegger switches positions and attempts to think the openness of Being from the things themselves, a possibility that occurs in the later phase of his writings on technology, art and the event of Being (*Ereignis*).

Heidegger's later writings on technology refocus attention from things as equipment ready-to-hand to things as *techne*, meaning 'to grasp beings […] in their outward look, *eidos*, *idea*, and, in accord with this, to care for beings themselves and to let them grow' (qtd. in Rojcewicz 2006, p. 44).[2] *Techne* means to 'care' for things as beings brought forth out of their concealment in Being and into a particular way of being seen.[3] As *techne*, things are already carrying Being with them in their coming-to-be-seen. When practiced as a 'way of life', a particular *techne* brings about a world by calling it into being as a certain way of seeing, for instance in Heidegger's proposal of an age of the 'world picture', where 'the world [is] conceived and grasped as picture' (Heidegger 1977, p. 129). Crucially, *techne* is not an independent practice set apart from nature, but is itself part of the 'bringing-forth' of nature as *poiesis*: '*techne* belongs to bringing-forth, to *poiesis*; it is something *poietic*' (p. 13). The complex relation between *techne* and *poiesis* in things will be the focus of this chapter.

An age of technology

A brief note on the possibility of an age of technology is warranted here. Rather than indicate an existing historical age of technology, for instance the one we are already in now with its computers and electronic devices, as distinct from an earlier technological or pre-technological age, I propose to consider only the possibility of an age of technology. What would it take to think such an age? An age of technology will need to see nature coming forth in things as technical facts.[4] That is, an age of technology will need to conceive and grasp the world *as* technology. In this case, the fact of the thing, its irreducible 'thereness', is made possible by a doubling of things as both 'things of nature' and as technically produced artefacts, a simulation that recapitulates back into nature as if it were already its own technology.[5] Jean-Luc Nancy calls this *denaturing* (Nancy 2007, p. 82 ff.).[6]

A technological age continually announces the end of (the coming into being of) nature; it replaces nature with technology, but technology already 'naturalized' and hence *renatured*. In an age of technology it is technology itself that withdraws, illuminating the world with things as 'naturally given'. Yet such things are already enabled by a *techne* concealed within them. This double illusion is with us today and should not be confused with openness. Things as technical facts may shine brilliantly (as phantasmagoria) but they do not lead to an opening in Being; rather they consolidate the same being already opened by, and hence closed in, its own technical limits. The aim of critique must therefore be to denature renatured technology; to expose the *techne* hidden in (the way we see) things to its own limits in the production of nature as technology, thereby releasing things into 'the opening of an empty space wherein the 'infinite' creation of the world is (re)played' (Nancy 2007, p. 90).

Poiesis and the artwork

In his book *Žižek and Heidegger: The Question Concerning Techno-capitalism*, Thomas Brockelman, following Žižek, argues that Heidegger's position on technology presumes that humans miss a 'broader horizon' because they are enframed by Cartesian subjectivism:

> In his technology writings, Heidegger presumes from the start that the fatal 'untruth' [of Cartesian subjectivism] today lies in the way we miss a broader horizon [...] the necessity of seeing such technology in terms of a wider 'destining of Being' indicated by the transformation from Greek technology to its modern avatar [...] Heidegger equates 'questioning' technology with seeing the limited 'truth' of calculation in relationship to the broader horizon of *poietic* un-concealment, of which it is, nonetheless, an interpretation.
> (Brockelman 2008, p. 29)

Here Brockelman argues that Heidegger's position is that, in the modern age of technology, our vision is limited by subjectivism – the reduction of things to representational objects for the perceiving subject projected onto a 'world picture' – that prevents us from seeing the broader horizon of Being as *poietic* unconcealing. As we shall see shortly, Brockelman rejects Heidegger's appeal to a 'broader horizon' as dangerous and fantastic. But Heidegger's argument is not that humans miss 'the broader horizon of *poietic* un-concealing' as a 'wider "destiny of Being"'; rather, it is that humans in their 'subjective' mode miss Being altogether (we 'forget Being'), and so the horizon, insofar as it is only possible to be a horizon as something see-able by human *Dasein* (the one for whom Being appears), is in fact too broad: it overshoots the mark; it looks over things instead of with them.[7] Instead, Heidegger argues, we need to look more closely around us, at the things that command our attention and pose questions to us about their way of being. Indeed the section of the essay 'The Question Concerning Technology' Brockelman quotes here is itself a careful consideration of a specific thing – an ancient Greek silver chalice – that poses questions about its way of being, answered by Heidegger through a detailed analysis of Aristotle's theory of causality and the implications of employing it in critique. For Heidegger, *poietic* unconcealment does not take place on a 'broader horizon' but through encounters with specific things.

Interestingly, Brockelman has nothing to say about the role of art in *poietic* unconcealing.[8] For Heidegger, who, in 'The Question Concerning Technology', follows Aristotle's analysis of the four causes of becoming as 'bringing-forth' (Heidegger 1977, p. 11), *poiesis* is not a force of nature operating on things, but a bringing-forth working through things themselves. *Poiesis* shapes things according to their immanent possibilities, in the way they come forth and appear through time and space as singular things. In terms of *poiesis*, the thing *is* art: 'what is brought forth by the artisan or the artist, e.g. the silver chalice, has the bursting open belonging to bringing-forth not in itself, but in another (*en allōi*), in the craftsman or artist' (Heidegger 1977, pp. 10–11).[9] *Poiesis* is not 'in' the silver chalice, nor is it 'in' the artist; rather, the silver chalice partakes of the 'bursting forth' of *poiesis*, which is also part of the artisan or artist.[10] Heidegger's thinking about technology is initiated through an encounter with the thing-as-artwork as a movement of *poiesis*.

To ignore this beginning with the artwork is to overlook the concern in Heidegger's analysis for finite openings in encounters with things as they already are, as products of *techne*, 'prehended' by *poiesis* that opens them to absolute possibility.[11] By equating *poiesis* with a broader horizon of Being 'missed' by the human subject, Brockelman risks turning *poiesis* into the 'force of nature' independent of things, an 'ontic' concept specifically proscribed by Heidegger as inadequate for thinking Being as such. It leads to an all-too-common metaphysical reading of Heidegger that thinks Being as an overarching 'thing' (a mysterious *plenum* or, in this case, a horizon) shaping beings, and construes his philosophy as mystical, anti-technology, and anti-modern, unable to engage with and think through the experience of technologically mediated life in its historical finitude. Indeed, in the very next paragraph, Brockelman asserts:

In this way, of course, Heidegger's thought here is not only mistaken but *dangerously so*, since it marks a *powerful* temptation. Take for example, what Yannis Stavrakakis calls the dominant fantasy of contemporary 'Green' visions, a fantasy that has frequently been tied back to Heidegger's technology-critique. This fantasy, beginning from the now-problematized foundation of 'Ecology' in systems-theory, posits nature as a harmonious interdependent system, always tending toward 'a balance or equilibrium state' only disturbed by human activity.

(Brockelman 2008, pp. 29–30)

Heidegger's 'mistake', according to Brockelman, is in encouraging a way of thinking of nature as entirely other to technologically mediated human being, an otherness recouped by green ecologists as a harmonious whole, but which turns out to be nothing more than a fantasy. Setting aside the erroneous assumption that Heidegger's thinking on technology could possibly be associated with a theory of nature as 'a harmonious interdependent system', in what sense is Heidegger's philosophy dangerous?[12]

In an accompanying footnote Brockelman refers to the environmental philosopher Bruce Foltz's book *Inhabiting the Earth: Heidegger, Environmental Ethics and the Metaphysics of Nature*, as an example of this 'fantasized' Heideggerianism (Foltz 1995). In what follows in this chapter I will undertake a reading of Foltz's book in relation to Heidegger's later writings on technology and art. My reading is undertaken not to support Foltz against Brockelman, but to show how both are limited in their respective readings of Heidegger by avoiding Heidegger's explicit employment of the artwork in his analysis of technology and the human relation to it. My argument is that Heidegger sets us on a path to think *through* the human relation to technology as other, not against it, thus making him a postmodern, rather than an anti-modern thinker. My reading will suggest that Heidegger's later philosophy offers an engagement with the openness of Being in specific encounters with things, such that they are opened to *poietic* becoming right at the place of the encounter, thereby countering any 'temptation' to think of nature in reactionary terms as a broad horizon *poiesis* based on a harmonic principle set apart from the modern world.

Things and art

In what follows I will outline some key ideas in Heidegger's thinking about things in relation to technology during his turn (*Kehre*) from an ontological analysis of *Dasein* (the self fated to free existence) to a reflection on the historical emergence of Being as event (*Ereignis*).[13] For Heidegger modern technology orders nature into 'standing reserve' (*Bestand*) – material made ready for technical use (Heidegger 1977, p. 17). Unlike pre-modern technology (*techne*) that works with nature, modern technology '*sets* upon nature' (p. 15), which yields to it.[14] Humans do not control technology; rather, human being is delivered over to ('destined' or made fit for) technological enframing (*Ge-stell*), so that thinking about nature is limited to 'lend[ing] a hand to the coming to presence of technology' (p. 37).[15] This leads to the 'danger' that the 'truth' of technology – its essential revealing of what it is – will be hidden from humans who only see nature through technological means as standing reserve, and thus fail to see the 'saving power' of technology that opens 'toward a special moment that sends it into another destining' (p. 37). Technological enframing (*Ge-stell*) 'turns' into otherness through an epochal event of opening in the technology itself (*Ereignis*), where 'another destining, yet veiled, is waiting' (p. 37). In following Heidegger's thinking about the things of nature, we need to address this sense of other destining; this 'other beginning' (1999, p. 289) within and through technology, calling for a '*free* relation to it' (1977, p. 3, emphasis added).

To gain a sense of this epochal aspect of technology, I will turn to Heidegger's analysis of things in relation to art and the artwork that has a special place in his thinking about the turn into otherness through technology.[16] In 'The Origin of the Work of Art' Heidegger returns to things as singularities or 'whatever is not simply nothing' (Heidegger 1971, p. 21). Heidegger is here critiquing Kant's 'thing-in-itself' (the unknowable absolute posited as the limit of what the subject can know) by proposing the idea of things as revealed entities in excess of *logos*. Grasped *as* things, things announce or 'say' the possibility of worldliness as the openness of Being in the breaching of the ordering of discourse (*logos*).

Heidegger also uses another term to describe this 'saying' of things in the openness of Being. He uses the verb 'to thing'. A thing 'things' (announces or 'says' possibility) by gathering other things to it to form a world of meaning (Heidegger 1971, p. 177).[17] Here it is important not to confuse things with objects. While an object can always be replaced, a thing is irreplaceable (we cannot replace one thing with another without sacrificing its singularity – its being there at *this* place and time). In modern formations, things 'thing' by resisting objectification, while objects themselves become 'thingly' when materialized into singularities.[18] According to Heidegger, anything that 'things' is a work of art. In western antiquity and pre-modern cultures, the work of art maintains a world of already shared meaning, whereas in modern cultures the artwork is the beginning of otherworldliness announced by the singular fact that it *is*.[19]

My aim is to trace the outlines of a nature philosophy in Heidegger's later writings insofar as they address art's capacity to make things 'thing', thereby opening up other-world possibilities through, but in resistance to technology. Heidegger's writings on technology ask that we think of things from the standpoint of art as *poiesis* – the 'bringing into appearance' of both human-made and natural things (Heidegger 1977, p. 10). For Heidegger *poiesis* does not precede things as their motivating cause but is transimmanently located in them as part of their way of being. Consequently, things are not the end product of overarching natural forces, but finite singularities, opening up possible ways of being. *Poietic* immanence is not a substrate of Being with its own internal dynamism that pushes things along, but an 'event' of the openness in Being itself (Ziarek 1998, p. 163). To be part of the event of Being (that is, to be able to 'thing'), the thing must be wrested from objectification. The thing must resist. As part of *poiesis*, art actively enables the thing to 'thing' by resisting technological ordering, thereby affirming its 'thingness' in the singularity of the artwork, and announcing that the thing could always be otherwise.

In a late essay 'Art and Space' (Heidegger 1969a) Heidegger questions the kind of space opened up by the artwork in the technologically enframed modern world, suggesting that this space is defined by an 'indeterminateness' that resists the unity of the 'physical-technological' space in which it is encountered (p. 5). Not only does the work of art resist technologically ordered space, it also carries with it a capacity to reveal the truth of this space: 'Once it is granted that art is the bringing-into-the-work of truth, and truth is the unconcealment of Being, then must not genuine space, namely what uncovers its authentic character, begin to hold sway in the work of graphic art?' (p. 5). Art opens up an indeterminate space within technologically mediated space itself, an indeterminacy that makes the truth of this space, its singular 'event', happen but otherwise. The artwork affirms technologically ordered space by resisting it at the same time. To explain this kind of affirmative resistance we need to turn to Heidegger's use of the term *Gelassenheit* or the 'letting be' that releases things from technological enframing in readiness for *poietical* becoming otherwise: where 'freedom now reveals itself as letting beings be' (Heidegger 1998, p. 144).[20] Art is the exemplary case of *Gelassenheit*: the releasing of the thing from capture by the power of technological ordering, to 'be itself' otherwise. Art participates in the epochal event of the turning of technology out of itself and into the 'other beginning' of open possibility when it hears the 'call' of Being otherwise.

Not poetic dwelling, but being open to *poiesis*

My argument counters that of Bruce Foltz who, in his book *Inhabiting the Earth: Heidegger, Environmental Ethics and the Metaphysics of Nature* (Foltz 1995) also makes a claim for Heidegger's later philosophy to be taken as a nature philosophy. Foltz offers a reading of Heidegger's philosophy that leads to an ethics of 'dwelling' on the earth with a concern for developing a care-full or pastoral relation with nature. His idea of dwelling with nature, drawn from Heidegger's later essays and lectures, is proposed through a 'leap out of technology' (p. 105) and back into nature as poetic dwelling – a dwelling with nature in the manner of pre-Socratic Greek *techne*, where human techniques for making things were 'attuned' to the *poiesis* of nature in a non-exploitative way: 'the revealing of *techne* is always attuned to self-emergence – remaining in harmony with the self-disclosure of phusis and cooperating with it' (p. 102). For Foltz, the attitude towards things required by *techne* is associated with poetic dwelling on earth and attuned (in harmony with) nature, which he sees as an alternative to the attitude required towards things by modern technology: 'There is also the possibility of a very different bearing and comportment toward entities than that prescribed by technology […] [T]his possibility is simply that of dwelling poetically upon the earth' (pp. 169–70).

For Foltz, to dwell poetically on the earth and reclaim our closeness to nature, we can 'leap out of technology and out of metaphysics as well, with its insistence on constant presence – a leap that is at the same time a leap back into that vicinity in which we already reside' (p. 105). Foltz characterizes this leap as the realization that I am suddenly somewhere else, in a 'primordial dimension of being-in-the-world' (p. 50) characterized by a closeness to the things of nature: 'It is the primordial involvement of finding myself here. Alive for a time, upon just this stretch of beach with this particular wave at my feet and that very seagull overhead' (p. 50). Thus Foltz identifies special technologically-free places, such as a lonely beach, a nature reserve, a country path 'or equally so, the neighbourhood park or the town square' (p. 89) as places that allow us to be close to nature, free from technology. But are these places really free from technology? Is it possible to separate the technological from the non-technological so that we can leap from one to the other? Clearly there are difficulties in making this claim; for instance places of nature such as nature reserves and beaches are already set up according to predetermined views and ways of occupying space. If this is so, then there can be no leaping out of technology as Foltz suggests without becoming subject to the illusion of a technologically free nature produced by technology itself.

In support of his claim, Foltz draws from Heidegger's view of nature that he (Foltz) construes as '"primordial nature"' (p. 32). For Foltz, Heidegger's view of nature as 'primordial' links to classical and romantic views of nature as *natura naturans* and 'the power of nature'. However, as I will demonstrate, by 'primordial nature' Heidegger does not mean either the classical or romantic sense of nature, which, for him, are metaphysical concepts and hence unable to access nature in its being as such. Rather he means something else: a nature that can only *be* in the in-between of the technological and its other. Instead of seeking a 'primordial involvement' with nature in specially reserved non-technological places, we need to attend more closely to places and things already ordered by technology, and discover through them the possibility of nature as the 'other beginning'.

Foltz's reading of Heidegger overlooks crucial points regarding the concept of *Gelassenheit* – the releasing that comes from 'turning' within and out of technology; a releasing 'for the possibility of' that exposes the thing released into *poietic* openness.[21] Dwelling in this openness should be understood not as a leaping out of technology and back into another space of poetic dwelling, but as a 'twisting free' (Davis 2007, p. 180) within technology itself.[22] Twisting free involves a 'sojourning within the open space of destining [where] we find ourselves unexpectedly taken into a freeing claim' (Heidegger 1977, pp. 25–26). This 'freeing claim' concerns the 'saving power' (p. 42) of technology – its counter-capacity to open up free space for the 'other beginning' of human destiny (Heidegger 1999, p. 289) as part of *poietic* becoming. This counter-capacity is not willed, but comes 'unexpectedly', as a possibility opened in the twisting itself. Heidegger identifies twisting free in terms of art's capacity to both resist and affirm technology at the same time.

Heidegger argues that there is something about our relation to art that frees us up for rethinking our being with nature in a different way. By being attuned to the saving power of art in its resistive stance towards technology, we are released towards the claim of *poiesis* in its 'call' upon us (our other destiny as beings given over in the freedom of being-as-becoming) from within the 'rift' (Heidegger 1971, p. 63) or disjuncture between ground and existence – in Heidegger's specific terms, 'earth' and 'world'[23] – opened up in technological 'turning', a call requiring our response. The claim is freeing because it releases us to be free, in the open possibility that comes to us as the beings that we could be in resistance to our subjectification to *Ge-stell* (modern technological enframing). In his commentary on Heidegger's analysis of the relation between art and technology, Richard Rojcewicz concludes that 'art reawakens trust' in Being as something other than technological production (Rojcewicz 2006, p. 206).

117

Art 'is not impositional but *poietic* [...] In the last analysis, then, art might save us because art brings home to us *poiesis*, the genuine alternative to the impositional [i.e technologically ordered] attitude, which is the danger' (p. 206). The event of art enables truth in Being, thereby countering the distrust engendered by *Ge-stell* where Being is reduced to 'nothing' or the meaningless *nihil* of standing reserve.

The face of nature

In an essay 'Nature's Other Side: The Demise of Nature and the Phenomenology of Givenness', Foltz argues that humans confront nature as a 'face' (Foltz 2004, p. 333). This face, according to Foltz, is the outside of an inside that is alive:

> A face requires an inside. A face is inside-out – *is* the inside facing out. From what had once been a surface alone, not yet even an exterior, now an interior faces us. What faces us has an inside, and what has an inside is alive.
>
> (p. 333)

The face of nature confronts us as the outward expression of an inner life concealed from us. To justify this claim, Foltz draws on precedents in phenomenology, leading to the claim for 'an inner life of nature' (p. 333) as mystery; that is, nature has a mysterious innerness, the meaning of which remains unknown except when revealed to individuals under exceptional circumstances. This inner life of nature is separated from humans in their ordinary existence in the same way that the presence of a face implies to some a living being secreted in 'holistic "inner life"' (p. 334) behind the face, a clear reference to hypostatic individuation.[24]

In developing this theme of the inner life of nature, Foltz suggests, a few pages on, that 'In the perceptual realm, things face us only because at the same time they turn away' (p. 335). To put this another way: something withdraws in revealing itself to us. But does withdrawal lead to innerness as Foltz suggests? To withdraw is not to disappear but to remain in the openness of revealing in a concealed way. In other words, to withdraw is to become concealed in such a way that awaits opening and revealing. It follows then that the 'mystery' of things is not in the fact that they exist more truly in a separate 'inner' world concealed from us, as Foltz suggests, but in the otherness that their concealment promises in this world – in the openness of possibility as such.[25]

Withdrawal does not reveal an innerness to the thing, but reveals yet more things in an opening and expanding of things into their many possibilities of being disposed in different ways. In his essay 'The Origin of the Work of Art', Heidegger offers the example of a stone lying on the ground (Heidegger 1971, p. 46). In appearing to us, the stone manifests withdrawal by pressing down on the earth. The stone 'presses downward and manifests its heaviness. But while this heaviness exerts an opposing pressure upon us it denies us any penetration into it' (p. 46). In lying there before us, the stone withdraws into the earth and in so doing, denies us any penetration into it. There is no question here that the stone might be penetrated; rather, any attempt to penetrate the stone simply leads to fragmentation: 'if we attempt such a penetration by breaking open the rock, it still does not display in its fragments anything inward that has been disclosed. The stone has instantly withdrawn again into the same dull pressure and bulk of its fragments' (pp. 46–47). By attempting to penetrate the stone, we have not got into its 'inner heart' but merely split it into pieces, producing more stones withdrawing into the earth.[26] The point Heidegger makes here is that the metaphor of innerness obscures the true mode of revealing of things; the breaking open of something does not reveal another thing in a different world inside the thing, but more things in different arrangements and dispositions in the same world. Things are, not because they have another thing inside them that makes them so, but because their being-a-thing is given to them in *physis* (physical emerging forth) as *poietic* becoming, which, in the case of the stone, redeploys the 'penetrated' thing into different constellations of yet more thing-fragments.

The phenomenon of withdrawal does not lead to an innerness behind the withdrawal but to an openness leading out of withdrawal itself. Withdrawal is future-oriented, opening into possibilities of appearing yet to take place. In appearing, the thing also withdraws, and in this withdrawal it gives what it is. Withdrawal is part of the giving of *poiesis,* its offering of what comes forth as being-as-becoming. Without the open cision of originary withdrawal-advancing (*Ursprung*) everything would already be melded into a monolithic whole with no separation between things.[27] However, as we have seen, Foltz wants us to accept that the withdrawal of the thing is really the concealment of a mysterious living innerness that remains separate from our encounter with the face of nature – an innerness that stays 'back there' in its own world, away from the 'worldlessness' of technologically enframed culture (Foltz 1995, p. 105). This innerness of nature, with its religious overtones of an 'indwelling' spirit that manifests the divine in the thing, leads Foltz to inevitable conclusions about the 'demise' or fall of nature (Foltz 2004, p. 338) in technologically mediated modernity and the possibility of accessing the concealed 'innerness' of nature through 'noetic' (p. 340) vision and insight.[28] For Foltz this is an 'aesthetic and religious vision' of 'nature's beauty and integrity as entailing a disclosure of its own other-sidedness' (p. 340) experienced through a pious contemplation of the things of nature. Drawing from the same and similar writings by Heidegger, but with different emphasis and conclusions, I will counter Foltz's noetic-religious aesthetics with a critical-ontological poetics based on the work of art as a 'saying' in its 'decisive confrontation' with technology (Heidegger 1977, p. 35).

The thinging of things

If things are singularities with no innerness to them, then in what way do they have their being? Heidegger argues that a thing has its being by gathering other things to it. Heidegger calls this gathering capacity the 'thinging' of the thing (Heidegger 1971, p. 174).[29] He uses the example of a pre-technological item of use: an earthenware jug. The jug 'things' by gathering other things to it – wine, someone to pour the wine and all the other things that allow the jug to be the jug that it is, including the earth on which it stands and the sky that opens up space to allow it to volume forth in its particular shape and size, as well as the use to which it is put, perhaps to provide refreshment, to give thanks to the gods or to share cordiality with others. There is no inner 'jugness' concealed by the appearance of the jug, but simply a range of uses whereby the jug can be the jug that it is. That is, the jug's thing-being is ineluctably future oriented in the opening of the 'void' of possibilities: 'the vessel's thingness does not lie at all in the material of which it consists, but in the void that it holds' (p. 169).[30] The thingness of the thing is its attunement to future possibilities concealed in its withdrawal from presence; its sinking back into the earth (its supporting material) while simultaneously opening up to the skies (its opening into possibility). In its gathering of other things to it, the jug 'things': 'the jug is a thing insofar as it things' (p. 177). The action of drinking from the jug is not to be understood in terms of human intentions, but as an enabling possibility enacted in the 'event' of the jug's thinging with respect to its attunement with the fourfold: 'the whole gathering of the drink as what is offered abides in the wine, which abides in the grapevine, which abides in the earth and in the gifts from the sky' (Heidegger 2010, p. 87).

The human is not the cause of the event of drinking the wine from the jug; rather, insofar as the event of the jug is meaningful in its fundamental attunement with the fourfold (i.e. insofar as the jug is able to thing), the human is 'called forth' to drink by the event itself. Human meaningfulness is related not to wilful intentions, subjective desires or needs, but to the event itself, in the revealing of its fundamental 'truth' as a gathering of meaningful things. Thinging is a bringing near of whatever is distant; a grounding in local events of disclosure (*Ereignis*) that affirms things as placed in their thingness – in their 'originary' attunement to the world as part of *poietic* becoming, including the human being itself as part of the event enacted. Human being receives its meaning from the event and not the other way around.

The thinging of the jug reveals a world already opened up with its own mode of being. The jug 'things' in such a way that maintains the meaning of this world in attunement with the 'fourfoldedness' of being: the configuration of earth, sky, divinities and mortals that prevails for any given world. Unlike objects, which gain their meaning from their position in the universal coordinates of space and time, things gain their meaning by thinging from their finite place on the earth in configuration with the sky, and with regard for the divinities and mortals that dwell there. While objects have value within infinitely exchangeable positions in abstract space, things have meaning in situated places of the finite world in its coming-to-be, as part of the material (earth) and ideational (sky) terrain of *poietic* becoming.[31] Meaning as original attunement is always relative to the world in which the thing is capable of thinging: a world in which the earth, the sky, the mortals and divinities are aligned in particular ways. If a thing things in one world, it cannot do so in another (Wrathall 2011, pp. 208–09).

The relativity of meaning to the world in which things are able to thing means that there can be no stepping out of the present world and back into a relation with things from a past world in the hope of retrieving their original meaning. Earthenware jugs no longer 'thing' in today's technologically mediated world. However this does not mean that meaning is locked into a particular world (the condition of nihilism). Meaning is never fully lost across epochs; rather it is recapitulated in, through and ahead of them as part of *poietic* becoming.[32] To access meaning in this recapitulated sense, one does not step out of the present world and into another world separated from it; rather, one must 'step back' within the constraints of the present world, to 'glance ahead to what comes':

> The 'step back' (the step that retreats from metaphysics) has the sole meaning of enabling, in the gathering of thinking upon itself, a glance ahead to what comes [elsewhere Heidegger calls this glancing ahead *Augenblick*: the 'blink of an eye']. It means that thinking begins anew, so that in the essence of technology it catches sight of the heralding portent, the covering pre-appearance, the concealing pre-appearing of enowning itself.
>
> (Heidegger 2003, p. 61)[33]

Stepping back in order to glance ahead (*Augenblick*) at the event (*Ereignis*) of what comes requires an 'unwilling' of the will to power over things. It means that things must not be forced into technological being (for example, by seeing them as equipment or useful items). Rather, things must be allowed to be, which turns out to be 'the most difficult of tasks' (Heidegger 1971, p. 31). 'Letting be' is by no means a simple matter of re-acquainting ourselves with the pristine things of nature waiting there for us. Rather, it means twisting free from technology to release a mode of seeing things otherwise. Twisting free can take place, I suggest, through a recapitulating counter-*techne* that moves forward by stepping back, to release objects into things as part of the event of *poiesis*.

The Open

Things thing when they are attuned with the 'fourfoldedness of Being,' an 'originary' way of being with nature as *poiesis*. How might this occur in technologically enframed worlds? In such worlds, things cannot thing in attunement with nature because their relation to nature has already been denatured (Nancy 2007, pp. 86–87); they are doubly reified into systems of value exchange. Denaturing is a double movement: 'This movement, which will always already have begun with "humans", and which consequently through humans, in humans and before humans comes from "nature" itself, this very movement takes on another form: instead of ensuring subsistence, it creates new conditions for humans, or even produces a strange "surplus-subsistence" [*sursistance*] in nature or outside of it' (p. 86). The human, as the animal 'in lack' – as the animal without a world and hence requiring technical supplementation – is initially removed from nature (first move) and then, removed yet again in the production of a 'strange surplus subsistence' as a substitute nature (second move). This second move is a renaturing of denatured nature – a renaturing that should not be confused with a restoration of, or to nature, but a further removal from nature as renatured-denatured-nature (redenatured nature). In effect nature is doubled away from itself. The more we try to get 'in tune' with nature, the more we find ourselves using technical means to do so. How, then, do we get around this double bind?

Heidegger provides a way out of the double bind of redenatured nature by suggesting that we affirm and resist technology at the same time: 'we can affirm the unavoidable use of technical devices, and also deny them the right to dominate us, and so to warp, confuse, and lay waste our nature' (Heidegger 1966, p. 54). Instead of blindly employing technology to 'warp, confuse, and lay waste our nature' we can engage in a decisive confrontation with/against technology that releases the 'thingliness' concealed in technically produced 'objects' – items of standing reserve and the ordered environments in which they are encountered – into *poietic* becoming.[34] This confrontation takes place in the realm of art:

> Because the essence of technology is nothing technological, essential reflection upon technology and decisive confrontation with it must happen in a realm that is, on one hand, akin to the essence of technology and, on the other, fundamentally different from it. Such a realm is art.
>
> (Heidegger 1977, p. 35)

By being part of, yet different from technology, art leads us into the Open: a place of 'unshieldedness' to the immanence of *poiesis* as 'forces serried [pressed together], boundlessly flowing into one another' (Heidegger 1971, p. 124).[35] The Open is not a place separate from technology, but a disjuncture in technology itself, opened by the stirring and striving of *poiesis*. The Open operates as free possibility, right at the limit of what technology controls and orders. To enter the Open and hence partake of 'the other beginning of immeasurable possibilities for our history' (Heidegger 1999, p. 289), one must engage in 'essential reflection upon technology' that, Heidegger argues, takes place in the realm of art and in particular through the singular artwork: '[the work of art] does not cause the material to disappear [into the nullity of negation], but rather causes it to come forth *for the very first time* and to come into the Open of the work's world' (Heidegger 1971, p. 46, emphasis added). The singularity of the artwork is its coming forth 'for the very first time', in open possibility.

Keeping the Open open

In what sense is an artwork singular? In 'The Origin of the Work of Art', Heidegger makes the following comments: 'Art is real in the artwork. Hence we first seek the reality of the work. In what does it consist? Art works universally display a thingly character, albeit in a wholly distinct way' (Heidegger 1971, pp. 39–40). In the 'reality of the work', a work of art affirms itself as a thing by holding itself apart in 'a wholly distinct way'. An artwork exhibits an other-than-object aspect in terms of its capacity to open up a world hitherto concealed.[36] The artwork 'opens up a *world* and keeps it abidingly in force' (p. 44). In being there in its singularity, it 'holds open the Open of the world' (p. 45). That is, it opens up a world in 'openness' (the Open) – in enabled readiness for the other beginning. The artwork does this by resisting the tendency of the work-material from which it is made to disappear into usefulness; unlike a piece of equipment such as an axe that 'disappears into usefulness' (p. 46), the artwork resists usefulness by the very fact that it *is*. In doing this, the artwork says 'yes' – it locates and puts on display an array of things, shapes and forms; at the same time, it says 'no' by the very existence of the display itself, which, for it to *be* art, must be experienced 'otherwise' *as art* and not as something else.[37] In opening up a world, the artwork 'says' what it is otherwise (yes ≠ no), as a singular event of art.

In Heidegger's well-known discussion of Van Gogh's painting of a pair of field worker's shoes, he says: 'This painting spoke. In the vicinity of the work we were suddenly somewhere else than we usually tend to be' (Heidegger 1971, p. 35). The artwork says something so that we are taken somewhere else. In contemplating the artwork we do not reflect on our own subjective state; rather, the artwork does something to us, transports us away from where we are to another place. In our encounter with it, the artwork makes the shoes 'thing', thus 'saying' the possibility of 'otherness'. Heidegger is not arguing that we are taken back to a context of references and intentions that would fix the painting's historical meaning, nor is he saying that we are taken back to the actual historical moment in which the shoes were originally painted or worn. Rather, he is saying that we are taken into the openness of possibility through the way in which the artwork returns the shoes to the materiality of the art-work – its 'work-being' (p. 41). This being-taken-into-openness is neither hermeneutic nor aesthetic, but *poietic*.

We can get a better understanding of the *poietic* by taking a detour through Heidegger's elucidations of the 'poetizing' at work in Hölderlin's river poetry, where he writes of *poietic* movement as the 'telling' (poetizing or *Dichtung*) that brings things into Being (Heidegger 1996). It is important to keep in mind here that Heidegger is not providing a 'symbolic' reading of the poem (interpreting the poem in terms of a symbolic register not presented by the poem itself), but elucidating what the poem itself says about the river 'Ister'. The poem 'poetizes' the river – brings it into another way of being. Heidegger's concern is to elucidate how this poetizing is announced by the poem itself.[38]

In the introduction to the river poem 'The Ister' Heidegger presents a detailed account of poetizing in terms of the 'symbolic image'. In this account, which bears similarities to Schelling's account of the symbolic image in *The Philosophy of Art*, Heidegger argues that poetic saying is an allegorizing of the symbolic image such that its 'spiritual content' (its nonsensuous meaning) can be made meaningfully available to a 'gathering of people'. Here is the passage in full:

> the rivers and waters that are sung in a poetic work, for example, are grasped as perceivable events of 'nature'. Which indeed they are. In the poetic work, however, these things of nature assume the role of appearances that can be grasped as something sensuous [*sinnlich*], as something that offers a view and thus provides an 'image'. Yet in the poetic work such images present not only themselves, but also a nonsensuous

meaning. They 'mean' something. The sensuous image points toward a 'spiritual' content, a 'sense' [Sinn]. The river that is named and that appears in the image [Bild] is a 'symbolic image' ['Sinnbild']. Under the broadly conceived concept of a symbolic image, we also include what is called 'allegory'. This word, which stems from the Greek, aptly says what is at issue: [...] ([...] the open, public place for a gathering of the people): to openly and publicly proclaim in a manner that everyone can understand. ἄλλο, something other, namely, to proclaim something other than what the image by itself allows to appear.

(Heidegger 1996, p. 16)

Here Heidegger repeats the conventional distinction between symbol and allegory, where the former unifies meaning and being (the symbol 'bring[s] together') in a 'belonging together' (p. 16), while the latter is an 'other saying', signifying otherness and difference. If we follow this distinction to the letter, then the gathering of people in the open public space belongs to the other-saying of allegory and not to the symbol, and suggests that what is said there is not the saying of Being in the unmediated sense of what is carried by the symbol, but something else: a saying by other means. However, this is not what Heidegger says about Hölderlin's poetry. Rather he argues that Hölderlin's nature poems say Being-otherwise; that is, they *say* Being in the way that the symbol does but otherwise in an allegorical mode. How does he argue this?

To argue that Hölderlin's poetizing says Being otherwise, Heidegger has to reverse Hegel's argument about art as nonsensuous being. This is what he has to say about Hegel's 'metaphysics of art':

Hegel says in his *Lectures on Aesthetics* (*Werke X*, 1, 48): 'What is sensuous in the work of art is meant to have existence only insofar as it exists for the human spirit, and not insofar as it itself exists as something sensuous'. As Hegel understands it, an example of something sensuous existing for itself is a piece of material painted over in many colours; such a thing, however, is not a painting by Rembrandt. Yet the painting is not merely placed onto this material thing either; rather, this material thing is sublated into the painting and now is what it is only *through* the latter.

(Heidegger 1996, p. 17)

Hegel's idealist theory of art says that the sensuous material of the artwork (the 'material thing') does not exist prior to the painting, but is sublated into it so that its mode of being is through it. The painting is not 'in' the sensuous material but the nonsensuous 'sense' [Sinn] (spiritual, ideal or value), appearing in the work of art as a 'symbolic image'. (Note here that we have already encountered the symbolic image in Schelling's philosophy of art; the symbolic image synthesizes the sensible and the intelligible in myth). The material 'thing' merely supports the painting whose essence lies somewhere else, in the nonsensuous symbolic image. Thus, in Hegel's aesthetics, there is always an ontological gap between the sensuous and nonsensuous elements of a work of art, where the material presentation of the nonsensuous idea can never measure up to the idea's truth.[39] For Hegel, modern art and poetry can no longer reveal the truth of Being because the event of Being that inaugurated western art in the Greek beginning has now run its course; in the modern epoch, art is supplanted by science and logic, and only these now carry the responsibility of revealing the truth of Being.

To counter Hegel and demonstrate that art is still able to reveal the truth of Being, Heidegger must get around the ontological gap between the nonsensuous idea and the sensuous materiality of the artwork. To do this he reverses Hegel's position so that the idea is made to come out of the materiality of the artwork, and not the other way around. This means that the 'truth' revealed by the artwork is not in the idea that it presents, but in the artwork itself, in its 'work-being' (Heidegger 1971, p. 41). The truth of the artwork is in being the artwork that it is, in its capacity to 'say' the truth of Being. In being and doing this, the artwork participates in the event of Being. The material 'thing' no longer acts as a mere support for the 'true' painting lying behind it; rather, in its work-being, the thing shown in the artwork leads into an openness 'in-between' nature and some other possibility not yet known: '*What* the river does, therefore, not even the poet knows' (Heidegger 1996, p. 20).

Thus, Heidegger argues that the things of nature in Hölderlin's poems (e.g. the river described in 'The Ister') are not symbolic images (that is, they are not symbols of some higher or deeper spiritual content manifesting itself as a poetic image), but events of Being 'concealed' from us. For instance the flow of the river 'takes its own time' (p. 19), a time-taking concealed from us when we think of the river as a geographical feature or resource for transporting goods. The poet's task is to reveal what this concealed time-taking is in a poetic saying: 'the poetic word unveils this concealment of the river's activity [its flow, its time-taking], and indeed unveils it as such an activity. This unveiling is poetic' (p. 19). The 'activity' of the river that flows in 'its own time' is revealed by the poem as *poietic*. In this case, the river is neither represented nor symbolised by the poem; rather, the river's being and the poem's being come together in a *poiesis* enacted in the saying of the poem itself. *Poiesis* is not 'in' the river as an actual physical feature, nor is it 'in' the poem as some special poetic device. Rather *poiesis* 'happens' when the river and the poem come together, opening up a possibility of what the river might mean 'otherwise'. By revealing that the river 'takes its own time' as distinct from the time of the clock, the deadline and the calculated rate of flow, the poem announces *poietic* becoming to whomever listens, and re-attunes these listeners to nature in its possibilities, other than in terms of its objective and technologically enframed life.

In order to stay in the 'in-between' of nature and its possibilities opened up in poetic saying, Heidegger equivocates about the river: 'The river's activity is its flowing, and therein it has its actuality and is the actual river. Yet surely we are familiar with what the actual river, the actual Donau does. If we are unfamiliar with it, then that description of the earth that is concerned with this kind of knowledge, namely geography, will provide us with precise information. Or is the actual river, as ascertained by geography and knowable through everyday experience, not the river as it truly is?' (p. 20) In other words, Heidegger asks rhetorically: 'Is the poetic river other than the actual one?' The question remains undecidable. If one were to come down on one side or the other, the 'in-between' position would immediately be annulled and we would be taken into either the actual river or the 'idea' of the river in its nonsensuous fulfilment. That is, in order for the artwork to make the river 'thing', there must be a movement that stays in the 'in-between' without leaving it. However, by having to stay in the in-between position, the poetic saying can never consolidate itself into a gathering around the symbol. Rather, as 'other-speaking' the saying must allegorize its own act of saying, its own 'work-being', such that the possibility of a full gathering is held forth but never realized. The saying must demythify the mythic sense of union between meaning and Being offered by the symbol. In terms of a politics based on poetic saying, the consequences are as follows: the gathering of the people in the poetic saying can only take place as a consolidation of their 'togetherness' with the river-thing as myth so long as this togetherness is itself dispersed into open possibility. The thinging of the thing does not lead to a gathering that consolidates people into mythic union but precisely its opposite: a demythification that perpetually keeps the Open open.[40]

We can see a similar type of poetizing analysis at work in Heidegger's account of the field worker's shoes in Van Gogh's painting. The fact that Heidegger imagines what this possibility of the shoes might be in invoking a fictional account of the wearer of the shoes (a woman who is taken back to the earth), indicates that he is offering his own 'saying' as *poietic* truth. This saying is a mythic account of the shoes but said 'otherwise' as the ἄλλο or 'proclaim[ing of] something other than what the image by itself allows to appear' (Heidegger 1996, p. 16). This allegorizing of the painting by Heidegger's own words invokes a symbolic or originary experience of fulfilment in a return to the earth. But this return is not a matter of going back historically to the actual time of the shoes in the earthy fields; rather, it is a telling that calls the shoes into being as poetic shoes through the materiality of the painterly gesture itself, just as the 'sonic' sense of Hölderlin's poetry enacted in the telling calls the river into being.

In its very materiality the artwork is a 'bringing-forth of the earth' (Sinclair 2006, p. 151) in the special sense that Heidegger gives to the concept of earth as a revelation of 'what shoes are in truth' (Heidegger 1971, p. 35). The truth of the shoes is their exposure to the fact that they simply *are* in the singular 'there' of being-there, seen only in the breaching of representational order enacted by the artwork in its 'saying' of things. Here earth is not to be understood as actual material ground (some place that we might travel to, dig our hands into and stand on), but the grounding of the beginning of a possibility opened up by the artwork in its revelation of the shoes as things that thing.[41] Earth is thus an *Unground* in Schelling's sense of the word: a grounding that is simultaneously an ungrounding in its possibilities. The shoes are demythified *through* their mythic 'origins', in a *poietic* saying that opens them to an absolute possibility *through* the 'thing' itself – the 'work' that the artwork undertakes to keep itself *there*, grounded in a singular painterly gesture yet ungrounded at the same time.[42]

In its singular occurrence – in its positivity – each time for 'the very first time,' the artwork exhibits a decisive resistivity to use, thereby affirming itself in the Open of absolute possibility.[43] In its resistance to objectification, the artwork opens up a *poietic* becoming otherwise: another beginning and a different mode of being-possible, unthinkable in current modes of utility and objectification where things are encountered as useful objects or stockpiles of standing reserve.

Gianni Vattimo has provided a way of reading Heidegger's approach to the work of the artwork as follows:

> the work opens up a new 'epoch' of being as an absolutely originary event, which cannot be reduced to what it already was, and it grounds a new order of relationships within beings, a true and actually new world [...] the artwork suspends in the reader all natural relationships, making strange everything that until that moment had appeared obvious and familiar.
>
> (Vattimo 2008, p. 152)

Unlike the thinging jug discussed previously, which opens into an already opened world, the work of the artwork inaugurates a radically new world-opening by 'put[ting] in question our way of seeing and standing in the world' (p. 69). The challenge for a nature philosophy is to think with the artwork in its capacity to breach the familiar, technologically ordered everyday world, opening us into the nothing or void of a not yet present world: a world to come.

If we are to work with Heidegger's philosophy of art and technology in pursuit of a nature philosophy, we cannot get around this issue of the fact of art in its confrontation with technology by sliding into a poetic dwelling with nature in the way Foltz suggests. Rather we need to recover what Vattimo calls 'the ontological bearing of art' (Vattimo 2008, p. 47) in its decisive confrontation with technology as offering an opening to nature in its call to us otherwise.

Seeing otherwise

In following Heidegger's thinking about the artwork as openness to Being, it becomes apparent that any attempt to get out of technological enframing cannot take place by way of a *techne*, since *techne* cannot get beyond the 'circumspective' looking that comes with using things that are ready-to-hand.[44] *Techne* can only 'see' in terms of the familiarity of an already known world. However the artwork has the ability to open up otherworldliness from within the familiarity (*heimlich*-ness) of the everyday, through a seeing otherwise: 'a look of an eye in the blink of an eye, a momentary look at what is momentarily concrete, which as such can always be otherwise' (Heidegger 1997, pp. 112–13). This 'blink of an eye' (*Augenblick)* is the visionary 'seeing' that allows the artwork to open up otherworldliness from within the circumspective seeing of *techne* and routine use.[45]

The *Augenblick* is not a projection of sight by a subject looking into the future (Heidegger calls this theoretical seeing – the seeing of science), but a seeing that comes from the future to the one who 'tarries' in the disjunctive in-between of the artwork and the space of the Open, as openness to the event of *poietic* becoming. *Augenblick* is thus experienced not as an initial breakthrough vision of pure futuristic seeing that sees beyond the things in front of it, but as a 'having seen': a seeing that comes to the one who sees when she gives herself over to the thing as it is; when she lets the thing be in its being other than as an object or item of use.[46] Otherwise seeing is the look of *Gelassenheit*: the thinking-seeing that releases the thing to be other than what it has already become as the *nihil* of *Ge-stell*, the nothing of standing reserve.

This otherwise seeing is not an anticipating-seeing that sees the thing coming to it in advance through the grid of calculation and perspective. Nor is it a random seeing that takes flight from the thing into fanciful visions. Rather, it is a seeing that comes in the 'already seen', discovered there as a possibility of seeing otherwise. This otherwise seeing is both resistive and retroactive in the same sense of the retroactive decisiveness we saw in the artistic stroke (see Chapter 5). In his book *Material Thinking*, Paul Carter provides an account of seeing otherwise through the deframing of the artwork as an 'eidetic consciousness' able to 'bear witness to a ground of seeing that can never be focused' (Carter 2004, p. 26). Such seeing is the seeing of 'non-events' or the nothing that opens in-between objectification and non-objectification that the deframing of the artwork enacts. Eidetic consciousness is a seeing that holds itself back – a seeing otherwise that 'unwills' the will of the already seen. This retroactive, resistive way of seeing is free in the positive sense when it sees the unfocused ground as 'constitutionally many' (p. 26); that is, as a ground of parts whose wholeness is always incomplete and ever forming. Seeing otherwise in this positive sense involves care and respect for being-with things, not insofar as they relate to a whole that precedes them, but in terms of the relation that the seer has with the thing itself, in what it calls for, what it wants in this emergent whole just coming into being.

Justice

In Heidegger's general philosophical orientation, the fragmentary texts and sayings of the pre-Socratic Greek philosophers present a world view in an unmediated relation with nature, unrestrained by modern considerations of subjectivity and self-reflective thinking. Speaking is not a matter of subjective speech, but a 'saying' that includes both human beings and things insofar as they come together in particular places and times as part of the event Being. Speaking or 'saying' gathers things to language: 'that which comes to language in the saying' (Heidegger 2002, p. 250). In the essay 'Anaximander's Saying' Heidegger undertakes a reading of the Anaximander fragments of Greek philosophy in order to listen to what they say. What do the things of nature say? And how do we respond to them?

Listening is an attentiveness to things in their becoming that attunes us to 'the fundamental trait of what is present [which is] injustice' (Heidegger 2002, p. 266). As things that arise and come to be, their presence testifies to an injustice in that by being there as they are and persisting in the same way, they try to hold being to themselves, thereby denying the just sharing of being with others. Being present-at-hand suggests a selfishness that values the persistence of the same and denies being-with others in future possibilities: 'The things that stay awhile are without consideration toward each other: each is dominated by the craving for persistence in the lingering presence itself, which gives rise to the craving' (p. 271). The craving of things to endure in self-presence closes off saying otherwise and consolidates saying into a discourse of the same that, in the age of technology, seeks "'unlimited domination over the earth'" (qtd. in Schürmann 1990, p. 193). However, to hear the call of things otherwise is to be attentive to the injustice of being-as-presence and to think the possibility of the thing's being otherwise in terms of a *poietic* justice: a redistribution of being-as-difference; a setting right of the wrong that makes being come to a stand in selfish self-presence.[47]

Heidegger calls this setting right *Gelassenheit* – the 'letting be' of the things of nature.[48] *Gelassenheit* is the critical task of non-willing releasement of things such that openness is 'let in' by 'waiting' for the event of Being as it comes to us (Heidegger 2010, pp. 75–76). One does not will releasement, but waits for it: you wait 'to let yourself be involved in releasement' (p. 76). To wait is also to wait on, to tend, to care for something. Thus waiting should not be confused with inactivity, as it involves twisting free from already committed ways of being in order to be able to wait on things, to care for them rather bending them to a will. A nature philosophy will need to think the letting-be of the things of nature so they are able to partake of the 'event' of nature, not as a wilful self-appropriation, but in a non-wilful releasement where things are accorded their due respect and place with regard to their being-with other things, and in accordance with *poietic* becoming.[49]

By linking the saying of nature with justice, Heidegger suggests an ontological ethics based on *poiesis* as the sharing of the gift of nature's giving. The good of nature can only be itself, its own providence, which is the fact that it gives in being what it is (see Chapter 5). The good of what is good is the fact that it gives what it is, not its selfish craving for self-presence. Goodness and hence justice is in giving, not having or possessing. The good of nature is the gift of itself shared out, for instance, in the turning of the earth around the sun that gives rise to the seasons, the weather, rivers, rainfall, tides and currents of the oceans, the blossoming of plants, and more generally, as a cosmic giving, shared through renewal and decay played out in the contractions and expansions of time and space that affect all things at all times and places. In giving what it is, in its 'goodness', nature massively exceeds the 'goods' of technological ordering and the authority of discourses that provide jurisdiction over nature (e.g. the good of technical efficiency, calculability, predictability and sustainability). Through its cosmic reach, nature breaches the ordering of *Ge-stell* with a shine in all things that is everywhere around. Nature gives even when challenged and ordered into standing reserve. Its giving is given in the chaos of eternal recurrence as 'existence as it is, without meaning or aim, yet recurring inevitability without any finale of nothingness' (Nietzsche 1967, p. 35). In their givenness, in the shining of nature through them, things are already otherwise.

An ontological ethics responds to the 'just' giving of nature in the singularity of its 'event' as openness to Being. Justice in this finite-absolute sense (ontological justice, concerned with being-as-giving) is, in Derrida's words, 'a *doing* [of justice] that would [...] be rendered to the singularity of the other [...] as the very coming of the event' (Derrida 1994, pp. 27–28).[50] An ontological ethics is not concerned with the restitution of justice according to rules and norms, but with the 'doing' that makes justice – the 'just' giving-sharing of being as becoming-possible in an inaugurating sense. The task of ontological ethics is to guard over the openness of Being to enable another beginning, another, more just way of being-with nature beyond the technological enframing (*Ge-stell*) of the modern world, without leaving that world.

Art as *poietic* event

In an age of technology things cannot thing because *poiesis* is concealed from them. Heidegger writes:

> Above all Enframing conceals that revealing which, in the sense of *poiesis*, lets what presences come forth into appearance.
> [...]
> Thus the challenging Enframing not only conceals a former way of revealing, bringing-forth, but it conceals revealing itself and with it That wherein unconcealment, i.e. truth, comes to pass.
>
> (Heidegger 1977, p. 27)

Enframing (technological ordering) not only conceals *techne* (the 'former way of revealing'), but conceals *poiesis* itself: As Krzysztof Ziarek has argued: 'in this way, *techne* belongs to and yet does not happen as *poiesis*: it conceals *poiesis*, instituting the technological as the sole standard of what obtains as real' (Ziarek 1998, p. 176). Ziarek concludes that 'technology is a doubling of *poiesis* that, instead of letting come to presence, "enforces" and disengages experience from *poiesis*' (p. 176). In short, technology blocks the *poiesis* concealed in it from coming forth. However, *poiesis* must itself *be* part of the *poietic* event doubled into it. It must mark itself there as the other way. In revealing this fact, *poiesis* turns technology against itself. Heidegger calls this capacity of technology to turn against itself the 'saving power': 'the essence of technology must harbor in itself the growth of the saving power' (Heidegger 1977, p. 28). The saving power of technology is the unconcealment of the concealment of *poiesis*; the 'undoubling' or 'un-denaturing' of the thing so that it remains there exposed ('unshielded') in the Open.

Thus we need to reconsider what it means to speak of *poiesis* in technologically enframed worlds. *Poietic* revealing is the revealing of a concealing already revealed, already *there*: This 'already-there' is the place of art, where, in Schelling's terms, 'something figural comes to be out of the non-figural' (Schelling 2000, p. 38). As *poietic* figuration, the artwork 'says' being-as-becoming otherwise to the calculative rationality of modern technology.[51] Art does not reveal something concealed by technology; rather its task is to release the *poiesis* blocked by technology in its current phase from coming forth. Art does this by carrying the figure as a *poietic* saying otherwise. Art's task is to begin from the figure already revealing itself in the opening of technology turning against itself. In this way, art becomes the *poietic* event of technology in its otherwise saying.

Renaturing

As *poietic* event, the artwork keeps the Open open, thereby ensuring that meaning is not blocked in the nihilistic sameness of technological enframing but available for *poietical* becoming. I have argued elsewhere that the task of maintaining openness to the other is essential for democracy (Mules 2010). At this point I want to suggest that we can think of *poietic* 'non-willing' as serving a democratic purpose in keeping openness open, thereby ensuring the necessary freedom and justice to take place in the open-gathering of human beings that makes democracy happen in particular places and times. We need to think of this open gathering as something that the artwork prefigures in its very materiality; in its resistance to everyday use, and in its singular thereness, as *this* thing in its 'thinging' into openness.[52]

As *poietic* event, the artwork leads into a space in which the *demos* (the people in open freedom with one another and within the world in which this freedom is enacted) is renatured, to bring this world into a just (i.e. non-exploitative) relation with the things of nature. By renaturing I do not mean returning to primary nature, but undoing the denaturing of nature that produces nature as something already available for use as standing reserve and technical fact. To do this is not to leap out of technology and into some non-technological ground more attuned to nature, but to re-attune ourselves with *poiesis* in unblocking and releasing of things as part of nature to come. This can be achieved in two ways: first, by recovering 'the ontological bearing of art' (Vattimo 2008, p. 47) – art's singular capacity to open up the otherness of Being by both affirming and resisting technological ordering at the same time; and second, by reawakening trust in Being (Rojcewicz 2006, p. 206), so that nature is no longer thought of as an 'empty signifier' circulating within the discourses of power, but as an open possibility in the shining of the things already giving and all around.

Chapter 8

Poetics: Benjamin and Celan

The age of the poets

I argued in the previous chapter that in an age of technology, nature philosophy needs to think with the artwork as counter-*techne*, providing a transition into openness in the event of nature as such. At this point, I want to extend the concept of the artwork to a general poetics and employ the poem as exemplary for poetic work as *praxis* – a saying that does what it says. By doing what it says, the poem carries the ontological truth of its own being and opens itself to the event of Being; it places its own being at stake by virtue of the fact that it says what it does, questioning its own status as a poetic act. In supporting the poem in its transitive capacity to invoke ontological truth, my argument counters that of Alain Badiou who has said that the era of the 'poetic suture' of philosophy to the poem has come to an end, to be replaced with a suturing of philosophy to the *matheme* (Badiou 1999, pp. 69–77). Badiou's argument depends on a historical identification of the beginning of the modern epoch with the obscure event of Hölderlin's poetry at the beginning of the nineteenth century and its ending with an equally obscure event of the poet Paul Celan's visit to Heidegger in his mountain hut in 1967. This 'age of the poets' is characterized by the poet's vocation, which is to respond to the question of Being as truth (p. 50). From Hölderlin to Celan, philosophy is sutured to the poem in its mythic enactment of the truth of Being.[1]

Badiou's target here is Heidegger, whose ontological critique of Being in its later phase begins from his engagement with Hölderlin's poetics that attempts to retrieve a sense of absolute Being from human fallenness into mortal life and, more broadly, proposes a resacralization of nature (p. 56) as the site of the 'holy' to overcome the nihilism of the modern age. In Heidegger's words: 'The holy is the essence of nature' (Heidegger 2000, p. 82). Badiou identifies Heidegger's attempts to revive an absolute sense of Being from Hölderlin's poetics as symptomatic of the mythologizing tendencies of the age of the poets with dangerous political consequences (including Heidegger's own notorious relationship with the German Nazi party), and argues that Celan's visit to Heidegger announces the end of the poem's capacity to carry the ontological burden of truth (Badiou 1999, p. 77, pp. 86–87).

Badiou argues that it is not the resacralization of nature that humans need to overcome nihilism, but a continuation of its desacralization through science and technology. Invoking Marx, Badiou claims that 'desacralization is not in the least nihilistic, insofar as "nihilism" must signify that which declares that the access to being and truth is impossible. On the contrary, desacralization is a *necessary* condition for the disclosing of such an approach to thought [...] [which] exposes the pure multiple as the foundation of presentation' (Badiou 1999, p. 56). For Badiou, desacralization exposes the 'barbarity' (p. 57) of Capital and its foundation on *mathesis* as 'the pure multiple'. He sees this exposure as a 'departure point' for a renewed thinking of the truth of being. Badiou exhorts philosophers (and critical theorists) to abandon the poem and begin to rethink being as *mathesis* from this departure point. Badiou's aim is to return philosophy to its Platonic task of realizing ideas in numerical proportions. The truth of the poem is to be replaced by mathematical 'truth procedures' (p. 33) based on the 'count-as-one' (Badiou 2005a, p. 24). Badiou's mathematical transcendentalism counters the immanent poetizing of the 'age of the poets' by relocating the ontological burden of truth from the poem to the *matheme*.

I argue that Badiou's strategy cannot live up to the transitive task of critique. As I have indicated in Chapter 1, critique needs to realign *praxis* (the work undertaken by humans in doing things) with *poiesis* (the shaping force of nature), thereby restoring a critical stance within global ecotechnological production and engaging in a demythification of the mythologizing of the subject in the aura of technologically renatured nature (see Chapters 1 and 9). This restoration requires an interruption to the system by the artwork – an interruption that enables critique to think in the turning otherwise, when thought is taken elsewhere by the artwork in the singular act of simply 'being there' (see previous chapter). I argue that this task is fundamentally *poietic* in that it works with *poiesis*, opening itself to a free relation with otherness and hence with possibility as such. Critique must accept responsibility for this freedom from within the finite event that it enacts, thereby enabling a thinking otherwise, in its turning in and out of technological enframing. In this way, I argue, another human-nature relation is enabled by realigning *praxis* (critique) with *poiesis* (the free becoming-shaping of nature). Because Badiou's 'truth procedures' reject the suturing of philosophy to the poem, they actively disavow any concern for the artwork in its immanent-active capacity to say the event, and constitute a retreat into subjective transcendentalism along Kantian lines (Strathausen 2005, p. 282). Badiou's transcendental subjectivism cannot disengage itself from the subject's rule over nature; it wipes out the contingency of the event – its affect-laden power of 'intimate contact' with things – that opens being to possibilities yet to come, yet to be named.

A nature philosophy needs to restore the ontological contingency of the event of nature. The way to do this is to follow post-Kantian responses to the paradox of freedom uncovered in Kant's critique by identifying a differential movement in being that exceeds the critical gap between subject and object, thereby encountering the dilemma of the self exposed to otherness in the disjunctive movement of being-as-becoming. Transcendental reason is folded back into an immanent opening of its possibilities, thought 'otherwise' (not purely in terms of reason's own applicability), in the finite moment of singular acts of being as such. This folding back of reason onto absolute singularity is what I call the event of nature: the *poietic* enactment of nature as such.

Badiou's argument follows a similar path, but only to a point. Having opened up the contingency of reason exposed to otherness, he, like Kant, withdraws into schematic transcendentalism in order to save the subject for the critical project, but at the cost of covering over the critical moment itself. Critique that speaks for the subject will always remain blind to its own *praxis* – its own event of speaking – in encountering what it critiques, thereby covering over the otherness of the other, rendering it always in terms of the same. To recover the critical moment from transcendental subjectivism requires a mode of critique that speaks in a non-subjective voice; that speaks *with* the voice of the other. In what follows I will counter Badiou's subjective transcendentalism with a poetics in which the poem is read in terms of its ability to say the truth of being 'otherwise', in its speaking with nature as such.

But having said this, I have yet to address Badiou's specific objections to Heidegger's poetic ontologizing. These are based on Heidegger's lapse into mythic thinking, in particular, in his analysis of Hölderlin's poetics as exemplary for a recuperation of the mythical foundations of human being in non-technological life (Badiou 1999, p. 54).[2] Badiou's objections extend to Heidegger's portrayal of the modern epoch as one enframed by technology, leaving open the possibility for Heidegger of positing a non-technological solution to the nihilism of the modern epoch, which, according to Badiou, leads to technophobia and 'reactionary nostalgia' (p. 53) for a lost, pre-technological age. Hölderlin's poetics as elucidated by Heidegger, so Badiou suggests, encourages this kind of thinking.

My arguments in the previous chapter lead to a different view of Heidegger's analysis of technological enframing, an analysis that works both with and against technology at the same time, in the turning of technology out of its own being and into an otherness to come. Heidegger's analysis of technology is not anti-technological as such, but concerned with preserving an explicitly human element within the technological (one that is not reducible to a function within the system), in the disjunctive moment of openness (*Augenblick*) offered in technological turning triggered by the art event. The art event is part of, yet other to technological enframing, responding to an active non-willing that opens the event otherwise. Badiou's objections to Heidegger's stance on modern technology can thus be countered by reaffirming the artwork in its relation to technology, not in terms of a return to the mythical foundations of human being, but in terms of a radically conceived demythification of the modern epoch catalysed by the art event, and affirming the possibility of a *poietic* thinking that thinks with the artwork as a transitive act. But does Heidegger's analysis of the poem live up to this affirmation? In what follows I will suggest it does not. To counter Badiou's argument and to retain the poem as the bearer of truth, it will be necessary to show how the poem enacts a demythification of its own mythic foundations, sending critique past Heidegger's exposure of the other beginning as destined otherness for (certain) human beings, towards a beginning that opens within the turning of technology itself – in the very act of transitivity as *poietic* demythification.

The demythification of the modern epoch is necessary, not because of the mythologizing of the poets as Badiou argues, but because of the labour undertaken by humans on nature, which, in its current phase, denatures nature into a simulated form by renaturing it in terms of myth (see Nancy 2007, p. 87). Modern myths of nature are not myths that hark back to a pre-technological time, but myths of nature's immediacy, its endless productivity, its timeless presence as both a nurturing and destructive force. Mythic nature circulates for the benefit of the autonomous free subject opened to a world of opportunity in a capitalized global economy. Unlike the retroactive myth of tradition that excludes technology, modern myths of nature require a relation to technology in order to be experienced as such. The function of technology in the modern epoch, then, is not one of enframing as Heidegger proposes, but enabling in the sense that it tries to make possible the fulfilment of the subject in mythic essence – in the immediacy of technological contact that endows the body with natural affectivity. Technology disappears into a nature-machine.[3] The 'age of the poets' may have come to an end, as Badiou suggests, but we nevertheless still require a *poietic* response to the modern epoch in order to engage in a demythification of technology and its promises of a new age of affective life founded on the providential myth of the nature-technological system. This *poietic* response will need to speak in a subjectless voice, or at least be aware that what it says is not said on behalf of a subject already identified and waiting to have its needs and desires satisfied by the nature-machine disguised as myth.

My suggestion is that we follow the counter-enablement offered by the artwork from within the technological enablement itself. We cannot enter into a post-mythic age by dispensing with myth altogether, as myth is fundamental to any justification of human existence. Myth humanises existence for good or for ill. We cannot live without myth, but we do not have to live in mythic ignorance of our mythic foundations. Rather we can begin again by demythifying the mythic foundations themselves, seeking a more just relation with the things of nature as they call to us from within technological enabling. In order to develop a *poietic* response adequate to this task of a demythifying beginning, I will turn to Walter Benjamin's concept of 'the poetized' (Benjamin 1996, p. 24) that he develops out of a reading of Hölderlin's poetry. I will then discuss the poetized in terms of Paul Celan's transitional poetics in which the poetic voice is made to speak from the position of the other. In the chapter following this, I will extend this concept of the poetized to Benjamin's writings on technology and the possibility of a resistive gesture within it.

The poetized: Heidegger and Benjamin

In this section I develop the concept of transitivity as it can be applied to the poem as the saying of myth. My aim is to shift focus from Heidegger's account of poetic saying as the other beginning not yet arrived, to Benjamin's account of the same poetic saying, as an indeterminate site of already operating otherness '*immediately* effective qua possibility itself, and not merely as an anticipation of a possible realization' (Weber 2008, p. 45). In doing this I aim to counter the tendency in Heidegger's critique to fall back into a mythologizing of the poetic event in terms of a mythic reunion awaiting a chosen folk, with Benjamin's deconstruction of the event of myth as part of an indeterminate *poietic* becoming. I take my lead here from two sources. The first of these is Phillipe Lacoue-Labarthe's critique of Heidegger's mythological reading of Hölderlin's poetry (Lacoue-Labarthe 2007) that sets the scene for a post-Heideggerian poetics based on *das Gedichtete* or the 'poetized', which both

Heidegger and Benjamin employ in their respective readings of Hölderlin's poems (p. 42).[4] The second source is Samuel Weber's reading of Benjamin's writings on Hölderlin's poetry in *Benjamin's – abilities* (Weber 2008), which proposes that Benjamin's poetized is the poem's self-interruption, releasing possibility as other speaking (p. 18).

Thus a politics based on poetic interruption is proposed here (Weber 2008, p. 222). Benjamin announces this as follows: 'That is as little the case here as that the life of any pure [i.e. singular] work of art could be that of a people; and as little the case, too, that what we find in the poetized might be the life of an individual and nothing else' (Benjamin 1996, p. 35). The poetized can be attributed to neither the people nor to any individual, but only to itself in its singular act. Poetic interruption – the exceptional event of art as singular 'truth' – is itself the political act *par excellence* insofar as it keeps openness open, ensuring transition and connectivity to happen, and enabling otherness to be; as Lacoue-Labarthe writes: 'the poem is the archi-ethical act' (Lacoue-Labarthe 2007, p. 79).

In his essay 'Two Poems by Friedrich Hölderlin' (Benjamin 1996, pp. 18–36), Benjamin describes the poetized as a 'limit-concept' (p. 19). A limit-concept relates thinking to the absolute as openness to possibility. In Benjamin's terms, the poetized opens thought to 'potential existence of those that are effectively [*aktuell*] present in the poem – and others [...] [by] a loosening up of the firm functional coherence that reigns in the poem itself' (p. 19).[5] The concept of the poetized allows Benjamin to undertake an immanent reading of the poem for what it promises to bring into existence as life to come. The addition of the '– and others' is significant here, as it suggests an extended sense of the event of Being that, as I will shortly show, is opposed to Heidegger's intensive, punctual sense of the same event in which dispersed beings are gathered back into the event rather than distributed through it.[6]

Heidegger's poetized

As we have seen in the previous chapter, Heidegger's analysis of the 'thinging' of the thing involves a 'gathering' of things towards the thinging thing, an intensification of the event of Being in a moment of revelation opening towards an enactment of the 'other beginning'.[7] Whatever is to be opened into this other beginning is already gathered in the moment of thinging, already turned and waiting for the event to happen. Access to this beginning is, of course, not limited to 'things' but extends to beings, that is, things that *are*, that have their being for them, for instance, a *Dasein* that knows itself as a chosen people, a certain national type or folk, gathered in a 'special moment' (Heidegger 1977, p. 37) of 'resolute' (Heidegger 1962, p. 443) preparation for the mythologized destiny awaiting them.

The specifically identified human type stands already turned and readied for the event (for Heidegger this type was the German people, the inheritors of the 'Greek beginning'). Lacoue-Labarthe demonstrates how this mythologizing of human destiny operates in Heidegger's reading of Hölderlin's poem 'Remembrance' ('*Andenken*') that involves an act of 'bad faith with very precise intentions, in order to deny *a priori* what I will call the [...] sense of *reality* in the late Hölderlin. Or, if you prefer: his "urgent demand [*exigence*] for truth'" (Lacoue-Labarthe 2007, p. 42). Lacoue-Labarthe discusses Heidegger's reading through Adorno, who criticizes Heidegger in the strongest terms for his handling of a line in the poem that covers over a non-Germanic, racialized difference marked in it, in order to read Hölderlin's poem in terms of a specifically 'German ideology' (p. 44).

The point of contention is Heidegger's elucidation of the line 'The brown women in that place', which Heidegger introduces as 'the women', leaving out the adjective 'brown'. This enables Heidegger to speak of the poem in terms of the traditional idea of the place of *German* women in the myth of homeland: 'the German women save the appearance of the gods, which remains the primal event of the history [of 'Germania']' (Heidegger 2000, p. 131). It is only after he has glossed 'the brown women' as 'the women' thereby justifying a mythological reading of the poem in which (German) women are depicted as the 'saving' women of Germanic myth, that Heidegger then reads the whole line as 'the brown women there too' that, although not Germanic (because of their colour, one presumes – the assumption here is that German people are white), also partake in this Germanic mythology, but in a supplementary way: 'And yet, just as in the naming of the *mill*, the *elms*, and the *courtyard*, a thinking back to the foreign speaks out of a thinking ahead toward the homelike, so here the greeting of the brown women is a fulfilled remembrance' (p. 131). The 'foreign' brown women serve as reminders of the 'distant presencing' (p. 131) of the homeland so that they 'too' become absorbed into its mythic presence.[8]

Lacoue-Labarthe accepts Adorno's criticisms that Heidegger was being deliberately self-serving in his misreading of Hölderlin's poem, but only up to a point. He sees both Adorno and Heidegger as complicit in an 'attempt to pull Hölderlin away from the speculative dialectic' (Lacoue-Labarthe 2007, p. 50), that is, from a poetizing ('speculative dialectic') open to radical possibility. This retreat from the radical possibility of Hölderlin's poetics is confirmed by Lacoue-Labarthe when he criticizes Heidegger for his inability to engage explicitly in the poetic language itself, suggesting that Heidegger 'has no understanding of what is "specifically poetic"' (p. 46) about Hölderlin's poetry (a charge, one must assume, Lacoue-Labarthe would also need to make against Adorno).[9] Rather, 'he treats only the gnomic element, the pronouncements and maxims'. That is, he reads the poem in terms of the voice of the poet himself, who, in Heidegger's eyes, is the supreme poet of the Germanic myth of homeland and the Germanic folk. This reading gives him excuses to overlook the clear evidence of what is written there, in favouring a mythologizing of the poem, where the non-white women are drawn into the mythic domain of the white homeland – where difference is absorbed into the same. Heidegger's reading is not simply an attempt to mislead the reader, but is, more importantly, a failure to read the poetic movement of the poem – its poetizing – as a movement of demythification.

Like Schelling before him, Heidegger understands the human-nature relation as one of mythologizing, in the sense that it is only enabled in the possibility of a mythic reunion with nature as Being, understood as a 'to come' not yet here. This mythologizing of his own project, enacted in his (mis)reading of Hölderlin's poem suggests that Being is a destiny towards which certain beings are directed, and causes Heidegger to betray his central insight, which, as I have already indicated (see Chapter 1), could be stated thus: nature as Being can only be accessed by holding the opening of Being open and staying there, in the event of nature as such, right at where it happens. In his elucidations of Hölderlin's poetry, Heidegger's critique abandons this transitional place where the fundamental task is to keep the Open open so that openness always remains absolutely possible and hence indeterminate with regard to the enablement of Being. Instead Heidegger returns the poem to its mythic origins in which a specifically selected kind of being (the German people) is identified as enabled to enter the other beginning.[10] The suggestion here is that Hölderlin has an insight into the radical possibilities of poetic language that Heidegger overlooks.

Heidegger's mythic thinking leads inevitably towards certain political conclusions, in which the historical *polis* is understood as a place not yet established and yet to be created by the poet-philosopher acting as a demiurge in founding decisional acts: 'because they *as* creators must first ground all of this [the various elements of the historical *polis*] in each case' (Heidegger 2000a, p. 163). To counter this mythifying of the *polis* by the decisional acts of the demiurgic poet-philosopher, I propose a demythified thinking in which the poetic-creative act is one of 'defounding' within the already founded *polis*. Through singular moments of interruption, the creative act affirms itself by resisting the already founded mythological *polis*, thereby maintaining the opening into otherness necessary for the *polis* to be truly free.[11]

Lacoue-Labarthe finds support for Hölderlin's insight in Benjamin's concept of the poetized – the *poietic* movement (transitivity) that works through the poetic text, turning it towards absolute otherness.[12] By turning to Benjamin's rendering of the concept of the poetized in Hölderlin's poetry, Lacoue-Labarthe counters the turn to myth in Heidegger and reinstates the poem as a suitable vehicle to carry critique. In this way, Badiou's rejection of the poem as mythification can be countered by a poetics of demythification enacted in the critical task itself.[13] My task in what follows will be to provide a reading of Benjamin's essay on Hölderlin's poetry to show how such a task is enabled. By engaging with the *poietic* movement of the poem in its self-enactment, the critical task remains within the transitional place of *poietic* becoming, thereby enabling an encounter with otherness without falling back on myth.

Benjamin's poetized

In 'Two Poems by Friedrich Hölderlin' (introduced previously), Benjamin shows how the poetized works, through a detailed reading of two drafts of Hölderlin's poem 'The Poet's Courage' retitled 'Timidity' in the later version. Benjamin analyses the two versions of the poem in terms of the two worlds they present: the first version founded on the mythology of the 'Greek world' where the gods and mortals exist side by side in the same continuum of heroic life, and another 'weakly articulated' (Benjamin 1996, p. 23) world within and moving out of the Greek world, which introduces life as 'living death' (the 'vague abyss') as the finitude of mortal existence.[14] The 'joyful day' of instantaneous connection to the gods of the heroic Greek world of the first version is transformed into the 'thinking day' of the fallen world of mortal life in the second version in which the human becomes aware (is able to 'think') of its separation from the gods as a confrontation with death.

These two worlds are not entirely separate; rather, their difference is connected by a movement of indeterminate poetic becoming that signifies 'a nonperceptual concept of life, an unmythic, destiny-less concept of life stemming from a spiritually exiguous sphere [which proves] to be the binding precondition of the early draft' (p. 24). That is, the second version demythifies the first as its 'binding precondition' by relocating the poetic movement of figures from an intransitive to a transitive mode; from an absolute world of living with the gods that negates mortal human life, to a relativized world in which human life must accept mythic disconnection in the fall into mortality, in its 'thinking' about it. Importantly, this transition retains a connection with the absolute, but in an attenuated way; it becomes 'a spiritually exiguous sphere' that opens life in its finite possibilities. The demythification of the human in the second version of the poem does not lead to a banishment of myth from human existence, but to a dwelling in attenuated mythic connectivity. The poem affirms human life as the negated 'other' of myth. To do this, the poem enacts its own demythification *as* myth, as mythic connectivity.

The two versions are connected in such a way that the principle of connectivity – the poetizing or 'shaping principle' (p. 23) – is 'said' by the second version in relation to the first. That is, the second version *interrupts* the first by 'saying' its own demythification. As Benjamin points out, Hölderlin's 'method requires from the outset that connected things be taken as a point of departure, in order to gain insight into [i.e. by 'thinking' about] their articulation' (p. 24). Working its way through the two versions of the poem, the poetizing principle exposes 'the underlying foundation of all relations' (p. 25), which, for Benjamin and Hölderlin, is the activity of *poietic* immanence in all things. In Hölderlin's terms, *poietic* immanence takes the form of 'life': 'Life, as the ultimate unity, lies at the basis of the poetized' (p. 20). Here we see Benjamin working with the legacy of Romantic and Idealist poetics, shaping it towards an immanent materialism without transcendence.[15] By invoking 'life' through Hölderlin's poems, he remains within the movement of the poetic work, so that his own essay mobilizes the concept of life as part of the poetic movement itself: 'But now the law, which appeared formally and generally to be the condition of the building of this poetic world [the world of myth], begins, foreign and powerful, to unfold' (p. 25). That is, through Benjamin's exegetical *praxis*, a *praxis* enacted in his very essay, the mythic world of the first version unfolds in the second in a process of demythification that reveals life exposed to otherness – in the ruins of a demythified world, but a world still enlivened by residual mythic connectivity.[16] The poetic task, then, is no longer one of courage in the face of the gods (the Hellenic stance to life), but 'timidity' or acceptance of the absence of the gods within the still mythified connections that make life possible in its openness to otherness, in its hope for future being.

Demythification becomes, for Benjamin, the poetic principle *par excellence*, which he locates as an operation of writing (marking, inscribing) in the mythologizing of the poem itself. Unlike Heidegger who reads with the voice of the poet in order to invoke a life of 'fulfilled remembrance' in myth, Benjamin allows a life to emerge from the poetizing of the writing itself: 'Here "life" lies outside poetic existence; in the new version it is not the precondition but the object of a movement accomplished with a mighty freedom: the poet *enters into* life; he does not wander forth in it' (p. 28). Unlike the first version where life is already determined by its relation to the gods, the second version produces life through a poetic 'movement' into a 'mighty freedom' in an attenuated mythic relation that nevertheless remains in the process of becoming demythified throughout. In effect, this shifts the register of critique from one of ontological pronouncement (the pronouncement of the event of Being) to its deconstruction. It shifts the burden of ontological truth from the voice of the poet to the event of *poiesis* enacted in the poem itself, in its specific de-figuration of mythic presence. Following Benjamin's exegetical *praxis*, ontological critique becomes positive deconstruction, where the 'shaping force' of *poiesis* is seen to be part of the transitivity of the poem in its writerly operation, as a chiasmic opening into an indeterminate otherness triggered by the *praxis* of criticism itself.

Benjamin's ontological deconstruction of Hölderlin's poem allows us to shift criticism away from a Heideggerian concern for the 'other beginning' as destinal, as prophetic, as demiurgic, and instead locates the 'event' of Being in precisely textual ways as part of the 'shaping force' of *poiesis*. It repositions critique as a *praxis* of reading and commenting on poetic and cultural texts to a more central position without mythifying the poetic voice. It remains focused on the onto-theological-political problem of countering nihilism in trying to think the possibility of a demythified yet meaningful human being open to otherness without resorting to a solution in remythologized foundations.[17]

Singular poetics: Celan

In this section I examine the poetics of Paul Celan for what it tells me about poetic speaking as nature philosophy. As transitive speaking, a nature philosophy requires a speaking with nature; a speaking that does not refer itself back to a subject speaking in relation to its object, but a speaking that speaks with the otherness that nature already *is*; that is, a speaking that speaks back from the position where the speaker 'will have been' in speaking with nature as other. This complex mode of address finds precedents in the ontological logic of 'lifedeath' addressed by Romantic and Idealist philosophers and poets; a thinking of the Hölderlinean 'living death' of human life within this world.[18]

Celan's poetizing thinks life not as lifedeath, but as deathlife or the possibility of a 'living on' after the death event, which, for Celan, is the Holocaust. From this perspective it becomes impossible to think of an original living nature, a nature that gives life; rather all events are now marked by their death, such that life is what comes after death, or the life-to-come-already-here in the finitude that marks human existence as fated for death. Thus Celan's poetizing goes past Heidegger's thinking of Being-towards-death in which *Dasein* must confront the singularity of its own death in order to *be* (Heidegger 1962, p. 294), and thinks of *Dasein* in a co-originary sense of being-with others after death.[19] However, Celan's poetics stops short of Levinas's ethics of transcendence of the '*other-in-the-same*' (Levinas 1996, p. 106), and holds fast to the singularity of the poem itself, in the mark that it leaves as a historically specific event. Celan's poetics is thus post-Heideggerian rather than Levinasian; it enacts an ontological deconstruction of the poetic voice.[20] I read Celan's poems in terms of the poetizing of their own event 'after death'. I refuse to let them dissolve into the 'other in me' but listen to the way the voice speaking in them draws attention to itself as a poetic act, and how it enables otherness to be encountered as such.

My reading of Celan's poetry differs from Michael Eskin's in this regard (Eskin 2000). Following Levinas's ethics, Eskin takes Celan's poetry to be fundamentally concerned with the other in terms of a transcendent act of human co-existence that he employs as a counterpoint to Heidegger's 'individuation' of *Dasein* in facing absorption into the 'they' (pp. 151–52). Countering Eskin, I argue that Celan's poetics does not repudiate the question of being in favour of human co-existence, but rethinks this question by going past Heidegger to think being as a 'being-with' disconnected from the other, as interrupted connectivity, and is thus equivalent to Benjamin's idea of mythic (dis)connectivity.[21]

Bearing witness

In his book *Sovereignties in Question: the Poetics of Paul Celan*, Jacques Derrida reads Celan's poetry as a case of 'bearing witness'. Bearing witness is a transitive act; it 'bears' or carries a witnessing of 'what happened' as a truth that must be believed: '*you have to believe me*' (Derrida 2005a, p. 76). To bear witness is to see something happen and on the strength of this seeing, to be party to a truth that must be carried away. Derrida suggests Celan's poetry asks to be read as bearing witness to something such that its truth has to be believed. In what sense does this truth have to be believed? Derrida points out that this imperative of truth involves the mode of address that witnessing requires in order to be believed. A witness cannot be a first or second party (an I–you speaking in dialogue) but a 'third': 'the one testifying, is the one who is present as a third' (p. 72).[22] That is, the speaking is neither a monologue (the 'I' speaking to itself), nor a dialogue (the 'I' speaking to a 'you'), but an oath spoken by a survivor of the event: a third person who has witnessed the event and is capable of swearing to it, thereby testifying the truth of the event to others after the event.[23] This casts the speaking into the future anterior tense: 'the one who testifies is the one who will have been present' (p. 74). Thus, to bear witness is to carry the truth of the event into the future as something that 'will have happened'.[24] Bearing witness is a case of speaking in the future anterior tense.

To bear witness is to live the event after the event, a condition that Derrida describes in an earlier essay (on Freud) as that of '*life death*' (Derrida 1987, p. 259), which he relates to the 'question of positionality' or the logic of the beyond:

a 'logic' of the *beyond*, or rather the *step beyond* [*pas au-delà*], would come to overflow the logic of the position: without substituting itself for this logic, and above all without being opposed to it, opening another relation, *a relation without relation* [emphasis added], or without a basis of comparison, a relation with what it crosses over via its step or with what it frees itself from at a stroke.

(p. 260)

The step beyond steps back into the position that it leaves, constituting a 'relation without relation' in the poetic leap, which is, I argue, precisely the condition of poetic speaking in Celan's poetry. As Celan says in his 'Meridian' speech: 'The poem holds its ground, if you will permit me yet another extreme formulation, the poem holds its ground on its own margin. In order to endure, it constantly calls and pulls itself back from an "already-no-more" into a "still-here"'(Celan 2005, p. 164). In being the poem that it is, the poem 'holds its ground', pulls itself back from where it is headed and from where it came. In holding its ground, it *is* the stillness of the chiasmic movement of the before/after; the deathlife moment in-between the step beyond and the step back – a movement of *Gelassenheit* or 'letting be', opened to absolute temporality in readiness for the advent of the other.

In Celan's poetry the poem becomes the third party, the witnessing of the event, by instituting a voice that is neither the 'I' of the poet nor the 'you' to whom the poet addresses his words, but the 'saying' of the poem itself, as the mark left after the 'I' and the 'you' have spoken. That is, the poem enables a retroactive 'bringing-to-life' of the finished event by speaking right at the place of what remains of it – the poem itself in its presentation of 'what happened'. In doing this, the poem sets in train a '*bearing witness to bearing witness*' (Derrida 2005a, p. 70). Bearing witness to bearing witness is not a simple repetition of the initial bearing witness as a self-evident fact, but a speaking from the 'third' position retroactively present to the bearing witness itself. Bearing witness always catches sight of itself in its own act of seeing. Thus, the task of Celan's poem is not simply to bear witness to an initial act of seeing, but to catch sight of its own bearing witness so that it remains open to repeated seeing and witnessing as a truth that must be believed. To do this it must keep itself *there* as the bearing witness that it already is, opening itself each time for repeated and different readings by speaking with a voice from the third position, from 'beyond' the I-you relation (as 'a "logic" of the beyond'), enacted in the poem's invocation of the I-you relation itself. This poetic voice comes between the I-you relation (it intervenes, mediates, makes possible) and opens the relation otherwise, taking it elsewhere to an unknown destination.

Derrida points out that this condition of bearing witness enacted in Celan's poetry is not something out of the ordinary; bearing witness is not an extra-ordinary act of oath-making done under exceptional circumstances, but something that happens in every act of speaking to another. At its heart, speaking to another is an act of poetic transitivity that carries ontological truth: 'Logically, it obliges one to take any address to another to be a testimony' (p. 86). In its singular enactment, the poem carries the very possibility of a truthful mode of address. Celan's poetic speaking is thus, to use Heidegger's terms, the limit case of ontological 'mineness' (*Jemeinigkeit*) – the possibility of an individuated singular being in being-with-others (*Mitdasein*) (Heidegger 1962, pp. 149–50, 153 ff.), but in the aoristic sense of coming after the death event, beyond its finite limits.[25] The saying of the poem does not represent the speech of a subject; rather, it belongs ontologically to the poem itself. Unlike Heidegger's poetizing that gathers others to it, Celan's poetizing *disseminates* truth as an open possibility. It 'bears witness to bearing witness' (p. 70), thus guaranteeing the possibility that the truth will live on after the finite event to which it testifies has ceased to happened; that is, after its 'death' in any singular event of its poetic saying.

The poetic voice

In his book *The Song of the Earth*, Jonathan Bate offers a reading of Celan's poem 'Todtnauberg' ('Death Mountain') written by the poet after his visit to Heidegger in his mountain hut in 1967. Bate's reading is informed by what he calls 'ecopoetics', a reading that enables the poem to reveal the things of nature as the opening of *poiesis*: 'to read ecopoetically is […] to find "clearings" and "unconcealments". In the activity of *poiesis*, things disclose or unconceal themselves' (Bate 2000, p. 268). On this basis, ecopoetics is a poetics of revelation, where the things of nature are revealed in their being as part of poetic making. Bate's own reading practice focuses on how the poem describes nature, its naming of the things of nature and their powers of restoration.

However, ecopoetics cannot limit itself to a revelatory poetics of the things of nature in the way Bate suggests. It must 'say' (*énonciation*) that it reveals something and so must adopt a stance with respect to what it reveals (the *énoncé*).[26] In its performative act, the poem must make a stand with respect to what it says it reveals. Ecopoetic reading needs to draw out the poem's conditions of speaking: its self-accounting of the very poem that it is; and how it bears witness to the event of what it reveals. It needs to ask: in what way does it stand in its enunciation of the event? In what follows, I offer a reading of Celan's poem 'Todtnauberg' with these questions in mind. My aim is to see how ecopoetics might be employed for a nature philosophy attentive to the stand taken by the poem in its poetizing of the event. Here is the translation of the poem in English as it appears in Bate's book:

TODTNAUBERG[27]

Arnica, eyebright, the
draft from the well with the
starred die above it,

in the
hut,

the line
—whose name did the book
register before mine?—,
the line inscribed
in that book about
a hope, today,
of a thinking man's
coming
word
in the heart,

woodland sward, unlevelled,
orchid and orchid, single,

coarse stuff, later, clear,
in passing

he who drives us, the man,
who listens in,

the half-
trodden wretched
tracks through the high moors,

dampness,
much.

The poem offers an account of Celan's visit to Heidegger in his hut, where the celebrated Jewish poet and the philosopher with dubious National Socialist connections engaged in conversation and walked in the woods together discussing plants. Bate suggests that the poem is not a dialogue between the poet and the philosopher but a monologue in which only the poet speaks: 'The poem does not report a dialogue; it is itself a monologue. Heidegger is absent. The only voice is that of the poet' (p. 271). It is clear here that what Bate means by the 'voice' is the voice of Celan himself: the poet whose identity belongs to the one who has met, talked and walked with the philosopher Martin Heidegger as a living being. However, keeping in mind the previous discussion of 'bearing witness' (in which Celan's poems are understood to be neither monologues nor dialogues, but acts of witnessing and hence truth-tellings), then what kind of voice is this?

Here are the pertinent lines:

—whose name did the book
register before mine?—,
the line inscribed
in that book about
a hope, today
of a thinking man's
coming
word
in the heart,

Bate reads these lines as follows: 'the poet inscribes in the visitors' book of the philosopher the hope that his host might find in his heart some word of penitence or sorrow' (p. 271). But this reading fails to address the specifically tensed mode of voice enacted here. The poetic voice invokes a question about whose name was registered by the previous visitor ('before mine'), but then goes on to describe the line of writing left there as if it were his own writing – as if it were Celan himself hoping for an apology from Heidegger for his association with the National Socialists and their appalling treatment of Jewish people. If we accept that at a certain factual level the poet is indeed speaking about the line he himself had written in Heidegger's visitor's book, then this makes the question 'whose name?' problematic. Is the author of the line the person who asks the question 'whose name' or is it the 'mine' in 'before mine'? Many commentators, including Bate, assume the latter – that it is Celan himself who is asking, through the poem, whose name is registered prior to the line he himself had written in the book.[28]

However, the line could be read differently. The voice could simply be asking: who wrote this line that comes next in the book? (and there is no reason not to read it this way, given the syntax).[29] The 'mine' (the identity of the voice asking the question) would thus be someone different from the author of the line written in the book. If we read the poem like this, this 'mine' must be someone else (not Celan), someone speaking after the event of writing of the line in the book. But at the same time, we are also obliged to read the poem in terms of a certain historical veracity: Celan did actually write a line similar to this in Heidegger's book, a fact that we would be expected to accept as part of the truth enacted by the poem.[30]

If we hold onto the thought that both these identities are valid, then we are led to the following conclusion: that the voice that asks the question 'Whose name …' is that of Celan speaking 'otherwise', in the voice of those to come. The 'mine' is not Celan's own personal 'myself', but an anonymous 'mine' made available as a possibility-in-general (in Heidegger's terms the mineness of *Jemeinigkeit* or 'mine-to-be').[31] Celan's voice speaks in the aorist tense, bearing witness to the encounter as a true testimony of what happened, or in this case, of what failed to happen (perhaps an apology from Heidegger for his association with the

National Socialists – historical information about what Celan might have had in mind is not conclusive on this matter). The happening of this event (which fails to happen at this time) is made possible in some future time by the poetic speaking itself.[32]

The poet speaks, but not in terms of his own subjective thoughts; rather, he speaks as part of the *poietic* possibility of 'bearing witness' to the encounter and carrying the truth of the event. The poem will have already enacted the truth of the event in its next reading by some unknown other. Celan's poetizing enables a speaking with a non-subjective voice, a voice that speaks in the place of the other, held open by the poem as a possibility. Furthermore, this possibility is an absolute possibility insofar as it enables anyone-at-all (and not just a select few or a specific identity) to fill the place left open by the poem.

The voice that speaks through the poem does not take its own self as its subject (it is not a monologue), nor does it address others intersubjectively as a 'you' (it is not a dialogue in which multiple parties speak in turn thereby consolidating their identities in an intersubjective relation). Rather it speaks in the mode of the future anteriority ('I will have been') by anticipating a future position from which to speak, as if it had already happened. This kind of speaking requires a collapse of causal temporality so that the voice speaking does not remember the past in the perfect sense, but speaks from the future as having already taken place. In this case, the identity of the voice cannot be that of the poet remembering the past, but must remain anonymous as the voice of possibility, leaving the question 'who speaks' open. In its mode of address, the poem keeps itself open, thereby enabling the other to inhabit it at any future time, as part of its bearing witness, its capacity to bear ontological truth. In keeping itself open, the poem 'holds its ground' and stands in its truth.

In his Meridian speech, Celan makes the following comments about the poem's ability to speak: 'But the poem speaks. It is mindful of its dates, but it speaks. True, it speaks only on its own, its very own behalf' (Celan 2005, p. 163). Here Celan makes it clear that the poem does not speak on behalf of any person, not even Celan himself; rather it speaks 'only' on behalf of itself, in its singular 'saying' ('mindful of its dates', its specific utterance as a unique poetic event). However, in speaking only for itself, the poem is not closed in on its own solipsistic moment, but opened to the 'other' as the 'strange' – as 'altogether other':

the poem has always hoped, for this very reason, to speak also on behalf of the *strange* – no, I can no longer use this word here – *on behalf of the other*, who knows, perhaps, of an *altogether other*.

(p. 163)

This otherness that Celan mentions here is not an other that a 'self' might confront in a face-to-face encounter (e.g. in terms of 'Todtnauberg', an encounter between the poet and the philosopher), but an 'altogether' or absolute other, called forth at the very limit of the poetic mode of address, where the poem 'holds its ground on its own margin' (p. 164).[33]

This absolute other is not an other that might someday be known to the self, but an other that is hoped for yet remains out of touch and hence unknowable:

This 'who knows' which I have reached is all I can add here, today, to the old hopes.

Perhaps, I am led to speculate, perhaps an encounter is conceivable between this 'altogether other' – I am using a familiar auxiliary – and a not so very distant, a quite close 'other' – conceivable, perhaps, again and again.

The poem takes such thoughts for its home and hope – a word for living creatures.

(p. 163)

Celan's poetic voice (here we need to imagine the same disconnected voice that we encountered in 'Todtnauberg') is here 'led to speculate' on the possibility ('perhaps') of an encounter with the other, an encounter that coincides with an experience of the absolute (the 'altogether other'), but realizes that such possibility leads to its repeated deferral ('perhaps, again and again'). The poet can only reach the 'who knows' or querying of possibility, rather than the certainty of a union with the other. In speaking on its own behalf, the poem 'says' these 'thoughts', makes them thinkable for living creatures (not just human beings) allowing them to live on in hope. Without such hope, life would not be transitively open (it would not 'do' its own being and hence cease to be open to otherness), and instead be permanently closed in intransitive being (as a solipsistic monologue of the self affirming 'I' or closed dialogue between an 'I' and a 'you').

An encounter with absolute otherness (the moment when otherness becomes totally absorbed into absolute otherness – the apotheosis of the ideal and the materially real in the Idea) 'is conceivable', that is, it can be conceptualized through philosophical argument (e.g. Hegel's dialectical *Aufhebung*), but its actuality is always deferred: 'perhaps, again and again'. The non-coincidence of 'others' and the 'altogether other' is the truth that the poem enacts. This truth is the truth of the other as such, enacted by the poem in 'holding its ground', and leaving itself open in an absolute sense for anyone-at-all to share in what it makes possible, what it attests to as having happened. For Celan, a poem is a 'message in a bottle, sent out in the – not always greatly hopeful – belief that somewhere and sometime it could wash up on land, on heartland perhaps' (qtd. in Felstiner 1995, p. 115).

In Celan's poetry we see the same kind of poetizing that Benjamin identified in Hölderlin's poem 'The Poet's Courage' where the poetized opens thought to the 'potential existence of those that are effectively [*aktuell*] present in the poem – and others [...] [by] a loosening up of the firm functional coherence that reigns in the poem itself' (Benjamin 1996, p. 19). The poem does not retreat into mythic originariness, but opens itself to absolute otherness as enabling connectivity. Celan's poetry announces the end of the 'age of the poets', but not for the reasons Badiou gives. Rather it announces the end of the poetic task of mythologizing being and the beginning of a new task: that of a thinking of being in its truth in the absence of mythic reunion, in the impossibility of a fulfilled experience of otherness, yet opened to others at the same time.

Celan's poetic voice is equivalent to Schelling's creative decision (see Chapter 5). For Schelling the creative decision is a decision enacted in indecisiveness – in the decision *to be* when faced with the indecisiveness of absolute otherness. This decisiveness is not a decision made by a subject enacting its own freedom to decide (intransitive freedom), but a decisiveness that comes to the subject in its being for the event, in its 'becoming' as part of the 'free being' of the event itself (transitive freedom). Unlike Badiou's deciding subject 'induce[d]' by the event and consequently enabled to decide what this event then means (Badiou 2005, pp. 46–47), Celan's poetic voice is a subject-less voice that speaks after the event, but in such a way that allows the event to be carried forward in its possibility as such. The event is free to be otherwise, for whomever is able to live up to it. Celan's poetry thus carries the ontological bearing of truth.

Nature

In his prose piece 'Conversation in the Mountains', Celan provides a description of poetic speaking as part of the *poiesis* of nature. The essay describes a meeting between two Jewish cousins mysteriously called to travel high into the mountains where they meet on a path surrounded by beautiful plants: 'So, there they are, the cousins. On the left, the turk's cap lily blooms, blooms wild, blooms like nowhere else. And in the right, corn-salad, and *dianthus superbus*, the maiden-pink, not far off' (Celan 2005, p. 150). Here they engage in a conversation, reflecting on the things of nature around them and on why they have been summonsed there. Their conversation takes the form of an oblique commentary by another voice (a third voice) speaking through them.[34] This other voice does not talk in the sense of conversing, rather it speaks in the form of pronouncements on the ontological condition of the meeting of the two cousins: their 'being' as part of, yet separate from nature:

> You know. You know and see: The earth folded up here, folded once, twice and three times, and opened in the middle, and in the middle there is water, and the water is green, and the green is white, and the white comes from even farther up, from the glaciers, and one could say, but one shouldn't, that this is the language that counts here, the green with the white in it, a language not for you and not for me – because, I ask you, for whom is it meant, the earth, not for you, I say, is it meant, and not for me – a language, well, without I and without You nothing but He, nothing but It, you understand, and She, nothing but that.
>
> (p. 151)

The voice that speaks here is neither the 'I' (first) nor the 'you' (second) of the conversation, but the 'third' voice, coming between the two cousins and inhabiting their speech. What this voice says is in the mode of a philosophical meditation on the evolution of nature: 'the earth folded up here, folded once, twice and three times, and opened in the middle'. The shaping force of nature – *poiesis* – is described here as folded three times on itself and 'opened in its middle', a dialectical opening of self-differentiation that produces the in-between as the place of abundant nature – the place of life giving water and its source in the glaciers above.

Nature speaks through this third voice, using a language which is not meant for 'you' and 'me', but for the 'earth', a speaking that is 'without I and without You nothing but He, nothing but It, you understand, and She, nothing but that'. The *poiesis* of nature is all for the third person whomever this may be (He, It, She). We need to be mindful of the syntax of this line. The question 'for whom is it meant' is immediately followed by what could be taken to be the answer: the 'earth', but this is then followed by two negations: 'not for you' and 'not for me'. The line could be read as saying that the *poiesis* of nature, its life-shaping force, is for the earth *and* the negated 'you' *and* the negated 'I', as a series of additions, all connected together. In being for the earth, nature includes the negated 'you' and 'I'. Thus the 'you' and the 'I' are placed in *partage* with respect to the being of nature and its *poietic* becoming (they are included by being excluded at the same time). This 'inclusive disjunction' means they are both enabled and disabled from being: they are capable of seeing and not seeing the things of nature; of hearing and not hearing nature's call, its voice, and the speaking of the things of nature drawn together in this place in singular ways. The cousins 'have no eyes' (p. 150) yet they see; they 'talk' but they cannot 'speak'; they have memory and they don't have memory (p. 151). These paradoxes of being bring to mind the demythified life of human existence in Hölderlin's poetry[35] – a living death in destiny-less mythic disconnectivity, and confirms the cousins' *unheimlich* status (not being at home).[36] The voice declares that 'the Jew and nature are strangers to each other' (p. 150), and, through one of the cousins, says that 'I [...] stand here [...] where I do not belong' (p. 152). As a poetic speaking, the voice speaks from within the dialogue of the 'I' and the 'you' but in an ecstatic 'outside' way, enabling it to 'say' what the cousins cannot say in their stuttering, half-grasped attempts to come to grips with why they have been summonsed, and why they feel compelled to talk ('when their tongues stumble dumbly against their teeth and their lips won't round themselves, they have something to say to each other' (p. 150).

Unlike the noisy talk of the cousins (the voice calls them 'windbags'), nature speaks with a silent voice, most evidently the silence of the stones:[37] 'The stones, too, were silent' (p. 150). As the things of nature closest to the earth, stones do not talk like you and I, they speak[38]: 'They do not talk, they speak, and who speaks does not talk to anyone, cousin, he speaks because nobody hears him, nobody and Nobody, and then he says, himself, not his mouth or his tongue, he, and only he, says: 'Do you hear me?' (p. 151). In their silence, their rectitude, their being withdrawn into the earth, the stones speak, but this speaking is not talking, it is not with 'mouth' or 'tongue', but silently; they speak silently, an appeal for someone to hear them. This call is made not to any particular person as one might speak to another in conversation, but to nobody in particular; to a general Nobody, a univocal call of nature's being, a call that gathers the cousins to the place high in the mountains without their knowing why.

As a Kafka-like parable, 'Conversation in the Mountains' imagines a poetic space – in the Meridian speech Celan describes this space as a place where poetry 'moves with the oblivious self into the uncanny and strange to free itself' (p. 160) – where words, images and things occupy the same place and share the same ontological truth: 'No word has come to an end and no phrase, it is nothing but a pause, an empty space between the words, a blank – you see all the syllables stand around, waiting' (p. 150). In this space, the voice of nature is enabled to speak through the speech of the cousins. The essay invokes similar themes developed in Schelling's *Naturphilosophie*, concerning the 'unconscious' activity of the ungrounding of nature as primary becoming, suggesting the reparative capacity of nature to enable new beginnings, new pathways forward from the place where humans find themselves in free existence. *Poiesis* works through the subject, a movement of free being that opens the subject to nature as such. But there is a further aspect to 'Conversation in the Mountains' that needs attention. This is the question of justice it invokes. This question relates to Celan's concern for the possibility of a life after the death event of Auschwitz. *Poiesis* must enable free being after the death event.

Justice

One of the cousins carries a stick, something that guides him on his journey to the mountains. The stick is the blind man's guide, but also a weapon. In Büchner's *Lenz*, Lenz carries a 'bundle of birch-rods' which he asks his protector, Oberlin, to beat him with (Büchner 1993, p. 158). Lenz wants to be punished for a transgression against God. In Celan's essay, the stick becomes a duelling weapon, where the duel is won by 'silencing' an opponent's stick: 'and Klein the Jew, silenced his stick before the stick of the Jew Gross. The stones too were silent' (p. 149). Talking can be done with the stick: one talks with the stick by using it to dominate others, to dominate the things of nature; it becomes a weapon that can be used to defend oneself and settle arguments when talk fails, and with references to the Holocaust: 'I lay on the stones back then, you know, the stone tiles; and next to me the others who were like me, the others who were different and yet like me, my cousins' (p. 152). This lying down on the stones echoes the line in Celan's Holocaust poem 'Death Fugue' that speaks of a place in the death camps 'where it's roomy to lie' (p. 46), a place of death. But in the case here, lying on the stones is a resurrection, an enabling possibility that comes to the cousins. These cousins are survivors of the death event, rendered speechless by it, yet, through the speaking of the 'third' voice, able to see and hear the possibilities of a life beyond. They bear witness to the death event, but not by talking about it, rather by letting the voice of nature speak through them. The voice calls them and enables them to be 'otherwise' in the opening of poetic saying.

The speaking of nature makes possible the inauguration of a new event of being, one that cannot be spoken of in terms of talk; that is, it cannot be 'said' in terms of dialogue between an 'I' and a 'You', but through the mediating 'moment' of the 'voice' of nature as it speaks through the interlocutors, in the opening of being as such. Such a speaking is a speaking with a just voice, insofar as it makes possible a renewed sense of being-with nature and with others, without reducing this sense back to a dialogical play between subjective claims over how the justice should take place; without reducing it to a matter of fighting with sticks: 'I've come with my stick, me and no other, me and not him, me with my hour, my undeserved hour, me who have been hit, who have not been hit, me with my memory, with my lack of memory, me, me, me' (p. 151). This 'me' here is the survivor of the death event, the witness who must speak not for himself or herself, but for the others to come. But here we see that his speaking is locked into the endless repetition of his own subjectivity. It is only through the poetic voice that speaks through him that justice can be done.

Justice is neither a matter of using a stick (violence), nor a matter of talking (dialogue). Rather, as discussed in the previous chapter, in its ontological sense, justice is a matter of enabling 'just being'; of letting beings be in their being, and not as beings given over to others. As being for others, beings cannot be the beings that they can be and hence are denied their just being. For instance, the things of nature cannot be the things they can be because they are destined by technology for human being. But, in this very destining, they are already the things of nature. The 'injustice' of their being (that they are given over to human being and cannot therefore be themselves) is thus already marked on them – a violation that 'speaks' to anyone able to listen. This anyone-who-can-listen, is, in Celan's terms, a general 'Nobody' who hears what they have to say not in terms of a subjective knowing that objectifies the things of nature as categorical objects, but in a listening to what they want, in the 'to come' of possibility that listens with them, and enacts in this listening the very possibility that they call for. Such is, I argue, the *poietic* event.

Part IV

Technology

Chapter 9

Benjamin: Collapsing Nature

Dispersed gathering

A common thread running through Heidegger and Benjamin is their reworking of Romantic and Idealist responses to Kant. In particular, they are both concerned with working from the indeterminate contact with the thing – the affect domain of non-cognitive life – exposed in the *aporia* between sense and reason in critique (for affect see Chapter 2, note 3). While Heidegger takes this contact to be the beginning of the opening of Being, Benjamin sees it in terms of a collapse of Being (Origin or *Ursprung*) as 'an eddy in the stream of becoming' (Benjamin 1998, p. 45).[1] Being collapses, proliferating beings in an 'eddy' of chaotic connections. This collapse of Being into a dispersal of beings becomes a key idea throughout Benjamin's writings on poetics, art and technology. For instance, in 'Two Poems by Friedrich Hölderlin', an essay we have already encountered in the previous chapter, Benjamin reads Hölderlin's concept of life as an 'extension [*Erstreckung*] of space, the plane spread out, in which […] destiny extends itself' (1996, p. 26, trans. Stanley Corngold). That is, life becomes something like a chaotic dispersal whose elements are held momentarily in check within one of a multitude of single life-forms (a body, a poem, a photograph, a film) that can be released through *poietic* shaping and unshaping. I propose to define this singular-multiple interconnectivity as a 'dispersed gathering'.

In his discussion of the passage from Benjamin's reading of Hölderlin quoted above, Samuel Weber translates the word *Erstreckung* as 'stretching':

> Benjamin's reading of Hölderlin opens a *space* in which an alternative notion of *Schuld* [debt-as-guilt], and of its relation to nets and networks, begins to emerge. Similarly the space opened by Benjamin in this text relates to his surprising interpretation of the 'living' in Hölderlin's 'world' precisely *as a certain kind of space*, or rather as a kind of *stretching*.
> (Weber 2008, p. 276)

Life does not 'extend' as Corngold's translation suggests; rather, it stretches in the sense of a net or mesh expanding and contracting through space and time. Here we can detect resonances with Schelling's proposal of world soul as a 'joint and intertwined continuing' (Schelling 2000, p. 37) – a dynamic movement of material-ideational becoming, recapitulating between ground and unground in terms of actual-virtual connectivity (see Chapter 6). Following Weber's cues, a 'dispersed gathering' describes life stretching across the actualizing-virtualizing of space through the collapsed opening of Being enabled by singular acts of the poetized, responding to the *Schuld* or debt owed to the gathering as a network of connectivity. This debt becomes 'the *obligation to respond*, not just to persons, things, or subjects, but to the "sole rule of relation" that for Benjamin is the "principle of the poetized"' (Weber 2008, p. 280). I will return to this obligation and responsibility shortly.

In his later writings, Benjamin develops the idea of what I have called a 'dispersed gathering' in terms of 'a decay of the aura' (Benjamin 2002, p. 104) produced in technological mediation, as 'a strange tissue of space and time: the unique apparition of a distance, however near it may be' (pp. 104–05).[2] This felt presence of distance in proximity is described by Benjamin in the following way: 'To follow with the eye – while resting on a summer afternoon – a mountain range on the horizon or a branch that casts its shadow on the beholder is to breathe the aura of those mountains, of that branch' (p. 105). Aura is a breathing in – a contraction into the body – of both distant and proximate things, giving life to the present moment, and simultaneously a breathing out, or expression expanded across the continuum of space and time that connects them.[3] Aura is a 'gathering' in the moment of inhaling, and an exhaling 'decay' – a fading dispersal of gathered things.

In gathering and dispersing things aura is associated with myth.[4] In technologically mediated experience, aura retains its mythic power to unify human being and nature, but as a waning affect. Unlike Heidegger's event of the openness of Being (*Ereignis*) that retreats to a remythified space in-between technology and its other, Benjamin's open auratic connectivity produces a mythified natural plenitude becoming demythified through technological obsolescence, fading and decay. Auratic fading foretells the death of things as an event of technological demise and renewal. Encounters with such things do not involve their appropriation into mythic self-presence; rather, they are followed into an openness obliquely seen in the flash of their enigmatic survival.

A dispersed gathering is the reverse of Heidegger's idea of a gathered dispersal where dispersed things are gathered in the opening of Being in one special place (the site of the 'holy'), in the 'thinging' of the thing in terms of the fourfold (as discussed in Chapter 7). In Heidegger's version of the gathering of things in Being, Being reveals itself as the 'impending' (Heidegger 2012, p. 79): something waiting in front of us but not yet here.[5] Being waits for us over there as our destiny, the place where we are headed. However, in Benjamin's version, Being is already here but fading in the dissemination of things in connected life. Benjamin's critique thus sets in train a de-destining of Being in what Weber describes as 'the unstable dynamics of an ongoing relation' (Weber 2008, p. 278). Unlike Heidegger's account of the event-opening of Being in which dispersed things are gathered back into the event in a special moment of destining, Benjamin's account of the same event-opening (Hölderlin's poetics) suggests an emptying of the destined event into a disseminating mesh of connectivity stretching endlessly through time and space.

Benjamin characterizes this stretched 'moment' of dynamic relational being in terms of a passive seeing occurring 'while resting on a summer afternoon'; that is, with a languid following with the eye that delineates the connection between the things connected. Seeing here is not a matter of a subjective sight that connects things according to a predetermining *eidos* (a subjective 'way of seeing'), but of a letting go of seeing that allows itself to be taken up by the connectivity from one thing to another. Seeing takes its place, together with the things connected, as part of the moment stretching out between them. Seeing traverses the connected things without coming back to the seer. The seer is dissolved into the dynamic process of seeing spreading across an open-ended space-time continuum.[6]

This dissolution of seer into the seeing means there can be no return to a subject-seer converting everything seen into an objectified vision or sight. Rather it suggests what Nelson has termed 'inappropriable connectedness' (Nelson 2008, p. 139, see Chapter 1): a connectivity always ahead of itself, emptying itself out in recapitulating-ecstatic movements of sense. The principles underlying Benjamin's analysis of Hölderlin's poetry extend to issues of technological connectivity, suggesting that poetizing applies not only to the poetic text, but also to a more broadly conceived activity of *poietic* seeing that sees from the 'unstable dynamics of an ongoing relation' (Weber 2008, p. 278) in technologically mediated events expanding and contracting in open connectivity.

The life enabled in this connectivity is obliged to respond 'not just to persons, things, or subjects, but to the "'sole rule of relation'" that for Benjamin is the "principle of the poetized"' (Weber 2008, p. 280). To live life in open connectivity is to be enabled such that one's enablement is indebted to the enabling relation itself, insofar as it sustains connectivity and allows life to go on in the possibilities that it makes happen, including all things connected with it. This is not an intersubjective relation, but a radically conceived relation of 'free beings' whose being is given over to securing each other's freedom in open connectivity. In this case, there is no sense of a common being shared by such beings: no national type, race, ethnicity or species being, but the commonality of the free relation itself. This commonality of freely associated beings is not limited to human beings, but extends to non-human beings as well – those able to speak in a subject-less voice and hence share in the possibility of other being that such an open connectivity enables.[7]

Benjamin's concept of open connectivity retains a sense of auratic presence as fading affect – the always escaping sense of fulfilled presence disseminated in technologized culture. In his essay 'The Doctrine of the Similar', Benjamin sets out a way of understanding this disseminated sense in terms of the mimetic power of nature: 'Nature produces similarities – one need only think of mimicry' (Benjamin 1999, p. 694). For Benjamin the human is closest to nature in the full power of mimicry, which is based on 'magical correspondences' (p. 695) that enable a direct reading of the 'script' of nature (p. 696). In its full mimetic power, language has yet to separate itself out between the signifier and its idealized content, and unifies the meaning of human being and nature in the same way that the mythic symbol does in Schelling's theory of art (see Chapter 6). This power is now waning, but its traces are nevertheless carried as 'an archive of nonsensuous similarities [and] correspondences' (p. 697) communicating a natural connection between the signifier and the signified all but lost in modern technologized culture. At its root, language is composed of signifier and signified threads: the signifier thread mimics the signified thread as a kind of reading, in the same way that an astrologer reads the pattern of the stars as a writing of nature that foretells the future (p. 697). The signifier reads the signified allegorically, announcing the death of the union of the human and nature (Benjamin 1998, p. 166). Allegorical reading becomes a key strategy for a Benjamin-inspired ecopoetics.

Ecopoetics

According to Jonathan Bate, ecopoetics should be concerned only with pre-industrialized things. Unlike the silver chalice from Greek antiquity discussed by Heidegger in 'The Origin of the Work of Art', industrialized products such as styrofoam cups cannot 'thing' because they lack an attunement with nature: 'The silver chalice was a vessel to experience and to live with, whereas the styrofoam cup is an object to use and to dispose of – in Rilke's and Heidegger's special sense, that which is mass produced is not a true "thing". The task of the poet is to sing of things' (Bate 2000, p. 265). On these terms, ecopoetics is pre-technological and pre-political: 'the controlling myth of ecopoetics is a myth of the pre-political, the prehistoric: it is a Rousseauesque story about imagining a state of nature prior to the fall into property, into inequality and into the city' (p. 266).

Ecopoetics, as understood by Bate, is controlled by a myth of pre-industrialized nature before the 'fall' into property and the 'inequality' of the city.[8] Bate proposes a mythified ecopoetics that seeks to restore human being to nature before the Fall. However, as I have argued in the previous chapter through Benjamin's reading of Hölderlin's poetry, poetizing in the modern age does not restore human being to myth; rather it demythifies myth so that human being can live on in demythified connectivity. Following Benjamin, an ecopoetics would begin not by imagining a Rousseauesque state of nature before the Fall, but in the 'otherwise' opened up in encounters with already fallen things on their way to obsolescence, yet still resonating with mythic affectivity and mimetic power.

Despite their fallenness, industrialized commodities are able to 'thing' when encountered in their otherwise possibilities. Benjamin associates these possibilities with mimetic power – the power to realign according to the 'sensuous shape-giving' power of nature (Benjamin 1999, p. 695); that is, through the power of *poiesis*. In 'The Doctrine of the Similar', he asks: 'Are we dealing with a dying out of the mimetic faculty, or rather perhaps with a transformation that has taken place within it?' (p. 695), suggesting that mimetic power continues to operate within technology to transform it into something that we do not yet know – a realignment to come.

The lamp

Jonathan Bate argues that while an ancient Greek silver chalice is able to 'thing', a styrofoam cup cannot do so. In this section I want to challenge this view, and propose that industrialized products 'thing' when encountered as 'fallen' objects. A fallen object is one becoming de-objectified by technological obsolescence. Out of date and no longer useful, such objects become things by retaining themselves in their singular 'thereness'. As *this* thing, they obtrude into everyday life, and pose questions to the technologies that support and reproduce the smooth functioning of the contemporary world. In their proximity to us, they are already moving away and remote. They resonate with aura. Encountered thus, such things open onto an uncertain ground – a matrix of forgotten technology intermingled with auratic life glimmering in the twilight of cultural memory. In such encounters we can begin to see and think otherwise.

In an essay fragment entitled 'The Lamp' (Benjamin 1999, pp. 691–93), Benjamin describes how the mimetic power is at its strongest in memories of things encountered in childhood, for instance an old lamp that he recalls as one of the 'objects that surrounded me in my childhood' (p. 692). In describing his memories of the lamp he begins as follows:

> unlike our lighting systems, with their cables, cords, and electrical contacts, you could carry [the lamp] through the entire apartment, accompanied always by the clatter of the tube in its casing and the glass globe on its metal ring, a clinking that is part of the dark music of the surf which slumbers in the laborious toil of the century.
>
> (p. 692)

Memories of the lamp transport Benjamin from the contemporary world of electrical lighting systems to another time in which rooms were lit by lamps that could be carried 'through the entire apartment'. Oil and coal fuelled lighting connected the senses more intimately to the household environment, suggesting a time now past when humans were closer to their birth before the 'fall' into the adult world where sense and meaning are no longer fused into a single experience but disconnected by language and conceptual thought.

Benjamin's encounter with the lamp triggers a memory flash, where he feels similarities and connections between his past and an indiscernible future he associates with mimetic power: 'the gift we possess for seeing similarity is nothing but a feeble vestige of the formerly powerful compulsion to be similar and behave mimetically' (p. 691). These memories are not however particularly pleasant ones. Benjamin notes that the taking of studio photographs when he was a child was not a pleasing experience and the smile he sees on his face in now looking at the photographs belies the 'torture' of having to stand still and display himself for others: 'For this was the torture: we had to display ourselves, even though nothing lay further from our wishes. Thus, we made ourselves more like the embroidered cushion that someone had pushed toward us, or the ball we had been given to hold, than like a moment from our real lives' (p. 693). This desire to disappear into the background by mimicking the things around him, to escape the controlling stare of adults, belies the image itself with its presentation of a childhood anticipating the camera's gaze with a 'forced smile [and] carefully rehearsed gracefulness'.

Thus Benjamin's memories stand on uncertain ground, suggesting 'the unstable dynamics of an ongoing relation' (Weber 2008, p. 278); they cannot decide whether the past was a happy or unhappy one, whether the experience of the memory flash is a reliable indicator of 'our real lives' (Benjamin 1999, p. 693). Indeed, in its fragmentary form, the essay breaks down into repetitions and displacements that fail to pull themselves into a coherent whole. Mimesis invades the essay everywhere and the memories raise more questions than answers. For instance, Benjamin tells us that he holds the lampshade to his ear, mimicking the gesture of placing a seashell to one's ear to hear 'the dark music of the surf', but hears 'something else', a series of childhood memories: the 'rattling noise' of anthracite, the 'dull pop' of igniting flame, the 'jangling' of keys, the 'clatter' of the tube casing, the 'clink' of the metal ring against the glass cover. Like Celan's 'Conversation in the Mountain' (see Chapter 7), Benjamin's essay invokes a transitive sense of *poietic* mimesis in that it does what it says, thereby mimicking the chaotic collapse of memory triggered by the lamp. The essay allegorizes the past as fulfilled presence now no longer possible, yet holding out hope for a (weakly articulated) future within the ruination of memory triggered by the encounter itself.

In an earlier essay entitled 'On Language As Such and the Language of Man' (Benjamin 1996, pp. 62–74), we come across the lamp again but this time in terms of the 'communicability' of language (pp. 62–63). All things have communicability, that is, a capacity to communicate 'that it is' – its being as such. Benjamin describes this capacity in terms of the thing's 'mental being' (p. 63), its capacity to be conceptualized, which he relates to communicability through language: 'Mental being is identical with linguistic being only insofar as it is capable of communication' (p. 63). Thus, with reference to the lamp, Benjamin proposes that 'The language of this lamp, for example, communicates not the lamp (for the mental being of the lamp, insofar as it is *communicable*, is by no means the lamp itself) but the language-lamp, the lamp in communication, the lamp in expression' (p. 63). What does Benjamin mean by this? The lamp, insofar as it is *this* lamp (it is important that the lamp be singularly there, and not lamp as 'object-in-general'), communicates itself as a 'mental being' by the fact that Benjamin happens to have encountered it and is now presently writing about it. In its factical thereness, the lamp exceeds the language that names it and brings it into meaning. Without this capacity, this 'communicability', the lamp would be a mere thing and nothing more. That which is communicated is the lamp's capacity to be a *Thing* in resistance to the signification that assigns it a meaning.

We are now getting closer to demonstrating how industrialized objects carry a capacity to thing. The lamp's capacity to be a thing is bound up in its resistance to meaning and objectification. By being the thing that it is, it already 'things' insofar as it is encountered *there* as other, as that which survives the loss of significance in obsolescence and fading. Its auratic presence however, does not lead to a retrieval in myth, but dissolves memory on the uncertain ground of a *poiesis* still at work and shaping the future. This *poietic* shaping realigns the human relation with the lamp by triggering a sudden break between the present and the past that, in the essay 'The Doctrine of the Similar', Benjamin describes as a 'moment of birth':

> The moment of birth, which is decisive here, is but an instant. This directs our attention to another peculiarity in the realm of similarity. The perception of similarity is in every case bound to a flashing up.[9] It flits past, can possibly be won again, but cannot really be

held fast as can other perceptions. It offers itself to the eye as fleetingly and transitorily as a constellation of stars.

(Benjamin 1999, pp. 695–96)

The possibility of otherness triggered by Benjamin's encounter with the lamp comes between the present and the past, in the momentary opening that 'flits past' and cannot be 'held fast'. In recalling Nelson's term (see Chapter 1), it is the 'inappropriable connectedness' of an ongoing relation enabled in encounters with contingent things. These encounters are enabled by coming in-between technologies, and not from within them. Following Benjamin, an ecopoetics needs to begin here, on the uncertain ground of the in-between of past and present technologies.

First and second technologies

In order to show how this in-between beginning might be achieved we can turn to Benjamin's account of the arrival of technological reproduction in the modern industrialized age, keeping in mind Heidegger's own account of this arrival in terms of technological enframing (*Ge-stell*). In 'The Work of Art in the Age of Its Technological Reproducibility' (Benjamin 2002, pp. 101–33), Benjamin makes a distinction between first and second technologies.[10] First technology is the technology of ritual, where humans are entirely inscribed within its marks and notations: 'the subjects for these notations were humans and their environment, which were depicted according to the requirements of a society whose technology existed only in fusion with ritual' (p. 107). First technology is total in the sense that it 'fuses' the human and nature through rituals of magic and religion, whereas 'the origin of the second technology lies at the point where, by an unconscious ruse, *human beings first began to distance themselves from nature*. It lies, in other words, in play' (p. 107, emphasis added). Second technology does not strive for total command over the human relation to nature, but produces an 'interplay' between them: 'the first technology really sought to master nature whereas the second aims rather at an interplay between nature and humanity' (p. 107). While first technology fuses human beings with nature, second technology releases them through an 'unconscious ruse' that Benjamin defines as 'play'.[11]

Benjamin's historicizing of the relation between first and second technology requires some attention. He argues that ancient Greek technology was a first technology because it could only produce eternal art works: 'the Greeks had only two ways of technologically reproducing works of art: casting and stamping. Bronzes, terra cottas, and coins were the only artworks they could produce in large numbers. All others were unique and could not be technologically reproduced. That is why they had to be made for all eternity. *The state of their technology compelled the Greeks to produce eternal values in their art*' (pp. 108–09). Here Benjamin makes a crucial point: first technology does not do the bidding of the technical producers; rather the producers are themselves obliged to produce works of art according to the determinations of the technology (a point also made by Heidegger in proposing modern technology as *Ge-stell* to which I will turn shortly).

It follows that Benjamin does not identify first technology exclusively with ancient Greece; rather, ancient Greek technology simply falls into the category of 'first technology' due to the 'eternal' nature of the artworks it produces. Presumably, other technologies whose products have taken on an aura of permanence and eternality must also qualify as first technology. What conclusions can be drawn from this? It means that a second technology may in time become a first technology, when its production settles down into a 'natural' state for those whose lives are enframed by it. This is especially so when the settled technology is seen from the perspective of a newer technology that comes to replace it. For instance, in his essay 'A Little History of Photography' (Benjamin 1999, pp. 507–30) Benjamin shows how this naturalization of technology takes place when he reads two photographic images: one older image (a photograph of the photographer Karl Dauthendey and his fiancé) and a more recent image (a photograph of the boy Franz Kafka), such that the latter appears to have broken away from the naturalized aura of the former (p. 517) (see Mules 2007). From a historical perspective, the 'interplay' by which Benjamin defines second technology must therefore be an interplay between the 'nature' produced by the totalizing enframing of first technology and the releasing gesture of second technology that seeks to 'distance [human beings] from nature' (Benjamin 2002, p. 107). The releasing gesture of technology is a releasement not from Nature, but from the 'nature' produced by technology itself; that is, a releasement by technology from itself.

Benjamin establishes the principle that first and second technologies are not separate, but recapitulated into one another in a dialectical interplay that produces the human relation to nature historically as a releasement. To make this point Benjamin uses the example of film:

> *The function of film is to train human beings in the apperceptions and reactions needed to deal with a vast apparatus whose role in their lives is expanding almost daily.* Dealing with this apparatus also teaches them that technology will release them from their enslavement to the powers of the apparatus only when humanity's whole constitution has adapted itself to the new productive forces which the second technology has set free.
>
> (p. 108)

As a second technology, film releases human beings from enslavement to first technology – here described as a 'vast apparatus' – through its power to 'interplay' between nature and humanity. How does film do this? Benjamin suggests here that the setting free of enslaved human being occurs when 'humanity's whole constitution has adapted itself to the new production force' released by film. However, this could not be the case as it means that film, as the bearer of this productive force, would have shifted from second to first technology, leading to further enslavement of humans into yet another 'vast apparatus' – an apparatus of film and media images (as is the case, for instance, in the age of the simulacrum where human subjects become enframed by simulated images). Benjamin must mean something else.

I suggest the following: the setting free can only occur in the interplay between nature and humanity opened up in-between first and second technologies. In this interplay, the second technology 'set[s] free' 'new productive forces' (the 'shaping force' of *poiesis*) that momentarily releases human beings from technological enslavement. As we have already seen in 'The Doctrine of the Similar', Benjamin characterizes this releasing in terms of a perception of nonsensuous similarity that 'flits past, can possibly be won again, but cannot really be held fast as can other perceptions' (Benjamin 1999, p. 695). Nonsensuous similarity is similarity-in-difference – the mimesis of something by means of something else, for instance in words that sound like their referent (onomatopoeia). Nonsensuous similarity constitutes the hidden connectivity threaded through all things: 'an archive of nonsensuous similarities, of nonsensuous correspondences' (p. 697). Another nature opens up in the momentary perception of nonsensuous similarities and correspondences in-between first and second technologies.[12]

Contact with this other nature is fleeting and momentary; it cannot be 'held fast'. Once set on its way, the productive forces lose their free creative potential and become totalizing, so that the sense of freedom produced becomes part of technology's own nature, remaining bound up in it.[13] The technology withdraws into the affect regime, thereby denaturing nature while renaturing it at the same time (see Chapter 6). Humans caught in this renatured-denatured-nature sense themselves as naturally free. But this freedom is no freedom at all, since it is entirely dependent on the technology concealed in the natural affects so produced.

Benjamin's first technology is equivalent to Heidegger's *Ge-stell* or second technology. For Heidegger, *Ge-stell* enframes human being: summons it into being such that human *praxis* is given over to 'lend[ing] a hand to the coming to presence of technology' (Heidegger 1977, p. 37). *Ge-stell* comes after *techne* attuned to nature as defined by the Greeks and as practiced in pre-modern technology (e.g. pre-industrial modes of agriculture) (p. 15). In order to be released from *Ge-stell*, one must move backward to the free being-with nature of attuned *techne*. However, with Benjamin, we see a different kind of movement. In order to be released from enslavement to technological totalization, one does not move backward into a more original *techne*; rather, one is already being released by the new technology as it interrelates with the older technological form, but only momentarily. This means that Benjamin begins from the place where Heidegger leaves off. He does not wait for the turn to happen; rather he is already beginning to think with the turning of technology against itself – in the 'interplay' between first and second technologies – as it frees itself from the historical ground through which it emerges as something new. This historical ground is already technologically mediated, but in such a way that, from the perspective of the newer technology, it can only be seen there as a fading auratic presence – as nature withdrawing from itself. The interplay between human being and nature is thus played out in-between emerging and receding technologies, where the lost connection to *poietic* mimesis is found in encounters with auratic things marked on them, so that 'nature appears as a textual network to be read rather than as an image to be seen' (Weber 2008, p. 264).

The thing exists in a technical milieu entangled in the ruins of older technologies. In its resistivity to the system, the thing announces the fact of nature's grounding on an unstable 'open matrix' of previous significations and calculations with residual affectivity that the current systems must constantly overcome and disavow.[14] The work of the system is to 'purify' itself from the contaminations of the previous technologies so that it can begin again on new ground entirely of its own making (Latour 1993, pp. 10–12). Such efforts are doomed to fail as the remnants of the earlier technologies continue to affirm the otherness necessary for the system to reproduce itself as different from what went before. The system is therefore constituted on the verge of a collapse, with a threatening chaos of indeterminacy constantly looming. What counts here are the possibilities opened up in the collapsing of the system: the creative potential occurring in-between the system and the resistive marks of *techne* forgotten and concealed in it. A nature philosophy needs to situate itself in moments of failure, where the system is interrupted by the surging forth of the archaic remnants encountered in their flashing potential – in the way they point otherwise.

There is no totalizing technology that is not already entangled with the technologies that it replaces. This means that any given technological enactment will consist of contradictory forces potentially open to all possibilities. Likewise, there is no *Ge-stell* that enslaves human being, only tendencies and counter-tendencies in any given moment opened to absolute otherness. An attunement with nature cannot occur from this in-between place by imagining a pre-technological nature – a nature before the Fall. Rather, attunement comes from holding one's place in the in-between moment of *poiesis*, opening into another nature. This other nature is not Nature on the other side of technology (nature 'in itself'), nor is it the nature produced by technology that comes to replace Nature in the modern industrialized age (nature 'for us'); rather, this other nature is the work of *poiesis* already releasing us from technological 'enslavement'. *Poietic* release enables us to discern this other nature as the mark of a withdrawal: a figuration tracing itself in-between first and second technologies that foretells of future possibilities from the withdrawn position now opened otherwise.

Figuration

Figuration is neither the material sign (signifier) nor its ideational value (signified) but the a-signifying trait that enables signification to take place while remaining exterior to it. Jean-François Lyotard identifies the figure in terms of art: 'The position of art indicates a function of the figure, which is not signified – a function around and even in the figure [...] a spatial manifestation that linguistic space cannot incorporate without being shaken, an exteriority it cannot interiorize as *signification*' (Lyotard 2011, p. 7). If signification seeks transcendence of the signified (ideational content) over the signifier (material vehicle), then the figure is already there, shaking and interrupting the space so produced.

For Benjamin, figuration is the *mark* of signification. In an essay entitled 'Painting, or Signs and Marks' (Benjamin 1996, pp. 83–86), Benjamin makes a distinction between marks and signs. Signs are lines inscribed or imprinted on a material surface, leading to meaning through signification and reference. But in perceiving signs, the material surface disappears. Perception thus harbours a hidden surface that Benjamin describes as a 'surge' – an expression of residual materiality inhabiting perception itself (p. 83). He calls this a 'mark'. The mark emerges from the medium on which the sign is printed or inscribed – a surging forth that persists and endures. This is not dead inert material, but rather a materiality that carries life itself, as experienced matter (that is, material capable of bearing experience). Marks prefigure the future in terms of possibilities other than those prescribed by signification; they carry the possibility of signification but otherwise, in the material enactment of the sign. Things mark themselves as figures – they carry possibility by refusing signification.

Figuration figures the future; it foretells or prophesizes rather than calculates or predicts. Figuration calls forth and announces possibility. It prepares the way for something to be brought into being without anticipating what this something is. In this sense, figuration is part of the *poietic* movement of things in their yearning for otherness. In terms of the poem, figures exhibit the 'law of the *poetized* [...] that all unities in the poem already appear in intensive interpenetration; that the elements are never purely graspable; that, rather, one can grasp only the structure of relations, whereby the identity of each individual being is a function of an infinite chain of series in which the poetized unfolds' (Benjamin 1996, p. 25).

As part of *poietic* unfolding, figures cross a threshold and enable connectedness with otherness. For instance, the lamp (discussed previously) is a figure-thing insofar as it yearns for a past by crossing the threshold of the present. In Benjamin's encounter with it, the lamp reaches out to another, enabling an 'indiscernible' figuration sensed in open connectivity. As figuration, the poetized is a '*loosening up* of the firm functional coherence that reigns in the poem' (p. 19, emphasis added), enabling transition between two meshings or 'functional unit[ies]': that of the poem and that of life. Likewise the lamp loosens up memory, precipitating a transition to open connectivity. In exceeding and resisting signification, figures are carried by the 'temporal plasticity of form [which] must lead in an extensive sense to an infinite configured form – to a plasticity which is, as it were, buried and in which form becomes identical with the formless' (p. 31). The plasticity of form is buried formless materiality waiting to be released in renewed figurations. Poetizing is the releasing of formless material into new configurations not yet discernible. Poetizing knows nothing of the future, only the struggle to release materiality from its internment in signification. It faces backwards while moving forward.[15]

Memento mori

Things allegorize the meanings of the present age; they announce the impossibility of a symbolic union with the idea, and act as a *memento mori* of the sign: a 'death's head' reminder of its materiality in finite temporal being and the inevitability of death and decay. For instance, in Benjamin's essay 'The Lamp', an encounter with a remnant from Benjamin's past – an old lamp – triggers the collapse of memory, signifying the impossible union of present and past. The symbolic power of the lamp is allegorized by failing to deliver on its promise to restore the past to full presence. In so doing, the essay does not despair but holds out hope; in the ruins of memory something held back as part of withdrawn nature can be found there leading elsewhere.

As other-speaking, allegories are movements of figuration operating in the ruins of memory opened to absolute possibility. In *The Origin of German Tragic Drama* (Benjamin 1998) Benjamin discusses allegory in terms of the classical distinction between allegory and symbol (p. 163 ff), showing how the unifying power of the symbol is countered by an allegorical movement working dialectically in the "'fluidity of time'" (p. 165). The transcendent qualities of the symbol, such as unity, clarity and beauty, are replaced by the affect laden qualities of disjuncture, contingency and expressiveness. Benjamin reverses the theory of the symbol, exposing it to an allegorical movement of demythification, grounded in an immediate experience of historical life.

For Benjamin, allegories operate in the contingency of modern life in terms of the impossibility of unified self-presence (promised but never delivered by the Romantic symbol). Allegories are thus reminders of the human's relation to nature as *lifedeath* (see Chapter 8, note 18):

> Whereas in the symbol destruction is idealized and the transfigured face of nature is fleetingly revealed in the light of redemption, in allegory the observer is confronted with the *facies hippocratica* of history as a petrified, primordial landscape. Everything about history that, from the very beginning, has been untimely, sorrowful, unsuccessful, is expressed in a face – or rather in a death's head. And although such a thing lacks all 'symbolic' freedom of expression, all classical proportion, all humanity – nevertheless, this is the form in which man's subjection to nature is most obvious and it significantly gives rise not only to the enigmatic question of the nature of human existence as such, but also of the biographical history of the individual. This is the heart of the allegorical way of seeing.
>
> (p. 166)

In the symbol, nature is fleetingly revealed in terms of human redemption, whereas in allegory the human faces the inevitability of death as a reminder of 'man's subjection to nature'. Reversing Schelling's privileging of the symbolic over the allegorical, Benjamin's argument suggests that the conjoining of human being and nature through the symbol is simultaneously disjoined by allegorizing as the rationalization of human existence after the 'fall'.[16] Benjamin's reversal must therefore be seen as a rejection of Schelling's idealist conviction of the priority of the symbol over allegory as the founding gesture of western art and literature. Benjamin does not abandon the symbol, but materializes its power in allegorizing events.

The symbol is a retroactive projection of the mythic fulfilment of human being with nature, while allegory is the presentation of this fulfilment such that human being with nature is rendered finite and facing its own death. The fleeting revelation of nature is not one of redemption but one of mourning and loss; a loss in which the human gains an acute sense of finite connectedness with things no longer seen in terms of symbolic transcendence but as an immanent otherness open to indeterminate possibility. The allegorical way of seeing thus reminds us that 'if nature has always been subject to the power of death, it is also true that it has always been allegorical' (p. 166), always grounding us in material lifedeath.

For Schelling, Greek poetry such as Homer's *Iliad* presents a 'true symbolism' (p. 47) in which the finite and infinite are fused in symbolic presentation. However, Benjamin's reversal of the allegory/symbol hierarchy indicates how a poem such as the *Iliad* might be read as an allegory of human life in-between god-like divinity and mortal existence. As Winkler has argued, the *Iliad* presents the dilemma of human existence caught between undying heroic greatness and the inevitability of death:

> The poet however, presents the hero's undying glory as an ambiguous quality: 'The Homeric hero is anxious for glory, and he faces the full horrors of death. But as there is no posthumous reward for the brave man in the other world, so the consolation of glory is a chilly one. … The hero dies, not so much for his own glory, not even so much for his friends, as for the glory of the song, which explains to a spellbound audience the greatness and fragility of the life of man'. This song is the *Iliad* itself, and its central concern is, 'the meaning and universality of human doom'.
> (Winkler 2009, p. 156, quotes from Griffin 1980, p. 102, p. 69)

In his struggles, the Homeric hero is abandoned to life without redemption, and dies neither for his own glory nor for his friends, but 'for the glory of the song'. The poem carries the heroic event with its 'saying', communicating the message of 'the greatness and fragility of the life of man' directly to its audience.[17] Human beings are fated to lifedeath struggle allegorized by the poem itself.

The war in the heart of nature

Here I offer a reading of Terrence Malick's film *The Thin Red Line* (1998) as an 'allegorical way of seeing' of the lifedeath fate of human existence. My aim in this reading is to demonstrate how this allegorical way of seeing exposes the relation between humans and nature as part of the 'event' enacted – the World War II battle of Guadalcanal in the Solomon Islands of the Pacific in 1942 – thereby enabling the film to see otherwise. As Bersani and Dutoit argue, 'Malick is not sending us the trite (if true) message that war violates nature's beauty. Rather, the war is the occasion for a demonstration of a universal relationality of which the violation is only a part' (Bersani and Dutoit 2004, p. 161). The film employs the battle to demonstrate the Schellingian point that nature grounds the possibility of both good and evil by withdrawing from them (as indifferent nature), and that the human-nature relation is itself part of this withdrawn ground as a *poietic* otherness shining through the 'death's head' face that looks at the horrors of war.[18]

Told through the experience of an American infantry company, the film allegorizes the battle by meditating on human life and its relation to death, nature, good and evil. Poetic voice-overs by the soldiers pose philosophical questions in response to the futility of war and the inevitable outcome of death, but illuminated by the light of the persistent beauty of nature that shines through the evil of warfare in every way. The struggle is as much a struggle with nature as it is a struggle between armies, as the soldiers find the terrain saps them of energy and blocks their way forward. The first line of the film, a voice-over spoken by one of the soldiers, asks: 'What's this war in the heart of nature?', a fundamental question about the evil of war and the part it plays in nature.

In concert with the film's visual revelations, the poet-soldiers sing of nature (through voice-over commentary posing poetically phrased questions) such that the battle is presented not in terms of some noble plan or outcome (a heroic victory or death, fighting for one's country, one's family or loved ones back home), but in terms of the wonder disclosed to them as glorious nature persisting and enduring through the horrors of war. The film depicts the lush tropical rainforests and rivers replete with life while the grassy hillsides sing with the wind, mimicked by the sound of whistling machine gun bullets.

Mimicry is an important component of the film: the behaviour of the soldiers mimics that of nature at war with itself. For instance, the bullying Colonel Tall steals Captain Staros's idea of a flanking move to capture a heavily fortified hill, claiming the credit for himself when the attack succeeds while relieving the captain of his command. Tall's usurpation of Staros's plan mimics the entwinement of the jungle vines that wrap themselves around the trees, strangling them to death, a point noted ironically by Tall himself when he tells Staros: 'Look at this jungle, look at these vines, the way they twine around the trees, swallowing everything. Nature's cruel Staros'. Tall also feels that he is like a dying tree, denied promotion and strangled by superior officers. Thus, all of human behaviour mimics nature at war with itself. Life and death, good and evil are mixed together in a lifedeath struggle into which the soldiers are fatally drawn. Yet hope remains in the *poietic* indifference of nature itself, reaching out into the rivers, skies and beyond.[19]

The film exemplifies the allegorical 'way of seeing' proposed by Benjamin, in that it carries the message of 'man's subjection to nature' as both a terrible fate and a wondrous openness, posing 'the enigmatic question of the nature of human existence as such' (Benjamin 1998, p. 166), a question that has no transcendent answers, no final triumph of good over evil, no resolution in elevated love, no redemption of human being restored to Nature, but simply the 'singing' of the film itself, its allegorizing of the event. The symbolic aspects of the film – the presentation of ideas of love, self-fulfilment and the restoration of the soldiers to a higher or more natural state – are undercut by an allegorical mourning over the loss of such ideals.[20] The film's stance to what it says demythifies the event, keeping it in a state of mythic disconnectivity. It bears witness to the battle, not by recalling its historical or ideal truth, but by announcing that 'man's subjection to nature' at war with itself destroys idealism and places the human in a state of mourning outside its own idealized self-image, yet open to a glorious otherness. Benjamin writes that at 'the heart of the allegorical way of seeing' is the face as a 'death's head' (p. 166) – the sorrowful face of mourning over the plight of human existence alienated from redemption in transcendent unity with nature. As everything around him lies in ruins and the soldiers' dreams have been shattered, one of the poet-soldiers asks 'what's stopping us from reaching out and touching the glory?' Yet he finds glory in the things of nature that shine all around him in the midst of war. The poetizing of the film allegorizes its own (im)possibility as a mourning over the loss of symbolic reunion with nature, thereby opening itself out to *poietic* otherness.

The wire bowl

I am looking at a bowl made of old fencing wire. It sits *there* on a long timber table, as part of the décor of an ultramodern house somewhere in rural Victoria. If I were to pick this bowl up, the wire would no doubt feel rough and flaked with rust, reminding me of its decay over time, and of the distance between its current use and the use it once had on some long forgotten farm. I cannot do this, however, as the bowl is not there in actuality. Rather, my gaze is framed by the photograph in which the bowl appears (see Figure 2). The photograph is there not to present the bowl as such, but to illustrate an article in a lifestyle magazine about the architectural design of the house (Carter and Kiely 2008). My gaze thus withdraws from the bowl while looking at it. However, in this withdrawal another possibility appears: a possibility of seeing the bowl otherwise. In the following discussion, I will outline what this otherwise possibility is.

The article accompanying the photograph describes the house in typical modernist terms of planes, angles and shapes, as impositions on the landscape. We are told that the house provides elevated views, where the owners look out over rolling hills behind a '40 metre-plus stretch of full-height glass' as if from the 'deck of a ship' (p. 168). However, there is something odd about this wire bowl; its irregular weaving of rusty old wire seems at odds with the flat surfaces, geometrical lines and futuristic styling of the house. This sense of being out-of-place poses questions to me. Where does this bowl come from? Who made it? How did it get here? The caption beneath the photograph provides some indication. It says that the bowl was woven by Lorraine Connelly-Northey, but says nothing about the artist or her work. Some personal recollection reminds me that Lorraine Connelly-Northey is an indigenous artist specializing in making artworks out of discarded objects found in the Victorian and New South Wales countryside.[21] The artist collects these found objects from old dumps and neglected corners of farms and paddocks once worked by white European colonists and their descendants, and reclaims them as part of her own indigenous culture. This suggests to me that the bowl is 'saying' something other than what it says about modern house décor; something not said in the article itself.

If the bowl reaches back to traditional Australian Aboriginal culture, then in what way does it stand in relation to that culture? As a woven mesh, the wire bowl cannot be used to contain things, and is not a replica of the bowls once used by traditional women in their daily lives. Rather, the bowl is a mime: it copies traditional Aboriginal bowls, but in a different material form.[22] Through mimicry, the bowl releases itself from its original indigenous *techne*. To effect this release, the bowl reuses discarded material from earlier white European farming practices found on traditional Aboriginal land, thereby retaining a connectivity with the past. This connectivity is a re-connectivity to 'country' – the original relation of indigenous people with the land – through the reclamation of the found material by the artist as a Waradjerie woman, born in the country where the material was found.[23] The bowl's stance is defined by its presentation as both a modern art object and something earthed in indigenous material history, its connectedness to country.

Does the magazine article recognize any of this indigenous history and art-making as part of the bowl's provenance? In an oblique reference to the bowl, the article records that the house owner 'bought an ultimately "perfect fit" of indigenous works without knowing where they might go' (p. 168). The bowl's connection to indigenous country is thus hidden

Figure 2.

by the *eidos* of modern *techne* – its 'way of seeing' that makes the bowl fit in with the décor of the house; as part of the overall design that imposes its shape upon the landscape. Yet there it is for the viewer to see. The bowl thus works against the modernist *techne* while partaking in it at the same time. How does it do this?

We are told in the caption to the photograph that a glass wall 'sets a wire bowl … into dramatic relief' (p. 169). The bowl comes into relief by being set against a glass wall behind it. But what is a relief? A relief is something raised above its support, standing out from the plane on which it is set. For instance a bas-relief stands out from the material of which it is made, thereby maintaining connectedness with it.[24] To set something in 'dramatic relief' is to make it stand out in a way that draws attention to itself, while retaining its connectedness with what gives it support. However, this support cannot be the *techne* that makes it a 'perfect fit' for the décor of the house (a perfect fit is something that works effortlessly, without support), but the *techne* that brought the bowl into being – the artwork of the artist in collecting and manipulating discarded things. The support is thus rendered invisible by the 'perfect fit' of the bowl to the décor, in accordance with an *eidos* that only sees things in one way – as design, shape and imposition.

Yet in this invisibility, the support becomes visible when the bowl is viewed otherwise, in following its stance against the place assigned to it on the table. It becomes visible not by returning to an original indigenous *techne*, but by something else: a capacity to say 'yes' and 'no' to the modernist *techne* at the same time, affirming *that* it is, against its function in the house design. The wire bowl stands obliquely to its assigned place, and 'says' that it is in another way. The bowl speaks back against its modernist functionality, reaffirming an indigenous connection to country without falling back into myth. In effect, the wire bowl allegorizes its symbolic function as a 'perfect fit' for the house, thereby re-indigenizing the view, and grounding it in earth.

The possibility I mentioned at the beginning of this analysis is that the wire bowl can be seen otherwise by following the way it turns against the *techne* already assigning it a place in a system of aestheticized objects. By following the resistive turning of the bowl, we allow it to retreat into its materiality so that it 'says' what it is otherwise. What it says reclaims country through the creative reuse of discarded material from past European farming practices. It renatures the denaturing of indigenous culture into possibilities awaiting their turn to be seen.

Ecopoetic openness

I began this chapter with a consideration of collapsed Being, drawing from Benjamin's idea of Being as an 'eddy in the stream of becoming' (Benjamin 1998, p. 45). In collapsed Being, things are released through a recapitulating *poiesis*, falling back yet moving forward at the same time in a temporal chiasm. To follow this *poietic* movement is to be taken by the thing 'otherwise' in dispersed connectivity. We saw how technology plays a part in this dissemination of chiasmic experience through the historical connectedness between present and past technologies, producing a fading-dissipating plenitude (aura) whose affects are weakly felt in the experience itself. Encounters with things trigger this weak power, enabling them to speak otherwise.

These ideas suggest that an ecopoetics needs to attend to the technological formats through which things are encountered and expose them to their historical limits. Ecopoetics must show how the current way in which a thing *is* blocks it from becoming what it can be as 'other'. To show this, we can deploy Benjamin's idea of an 'interplay' between first and second technologies, where the latter releases things from 'enslavement' by the former. In this chapter I have shown how technological interplay naturalizes perception so that the more recent technology breaks away yet remains entangled in earlier technologies. The place in-between these technologies is uncertain ground: a matrix of possibilities with no discernable goal or end in sight. This uncertain ground can also be identified within technical formats such as poems, films and art objects, as the allegorizing of ideational (i.e. symbolic) content, thereby making the poem, film or artwork stand against itself.

Being on this uncertain ground loosens the ties of cognitive thinking and enables the perception of nonsensuous correspondences between things as a 'flashing up' of similarity-in-difference (Benjamin 1999, p. 695). By following the flashing up of the thing, we trace the outlines of another nature already beginning to reveal itself in connectivity with other things. This other nature is the shaping force of *poiesis* released from signification. Nature as *poietic* openness is neither nature 'in itself' nor nature 'for us', but a transitive event of Being; that is, Being carrying itself as becoming (being-as-becoming). Both Malick's film and Connelly-Northey's wire bowl carry Being as *poietic* openness; they refuse mythic transcendence and keep themselves in open possibility. They exemplify a transitive poetics in which the act of *poiesis* carries the openness of Being.

A relation of free beings cannot be closed in self-identity, but must remain open in the possibility of '– and others' (Benjamin 1996, p. 19); a possibility responsive to the 'sovereignty of relation' (p. 34) that I have called keeping the Open open. Keeping the Open open means keeping the possibility of connectedness open to relations not yet brought into self-identity. The being of such relations must remain free 'to be', and hence always open 'otherwise'. Ecopoetics must free itself from predetermining ways of being. It can do this by becoming transitive: it must itself *be* a carrying of the openness of Being, as part of a *poietic* 'stream of becoming'.

Chapter 10

Nancy: Renaturing and Bio Art

Bio life

A nature philosophy begins with the current saying of nature, turning it otherwise to expose its *techne* – its way of self-knowing in technological formats and modes of production – to the critical gaze. A *techne* produces nature as a 'way of life' in which beings gain their meaning by living this way of life and becoming accountable to it. I have suggested in Chapter 8 that nature is 'said' today in terms of the nature-machine – the entwining of life and technology to produce nature as technical fact.[1] We live today in a rapidly expanding world of the nature-machine as a multifarious set of technical facts to be managed, controlled and produced. Glimmering through this emerging world can be seen the beginnings of a 'new biological nature' (Tibon-Cornillot qtd. in Andrieu 2007, p. 62) led by bio science, producing a new kind of bio life now gaining control over modes of industrial production and the shaping and engineering of living bodies.

The concept of bio life, currently employed in much commentary about the new bio sciences, is drawn from Foucault's writings on disciplinary power (Foucault 1978, p. 141). In Foucault's terms, bio life is life managed by techniques of power: 'the maintenance of productive relations … as *techniques* of power present at every level of the social body' (p. 141). Bio-power is the technique for producing and maintaining life in disciplinary societies; in societies organized and controlled by social hierarchies and mechanical production based on the efficient use and circulation of energy as work. Bio-power is 'what brought life and its mechanisms into the realm of explicit calculations and made knowledge-power an agent of transformation of human life' (p. 143). However, as Gilles Deleuze has argued, the disciplinary societies of the eighteenth and nineteenth centuries have since given way to control societies (Deleuze 1995, pp. 177–82), where efficient use of closed system energy has been replaced by the modulated circulation of open system informational codes. In a control society, bio-power works through recapitulated feedback loops constantly travelling through and transforming living bodies and sites.

In control societies, life is distributed through informational networks managed according to the requirements of the code. Nature itself – as living being – becomes entwined in the code that spreads into the living body and into the cellular material of life made responsive and adaptive to the management of the code by technical means. Nature becomes a biotechnologically enlivened nature-machine: a distributed modulation of living material and technical data entwined in such a way that one cannot be separated from the other without losing its natural power. Bio-power is shifted from the management of life, in particular material things, to the management of the bio-system itself in which material things receive their living being. This 'new biological nature' dissolves the boundaries of fixed identity and the limits of the material body into a heterogeneous enmeshment of living and technical elements that challenges anthropocentric and providential ideas of nature as self-identical, consistent and fully formed.

This chapter is a critical response to the emergence of the new age of bio life as biotechnologically engineered.[2] I employ Jean-Luc Nancy's concept of denaturing to think about the kind of nature produced in biotechnologically engineered environments, in terms of globalization and its effects on localized means of world-forming. Denaturing is the withdrawal of Meaning from the world (Nancy 2007, pp. 82–90).[3] Nancy associates denaturing with technology (p. 87). A denatured world is one in which its meaning is supplied to it by technology. Nature is denatured when it is named as such, and is thus technologically produced: 'the very motif of "nature" is by itself "denaturing"' (p. 87). Biotechnological engineering is part of a broader denaturing of nature, underway since industrialization, which Heidegger calls *Ge-stell* or technological enframing (Heidegger 1977, p. 21) (see Chapter 7). The current globalizing phase of denaturing accelerates the tendencies of enframing to strip local connectivities and replace them with sets of abstract relations remote from their physical sites of application, leading to transformations of the world thus formed into a *Ge-stell* that we now define as globalized communication networks, reducing everything to material resource as 'standing reserve' (p. 27). This denatured world of virtual informational life makes existing worlds disappear, triggering realignments in the ownership of wealth, resources, information and the production and distribution of life-forms in new kinds of human/non-human power relations. Meaning is drawn away from these disappearing worlds and absorbed into the globalizing denatured world now emerging as total world transformation.

Both Schelling and Heidegger offer critiques of world-forming through their respective philosophies, where art plays a significant role. For Schelling, art provides the sensuous mediation between the finite and the infinite, uniting experience in the Absolute, while for Heidegger, art singularises experience into an open possibility from within technological enframing, turning into the 'other beginning'. Both philosophers are concerned with beginnings: how does one begin from the world that enframes and orders us into what we already are? Benjamin's poetizing of myth provides yet a further turning in the critique of technology, exposing technology to its ruined historical grounds. Benjamin's concept of allegory, as the demythification of mythic self-grounding, opens technology to its auratic remnant-past, allowing it to speak otherwise from these very ruins (see Chapter 9).

In this chapter I examine biotechnological denaturing of the world, and how it is challenged by art. I examine the possibilities opened up by the artwork's challenge as well as its limits. I will begin the chapter with a brief re-examination of Schelling's concept of recapitulation as a means of conceptualizing the human-nature relation *in media res*: in the uncertain contingency of the 'that' of things. This will be followed by a working through of Nancy's concept of finite world-forming out of and in resistance to globalization. The chapter then moves on to an examination of bio art as a critique of biotechnology. In particular I look at the artwork and ideas of transgenic bio artist Eduardo Kac as well as the collaborative artwork of Oron Catts and Ionat Zurr, two prominent bio artists working with tissue engineering.[4] My aim here is to show how bio art offers a way of caring for the things of nature confined within biotechnological objectification. The chapter concludes by considering a recent artwork by Patricia Piccinini as a retroactive allegory that exposes biotechnology to its ruined grounds. Piccinini's art provides another way to think of biotechnological denaturing of the world, less indebted to technology and more intimately and locally connected with the things of nature. I show how Piccinini's artwork maintains the openness required for free being to flourish with nature against the tendency towards its closure in technical fact.

Beginning again with Schelling

Iain Grant suggests that Schelling's *Naturphilosophie* lends itself to a materialist philosophy through the idea of recapitulated being-as-becoming as non-linear life (Grant 2006, p. 13). Recapitulated life is life 'acting on its self-construction [as] [...] the dynamic process of the self-construction of matter' (p. 13). Life emerges through a dynamic movement constantly turning back on itself in non-linear progression. Grant notes that there is a tension in Schelling's *Naturphilosophie* between linear and non-linear recapitulation (p. 12). Evolutionary progress is understood to be moving linearly to higher forms (with the human organism at the pinnacle) while, at other times, it is understood in non-linear ways as an opening in material beginnings. It is clear, however, that what Schelling seeks is the principle of recapitulation itself, as the emergence of difference from the indifference of being. If this is the case, then linear recapitulation must itself be part of non-linear emergence constantly turning back on itself in repeated differentiations of undifferentiated being. Linearity gives way to non-linear openness as the emergence of what Schelling calls 'unrestricted being' (qtd. in Grant 2006, p. 13) in absolute beginnings. Life is produced through a recapitulating movement that brings with it elements of the previous stage in new forms. Thus, the human-nature relation is not one based on simple linear progress, but dependent on a recapitulation of material and ideational becoming in uncertain contingency, leading to the possibility of new relations unthinkable in terms of the previous stage.

Schelling himself did not or could not foresee the consequences of this non-linear thinking about new life-forms and the possibility of new human-nature relations. Instead he fell back on a linear idea of the human-nature relation with the human as the most advanced life-form, calling for a new mythology from the beginning of the current age to seek higher revelations of the Absolute as the unity of being: 'But how a new mythology is itself to arise' (Schelling 1978, pp. 232–33). Schelling's philosophy proposes a solution to the uncertainty of non-linear, recapitulated 'free beginning' through a remythologizing of the human-nature relation reaching for a higher state of being. Against this linearity seeking the ideal in higher stages of being, a non-linear reading of Schelling's *Naturphilosophie* postulates that any evolutionary stage is always already an 'in-between', recapitulating itself into previous and future stages; there can be no forward movement without a simultaneous counter-movement such that the present stage is always beginning again in perpetual 'beginningness'. Any evolutionary stage is itself the site of an incessant ungrounding movement held in check by a 'free being' that blocks past and future beingness from coming about (see Chapter 6). A specific age of technology for instance blocks previous and future ages by constantly being the age that it is, in enacting its own 'freedom to be'. Foucault's genealogical-archaeological descriptions of the 'evolution' of institutional-discursive knowledge and conceptual truth through transformational leaps and disjunctures owes a debt to Schelling's philosophy of recapitulated being.[5]

Schelling's fluid and dynamic theory of 'virtual nature' provides a departure point for this chapter, which concerns the renaturing of nature. Renaturing refers to the process of recapitulating denatured nature into another nature, a new form of life. As I have indicated in Chapter 7, nature is denatured in human *praxis* (as *techne*) when it is turned into a projection of human will and desire. Denatured nature is nature produced by technology as 'naturally given'.[6] Thus denatured nature is already renatured in the technical fact that *it is*. Denatured nature is, in effect, redenatured nature, producing the illusion of nature as an *autopoietic* nature-machine. My concern in this chapter is to examine this process of denaturing and renaturing in terms of the production of bio life, or life produced through the connection of technology and materiality as engineered life-forms. My aim is to explore the challenges this production of new bio life-forms pose to thinking about a nature philosophy and the role that art, as transitive poetics, might play in it. Keeping in mind that the concern of a nature philosophy is to engage in critique by pursuing the 'as such' of nature as *poietic* openness and possibility, then in what way can bio art throw light on *poiesis* and in what sense does it help us to achieve a realignment of human *praxis* with *poiesis* leading to a more just, non-exploitative human-nature relation?

World-forming

In *The Creation of the World, or Globalization* (Nancy 2007), Jean-Luc Nancy argues that critical thought is faced with two ways of seeing the world: either as globalizing or as world-forming (*mondialisation*). Globalizing is a disconnecting, abstract process of total consolidation at the expense of contact with the finite world, whereas world-forming is a finite-expanding process of connectivity always in contact with itself and with the world that it creates (pp. 27–28). Globalizing and world-forming are not mutually exclusive world views, but simultaneous counter-processes: the former expands in an infinite spiral of unearthly exchanges, while the latter contracts back into finite contact with the earth. In Schelling's terms, globalizing and world-forming are rotatory drives incessantly turning in an eternal beginning in-between the ungrounding and grounding of ideation and materialization (Schelling 2000, p. 20); they turn in a 'beginning [that always] remains ungrounded' (Nancy 2007, p. 80).

Ungrounded beginnings denature the world. What does Nancy mean by this? Denaturing must not be thought of in terms of an original plenitude robbed of its nature, but as an incessant production of beginnings. Nancy argues this point through the founding gesture of western philosophy, which is always grounded in its own ungrounding (e.g. the Cartesian *cogito*, the Kantian subject), thereby producing a *logos* (a 'technology' of knowledge production), that 'can do nothing else [...] than open onto the abyss of its own beginning' (p. 82). Philosophizing since Plato constitutes a *techne* forever beginning in an encounter with the 'abyss of reason' opened up in its own self-questioning. Nancy argues that this gesture inaugurates the regime of modern technology as repeated attempts to master the world in incessant beginnings.

Modern technology is *autopoietic* in that it grounds itself in its own self-reflexion, itself inhabited by *poiesis* as an absolute openness: an 'allo-' or 'other speaking' that the auto-cannot hear as other but only as the same. Denaturing is not the 'other speaking' of *poiesis*, but the auto- preparing to begin again. This new beginning strips the world of its existing nature in order to renature the world with globalized *techne*. The human relation to nature is denatured in this auto-renewing activity, entwining it into an 'abstract process' (p. 27) of globalized renaturing. Denaturing thus excludes the other from having its own voice, and guides everything into the globalizing same.

Globalizing denatures the world – strips away the finite connectedness that enables the world to retain itself in earthly contact with itself, and to have its own localized voice. The world as a distinct place of finite connectedness disappears into an infinite series of technical facts connected by a *techne* that makes sense of things in abstract form. Thus, globalization destroys the connectedness of peoples, places and things in their pluralized being-together, and replaces it with the 'indistinct integrality' (p. 27) of an infinite totality abstracted and disconnected from the finite world.

The denaturing of the world occurs through what Nancy calls 'ecotechnology': the articulation of economic, technological and ecological elements in the production of 'life'.[7] Ecotechnology replaces the connected life of the world with an ecotechnological life; that is, life already living in the world as globalized *techne*:

[S]o called 'natural life', from its production to its conservation, its needs, and its representations, whether human or animal, vegetal, or viral, is henceforth inseparable from a set of conditions that are referred to as 'technological', and which constitute what must rather be named *ecotechnology* where any kind of 'nature' develops for us (and by us).

(p. 94)

Ecotechnology is 'the technological management of life' where 'such life has, in fact, already become *techne*' (p. 94). Ecotechnology produces and manages life, not as a self-sustaining plenitude, but as something indebted to globalized *techne*, abstracted from finite conditions of living. Nature, as the 'source of life' can no longer be distinguished from *techne*, leading to the powerful illusion that the world is simply made up of technical facts that are fully alive and capable of their own *autopoiesis*. Is this not the situation confronting us today? Take the case of the genetic modification of agricultural crops. Because they provide better yields and resistance to pests, genetically modified crops have taken over the world of agriculture. The bio artist and theorist Eduardo Kac writes:

> [T]he corporate monocrops of selected transgenic varieties of plants [...] have decreased biodiversity by pushing out local family farms and their unique cultivars,[8] which are genetically various and are often locally adapted not only to weather and soil but also to a given region's economic and cultural needs. In the age of molecular biology, rather than operating at the glacial pace of geological time, evolution both annihilates a percentage of the extant flora and fauna and produces new life and new relationships (symbiosis, parasitism, assistance, predation, hybridization, infection, cooperation) within the life cycle of a single human being.
>
> (Kac 2007, p. 4)

The production of new life by genetically based biotechnology 'annihilates' local forms of life, and produces new types of relations with humans beings. We see fields of wheat and corn stretching forever as the bounty of nature given to us with the helping hand of human ingenuity and technology. However, genetically modified life is by no means 'natural', if by nature we mean nature 'in itself' untouched by *techne*, but something entirely dependent on techniques of genetic manipulation owned and controlled by global corporations and institutions, producing new life relations in a massive evolutionary acceleration extending into the broader social, cultural and ecological environments.

Genetically modified seed is routinely engineered so that it cannot reproduce itself.[9] This means that farmers no longer set aside seeds from the previous crop to replant for the next, but obtain the latest genetically modified seed-type from the grain stores, thus guaranteeing uniformity and a healthy crop. Farmers become indebted to the grain stores and their connection to global corporations, working in synchrony with research institutions and state authorities to meet calculated yields, and, through their collective efforts, to reproduce the agricultural industry as a whole. This indebtedness is no longer confined to local conditions but stretches into the economic-technological articulation of the globalized state-capital nexus. Through this indebtedness, finite worlds disappear while the constant presence of a globalizing world of infinite interconnectivity is reproduced and maintained.[10] In this constant presencing, an illusion of natural bounty appears.

The globalizing world denatures things, replacing their finite diversity with infinite uniformity. Take a simple ear of wheat. The place that the ear of wheat takes up in the wheat field is no longer indebted to the local conditions of farming and managing, but to an abstract space of formal equivalence projected back onto the land to produce crops of consistent quality and yield. The ear of wheat thus has value but no meaning. In Heidegger's terms, the wheat is no longer experienced as something with a special connection to the earth but becomes 'standing reserve' in globalizing *Ge-stell* (technological enframing). The danger here is that the human being subject to the *Ge-stell* sees only a boosted natural bounty and becomes blind to its indebtedness to the *techne* that brings it about. The human being is thus blocked from seeing otherwise. Threats to the crops and the environment are countered by applying the same *techne* in the form of more technical facts. The *techne* itself – the way of seeing as a technical 'bringing forth' – remains hidden in the facts, thereby perpetuating the technical conditions that caused the problem in the first place, and disabling the 'other seeing' required to turn the technology around in seeking another way.

The challenge that this danger poses for critique is to expose the *techne* hidden in the facts such that it might be turned otherwise. To expose the *techne* requires a denaturing of a nature already renatured – a critical turning of the things of nature already entwined in a *techne* that produces them as natural things. This denaturing becomes a renaturing when nature 'as such' is grasped as an openness within the *techne* itself. The aim of critique should therefore be a double turn within technological environments, to give meaning back to things by showing how their value depends on a *techne* that orders and controls them, and blocks them from being the thing they already are.

Globalization is unjust in that it seeks to replace the meaning of things with abstract values; its injustice is derived from the fact that things are not able to simply *be*. Globalization mythifies things into what Marx calls phantasms: products of human labour disassociated from their material base and circulating as commodities that glitter as 'fantastic form[s]' (Marx 1976, p. 165). As phantasmic apparitions, commodities take on a peculiar grip on people's imagination, turning it upside down into an illusion that substitutes for real social relations. Globalization replaces social and material life with a false appearance (*Schein*) of the real carried by the phantasmic thing in its exchangeability with other things in infinite serialization. Through the exchange, this false appearance entwines itself back into the socially-materially real, which is shaped into an image of the exchange itself. The world, as a real, material base of social, cultural and personal relations, disappears into a globalizing network of infinite exchanges. Globalization is unjust not only because, as Marx argued, it denies those who labour to produce the commodities their rightful share, but also because it refuses to allow the world to be a world, by turning it into a site of infinite exchange.

However, world-forming is always already at work. In the irreducible remainders of sense that resist the globalizing of the whole into an infinite exchange of values, a just world is already forming. World-forming *renatures* the denatured world already being destroyed by globalization, giving back its meaning and right to be. Nancy writes:

> [T]o create the world means: immediately, without delay, reopening each possible struggle for a world, that is, what must form the contrary of a global injustice against the background of general equivalence. But this means to conduct this struggle precisely in the name of the fact that this *world* is coming out of nothing, that there is nothing before it and that it is without models, without principle, and without given end, and that it is precisely *what* forms the justice and the meaning of the world.
>
> (Nancy 2007, pp. 54–55)

185

To create a just world means creating it from the finite beginnings of localized encounters from the 'nothing' of the reserve held back in readiness for the 'other beginning'. It means seeing 'otherwise', against the false appearances of the commodity form and the myth of origins that circulates through it in which technology withdraws in order to present the world as a technical fact. It means renaturing the world from the ground up, from the merest encounters with things in demythified exposure.

Renaturing is not a return to an original natural plenitude, nor is it a retreat into a pre-technological world. Rather, it involves keeping the possibility of world-forming open in a perpetual struggle against the tendency of globalization to fold everything into its own infinite activity. Renaturing reverses the denaturing power of globalization to take us away from finite places and into the spirals of ecotechnological exchange, and expands itself into the world that it creates as its own being-together with things. Renaturing gives back to the world its capacity to *be* a world and to partake in a finite being-together of people, places and things.

Finite renaturing enlivens the capacity of things to connect in world-forming according to their meaning, and not their value, restoring their dignity – their worthiness as 'free beings' – to connect with other things. By contracting back to the earth, finite renaturing dissolves exchange value into non-relational indifference, and opens up the possibility of another relation with nature. This nature to come is not a nature known in advance, already out there waiting to be restored to the human, but something possible in the relation itself; the missing term of the relation yet to be filled. The nature to come is not a *physis* (a material 'coming forth' already on its way), but a void in being itself, an emptiness that calls for a connection. Renaturing is this reconnecting of the missing part of the relation, offering the possibility that things might be combined according to a renewed sense of justice: the justice of a non-exploitative sharing of things.

The dignity of the thing

In commenting on the science of biotechnology, the transgenic bio artist Eduardo Kac has said: 'The extreme difficulty in dealing with very complex biological interactions leads to the simplified treatment of life processes as quantified data that exhibit statistical patterns. In turn, this can lead to an objectification of life and a disregard for the subjects and their rights' (Kac 2007, p. 1). Things lose their complex relations with other things and thus their 'right' to be things, when objectified by biotechnology into a *techne* that controls, values and orders them as data and patterns of information. In confirming this point, Kac makes the following comment: 'If a private company can legally own the international rights to genetic sequences with which the reader was born, clearly this issue touches everyone on a profoundly personal level' (pp. 1–2). What is at stake here? By touching all of us 'on a profoundly personal level', the issue of genetic ownership is shifted from the rights of the subject, to the affect domain of the person.[11] What is at stake is not the subject's rights, but the consequences of an offence to the dignity of the person: to the person's capacity to be in possession of herself; to 'stand on her feet' and not be indebted to another.[12] The ethics of bio art to which Kac alludes are thus concerned not so much with subjective rights, but with protecting the 'personhood' or dignity of things threatened by the objectifying processes of biotechnology. In what follows in this section, I will pursue the idea of dignity as 'standing on one's feet', as it relates to bio art.

In a 2011 interview at the gallery of Modern Art in Brisbane, bio artist Ionat Zurr spoke of her response to seeing a media image of a mouse with a human 'ear on its back'.[13] Amazed and 'ethically challeng[ed]' by what she saw as 'a treatment of life as a sculptured art form', she set out in collaboration with Oron Catts to make artworks out of living tissue by employing the techniques of tissue engineering.[14] Here is how she describes her motivations and attitude to her art:

As artists, [we are concerned with] what is happening to life at the moment. We must be there and see what's happening, not just see, but contribute and subvert to what is happening in the land.

(21st Century Blog)

In their artworks Catts and Zurr 'contribute [to] and subvert' the practices of biotechnology by doing the very thing they critique. That is, they engage in a transitive art practice: a *praxis* that does what it says. It carries the practice of biotechnology into its own practice. They describe how their creation of 'semi-living art' – synthesized material whose life is entirely dependent on a laboratory environment and computer generated feedback – allows them to engage in 'a deeper exploration of the ethical and epistemological issues and concerns about the life-science industry in general' (Catts & Zurr 2007, p. 233).[15] For instance, in their creative endeavours they attempt to expose the practice of consumption as a form of 'ultimate exploitation' by humans of non-human things:

Consumption is also an issue our modern society is trying to conceal, and one we are attempting to expose. This discussion will raise issues in regard to society's hypocrisies toward living systems (let alone semi-living systems) and to the 'other' in general. Our semi-livings are 'evocative objects' that raise emotional and intellectual reactions and suggest alternative scenarios for a future.

(p. 233)

By collaborating with the life-science industry, their artwork – semi-living biotechnological products – become 'evocative objects' that also subverts it, suggesting the possibility of another beginning ('alternative scenarios for the future'). Their artwork bears witness to 'what is happening' with biotechnologically engineered life by catching the *techne* of biotechnology in its own act (for bearing witness see Chapter 8). The artwork exposes the *techne* to its limits, and presents those who encounter it with their own involvement in the 'hypocrisies' of western consumption. In doing this, their artwork plays with biotechnology through an ironized mimicry.[16] In order to 'get' the artwork and thus see it for the critique that it is, one must not mistake it for a work of biotechnology, but read the signal emitted by the artwork as 'this is play' (Bateson 1972, p. 179). The artwork ironizes its relation with biotechnology by saying it otherwise.

Another term for this kind of playful mimicry is parody. In parodying biotechnology, the artwork presumes an unstated norm.[17] To 'get' the parody an audience member must tacitly agree that something is being parodied, thereby appealing to an unstated norm by which to judge the work as parody and not the thing being parodied. For instance, Catts and Zurr describe how their art project entitled *Disembodied Cuisine* (see Figure 3) involving the synthesizing

Figure 3.

of living tissue over animal skeletal muscle as 'steak' for human consumption, 'deals with one of the most common zones of interaction between humans and other living systems, and probes the apparent uneasiness people feel when someone "messes" with their food' (Catts & Zurr 2007, p. 242). The artwork exposes an unstated norm about food consumption as a limit expressed in the 'uneasiness' felt by audience members' encounter with it, obliging them to confront their own hypocrisy with respect to the consumption of food.[18]

How might this exposure of an unstated norm apply to Zurr's own 'amazed' response to the ear mouse? Let me conjecture: the norm is that it is simply wrong to have a mouse with a human ear on its back.[19] The norm remains unstated as the limit of what is or is not acceptable to an audience.[20] This limit is reached when someone responds personally to something that she may feel uneasy about or offended by, and implies, in this case, that the mouse lacks something: a certain 'naturalness' that it would otherwise have without the ear grafted onto its back. This sense of naturalness does not come from any appeal to the 'laws of nature' or 'natural selection'; rather it comes from a sense that the integrity of the mouse as a living thing – the mouse's 'right' to be a mouse – has been violated by grafting a human ear onto its back. What is unnatural is not so much the mouse's hybrid physical make up, but its lack of dignity, its inability to 'stand on its feet' as a mouse. This would mean that natural life is not 'in' the mouse but part of the human-mouse relation itself.

What is it about humans that makes them feel uneasy or offended when presented with non-human life-forms manipulated into hybrid 'unnatural' things? It suggests that humans have something about them that should not be violated in this way: an integrity and freedom-to-be that they also want non-human beings to have as well. In Eduardo Kac's discussion of the birth of his transgenic creation Alba, the green fluorescent rabbit, he says: 'Alba was born like you and I were born, with an intrinsic justification that is irreducible to external factors, in other words with nothing but her life to justify itself' (qtd. in Osthoff 2009, p. 2).[21] Like any form of bio life created by artists, Alba has the same right to be, as we grant to ourselves. She, like us, has the right to stand on her own feet: she has a right to dignity.

The integrity of the thing is not related to its body, but to the fact that it is a thing. To be a thing it must be free to be that thing, and not forced into it.[22] If it were forced, then it would no longer be a thing but an object of power. The integrity of the thing cannot be reduced to a subject/object relation; rather it resists this relation in being-with the thing, together, in 'free being'. Zurr notes that the ethical aspects of her and Catts's artwork concern 'an empathy towards something that is alive [...] the liveliness that we all share with the living world around us' (21st Century Blog). This sharing is a being-with that has its own responsibility, its own integrity. It is, I suggest, a responsibility that can only be had in terms of a relation to the close proximity of things in 'touching distance'. For instance, Zurr describes the paradox of having to manipulate living cells without killing them. Once touched, the cells will die because they lack an immune system. In her and Catts's creative practice, she must touch/ must not touch her creations, triggering an ethical dilemma presented ritualistically in the 'life' of the artwork itself, as an enactment of the life/death cycle of the cells.[23] Thus, Catts and Zurr's practice of creative biotechnology requires respect for each cell and its 'right' to live, with the full expectation that, like all living things, the cell is destined to die as part of the living event that the artwork is. Despite its minuteness, the cell is respected for its own dignity, its right to 'stand on its own feet'. The 'Tissue Culture and Art Project' initiated by Catts and Zurr is informed by an ethics concerning the life and death of the living tissue created, predicated on respect for the single cell: its integrity and 'freedom' to live on and eventually die like all living things.

It is clear from these considerations, that Catts and Zurr's artworks resist the anthropocentric projection of will that forces things into objectification in the name of ecotechnological productivity. Rather, they concern a shared sense of 'free possibility' between the creator-artist and the created thing – a caring sensitivity that applies across their entire artistic project. The thing created is not an object of scientific experimentation, but a work of art that rescues the created thing from ecotechnological productivity and management, returning it to a life localized in the singular event of the artwork itself. The artwork mimics and subverts the forcing of living cells into altered forms by turning the technology against itself, releasing the thing created into a shared living environment animated by a sense of the creator's responsibility to it. The artwork gives back to the thing its dignity in a sharing of 'free being' with its human creator, resistive to the biotechnology that produced it.

In my consideration of Catts and Zurr's ethical approach to their bio art works, I have shown their art practice to be informed by a care for their living creations, characterized by an ironizing of the stance taken by the artwork to the technology that produces it; their artworks make the technology speak otherwise. By ironizing their stance, they maintain a critical distance from biotechnology, subverting it from within. Catts and Zurr's art practice is also an example of renaturing denatured nature – a returning of the things of nature to localized connectivities in resistance to the globalizing imperatives of modern technology. This is a step towards developing a nature philosophy that works both with and against technology, restoring a sense of justice to the things of nature.

The work of Catts and Zurr suggests that some forms of bio art may be able to provide a new kind of human-nature relation resistive to ecotechnology while working within it – a human-nature relation capable of restoring the dignity of things. However a question remains with regard to bio art in general. Can bio art escape the technology it attempts to subvert, or does it remain bound up in it? A common criticism of bio art is that it is easily recuperated into mainstream new life technologies, becoming a creative extension of the biotechnological project itself (Michaud 2007). This suggests that there are limits to bio art that need to be addressed.

The limits of bio art

Eduardo Kac has made it clear that he understands bio art in terms of the autonomy of art and its freedom of self-expression.[24] In a recent interview Kac makes the following comments on his own transgenic art practice: 'Transgenic art [as a form of bio art] is not here to 'comment' on science or any other field. Commentary is best carried out by pedagogy or academic exegesis. Transgenic Art exists, first and foremost, as a new creative realm in itself' (Kac in Osthoff 2009, p. 4). Transgenic art is entirely autonomous, creating its own aesthetic world independent of the world of commentary and debate. It has a responsibility to itself to be art, and not something else. However, further into the interview Kac suggests, in contradiction to his previous statement, that his transgenic art has another responsibility, this time in the ethical field. It 'sparks a new ethical dimension of art [...] prompting society to ask how it will prepare itself to welcome new citizens who will be, themselves, clones and transgenics' (pp. 4–5). This concern for the ethical responsibility of his artwork is also evident in Kac's introduction to the collection of essays on bio art entitled *Signs of Life: Bio Art and Beyond*:

> The writers and artists whose work forms this anthology [see their work as] engaged in shaping discourse and public policy, and in stimulating wide-ranging debate. The writers and artists in this collection also reveal an acute awareness of the ethical questions associated with biotechnology.
>
> (Kac 2007, p. 12)

These contradictory statements suggest that there may be a tension in bio art between the singularity of the artwork (its aesthetic integrity) and its openness to public debate (its ethical comportment). On one hand, bio art is responsible only to itself as art, yet on the other, it carries an ethical responsibility to open up debate in public forums to engage in fundamental questioning about life and to 'prepare' for the biotechnological age to come.[25] How does bio art reconcile these two imperatives? To answer this question we need to consider how Kac understands his work in relation to science.

Kac makes a strong distinction between art and science (*One on One*, Al Jazeera, 2008). In his own words, science requires the reproducibility of its experiments for verification within a community of experts, whereas art requires that the artwork should always remain singular. In other words, the artwork exists to resist reproducibility. Thus, the art work is itself a fundamental questioning of the technology – a living resistivity embedded in the technology itself. Here we are moving towards an immanent critique of technology, but does it go far enough?

For Kac, bio art is an attempt to turn myth into singular life: 'to move from myth to medium, from legend to life' (*One on One*, Al Jazeera, 2008). Kac understands myth as an imagining of 'new beings, different beings' found in the stories and legends of all societies and cultures. By creating such beings in his bio art, he seeks to subvert biotechnology from within. It is clear from these statements that Kac's idea of myth is poetic, but it is not sufficiently grounded in the work of myth as ontologically founding. That is, he imagines different 'stories and legends' concerning mythical beings in all cultures as possible new life-forms, but has an insufficient grasp of the work of the prevailing myth in his own culture – the myth of the nature-machine – to ground the 'being' of the artist in his or her own creations. Without engaging with the limits of this myth in enabling the possibility of his own artwork, Kac risks simply reproducing the myth in a new guise, thereby weakening his critical stance towards the technology he seeks to subvert.

In what way is myth ontologically founding? In *The Philosophy of Art*, Schelling argues that myth founds human existence in nature's free being, exemplified in the Greek beginning (Schelling 1989, p. 39 ff.). Myths are retrospective projections of reason to justify human existence to itself in terms of its free being with nature. As I have already shown in Chapter 6, myth closes human existence in mythic self-founding, blocking free possibility and the age to come. To unblock the current age from closing on its own mythic self-founding, Schelling calls for the creation of new myths to begin a new age where human being might partake of nature's free being in a more providential way. Schelling's demiurgic call for new myths announces the new age by repeating the founding gesture of the Greek beginning. However, in doing this, he risks also repeating the current myth in a new guise, thereby occluding the openness into absolute possibility his critique has uncovered. To retain this openness and hence the possibility of an absolute beginning, critique must not fall back in myth, but instead should engage in a demythification of the current myth by subverting it from within and displacing it at the same time. This can be done through allegory. By allegorizing the myth, its historical ground is exposed as the barely active remains of a forgotten event upon which the myth rests but which remains concealed in the myth's closure in its own self-founding (its 'tautegorical' sense of self-creation). From the remnants of these forgotten grounds a new life can begin.

Yves Michaud has warned of the dangers of bio artists acting in the role of the prophetic demiurge. By creating nature in terms of a prophesized new age of nature, the demiurge risks 'mak[ing] the scientist a wondermaker, largely immunized against what effectively determines most of the scientific research today – the competition between research teams and the profit of investors' (Michaud 2007, p. 393). In his prophesizing about the future of biotechnology and in the creation of transgenic life-forms, Kac risks eliding the indebtedness of bio art to its host technology, thereby reproducing the same myth all over again – the myth of the nature-machine in an age of ecotechnological life production. As Paul Carter has argued, 'to replace one discursive representation with another is to perpetuate a contest of masks' (Carter 2004, p. 23). Kac risks replacing one mythic mask with another in the guise of something entirely new, while leaving the *techne* through which we see ourselves and live out our lives undisturbed.

By mimicking the techniques of the bio sciences, bio artwork reproduces bio life in the specificity of a singular artwork. The artwork takes a stand; it signals its difference from the host technology by being the artwork that it is. In doing this, the artwork allegorizes the mythic enactment of nature as nature-machine, enabling it to turn otherwise. To do this is not to create new forms of life in the name of biotechnology as Kac suggests, but to parody such forms in terms of a one-off production that refuses the imperative of reproducibility. Kac's work thus requires a further turn to make it stand against itself, in order to make it touch the earth.

Kac's real aim in his artwork is to reclaim artistic freedom from the sciences by inhabiting it from within to produce singular artworks that resist reproducibility.[26] This 'reclamation of the artistic freedom of the demiurge tradition' (Michaud, p. 393) leads to a renewed sense of responsibility to the living thing produced: 'when you bring a life form in the world, you cannot treat that life form as a car, a vase or a bottle. That being is alive and immediately demands our responsibility in the sense of our response, being responsible for that being' (*One on One*, Al Jazeera, 2008). To make this claim, Kac must first accept the modernist principle of the autonomy of art, and its motivation to create new things. But in doing this, Kac's work remains bound to the technology that it inhabits and risks being recuperated into the mainstream project of progressivist science.[27] Instead I suggest we can turn to discarded things as a means of making the technology turn again, thereby slipping through the technology, releasing the thing to be otherwise (see the following section).

The dissolving of the boundaries between bio art and the technology it employs disables the critical stance and blends the artwork into mainstream biotechnological work. As Louis Bec has argued with regard to Kac's transgenic bio art, '[a]pparently nothing distinguishes a transgenetic "construct" from a living organism generated by natural procreation' (Bec 2007, p. 86). Here, bio art is taken to be an extension of the experimental sciences, seeking to discover a 'hidden dimension' (p. 86) of mutant gene production in the quest for knowledge of the genetic code. There is no sense that the work undertaken in revealing this 'hidden dimension' is anything other than a continuation of the science by other means. The work that the artwork does – the singular stance it takes with respect to what it copies – is elided by a stronger claim that the artwork is in fact part of the experimentalism of the scientific endeavour and hence under the sway of the nature-machine myth. Under these circumstances, bio art withdraws from poetizing, as it has no awareness of the distinction that needs to be made between the stance it takes and the content to which it bears witness. On these terms, bio art remains bound to the *techne* of biotechnology without interrupting or turning it otherwise.

Retroactive allegory

In this section I propose the concept of retroactive allegory to make a double turn within technological environments, which, I argue, is necessary to restore the dignity of things in their technological 'otherness'. A retroactive allegory is an allegory enacted 'after the event'. Unlike the bio art examined in the previous two sections that acts within the event it inhabits, a retroactive allegory allegorizes the event after it has already taken place, but as if it were about to happen for the first time. A retroactive allegory works aoristically as 'an anterior future of which death is the stake' (Barthes 1993, p. 96). In *Camera Lucida* Roland Barthes shows how the aoristic tense operates in the viewing of old photographs, where people who will soon be dead are seen alive, as if denying their own deaths.[28] The affect produced is to make life appear to resist its own death as lifedeath. A retroactive allegory of technology makes the technology live again from the lifedeath of its ruined beginnings as a possibility that will have already happened *but not yet*, and hence exposed by the allegory as other.

In this section I examine the artwork of Patricia Piccinini as a retroactive allegorizing of biotechnology exposed to deathly obsolescence. Piccinini's artwork counters bio art by returning the technology to its ruined grounds, thereby turning it otherwise.

If bio art looks forward into a new biotechnological future, the work of Patricia Piccinini looks backward to the abject things left behind in the wake of modern progress. Recalling Schelling's love of materiality (Schelling 2000, p. 57, see Chapter 3), she finds a lost love in encounters with these forgotten and discarded things. Her fabulous creations are not chimeras warning us not to 'mess with nature', but *faux* creatures: evolutionary side tracks and genetic mutant 'errors', 'forever dependent on the care of [their] creators and the provision of an artificial environment' (Millner 2001), and 'whose evolutionary and ecological habitats are the installation, the mall, the website, and the lab' (Haraway 2007). These 'abject' creatures allegorize our own technologically dependent lives by reminding us of this dependency and by turning us otherwise with them, calling for our response.[29]

Piccinini's artwork *Nectar* consists of a pink organic blob sitting on top of an old refrigerator (see Figure 4).[30] Made of silicone and fibreglass, the blob is covered in patches of wispy human hair and features two orifices. A thick brown liquid 'nectar' pours out of one of the orifices, piling up beside the blob. The refrigerator serves a double purpose: it acts as a plinth, holding the blob aloft, as well as acting as the blob's 'home' – the place where it belongs. The artist describes *Nectar* in the following terms:

This work represents the idea of the endless, productive capacity of the organic world. A beautiful honey-like nectar pours uncontrollably from one of the small amorphous organisms that I am so fond of. The abundance of this viscous liquid is both amazing and also disturbing. Where is it coming from? Is it safe? Will it ever stop? Is it delicious? Would we risk a taste? It sits on top an old refrigerator, which is an object that is designed to contain, and to hold things in stasis, stopping the natural process of decay. However, the new object sits on top of the fridge, and appears certain to overwhelm the ageing whitegood with its unstoppable abundance. In many ways, this small work encapsulates the combination of anxiety and wonder that motivates many of my figurative sculptures.

(Piccinini 2013)

Here, the artist listens to the artwork as it poses questions to her about the nectar pouring out of it: 'Where is it coming from? Is it safe? Will it ever stop? Is it delicious? Would we risk a taste?'. In posing these questions, the artwork opens the artist out to possibilities that are enticing yet dangerous, suggesting that she might be risking something in the encounter. What is being risked?

Nectar employs conventional installation art material to mimic biotechnology. As a reminder of transgenically engineered life-forms, the blob has no autonomy; to survive, it should be inside the refrigerator where the controlled environment provides safety and the conditions of life. But there it is, on top of the refrigerator, exposed to the dangers of heat, humidity and bacterial attack. In Benjamin's terms, the ageing refrigerator acts as a

Figure 4.

memento mori or figure of death (see Chapter 9). It reminds us that the blob exists in the lifedeath cycle of biotechnological production in the same way that technology in general is subject to obsolescence and decay. The silicone and fibreglass fabrication of the blob suggests a material inertness entirely at odds with the state of the art transgenic and living tissue creations of bio art. However, in this obsolescence a new life begins; the 'abundance of […] viscous liquid' threatens to 'overwhelm' the technology supporting it.

 Nectar enacts an allegorical saying of biotechnology such that a new life begins otherwise from its ruined remains. Unlike the saying of the bio artists' work that continues to be indebted to the technology it inhabits, *Nectar* exposes the technology to the lifedeath of obsolescence, freeing up the human relation so that it can begin again on the uncertain ground of technological 'ruinance' where it discovers things it did not see before; things now seen otherwise – other than as objects of technological control.[31] The myth of the nature-machine embodied in the power of biotechnology to reproduce itself as *autopoietic* life is undone by the refusal of the blob to be anything other than its abject self, placing it at risk of not being. In this 'not being' a possibility appears – a *poietic* line of flight yet to be followed.

Nectar stands in an ambiguous relation to the technology that it mimics. The blob falls back into the technological obsolescence of the ageing refrigerator that simultaneously lifts it back up again as a thing to be viewed, appreciated and loved. The artwork turns back to a 'low tech.' phase where it begins again but otherwise, producing a hardly recognizable life with a strange and delicious bounty. The artwork makes the blob live again retroactively, as if it were living for the first time. The effect is to produce a strange affinity to something not fully formed and recognizable, yet providentially giving as 'the endless, productive capacity of the organic world'. The artist's comments on *Nectar* are telling: she lavishes praise and loving attention on the blob and its delicious nectar as 'both amazing and also disturbing'. As a retroactively produced 'amorphous organism', the blob becomes an enigmatic Thing: a figure of possibility opened otherwise in the in-between of new and old technology (see Chapter 6 for further discussion of the Thing). In being exposed and vulnerable, the blob attracts a special caring attention from the artist, which restores it to the dignity of a Loved Thing.[32]

The blob-Thing can be understood in terms of what Heidegger calls the abandonment of being. In his book *Heidegger Amongst the Sculptors*, Andrew Mitchell discusses Heidegger's concept of abandonment in relation to the work of the early twentieth-century German sculptor Ernst Barlach, whose sculptures take the form of incomplete figures 'harboring a constitutive insufficiency that surrenders them wholly to the world' (Mitchell 2010, p. 22). Abandoned beings are 'already opened and spilled into the world' (Mitchell 2010, p. 22). We can relate this idea of abandoned being as something that spills into the world to Piccinini's blob. In its exposure on top of the refrigerator, the abandoned blob oozes nectar that spills into the world as an offering: something given without demand for return. The delicious nectar spilling out of the blob's orifice is an 'abundance' that exceeds biotechnological life, offering the possibility of life lived otherwise in an uncertain providence opening to an absolute outside. Its ceaseless flow, which may or may not stop at any moment, poses questions to the responding human concerning what it calls for and what it enables – 'Where is it coming from? Is it safe? Will it ever stop? Is it delicious? Would we risk a taste?' – and draws her into an openness without destination or purpose. The retroaction of the artwork draws the artist into a relation with the blob-as-other such that the relation itself is reconfigured in a place where 'meaning collapses' (Kristeva 1982, p. 2), yet strangely enabled by what is discovered there as the possibility of life to come.

Unlike the creations of bio art that reproduce the *techne* of biotechnology as parodic play but remain within the *techne* itself, Piccinini's art creations allegorize the technology such that it is made to begin again but in another way. To do this, her artworks take a double turn. First turn: the artwork denatures the already renatured thing. To do this requires that the *techne* that renatures the thing be turned against itself by doing the very same thing. The thing is made to stand against itself, triggering an *allo* or otherwise saying. But in doing this the thing has yet to touch the earth. It is yet to be renatured from its derenatured state. Second turn: the first turn must also turn under itself to speak through the *techne* in its ruined possibilities. In doing this the thing once again touches the earth as the void of another beginning. It begins again but in another way. The double turn renatures the derenatured thing such that it is opened into possibilities leading nowhere, remaining on the uncertain ground of a beginning otherwise.

Rederenatured things such as we encounter in Piccinini's *Nectar* are retroactive allegories; they trigger an openness, a possibility out of the barely visible ruins of past technologies, resisting and shining through contemporary technological enframing.

Art as renaturing

Renaturing is not returning nature to its natural form, but a turning within technology so that it opens against itself, enabling another nature to take shape. This other nature is a possibility carried in the disjunctive relation between technology's infinite drive to reproduce itself and resistive things inhabiting it. Encountered as such, things refuse *techne* and affirm themselves as other. By thinking with these things in their refusal, we open the technology otherwise, exposing a space in-between infinite reproducibility and finite singularity in which we see a prefiguring image that 'flits past' (Benjamin 1999, p. 695) and may never be seen again. By thinking with resistive things in their stance against technology, we connect with prefiguring otherness, initiating a *poietic* line of flight that keeps us in open possibility.

As transitive poetics, art carries *poiesis* such that its own saying is itself an act of *poietic* openness. By standing within but against technology, art keeps openness open, causing technology to turn against itself. In this way, technology enables renaturing but otherwise, by turning against itself through the work that the artwork does in enacting *poietic* openness. Denatured nature is renatured through the artwork when it keeps itself open to *poiesis*. In doing this the artwork becomes earthed in another beginning.

Conclusion: Towards Ecopoetics

Crossing over

In his essay 'What is Enlightenment', Michel Foucault argues we should continue the project of the Enlightenment through a 'permanent critique of ourselves' (Foucault 1997, p. 313). By this Foucault does not mean engaging in an individualist ethics of personal freedom, but an 'exercise of freedom' (p. 311) that risks what human being is in the present age by daring to think otherwise: 'to imagine [the present] otherwise than it is, and to transform it not by destroying it but by grasping it in what it is' (p. 311). The aim of this critical *praxis* is not to enhance individual human freedom but to enable 'the growth of capabilities [by disconnecting them] from the intensification of power relations' (p. 317). Through the exercise of freedom, capabilities can be unblocked from the power relations (*techne*) in which they are intensified, and released into articulations yet to form.[1] He sums up this idea as follows: 'The point, in brief, is to transform the critique conducted in the form of necessary limitation into a practical critique that takes the form of a possible crossing over' (p. 315). Foucault defines this possible crossing over as the 'undefined work of freedom' (p. 316); the work where 'we are always in the position of beginning again' (p. 317).

Foucault's proposal of critique as a 'possible crossing over' resonates with the factical-ontological critique proposed in this book. As an exercise of freedom, critique enables a crossing over by carrying what it critiques. Critique does not destroy what it critiques in a negating *Aufhebung* but 'grasp[s] it in what it is' by carrying it otherwise as a possibility not yet realized. Foucault's proposal for an ontological critique in free being reawakens the post-Kantian problem of the abyss of reason raised in Kant's critique with which I began the second part of this book. It indicates the necessity to attend to the 'undefined work of freedom' as a beginning of possibility. What is this undefined work of freedom? Foucault provides us with a clue: modernity 'does not "liberate man in his own being"; it compels him to face the task of producing himself' (p. 312). The undefined work of freedom concerns the responsibility of the human to produce itself in free possibility by responding to the challenge to *be* in its 'capabilities' (powers), blocked by the *techne* of the current age. By resisting the claim of *techne*, the human affirms free being with otherness, in what Schelling calls the third potency or the power to begin (Schelling 2000, p. 19). The work of critique is to initiate beginnings by unblocking human being from its restrictions in current *techne*, thereby releasing a capacity to be free with otherness in open possibility, carrying this relation otherwise.

My aim in this book has been to initiate a critique of the present human-nature relation by 'grasping it in what it is' in order to carry it otherwise. Foucault calls this critique positive (p. 315). Positive critique does not destroy nature by reflecting back into the human, but carries nature with it, in the beginning it enacts.

Fashioning a world

To grasp nature 'as such' in its conditions of possibility is fundamentally an ethical task. In his essay 'The Mythological Being of Reflection – an Essay on Hegel, Schelling and the Contingency of Necessity', Markus Gabriel defines this ethical task as a decision: 'the *decision* to grasp the constitutive elusiveness of the conditions of possibility of (epistemo- and onto-logical) determinacy and to refer to it in terms of the mythology of a domain of all domains is ethical' (Gabriel 2009, p. 75). In terms of this book, the decision to situate critique right at the human-nature relation in order to grasp its elusive 'conditions of possibility' is an ethical one, seeking the right way or right action, given the requirement of positing what is good. The decision is not simply a resistive reflex or creative gesture, but a *praxis* that makes what it is by what it does. Its good is in what it does, grounded in the proximity of what is called for.

If we live in an 'age of the world picture' as Heidegger argues (Heidegger 1977, p. 129), then it is up to us to decide what world picture we want to make happen and inhabit.[2] However, this new world picture cannot be actualized by proposing alternatives to the current one. To do this is to mythify the world in an exchange of world pictures. The world becomes, in Gabriel's terms, a 'mythology of a domain of all domains'. A mythified world repeats the *techne* of the current age and closes off possibility. A new world picture comes about not through extension and enhancement of the technological ordering of the current one, but by thinking it otherwise in our finite being-with resistive otherness as something technologically produced. This 'doing' is fashioning a world: '*we* do not fashion but rather that we *are* our hypotheses: that is to say, our *lives* express themselves in the way we objectify the unconditioned, in and as the world we inhabit' (Gabriel 2009, p. 75). We do not fashion ourselves as autonomous free beings; rather, a world is already being fashioned 'in the way we objectify the unconditioned' in our being-with otherness as free possibility. We do not choose the world picture by which we live; rather, in being with things in their resistive openness, we decide to be, affirming our free being otherwise. By deciding to be in this sense of resistive affirmation, we demythify the world in its current mythological presentation and partake of an emergent event of world fashioning. The ethical task is not one of choosing a world picture by which to live, but of ensuring the possibility that a world can *be* in demythified openness, by thinking right at the human-nature relation as unconditioned possibility. I have called this task keeping the Open open.

Ecopoetics

To fashion a human-nature relation is to produce the self as being with nature in free possibility. This is fundamentally a poetic task. Rather than reflecting back into subjective states or affects, poetics seeks to connect with otherness in what it does. Ecopoetics thus begins on the uncertain ground of open connectivity. It risks 'what is' in the possibility that something might be otherwise.

The ethical task of ecopoetics is to defend the connectedness of things – their right to *be* things together with other things in 'free possibility'. But insofar as we only encounter things in their resistance to *techne*, then the task becomes one of releasing things from *techne*, enabling them to connect with other things in open connectivity. A name for this releasing is art.

Being enabled in open connectivity is to stand at the place of the emergent event, already fashioning a world by connecting with otherness. In this way, the world comes into being through the flourishing of localized connections, where things find their place together with other things in finite connectedness. Emergent world fashioning returns the globalizing of the world to the earth. It relocates connectedness to earthly places resistive to globalizing abstraction. From these places things begin otherwise in *poietic* lines of flight, taking the human relation with them. The task of ecopoetics is to follow these lines of flight, where they begin in the finite connectedness of things as they partake of world-forming.

Restoring critique

To follow the *poietic* lines of flight we need to restore our capacity to think with nature, not against it. Critique holds the key to this restoration. In its positive mode, critique allows us to carry the human-nature relation into open possibility. But it must be kept there in the open to retain the power of critique. Critique is thus a never ending task to keep the Open open; to unblock the closure of the same. Foucault's call for a 'permanent critique of ourselves' continues the Enlightenment project of emancipating the human from the determinations of nature and unreason, but in the light shining through the post-Kantian abyss of reason that throws the self onto uncertain contingent ground. From this place, critique begins again …

References

21st Century Blog: Art in the First Decade 2011, *Talking About Contemporary Art,* online video, viewed 19 October 2012, <http://21cblog.com/category/interviews>.

Agamben, G. 1991, *Language and Death: The Place of Negativity,* trans. K. E. Pinkus with M. Hardt, University of Minnesota Press, Minneapolis.

Alliez, E. 1996, *Capital Times: Tales from the Conquest of Time*, trans. G. V. D. Abbeele, University of Minnesota Press, Minneapolis.

Alliez, E. & Feher, M. 1987, 'The Luster of Capital', *Zone* 1/2, pp. 314–59.

Anderson, A. 1997, *Media, Culture and the Environment*, UCL Press, London.

Andrieu, B. 2007, 'Embodying the Chimera: Biotechnology and Subjectivity', in E. Kac (ed.), *Signs of Life: Bio Art and Beyond*, The MIT Press, Cambridge, Mass.

Arendt, H. 1978, *The Life of the Mind: Two/Willing*, Harcourt, San Diego.

Arendt, H. 1958, *The Human Condition*, The University of Chicago Press, Chicago.

Aristotle 1941, *The Basic Works of Aristotle*, R. McKeon (ed.), Random House, New York.

Armstrong, P. 2009, *Reticulations: Jean-Luc Nancy and the Networks of the Political*, University of Minnesota Press, Minneapolis.

Auerbach, E. 2003, *Mimesis: The Representation of Reality in Western Literature*, fifteenth anniversary edition. trans. WR Trask, Princeton University Press, Princeton.

Badiou, A. 1999, *Manifesto for Philosophy* trans. N. Madarasz, State University of New York Press, Albany.

Badiou, A. 2005, *Infinite Thought: Truth and the Return to Philosophy*, trans. O. Feltham & J. Clemins, Continuum, London.

Badiou, A. 2005a, *Being and Event*, trans. O. Feltham, Continuum, London.

Bandari, N. 2012 'Indian Artist Samant Auctions Works to Raise Funds for Farmer Families' *India Voice*, 10 September, viewed 25 October, 2012, <http://www.india-voice.com/joomla/index,php?option=com_content&task=view&id=350&Itemid=39>.

Barnes, J. (ed.) 2001, *Early Greek Philosophy*, 2nd edn, Penguin, London.

Barthes, R. 1973, *Mythologies,* trans. A. Lavers, Paladin, London.

Barthes, R. 1977, 'The Third Meaning', *Image, Music, Text*, trans. S. Heath, Fontana, London, pp. 52–68.

Barthes, R. 1993, *Camera Lucida*, trans. R. Howard, Vintage, London.

Bate, J. 2000, *The Song of the Earth*, Picador, London.

Bateson, G. 1972, *Steps to an Ecology of Mind*, Ballantine Books, New York.

Bec, L. 2007, 'Life Art', *Signs of Life: Bio Art and Beyond*, E. Kac, (ed.) The MIT Press, Cambridge, Mass.

Beiser, F. C. 2002, *German Idealism: The Struggle Against Subjectivism, 1781–1801*, Harvard University Press, Cambridge, Mass.

Beiser, F. 2003, *The Romantic Imperative: The Concept of Early German Romanticism*, Harvard University Press, Cambridge, Mass.

Beller, J. 2006, *The Cinematic Mode of Production: Attention Economy and the Society of the Spectacle*, Dartmouth College Press, Lebanon, NH.

Benjamin, W. 1968, *Illuminations: Essays and Reflections*, trans. H. Zohn, Schocken, New York.

Benjamin, W. 1996, *Walter Benjamin: Selected Writings* M. Bullock & M. W. Jennings (eds), vol. 1, 1913–1926, The Belknap Press of Harvard University Press, Cambridge, Mass.

Benjamin, W. 1998, *The Origin of German Tragic Drama*, trans. J. Osborne, Verso, London.

Benjamin, W. 1999, *Walter Benjamin: Selected Writings*, H. Eiland & M. W. Jennings (eds), vol. 2, part 2, 1931–1934 trans. R. Livingston & others, The Belknap Press of Harvard University Press, Cambridge, Mass.

Benjamin, W. 1999a, *The Arcades Project*, trans. H. Eiland & K. McLaughlin, The Belknap Press of Harvard University Press, Cambridge, Mass.

Benjamin, W. 2002, *Walter Benjamin: Selected Writings*, H. Eiland, & M. W. Jennings (eds), vol. 3, 1935–1938, trans. E. Jephcott, H. Eiland & others, The Belknap Press of Harvard University Press, Cambridge, Mass.

Benjamin, W. 2003, *Walter Benjamin: Selected Writings*, H. Eiland & M. W. Jennings (eds), vol. 4, 1938–1940 trans. E. Jephcott & others, The Belknap Press of Harvard University Press, Cambridge, Mass.

Benveniste, E. 1971, *Problems in General Linguistics*, trans. M. E. Meek, University of Florida Press, Coral Gables.

Berlin, I. 1958, *Two Concepts of Liberty*, Clarendon Press, Oxford.

Bersani, L. & Dutoit, U. 2004, *Forms of Being: Cinema, Aesthetics, Subjectivity*, BFI Publishing, London.

Bird, D. R. & Robin, L. 2004, 'The Ecological Humanities in Action: An Invitation', *Australian Humanities Review*, no. 31–32, viewed 20 May 2013, <http://www.australianhumanitiesreview.org/archive/Issue-April-2004/rose.html>.

Bois, Y-A. & Krauss, R. E. 1997, *Formless: A User's Guide* Zone, New York.

Bowie, A. 1993, *Schelling and Modern European Philosophy*, Routledge, London & New York.

Breckman, W. 1999, *Marx, the Young Hegelians, and the Origins of Radical Social Theory*, Cambridge University Press, Cambridge.

Breitenbach, A. 2011, 'Kant on Causal Knowledge: Causality, Mechanism and Reflective Judgment', in K. Allen & T. Stoneham (eds), *Causation and Modern Philosophy*, Routledge, New York.

Brockelman, T. 2008, *Žižek and Heidegger: The Question Concerning Techno-Capitalism*, Continuum, London.

Büchner, G. 1993, *Complete Plays, Lenz and Other Writings*, trans. J. Reddick, Penguin, London.

Carew, J. 2011, 'The *Grundlogik* of German Idealism: The Ambiguity of the Hegel-Schelling Relationship in Žižek', *International Journal of Žižek Studies*, vol. 5, no. 1.

Carter, E. & Kiely, A. 2008, 'Vintage Point', *Vogue Living Australia*, July/August 2008, pp. 160–69.

Carter, P. 2004, *Material Thinking: The Theory and Practice of Creative Research*, Melbourne University Press, Melbourne.

Catts, O. & Zurr, I. 2007, 'Semi-Living Art', in E. Kac (ed) *Signs of life: Bio Art and Beyond*, The MIT Press, Cambridge, Mass.

Catts, O. & Zurr, I. 2008, 'The Ethics of Experiential Engagement with the Manipulation of Life', in B. da Costa & K. Philip (eds) *Tactical Biopolitics: Art, Activism and Technoscience*, The MIT Press, Cambridge, Mass.

Catts, O. and Zurr, I. 2012 'Introduction', in O. Catts & I. Zurr (eds), *Partial Life*, Living Books About Life, viewed 26 November 2012, <http//www.livingbooksaboutlife.org/books/PartialLife>.

Celan, P. 2005, *Selections*, P. Joris (ed.), University of California Press, Berkeley.

Chakrabarty, D. 2009, 'The Climate of History: Four Theses', *Critical Inquiry*, vol. 35, no. 2, pp. 197–222.

Clark, D. L. 2007, 'Lost and Found in Translation: Romanticism and the Legacies of Jacques Derrida', *Studies in Romanticism*, vol. 46, no. 2, pp. 161–82.

Clark, J. P. 1989, 'Marx's Inorganic Body', *Environmental Ethics*, vol. 11, pp. 243–58.

Crichtley, S. 2002, 'Calm – On Terrence Malick's *The Thin Red Line*', *Film-Philosophy*, 6.38, viewed 12 December 2012, <http://www.film-philosophy.com/index.php/f-p/article/view/688>.

Crichtley, S. 2012, *The Faith of the Faithless: Experiments in Political Philosophy*, Verso, London.

Davis, B. 2007, *Heidegger and the Will: On the Way to Gelassenheit*, Northwest University Press, Evanston Ill.

De Man, P. 1984, *The Rhetoric of Romanticism*, Columbia University Press, New York.

Delanda, M. 2002, *Intensive Science and Virtual Philosophy*, London: Continuum.

Deleuze, G. 1986, *Cinema 1: The Movement Image*, trans. H. Tomlinson & B. Habberjam, The Athlone Press, London.

Deleuze, G. 1990, *Expressionism in Philosophy: Spinoza*, trans. M. Joughin, Zone, New York.

Deleuze, G. 1993, *The Fold: Leibniz and the Baroque*, trans. T. Conley, University of Minnesota Press, Minneapolis.

Deleuze, G. 1994, *Difference and Repetition*, trans. P. Patton, The Althone Press, London.

Deleuze, G. 1995, *Negotiations: 1972–1990,* trans. M. Joughin, Columbia University Press, New York.

Deleuze, G. 2003, *Francis Bacon: The Logic of Sensation*, trans. D. W. Smith, University of Minnesota Press, Minneapolis.

Deleuze, G. & Guattari, F. 1983, *Anti – Oedipus: Capitalism and Schizophrenia*, trans. R. Hurley, M. Seem & H. R. Lane, University of Minnesota Press, Minneapolis.

Deleuze, G. & Guattari, F. 1987, *A Thousand Plateaus: Capitalism and Schizophrenia*, trans. B. Massumi, University of Minnesota Press, Minneapolis.

Deleuze, G. & Guattari, F. 1994, *What is Philosophy?*, trans. H. Tomlinson and G. Burchell, Columbia, New York.

Derrida, J. 1978, *Writing and Difference*, trans. A. Bass, Routledge & Kegan Paul, London.

Derrida, J. 1987, *The Post Card: From Socrates to Freud and Beyond*, transl. A. Bass, The University of Chicago Press, Chicago.

Derrida, J. 1994, *Specters of Marx: The State of the Debt, the Work of Mourning, and the New International*, trans. P. Kamuf, Routledge, New York.

Derrida, J. 1995, *The Gift of Death*, trans. D. Wills, University of Chicago Press, Chicago.

Derrida, J. 1997, *Politics of Friendship*, trans. G. Collins, Verso, London.

Derrida, J. 2005, *Rogues: Two Essays on Freedom*, trans. P-A. Brault & M. Naas, Stanford University Press, Stanford.

Derrida, J. 2005a, *Sovereignties in Question: The Poetics of Paul Celan*, T. Dutoit & O. Pasanen (eds), Fordham University Press, New York.

Dibley, B. 2012, '"Nature is Us": The Anthropocene and Species-Being', *Transformations*, no. 21, viewed 1 August, 2012, <http://www.transformationsjournal.org/journal/index.shtml>.

Dreyfus, H. & Kelly, S. 2011, *All Things Shining: Reading the Western Classics to Find Meaning in a Secular Age*, Free Press, New York.

Eskin, M. 2000, *Ethics and Dialogue in the Works of Levinas, Bakhtin, Mandel'shtam and Celan*, Oxford University Press, Oxford.

Felstiner, J. 1995, *Paul Celan: Poet, Survivor, Jew*, Yale University Press, New Haven.

Fichte, J. G. & Schelling, F. W. J. 2012, *The Philosophical Rupture Between Fichte and Schelling: Selected Texts and Correspondence (1800–1802)*, trans. & eds M. G. Vater & D. W. Wood, State University of New York, Albany.

Foltz, B. 1995, *Inhabiting the Earth: Heidegger, Environmental Ethics, and the Metaphysics of Nature*, Humanities Press, New Jersey.

Foltz, B. 2004, 'Nature's Other Side: The Demise of Nature and the Phenomenology of Givenness', in B. Foltz & R. Frodeman (eds) *Rethinking Nature: Essays in Environmental Philosophy*, Indiana University Press, Bloomington, pp. 330–41.

Foster, J. B. & Burkett, P. 2000, 'The Dialectic of Organic/Inorganic Relations', *Organization & Environment*, vol. 13, no. 4, pp. 403–25.

Foucault, M. 1972, *The Archaeology of Knowledge*, trans. A. M. Sheridan Smith, Tavistock, London.

Foucault, M. 1977, 'Nietzsche, Genealogy, History', in *Language, Counter-Memory, Practice*, ed. D. F. Bouchard, trans. D. F. Bouchard & S. Simon, Cornell University Press, Ithica, pp. 139–64.

Foucault, M. 1978, *The History of Sexuality: An Introduction*, vol. 1, trans. R. Hurley, Vintage Books, New York.

Foucault, M. 1980. *Power/Knowledge. Selected Interviews and Other Writings 1972–1977,* trans. Colin Gordon et. al. Harvester, Brighton, Sussex.

Foucault, M. 1997, *Ethics: Subjectivity and Truth*, P. Rabinow (ed.), trans. R. Hurley et al., Penguin, London.

Frank, M. 2004, *The Philosophical Foundations of Early German Romanticism*, trans. E. Millán-Zaibert, State University of New York, Albany.

Gabriel, M. 2009, 'The Mythological Being of Reflection – An Essay on Hegel, Schelling, and the Contingency of Necessity' in M. Gabriel & S. Žižek *Mythology, Madness, and Laughter: Subjectivity in German Idealism*, Continuum, London, pp. 15–94.

Garrard, G. 2012, *Ecocriticism*, 2nd edn, Routledge, London.

Gasché, R. 1986, *The Tain of the Mirror: Derrida and the Philosophy of Reflection*, Harvard University Press, Cambridge, Mass.

Giblett, R. 2004, *Living with the Earth: Mastery to Mutuality*, Salt Publishing, Cambridge.

Glaab, K. & Engelkamp, S. 2011, 'Writing Norms: Constructivist Norm Research on Scholarly Practice', paper delivered at the Millennium Annual Conference, London, October 22–23.

Goudeli, K. 2002, *Challenges to German Idealism: Schelling, Fichte and Kant*, Palgrave Macmillan, Basingstoke.

Grant, I. H. 2006, *Philosophies of Nature after Schelling*, Continuum, London.

Griffin, J. 1980, *Homer on Life and Death*, Clarendon, Oxford.

Haraway, D. 2007, 'Speculative Fabulations for Technoculture's Generations: Taking Care of Unexpected Country', viewed 29 November 2012, <http://www.patriciapiccinini.net/essays/30/printing>.

Harries, K. 2009, *Art Matters: A Critical Commentary on Heidegger's 'The Origin of the Work of Art'*, Springer, Dordrecht.

Hegel, G. W. F. 1970, *Hegel's Philosophy of Nature*, trans. M. J. Petry, vol. I, George Allen & Unwin, London.

Hegel, G. W. F. 1970a, *Hegel's Philosophy of Nature*, trans. M. J. Petry, vol. II, George Allen & Unwin, London.

Hegel, G. W. F. 1977, *Phenomenology of Spirit*, trans. A. V. Miller, Oxford University Press, Oxford.

Hegel, G. W. F. 1991, *The Encyclopaedia Logic*, trans. T. F. Geraets, W. A. Suchting, & H. S. Harris, Hackett Publishing Company, Indianapolis.

Hegel, G. W. F. 1993, *Introductory Lectures on Aesthetics*, trans. B. Bosanquet, Penguin, London.

Heidegger, M. 1962, *Being and Time*, trans. J. Macquarrie & E. Robinson, Basil Blackwell, Oxford.

Heidegger, M. 1966, *Discourse on Thinking*, trans. J. M. Anderson & E. H. Freund, Harper, New York.

Heidegger, M. 1969, *Identity and Difference*, trans. J. Stambaugh, The University of Chicago Press, Chicago.

Heidegger, M. 1969a, 'Art and Space', trans. C. H. Seibert, viewed 22 December 2012, <http://www.beyng.com/hlinks/hh.html>.

Heidegger, M. 1971, *Poetry, Language, Thought*, trans. A. Hofstadter, Harper & Row, New York.

Heidegger, M. 1973, *The End of Philosophy*, trans. J. Stambaugh, The University of Chicago Press, Chicago.

Heidegger, M. 1977, *The Question Concerning Technology and Other Essays*, trans. W. Lovitt, Harper & Row, New York.

Heidegger, M. 1982, *The Basic Problems of Phenomenology*, trans. A. Hofstadter, University Press, Bloomington.

Heidegger, M. 1984, *Nietzsche, Vol. II*, trans. D. Farrell-Krell, HarperOne, New York.

Heidegger, M. 1985, *Schelling's Treatise on the Essence of Human Freedom*, trans. J. Stambaugh, Ohio University Press, Athens, Ohio.

Heidegger, M. 1987, *Nietzsche, Vol. III and IV*, trans. D. F. Krell, HarperOne, New York.

Heidegger, M. 1996, *Hölderlin's Hymn 'The Ister'*, trans. W. McNeill, & J. Davis, Indiana University Press, Bloomington.

Heidegger, M. 1997, *Plato's Sophist*, trans. R. Rojcewicz & A. Schuwer, Indiana University Press, Bloomington.

Heidegger, M. 1998, *Pathmarks*, trans. various, Cambridge University Press, Cambridge.

Heidegger, M. 1999, *Contributions to Philosophy (from Enowning)*, trans. P. Emad, & K. Maly, Indiana University Press, Bloomington.

Heidegger, M. 2000, *Elucidations of Hölderlin's Poetry*, trans. K. Hoeller, Humanity Books, New York.

Heidegger, M. 2000a, *Introduction to Metaphysics*, trans. G. Fried & R. Polt, Yale University Press, New Haven.

Heidegger, M. 2002, 'Anaximander's Saying', trans. J. Young & K. Haynes, in *Martin Heidegger, Off the Beaten Track*, Cambridge University Press, Cambridge, pp. 242–81.

Heidegger, M. 2003, *Four Seminars*, trans. A. Mitchell & F. Raffoul, Indiana University Press, Bloomington and Indianapolis.

Heidegger, M. 2010, *Country Path Conversations*, trans. B. W. Davis, Indiana University Press, Bloomington.

Heidegger, M. 2012, *Bremen and Freiberg Lectures: Insight Into That Which is and Basic Principles of Thinking*, trans. A. Mitchell, Indiana University Press, Bloomington.

Hölderlin, F. 1988, *Essays and Letters on Theory*, trans. T. Pfau, State University of New York Press, New York.

Hölderlin, F. 1998, *Selected Poems and Fragments*, trans. M. Hamburger & J. Adler (ed.), Penguin Books, London.

Horn, L. 1989, *A Natural History of Negation*, The University of Chicago Press, Chicago.

Inwood, M. 1992, *A Hegel Dictionary*, Blackwell Reference, Oxford.

Jonas, H. 1966, *The Phenomenon of Life: Toward a Philosophical Biology*, Northwest University Press, Evanston, Ill.

Kac, E. 2007, 'Introduction: An Art that Looks You in the Eye: Hybrids, Clones, Mutants, Synthetics, and Transgenetics', in E. Kac (ed.), *Signs of Life: Bio Art and Beyond*, The MIT Press, Cambridge, Mass.

Kac, E. 2007a, 'Life Transformation – Art Mutation', in E. Kac (ed.), *Signs of life: Bio Art and Beyond*, The MIT Press, Cambridge, Mass., pp. 163–84.

Kant, I. 1929, *Critique of Pure Reason*, trans. N. Kemp Smith, Macmillan Education Ltd, Houndmills.

Kant, I. 1987, *Critique of Judgment*, trans. W. S. Pluhar, Hackett Publishing Company, Indianapolis.

Kant, I. 2005, *Groundwork for the Metaphysics of Morals*, trans. T. K. Abbott, revised L. Denis, (ed.) L. Denis, Broadview Editions, Peterborough, Ontario.

Kojevè, A. 1969, *Introduction to the Reading of Hegel: Lectures on the Phenomenology of Spirit*, trans. J. H. Nichols, Jnr. Cornell University Press, Ithica.

Krell, D. F. 1998, *Contagion: Sexuality, Disease, and Death in German Idealism and Romanticism*, Indiana University Press, Bloomington.

Kristeva, J. 1982, *Powers of Horror: An Essay on Abjection*, trans. L. S. Roudiez, Columbia University Press, New York.

Lacan, J. 1992, *The Seminar of Jacques Lacan: The Ethics of Psychoanalysis, 1959–1960, Book VII*, trans. D. Porter, Norton & Company, New York.

Lacan, J. 1996, *Écrits*, trans. B. Fink, W. W. Norton, New York.

Laclau, E. 1996, *Emancipation(s)*, London, Verso.

Lacoue-Labarthe, P. 1990, *Heidegger, Art and Politics*, trans. C. Turner, Basil Blackwell, Oxford.

Lacoue-Labarthe, P. 1999, *Poetry as Experience*, trans. A. Tarnowski, Stanford University Press, Stanford.

Lacoue-Labarthe, P. 2007, *Heidegger and the Politics of Poetry*, trans. J. Fort, University of Illinois Press, Urbana.

Lacoue-Labarthe, P. & Nancy, J-L. 1988, *The Literary Absolute: the Theory of Literature in German Romanticism*, trans. P. Barnard & C. Lester, State University of New York Press, Albany.

Latour, B. 1993, *We Have Never Been Modern*, trans. C. Porter, Harvard University Press, Cambridge, Mass.

Lauer, C. 2010, *The Suspension of Reason in Hegel and Schelling*, Continuum, London.

Lemmens, P. 2009, 'The Detached Animal – On the Technical Nature of Being Human', in *New Visions of Nature*, M. Drenthen et al., (eds), Springer, Heidelberg, pp. 117–27.

Levinas, E. 1969, *Totality and Infinity: An Essay on Exteriority*, trans. A. Lingis, Duquesne University, Pittsburg.

Levinas, E. 1996, *Basic Philosophical Writings*, A. T. Peperzak, S. Critchley & R. Bernasconi (eds), Indiana University Press, Bloomington.

Lewis, M. 2007, *Heidegger Beyond Deconstruction: On Nature*, Continuum, London.

Löwy, M. 1985, 'Revolution against "Progress": Walter Benjamin's Romantic Anarchism', *New Left Review*, no. 152, pp. 42–59.

Lyotard, J-F. 2011, *Discourse, Figure*, trans. A. Hudek & M. Lydon, University of Minnesota Press, Minneapolis.

Macherey, P. 2011, *Hegel or Spinoza*, trans. S. M. Ruddick, University of Minnesota Press, Minneapolis.

Mackenzie, I. 2004, *The Idea of Pure Critique*, Continuum, New York.

Malick, T. (dir.) 1998, *The Thin Red Line*, Fox 2000, US.

Malpas, J. 2006, *Heidegger's Topology: Being, Place, World*, MIT Press, Cambridge, Mass.

Marx, K. 1959, *Economic and Philosophic Manuscripts of 1844*, trans. M. Milligan, Lawrence & Wishart, London.

Marx, K. 1975, *Early Writings*, trans. R. Livingstone & G. Benton, Penguin Books, London.

Marx, K. 1976, *Capital: A Critique of Political Economy, Vol. 1* trans. B. Fowkes, Penguin, London.

Marx, K. 1981, *Capital: A Critique of Political Economy, Vol. 3* trans. D. Fernbach, Penguin, London.

Mathews, F. 2004, 'Letting the World Do the Doing', *Australian Humanities Review*, no. 33, viewed 20 May 2013, <http://www.australianhumanitiesreview.org/archive/Issue-August-2004/matthews.html>.

Matthews, B. 2007, 'Translator's Introduction', F. W. J. Schelling, *The Grounding of Positive Philosophy: The Berlin Lectures*, State University of New York, Albany, pp. 1–84.

McGrath, S. J. 2012, *The Dark Ground of Spirit: Schelling and the Unconscious*, Routledge, East Sussex.

McNeill, W. 1999, *The Glance of the Eye: Heidegger, Aristotle, and the Ends of Theory*, State University of New York, Albany.

Meillassoux, Q. 2008, *After Finitude: an Essay on the Necessity of Contingency*, trans. R. Brassier, Continuum, London.

Menninghaus, W. 2002, 'Walter Benjamin's Exposition of the Romantic Theory of Reflection', *Walter Benjamin and Romanticism*, in B. Hanssen & A. Benjamin (eds), Continuum, New York, pp. 19–50.

Merleau-Ponty, M. 2003, *Nature: Course Notes from the Collège de France*, trans. R. Vallier, Northwestern University Press, Evanston.

Michaud, Y. 2007, 'Art and Biotechnology', in E. Kac, (ed.) *Signs of Life: Bio Art and Beyond*, The MIT Press, Cambridge, Mass.

Millner, J. 2001, 'Patricia Piccinini: Ethical Aesthetics', viewed 29 November 2012, <http://www.patriciapiccinini.net/essay.php?id=4>.

Mitchell, A. J. 2010, *Heidegger amongst the Sculptors: Body, Space and the Art of Dwelling*, Stanford University Press, Stanford.

Mitchell, A. J. 2012, 'Translator's Foreword', M. Heidegger, *Bremen and Freiburg Lectures*: Insight into That Which Is *and* Basic Principles of Thinking, trans. A. J. Mitchell, Indiana University Press, Bloomington, pp. vii–xviii.

Morton, T. 2007, *Ecology without Nature: Rethinking Environmental Aesthetics*, Harvard University Press, Cambridge, Mass.

Morton, T. 2010, *The Ecological Thought*, Harvard University Press, Cambridge, Mass.

Moss, L. 2009, 'Detachment, Genomics and the Nature of Being Human', *New Visions of Nature*, M. Drenthen et al. (eds), Springer, Heidelberg. pp. 103–15.

Mules, W. 2000, 'Lines, Dots and Pixels: The Making and Remaking of the Visual Image in Visual Culture', *Continuum*, vol. 14, no. 3, pp. 303–16.

Mules, W. 2001, '"That Obstinate Yet Elastic Natural Barrier": Work and the Figure of Man in Capitalism' *M/C: A Journal of Media and Culture*, vol. 4, no. 5, viewed 21 December 2012, <http://www.api-network.com/mc/cover.html>.

Mules, W. 2006, 'Contact Aesthetics and Digital Arts: At the Threshold of the Earth', *Fibreculture*, no. 9, viewed 21 December 2012, <http://journal.fibreculture.org/issue9/issue9/mules.html>.

Mules, W. 2007, 'Aura as Productive Loss', *Transformations*, no. 17, viewed 2 January 2013, <http://www.transformationsjournal.org/journal/index.shtml>.

Mules, W. 2008, 'Open Country: Towards a Material Environmental Aesthetics' *Continuum*, vol. 22, no. 2, pp. 201–12.

Mules, W. 2010, 'Democracy and Critique: Recovering Freedom in Nancy and Derrida', *Derrida Today*, vol. 3, no. 1, pp. 92–112.

Mules, W. 2012, 'Heidegger, Nature Philosophy and Art as *Poietic* Event', *Transformations*, no. 21, viewed 3 January 2013, <http://www.transformationsjournal.org/journal/index.shtml>.

Mules, W. 2013, 'Mise-en-scène and the Figural: a Reading of Terrence Malick's *Tree of Life*', *Cine-Files*, no. 4, viewed 8 June 2013, <http://www.thecine-files.com/>.

Nancy, J-L. 1988, *The Experience of Freedom*, trans. B. McDonald, Stanford University Press, Stanford.

Nancy, J-L. 1991, *The Inoperative Community*, trans. P. Connor, L. Garbus, M. Holland & S. Sawhney, University of Minnesota Press, Minneapolis.

Nancy, J-L. 1993, 'Corpus', trans. C. Sartiliot, in *The Birth to Presence*, Stanford University Press, Stanford, pp. 189–207.

Nancy, J-L. 1997, *The Sense of the World*, trans. J. S. Librett, University of Minnesota Press, Minneapolis.

Nancy, J-L. 2000, *Being Singular Plural*, trans. R. D. Richardson & A. E. O'Byrne, University Press, Stanford.

Nancy, J-L. 2003, *A Finite Thinking*, trans. various, Stanford University Press, Stanford.

Nancy, J-L. 2003a, 'Originary Ethics', trans. D. Large, in J-L. Nancy, *A Finite Thinking*, S. Sparks (ed.), Stanford University Press, Stanford, pp. 173–95.

Nancy, J-L. 2007, *The Creation of the World or Globalization*, trans. F. Raffoul & D. Pettigrew, State University of New York Press, Albany.

Nelson, E. S. 2008, 'Heidegger and the Ethics of Facticity', in F. Raffoul & E. S. Nelson (eds), *Rethinking Facticity*, State University of New York, Albany, pp. 129–47.

Nelson, E. S. 2011, 'Revisiting the Dialectic of Enlightenment: Nature as Ideology and Ethics in Adorno and the Frankfurt School', *Telos*, no. 155, pp. 105–26.

New South Wales Government, Wilderness Act, 1987, No. 196, Viewed 12 December 2012, <http://www.legislation.nsw.gov.au/viewtop/inforce/act+196+1987+FIRST+0+N>.

Nietzsche, F. 1910, *The Birth of Tragedy*, trans. W. M. A. Haussmann, T. N. Foulis, Edinburgh.

Nietzsche, F. 1967, *The Will to Power*, trans. W. Kaufmann, Vintage Press, New York.

Nietzsche, F. 1973, *Beyond Good and Evil: Prelude to a Philosophy of the Future*, trans. R. J. Hollingdale, Penguin Books, Harmondsworth.

Nietzsche, F. 1997, *Daybreak: Thoughts on the Prejudices of Morality*, trans. R. J. Hollingdale, Cambridge University Press, Cambridge.

Nietzsche, F. 1997a, *Untimely Meditations*, trans. R. J. Hollingdale, Cambridge University Press, Cambridge.

One on One: Eduardo Kac. 2008, television program, Al Jazeera, 23 February, viewed 18 October 2012, <http://www.youtube.com/watch?v=evxlR3zJ11o&NR=1&feature=endscreen>.

Osthoff, S. 2009, 'Invisible in Plain Sight, and As Alive As You And I: An Interview with Eduardo Kac', *Flusser Studies*, no. 8, viewed 19 October 2012, <http://www.flusserstudies.net/pag/archive08.htm>.

Peirce, C. S. 1991, *Peirce on Signs: Writings on Semiotic by Charles Sanders Peirce*, J. Hoopes (ed.), University of North Carolina, Chapel Hill.

Piccinini, P. 2012, *Nectar 2012*: Silicone, Fibre Glass, Human Hair, Refrigerator, Edition of 6, viewed 13 October 2012, Heidi Gallery, Melbourne.

Piccinini, P. 2013, Artist's Statement. *Nectar*, 'Those Who Dream by Night', Art Exhibition, Haunch of Venison Gallery, London.

Pippin, R. 1999, *Modernism as a Philosophical Problem: On the Dissatisfactions of European High Culture*, 2nd edn, Blackwell, Malden, Mass.

Plumwood, V. 2008, 'Shadow Places and the Politics of Dwelling', *Australian Humanities Review*, Eco-Humanities Corner, no. 44, viewed 20 May 2013, <http://www.australianhumanitiesreview.org/archive/Issue-March-2008/plumwood.html>.

Raffoul, F. 2008, 'Factical Life and the Need for Philosophy', in F. Raffoul & E. S. Nelson (eds) *Rethinking Facticity*, State University of New York, Albany, pp. 69–85.

Raffoul, F. & Nelson E. S. 2008, 'Introduction', F. Raffoul & E. S. Nelson (eds) *Rethinking Facticity*, State University of New York, Albany, pp. 1–22.

Rancière, J. 2004, *The Politics of Aesthetics: The Distribution of the Sensible*, trans. G. Rockhill, Continuum, London.

Rancière, J. 2006, 'Thinking between Disciplines: an Aesthetic Knowledge', *Parrhesia: A Journal of Critical Philosophy*, no. 1, viewed 19 May 2013, <http://www.parrhesiajournal.org/past.html>.

Rawls, J. 1999, *A Theory of Justice*, revised edn, Oxford University Press, Oxford.

Rigby, K. 2004, *Topographies of the Sacred: the Poetics of Place in European Romanticism*, University of Virginia Press, Charlottesville.

Rojcewicz, R. 2006, *The Gods of Technology: A Reading of Heidegger*, State University of New York Press, Albany.

Rorty, R. 1980, *Philosophy and the Mirror of Nature*, Basil Blackwell, Oxford.

Rose, D. B. 1996, *Nourishing Terrains: Australian Aboriginal Views of Landscape and Wilderness*, Australian Heritage Commission, Canberra.

Rosen, M. 1996, *On Voluntary Servitude: False Consciousness and the Theory of Ideology*, Polity Press, Cambridge.

Ryan, M. 1984, *Marxism and Deconstruction: A Critical Articulation*, The John Hopkins University Press, Baltimore.

Sallis, J. 1999, *Chorology: On Beginning in Plato's* Timaeus, Indiana University Press, Bloomington.

Sallis, J. 1999a, 'Secluded Nature: The Point of Schelling's Reinscription of *Timaeus*', *Pli* no. 8, pp. 71–85, viewed 2 January 2013, <http://web.warwick.ac.uk/philosophy/pli_journal>.

Sallis, J. 2008, *Transfigurements: On the True Sense of Art*, University of Chicago Press, Chicago.

Sallis, J. 2008a *The Verge of Philosophy*, The University of Chicago Press, Chicago.

Schalow, F. 1995, 'Beyond Decisionism and Anarchy: the Task of Re-thinking Resolve', *Man and World* vol. 28, no. 4, pp. 359–76.

Schelling, F. W. J. 1978, *System of Transcendental Idealism*, trans. P. Heath, University Press of Virginia, Charlottesville.

Schelling, F. W. J. 1980, *The Unconditional in Human Knowledge: Four Early Essays (1794–1796)*, trans. F. Marti. Bucknell University Press, London.

Schelling, F. W. J. 1984, *Bruno or on the Natural and the Divine Principle of Things*, ed. & trans. M. G. Vater, State University of New York Press, Albany.

Schelling, F. W. J. 1988, *Ideas for a Philosophy of Nature*, 2nd edn, trans. E. E. Harris & P. Heath, Cambridge University Press, Cambridge.

Schelling, F. J. W. 1989, *The Philosophy of Art,* trans. D. W. Stott, University of Minneapolis Press, Minneapolis.

Schelling, F. J. W. 1997, *Ages of the World*, 2nd version, 1813 trans. J. Norman, The University of Michigan Press, Ann Arbor.

Schelling, F. J. W. 2000, *The Ages of the World*, 3rd version, trans. J. M. Wirth, State University of New York, Albany.

Schelling, F. W. J. 2002, *Clara or, On Nature's Connection to the Spirit World*, trans. F. Steinkamp, State University of New York Press, Albany,

Schelling, F. W. J. 2004, *First Outline of a System of the Philosophy of Nature,* trans. K. R. Peterson, State University of New York Press, Albany.

Schelling, F. J. W. 2006, *Philosophical Investigations into the Essence of Human Freedom* trans. J. Love & J. Schmidt, State University of New York Press, Albany.

Schelling, F. W. J. 2007, *The Grounding of Positive Philosophy: The Berlin Lectures*, trans. B. Matthews, State University of New York, Albany.

Schiller, F. 2004, *On the Aesthetic Education of Man*, trans. R. Snell, Dover publications, Inc., Mineola, New York.

Schuback, M. 2005, 'The Work of Experience: Schelling on Thinking Beyond Image and Concept', in J. Wirth (ed.), *Schelling Now: Contemporary Readings*, Indiana University Press, Bloomington, pp. 66–83.

Schürmann, R. 1990, *Heidegger: On Being and Acting: From Principles to Anarchy*, trans. C-M. Gros, Indiana University Press, Bloomington.

Shaw, D. Z. 2010, *Freedom and Nature in Schelling's Philosophy of Art*, Continuum, London.

Shiva, V. 2012, 'The Great Seed Robbery', *Deccan Chronicle*, 27 April, viewed 18 October 2012, <http://www.deccanchronicle.com/editorial/dc-comment/great-seed-robbery-394#comment-99262>.

Sinclair, M. 2006, *Heidegger, Aristotle and the Work of Art: Poiesis in Being*, Palgrave Macmillan, Basingstoke.

Sinnerbrink, R. 2006, 'A Heideggerian Cinema?: On Terrence Malick's *The Thin Red Line*', *Film-Philosophy*, vol. 10, no. 3, viewed 12 December 2012, <http://www.film-philosophy.com/2006v10n3/sinnerbrink.pdf>.

Smith, A. 2000, *The Wealth of Nations*, The Modern Library, New York.

Smith, M. 2001, *An Ethics of Place: Radical Ecology, Postmodernity, and Social Theory*, State University of New York Press, Albany.

Spinoza, B. 1992, *The Ethics: Treatise on the Emendation of the Intellect, Selected Letters*, trans. S. Shirley, Hackett Publishing Company, Indiana.

Stewart, S. 2006, 'Response to Brady, Phillips and Rolston', *Environmental Values*, vol. 15, no. 3, pp. 315–20.

Strathausen, C. 2005, 'The Badiou-Event', *Polygraph*, 17, pp. 275–93.

Sumič, J. 2004, 'Anachronism of Emancipation or Fidelity to Politics', in S. Critchley & O. Marchant (eds), *Laclau: A Critical Reader*, Routledge, Abingdon, Oxon., pp. 182–98.

Taminiaux, J. 1987, 'Poiesis and Praxis in Fundamental Ontology', *Research in Phenomenology*, no. 17, pp. 137–69.

Thacker, E. 2007, 'Open Source DNA and Bioinformatic Bodies', in E. Kac (ed.), *Signs of life: Bio-Art and Beyond*, The MIT Press, Cambridge, Mass.

The Thin Red Line 1998, motion picture, Twentieth Century Fox, video format.

The Tree of Life 2011, motion picture, Twentieth Century Fox, video format.

Toadvine, T. 2009, *Merleau-Ponty's Philosophy of Nature*, Northwestern University Press, Evanston.

United Nations Convention on Biological Diversity 1993, viewed 14 May 2013, <http://www.cbd.int/convention/articles/default.shtml?a=cbd-02>.

Vallier, R. 2003, 'Translator's Introduction', in M. Merleau-Ponty, *Nature: Course Notes from the Collège de France,* Northwestern University Press, Evanstone:, pp. xiii–xx.

Vater, M. G. & Wood, D. W. 2012, 'Introduction: The Trajectory of German Philosophy after Kant, and the "Difference" between Fichte and Schelling', in M. G. Vater & D. W. Wood (eds),

The Philosophical Rupture between Fichte and Schelling: Selected Texts and Correspondence (1880–1802), State University of New York, Albany, pp. 1–20.

Vattimo, G. 1987, '"Verwindung": Nihilism and the Postmodern in Philosophy', *SubStance*, vol. 16, no. 2, issue 33, pp. 7–17.

Vattimo. G. 2004, *Nihilism and Emancipation: Ethics, Politics, and Law*, trans. W. McCuaig, Columbia University Press, New York.

Vattimo, G. 2008, *Art's Claim to Truth*, trans. Luca D'Isanto, Columbia University Press, New York.

Vogel, S. 1996, *Against Nature: The Concept of Nature in Critical Theory*, State University of New York Press, Albany.

Weber, S. 2008, *Benjamin's Abilities*, Harvard University Press, Cambridge, Mass.

Westin, M. 2012, 'Recuperating Relational Aesthetics: Environmental Art and Civic Relationality', *Transformations*, no. 21, viewed 13 December 2012, <http://www.transformationsjournal. org/journal/issue_21/article_09.shtml>.

Whitehead, D. 2003, 'Poiesis and Art-Making: A Way of Letting-Be', *Contemporary Aesthetics*, vol. 1, viewed 21 December 2012, <http://www.contempaesthetics.org/>.

Wilden, A. 1980, *System and Structure: Essays in Communication and Exchange*, 2nd edn, Tavistock, London.

Wilson, S. 2002, 'Editor's Introduction', *Decadence of the Nude: Pierre Klossowski*, Black Dog Publishing, London, pp. 15–31.

Winkler, M. 2009, *Cinema and Classical Texts: Apollo's New Light*, Cambridge University Press, Cambridge.

Wirth, J. M. 2003, *The Conspiracy of Life: Meditations on Schelling and his Time*, The State University of New York Press, Albany.

Woods, C. 2006, 'Lorraine Connelly-Northey', *Xstrata Coal Emerging Indigenous Art Award 2006*, Queensland Art Gallery Publishing, South Brisbane.

Woodward, B. 2010, 'Inverted Astronomy: Ungrounded Ethics, Volcanic Copernicanism, and the Ecological Decentering of the Human', *Polygraph*, no. 22, pp. 79–93.

Wrathall, M. A. 2011, *Heidegger and Unconcealment: Truth, Language and History*, Cambridge University Press, Cambridge.

Ziarek, K. 1998 'Powers To Be: Art and Technology in Heidegger and Foucault', *Research in Phenomenology*, no. 28, pp. 162–94.

Zimmerman, M. 2004, 'What Can Continental Philosophy Contribute to Environmentalism?', in B. Foltz & R. Frodeman (eds), *Rethinking Nature: Essays in Environmental Philosophy*, Indiana University Press, Bloomington.

Žižek, S. 1992, *Looking Awry* The MIT Press, Cambridge, Mass.

Žižek, S. 1996, *The Indivisible Remainder: On Schelling and Related Matters*, Verso, London.

Žižek, S. 1997, *The Abyss of Freedom*, The University of Michigan Press, Ann Arbor.

Žižek, S. 1999, *The Ticklish Subject: The Absent Centre of Political Ontology*, 2nd ed. Verso, London.

Žižek, S. 2006, *The Parallax View*, The MIT Press, Cambridge, Mass.

Zizioulas, J. 1985, *Being as Communion: Studies in Personhood and the Church*, St. Vladimir's Seminary Press, New York.

Notes

Introduction: Wanted – A Nature Philosophy

1. Ted Toadvine has also addressed the issue of the forgetting of the philosophical question of nature in the sciences and humanities (Toadvine 2009, p. 3). He argues for 'a renewed philosophy of nature' (p. 7) along similar lines to what I am proposing in this book, but employs Merleau-Ponty's phenomenology to develop an 'ecophenomenology' (p. 8) of the human-nature relation.

2. In a more recent book *The Ecological Thought*, Morton has shifted to a positive position following Deleuzian-Spinozist lines (Morton 2010). But this shift, I argue, does not satisfy the requirements of an ecocriticism grounded in its own critical act. It risks losing sight of the critical act itself as a contingent and historical *praxis* facing the closure of nature in technology and myth. For further discussion see Chapter 6, note 2.

3. See for instance the debate in the journal *Environmental Values* (2006, vol. 15) concerning the diminished role of 'aesthetic experience' in environmental policy studies. Summing up the various positions, Susan Stewart notes the following: 'emphasising the centrality of aesthetics seems more and more to be a matter of wishful thinking – the aesthetic seems to set sail and disappear over the horizon while the sea of discussion churns beneath the winds of cost-benefit analyses. Over and over, sustaining the biodiversity of nature is put in conflict with the needs of economic development: efficiency and a certain form of blunt pragmatism (as if bluntness were a form of pragmatism) reign. Indeed, the selfishness of the instrumental comes into relief in its full impracticality: calculating our approach to natural resources as a matter merely of current economic pressures, acting within a framework of rationality that is in truth irrational when one takes the long view, valuing false needs as if they were vital to our existence all create an atmosphere of emergency that obscures the true unfolding disaster of our relation to nature's finitude' (Stewart 2006, pp. 316–17).

4. 'This third [power] must in itself be outside and above all antithesis, the purest potency, indifferent toward both, free from both, and the most essential' (Schelling 2000, p. 19).

5. In his book on Schelling, Heidegger says that what is required is a 'second beginning' in the thinking of nature as ontological fact, the first beginning being Schelling's own attempt to do so. (Heidegger 1985, p. 161).

6. The word *techne* is drawn from Greek philosophy and means making or 'coming into being' (Aristotle, *Nichomachean Ethics*, 1140a; 1941, p. 1025). In Heidegger's terms *techne*

is 'bringing forth' (Heidegger 1977, p. 13): a carpenter 'brings forth' a chair according to a *techne* – a preconceived knowingness put into practice to produce the chair – to 'bring it forth' from non-being into being.

7. Being with a capital 'B' refers to the fact that beings must share a common being irreducible to their own being, and is thus equivalent to Schelling's 'indivisible remainder' – the third potency, or the power of indifference in the 'in-between'. In Heidegger's philosophy, this common being is designated by the capitalization of the word 'Being'. The relation between Being and beings is what Heidegger calls 'ontological difference' (Heidegger 1982, p. 17). See also Chapter 7, note 3.

8. Ecocriticism defines an interdisciplinary alliance in the humanities and arts sharing a common concern for the environment and the human-nature relation, through critical engagement with literature and other modes of cultural representation and expression. In Greg Garrard's terms 'the widest definition of the subject of ecocriticism is the study of the relationship of the human and the non-human, throughout human cultural history and entailing critical analysis of the term "human" itself' (Garrard 2012, p. 5). Garrard argues that ecocritics are obliged to engage with the science of ecology to 'help to define, explore and even resolve ecological problems in this wider [cultural] sense' (p. 6). In this book I employ the term 'nature' to signal the 'other' of the human as something positive rather than the negativity of the term 'non-human'.

1. Nature Otherwise

1. Wittgenstein shows how this set up takes place in classical Newtonian physics. In Karsten Harries' words, Wittgenstein describes how Newtonian physics places a representational grid over the 'things' of nature, making them disappear: 'the grid provides the general framework used to represent these spots [i.e. things]. In that framework things have to take their place if they are going to be said "to be" in the scientific sense. But so understood, their being both conceals and presupposes what they "are" in another sense. And no matter how fine the grid, their representation by means of it does violence to what they really "are"' (Harries 2009, pp. 156–57).

2. Richard Rorty calls this self-reflection a 'quasi-visual faculty, the Mirror of Nature' (Rorty 1980, p. 163).

3. Jacques Lacan describes the 'this' as follows: 'the "this" [...] is not a this which can be the object of knowledge, but a this [...] which constitutes my being and to which [...] I bear witness as much and more on my whims, aberrations, phobias, and fetishes, than in my more or less civilized personage' (Lacan 1996, p. 437). Nature is this nature when I am caught off-guard in contingent interruptions and slippages.

4. Kant sums this situation up as follows: 'though we cannot know these objects as things in themselves, we must yet be in a position at least to think them as things in themselves' (Kant 1929, p. 27). We cannot know the thing 'in itself', but we can nevertheless think it in terms of the categories of transcendental reason. Thinking turns the thing into an object of thought, thereby blocking access to its 'thatness' – the fact that it is a thing. For Kant 'thatness' or

216

being does not play a constitutive role in the subject/object relation: '"*Being*" is obviously not a real predicate' (Kant 1929, p. 504).

5. Seeing as thinking relates to the Greek word Θεωρία (theoria). Seeing means gazing upon something in the sense of seeing-as-thinking.

6. See Weber (2008, pp. 4-5) for a discussion of possibility in Benjamin and Derrida and further commentary on the distinction between the possible and the virtual in Deleuze (p. 32). In Difference and Repetition, Deleuze draws on Heidegger's concept of ontologically contingent possibility as 'the potentiality of an Idea, its determinable virtuality' (Deleuze 1994, p. 201). Possibility is virtual so long as it is thought as ontologically enabling and not as a transcendent condition of the actual: where 'it is *immediately* effective qua possibility itself, and not merely as an anticipation of a possible realization' (Weber 2008, p. 45).

7. Jeff Malpas writes: 'The way in which, in virtue of the questionability of our being, we are caught up in the question of being *as such* reflects the way in which the fact of our existence always precedes us – we find ourselves already in a situation. Already living a certain life, already given over to a particular existence – and as such we find ourselves already involved with things, already engaged in a world' (Malpas 2006, p. 43, emphasis added).

8. The 'not' of thought as positive follows a line of thinking since Aristotle (Horn 1989, p. 5).

9. Schelling's nature philosophy (*Naturphilosophie*) is spread out in a number of publications in the early phase of his career. See Chapter 4 for details of these publications.

10. For instance in System of Transcendental Idealism, Schelling writes of the need for a 'new mythology [to] arise, which shall be the creation, not of some individual author, but of a new race, personifying as it were, one single poet – that is a problem whose solution can be looked for only in the future destinies of the world, and in the course of history to come' (Schelling 1978, pp. 232–33).

11. This quote is found in the section on resoluteness in *Being and Time* (first published in 1927), the culminating work of his early philosophy. In his later thinking on art – in the essay 'The Origin of the Work of Art' (1935–36) – we see a similar concern: 'In taking possession thus of the Open, the openness holds open the Open and sustains it' (Heidegger 1971, p. 61).

12. See Jean-Luc Nancy's comments on technology and sense in *A Finite Thinking* where he rejects the kind of critique that disengages with global technology by 'returning nostalgically to pious images (or essences) of the artisan and life in the fields' (Nancy 2003, pp. 26–27). Nancy has Heidegger in mind here, especially his discussion of the artwork in 'The Origin of the Work of Art' (Heidegger 1971). I will be dealing with these issues and Heidegger's discussion of art more fully in Chapter 7.

13. In his book, *Living with the Earth: Mastery to Mutuality*, Rod Giblett argues for 'a participatory, political ecology [that] would deconstruct and decolonise the hierarchical distinction [between nature and culture] and […] decolonise the conquest of the earth' (Giblett 2004, p. 38). The poetics I develop in this book are a response to the challenge Giblett poses for a participatory political ecology in terms of being with nature.

14. The artist Paul Klee makes the following comments: 'May I use a simile, the simile of the tree? The artist has studied this world in all its variety and has, we may suppose, unobtrusively found his way in it. His sense of direction in nature and life, this branching and spreading array, I shall compare with the root of the tree. From the root the sap flows to the artist, flows

through him, flows to his eye. Thus he stands as the trunk of the tree […] standing at his appointed place, the trunk of the tree, he does nothing other than gather and pass on what comes to him from the depths. He neither serves nor rules – he transmits. His position is humble. And the beauty at the crown is not his own. He is merely a channel' (qtd. in Harries, 2009, pp. 97–98). Klee's comments underline the *poietic* connectivity of the artist and the tree (the thing of nature), as a 'flow' of energy (sap) that comes to him from the 'depths', emphasizing the non-subjective character of the encounter in which the artist is a passive conduit that transmits something by passing it on.

15. Dignity is an idea circulating in the European enlightenment and employed by Kant in his critique of reason in terms of the rational subject's pursuit of a '*kingdom of ends*' (Kant 2005, p. 91). Kant argued that morality (how one should act) should not be based on private concerns or short-term practical motivations, but on 'the idea of the dignity of a rational being, obeying no law but that which he himself also gives' (p. 93). Dignity is neither value nor fanciful play, but the 'inner worth' of something that has an 'end in itself' (p. 93).

16. In the sections on rent, land and estranged labour in the Manuscripts essay, Marx spells out his anthropocentric views of nature and its function in the achievement of human emancipation. By eliminating private property, the human is able to overcome its 'alienated' state from nature and resume its Adamic role as keeper of the earth: 'This is because the earth ceases to be an object of barter, and through free labour and free enjoyment once again becomes an authentic, personal property of man' (Marx 1975, p. 320). Released from the selfishness of private property ownership, the human labours on nature in a dialectical *Aufhebung* that realizes its 'free being' (p. 327). In Marx's theory of alienated labour, the human worker is alienated not from nature as such, but from having possession of it.

17. Marx follows Hegel on this point. In *Philosophy of Nature* Hegel argues that material nature is an infinite process, not yet capable of organic form; it is nature as 'inorganic being' (Hegel 1970a, p. 222).

18. For the theme of denaturing in ecotechnological enframing, see Jean-Luc Nancy's book *The Creation of the World, or Globalization* (Nancy 2007), especially Chapter 3, 'Creation as Denaturation: Metaphysical Technology' (pp. 77–90). I discuss Nancy's concept of denaturing and world-forming (*mondialisation*) more fully in Chapter 10. Renaturing is not a term used by Nancy. I use it here and throughout this book to refer to the process of returning meaning to the world.

19. See Alliez's *Capital Times: Tales from the Conquest of Time* (1996), and Alliez and Feher's 'The Luster of Capital' (1987) where the authors argue that globalized capital exploits human work by dissolving the separation between labour and capital, releasing quantities of 'reserve time' (the time set aside from work in order to consume), which then becomes part of the capitalizing process itself. In this case workers become 'investors in their own lives (conceived of as capital) concerned with obtaining a profitable behaviour through information (conceived of as a production factor) sold to them (Alliez & Feher 1987, p. 347). Gilles Deleuze has identified this shift in terms of what he calls a 'control society' where the individuation of workers guaranteed by the disciplinary society gives way to a cybernetic modulation of 'dividuals' or cypher values regulated according to a code (Deleuze 1995, p. 180). For dividualized workers, the resource incorporated into capital is their own lived time, no longer divided between

work and leisure, but entirely 'consummated' in capital (Alliez & Fehrer 1987, p. 350). See also Mules (2001).

20. Deleuze and Guattari define a line of flight as a beginning in rupture, an escaping trajectory which leads nowhere in particular but away from where it begins, as part of rhizomatic connectivity (Deleuze and Guattari 1987, p. 9).

21. Vogel identifies the roots of this 'naturalist' philosophy in 'Romantic and Lebensphilosophische traditions' (p. 5), defended by the classical Frankfurt school (Adorno and Horkheimer, Marcuse), as well as the later Heidegger.

22. Drawing on different philosophical precedents, Hannah Arendt also notes the inherent nihilism of the modern age: 'The danger is that such a society, dazzled by the abundance of its growing fertility and caught in the smooth functioning of a never-ending process, would no longer be able to recognize its own futility – the futility of a life which "does not fix or realize itself in any permanent subject which endures after [its] labour is past."' (Arendt 1958, p. 135). The embedded quote in the previous quotation is from Adam Smith, *Wealth of Nations 1* (Smith 2000, p. 295).

23. In calling for scholars to undertake work in ecological humanities, Deborah Bird Rose and Libby Robin have argued for an approach based on connectivity (Bird & Robin 2004, 2 of 6). In proposing 'enlarged dialogue' with 'others' through connectivity, Bird and Robin go some way toward the ontological connectivity I argue for in this book. However their argument falls back on dialogue between subjects and hence risks eliding the relation with nature as such.

24. '[Critique] is a call to reason to undertake anew the most difficult of all its tasks, namely, that of self-knowledge, and to institute a tribunal which will assure to reason its lawful claims, and dismiss all groundless pretensions, not by despotic decrees, but in accordance with its own eternal and unalterable laws. This tribunal is no other than the critique of pure reason' (Kant, 1929, p. 9).

25. For a discussion of facticity in western philosophy see Raffoul and Nelson (2008).

26. Iain Grant's work is associated with the 'speculative realist' school of philosophy that rejects 'correlationism' – the assumption, since Kant, of a correlation between thinking and being: 'the idea according to which we only ever have access to the correlation between thinking and being, and never to either term considered apart from the other (Meillassoux 2008, p. 5). By rejecting the correlation between thinking and being, speculative realism claims to be able to think 'in terms of the existence of primary qualities' (p. 8).

27. According to Kant, a system is a self-immanent totality obeying universal reason (Kant 1929, 543). The key issue concerns the homogeneity of the system and its intolerance of a void. Though singular things are present in the system, they cannot be known 'in themselves' but only insofar as they are part of the system as a whole.

28. Bateson is here describing a closed system, but the same applies to an open system; any system, open or closed, implies a mentality that determines its operations (Wilden 1980, p. 203).

29. Kant demonstrates that a system is an 'architectonic' of reason sufficient to human thought (Kant 1929, p. 653). An ecosystem is no exception. Following Kant, there can be no system of nature in itself, outside human thought.

30. Schelling notes that any system is riven with the paradox of its own creation in which the creator must be both part of the system yet independent from it. If the creator lacked creative

independence then 'the creator ... would be degraded to an instrument of his system' (qtd. in Shaw 2010, p. 143).

2. Saying Nature

1. In sections 34 and 35 of *Being and Time* Heidegger develops the concept of 'saying' as 'uncovering something': 'for what is said is always understood proximally as "saying" something – that is, an uncovering something' (Heidegger 1962, p. 213). To 'say' something is to uncover it in its being, as opposed to 'idle talk', which is to close it off and leave it 'undone'.

2. In *Discourse, Figure*, Lyotard writes of a certain exteriority to language, a thickness of sense, a 'gesticulatory expanse that makes depth or representation possible, far from being signifiable through words, spreads out on their margins as what enables them to designate; and to show, too, that this expanse is the source of the words' power of expression, and thus accompanies them, shadows them, in one sense terminates them and in another marks their beginning. For one needn't be immersed in language [*langage*] in order to be able to speak; the "absolute" object, the language-system [*langue*], does not speak. What speaks is something that must remain outside of language as system and must continue to remain there even when it speaks' (Lyotard 2011, p. 8). To speak is to 'say' what one speaks of – to summon it to meaning – outside the system of language that has already assigned it a meaning.

3. Sense is not the same as the senses. We cannot reach sense through an examination of the senses (for instance, through empirical study of bodily reactions and perceptions). Sense is already sense the moment we sense the senses. Sense can only be described philosophically, as that mode of thinking that expresses being as positionality, for instance when we say 'that makes sense' thereby saying something about our relation with that which 'makes sense'. This is not to be confused with signification, which is the production of sign value, or the difference between thought and what is sensed. Sense and signification are mutually present in the thought of being (the thought that something *is*). Something may signify, but it may not make sense. Sense connects thought to the thing that is thought, while signification differentiates thought from the thing that is thought. Signification makes things significant in terms of signs, whereas sense makes things sensible in terms of the positional relation between bodies. Sense also needs to be distinguished from affect. Affect is disembodied sense.

4. '[W]hat is under discussion here are not the words *is* and *to be*, but what they say, what comes to words in them: Being' (Heidegger 1987, p. 191).

5. In the fourteenth letter of *On the Aesthetic Education of Man*, Friedrich Schiller writes of a certain 'play impulse [...] [which aims] at the extinction of time *in time* and the reconciliation of becoming with absolute being' (Schiller 2004, p. 74). *Poietic* saying is the enactment of this 'playful impulse' in the saying itself: the attunement of becoming and absolute being in a moment of achronic openness, which Schiller understands in terms of reconciliation. However, what I aim to show in this present work is that *poietic* saying is the 'playful' release

of being-as-becoming, not its reconciliation. The attunement with nature opens being-as-becoming to its possibilities, rather than reconciling it in the Idea.

6. For talk as discourse of the already said that closes off disclosure, see Heidegger, *Being and Time*, section 35 (Heidegger 1962, p. 213).

7. Mick Smith argues that the *techne* of scientific utilitarianism involves what he calls 'axiological extensionism', that is, the unreflective extension of current ways of thinking about the human-nature relation into non-human domains, for instance in applying the concept of rights to animals. This position does not change anything but 'operates to reflect and reinforce our current social structures' (Smith 2001, p. 15). Axiological extensionism 'defuses environmentalism's radical critique of Western society by marginalizing those who try to speak with "a different voice"' (p. 16).

8. For a discussion of aesthetics as subjective sense as distinct from ontology see Harries (2009, pp. 6–7).

9. Jelica Šumič offers the following critique of Laclau's concept of the empty signifier: 'What a signifier cannot by definition be stripped of, in my view, is not the remainder of signifieds [the anachronistic meanings still lodged in the signifier], rather, it is the very materiality of the signifier, which, however, only emerges as the ineradicable residue of the operation of emptying [...] The empty signifier thus points to an excess or surplus in the autonomous working of the signifier. This surplus, however, is not related to the remainder of the signifieds, as Laclau suggests, but rather to something inherent in the signifier, something "within" the signifier itself (whether sound or letter). And it is precisely this "materiality" which leads to its going beyond, exceeding, or surpassing itself' (Šumič 2004, p. 192). This 'something inherent' in the signifier, which Šumič describes as 'materiality', is, I suggest, the announcement of its very possibility; an announcement that interrupts the system of signification, sending it otherwise.

10. See Plumwood (2008) for a critique of the reclamation of place in ecocriticism. Plumwood criticizes the influence of Heidegger on ecocritics and bioregionalists in 'giving honour to place in terms of celebrating "*one's own place*" or "*one's place*" [...] that commands our identity and loyalty'. However, as I argue in Chapter 7, Heidegger's concept of place should not be reduced to the simplicity of 'a place of one's own'; rather it needs to be understood as an unstable, contingent possibility that must be won from the placelessness of modern technologically enframed being.

11. For denaturing see Nancy (2007, pp. 87–88). Denaturing and renaturing are discussed at length in Chapter 10. See also Chapter 1.

12. For a critique of this positing of a special place or time free from industrialization from which to rethink the world anew, see my article 'Open Country: Towards a Material Environmental Aesthetics' (Mules 2008, especially pp. 205–06). In the article, I argue that Raymond Williams's concept of 'working country' in eighteenth-century England is a romanticizing of the past trapped in a dialectical projection of its own desire to escape the present.

13. Nietzsche is here invoking the figure of the ancient Greeks and the 'plastic power of their eyes' to see colours in an immediate and joyous way (Nietzsche 1910, p. 29). But Nietzsche

is not suggesting a return to this way of seeing; rather, he wants to use it in a way that breaks with current experience through a 'critical' mode of thinking (Nietzsche 1997a, p. 75), 'a new, stern discipline [to] combat our inborn heritage and implant in ourselves a new habit, a new instinct, a second nature, so that our first nature withers away' (p. 76).

14. In German Idealist philosophy, the term *Schein* refers to the appearance of things as 'essence'. Things shine in their essence as possibility. For further on *Schein*, see Chapter 6, note 23.

15. See V, VI and IX of 'On the Concept of History', in *Walter Benjamin: Selected Writings*, H Eiland, & M W Jennings (eds.), vol. 4, 1938–1940 (Benjamin 2003, pp. 390–92).

3. Schelling after Kant

1. In its concern for possible conditions, Schelling's *Naturphilosophie* remains at the level of transcendence, but a transcendence conditioned by immanent material becoming. Thus Schelling's *Naturphilosophie* can rightly be called a transcendent-immanent philosophy of nature, or as I have suggested here, a factical-ontological philosophy, where facticity is understood as the necessity that nature *be* something, as distinct from Kant's transcendental philosophy in which nature is banished from being anything other than an unknowable thing-in-itself. See Bowie for facticity in Schelling's *Naturphilosophie* (Bowie 1993, pp. 42–43). Bowie argues that Schelling comes to a factical position of nature only in his later philosophy. However, I argue that a concern for facticity is present throughout Schelling's philosophy as a subtended necessity 'that nature be', and, as such, philosophizing about nature must begin from this fact.

2. See Zimmerman (2004, p. 209), for a discussion of the use of Heidegger's notion of 'letting things be' by deep ecologists. See also Mathews 2004. This slogan, used to justify an attitude of leaving nature as it is, as pristine wilderness, is a misreading of Heidegger's concept of *Gelassenheit*, as I demonstrate in Chapter 7.

3. See Schelling's *Philosophical Letters on Dogmatism and Criticism*, Tenth Letter (Schelling 1980, pp. 192–96). Glossing this letter, Lauer writes: 'reason in Kant's philosophy suddenly discovers its own finitude and realizes that no matter how successful it is in overcoming the gaps and traps of the understanding, it can never be its own ground' (Lauer 2010, p. 83). Beiser notes that Kant's gap was 'concerned about the apparent discrepancy between the categories of the understanding and specific empirical laws' (Beiser 2002, p. 183).

4. Jacques Rancière provides an example of this thinking otherwise. Drawing from Kant's *Critique of Judgment*, he points out that Kantian disinterested judgement requires the suspension of historical and social knowledge of that about which one judges. In the example provided by Kant, a judgement about the beauty of a palace (its well-formedness) must suspend knowledge about the 'sweat' of the labour that went into it. This leads to a doubling of knowledge: repressive and liberating on the part of the labourers. They are repressed because their knowledge of what they have built is confined to what is required to build the palace that 'prevents them from seeing in the palace something other than the product of the labour invested and the idleness appropriated from this labour' (Rancière 2006, p. 3). Rancière points out that this other mode of seeing – a seeing otherwise – is something

they 'cannot ignore [...] because their condition imposes on them the need to create another body and another way of seeing than that which oppresses them' (p. 3). This other way of seeing is built into the palace itself as the 'otherwise' seeing that makes what is seen possible.

5. This is also the case for Schelling: '*the concept of being as an originary substratum should be absolutely eliminated from the philosophy of nature*, just as it has been from transcendental philosophy' (Schelling 2004, p. 14).

6. Kant calls the mereness of things 'actuality' (*Wirklichkeit*): 'through the actuality of a thing I certainly posit more than the possibility of it, but not *in the thing*. For it can never contain more in its actuality than is contained in its complete possibility. But while possibility is merely a positing of the thing in relation to the understanding (in its empirical deployment), actuality is at the same time *a connection of it with perception*' (Kant 1929, p. 252, final emphasis added). Kant does not ascribe reality to actual things in their simple being there: '"*Being*" is obviously not a real predicate' (p. 504).

7. Atomism goes back to ancient Greek philosophy, but finds its seminal modern statement in Descartes' *cogito* as the 'thinking thing'. Atomism privileges things as monadic entities with quasi-autonomous power, over relations between things as part of a network in which things exist (see Wilden 1980, p. 215).

8. Here I draw on Grant's discussion of Kant with respect to Schelling's *Naturphilosophie* (Grant 2006). Grant argues that Kant's 'somatic' theory of nature follows Aristotle in that it privileges the things of nature as discrete bodies, as found for instance in Aristotle's *Physics*: 'the universe is composed of a plurality of distinct individual entities' (Aristotle, *Physics*, qtd. in Grant 2006, p. 67). Grant points out that Kant maintains a strict separation between material things and forces: 'the forces *themselves* cannot form part of material nature' (p. 68) so that nature is reduced to atomized things along Newtonian lines as 'a dualism of body and force' (p. 68).

9. Kant's atomization of things corresponds to classical mechanics in which things constitute discrete states governed by invariable principles that operate outside the state itself, obeying the 'law of inertia' (Beiser 2003, p. 160). The thing corresponds to an objectively determined state acted on by outside forces.

10. See Kant's example of the birds of nature in the *Critique of Judgment* (Kant 1987 p. 236). Our knowledge of the structure of birds' anatomy is in the first instance 'utterly contingent if we go by the mere *nexus effectivus* in nature and do not yet resort to a special kind of causality, viz., the causality of purposes (the *nexus finalis*); in other words, we are saying that nature, considered as a mere mechanism, could have structured itself differently in a thousand ways without hitting on precisely the unity in terms of a principle of purposes' (p. 236). Kant argues that judgements about the things of nature concerning their ends (teleological judgements) are reflective and not determinative judgements; that is, they reflect on absolute possibilities ('could have structured itself differently in a thousand ways') in the indeterminacy of 'what is' without appeal to a predetermining concept.

11. In this sense Kant radicalizes Descartes' *cogito*. For Descartes the cogito or thinking self is identified with thought itself as the substance of thought, whereas for Kant the self is simply the possibility of thought.

12. Kant argues that this pre-subjective self is a synthesizing activity, such that 'the representations given in intuition one and all belong to me' (Kant 1929, p. 154). But here Kant presupposes the 'me' as already known to the self, and so posits a prior identity for which he cannot account. There is no way out of this infinite regress unless an absolute identity is posited, the position taken by Fichte and the early Schelling in response to Kant.

13. In post-Kantian philosophy this revelation is often termed *Schein*. For a discussion of *Schein* see Rosen (1996, pp. 164–66). See also Chapter 6.

14. See Crichtley (2012) for a discussion of the paradox of freedom in Rousseau. Crichtley traces this paradox to Rousseau's analysis of sovereignty in the modern state (p. 22 ff.). Kant and his contemporaries took their lead from Rousseau's attempt to reconcile absolute sovereignty with that of the citizen.

15. Robert Pippin writes: 'If Kant is right, we don't find ourselves subject to anything, but determine ourselves to be subject to it. And if that is so, though, then free self-determination appears to be prior to, rather than equivalent to, rationality' (Pippin 1999, p. 63). On what grounds, then, does the self 'freely determine' its relation to things, if not reason? Kant's discovery of the free self (and his refusal to accept it as the basis of the thought of existence) opens up a long line of existential and phenomenological inquiry in modern philosophy and critical thought.

16. For an example of the application of the Kantian regulative principle to political philosophy, see John Rawls's social contract theory of justice in *A Theory of Justice*: 'they [principles of justice] are the principles that free and rational persons concerned to further their own interests would accept in an initial position of equality as defining the fundamental terms of their association. These principles are to regulate all further agreements; they specify the kinds of social cooperation that can be entered into and the forms of government that can be established' (Rawls 1999, p. 10).

17. See Hannah Arendt and the difference between will and possibility in classical Greek democracy (Arendt 1978, p. 19; Mules 2010, p. 93). The free self is the site of the political *per se*.

18. Thus Kant rejects the possibility of a speculative system of reason, that is, a system that could ground itself in the 'abyss' of unconditioned necessity. Kant proposes a purely regulative idea of reason.

19. This communicability of the other is Walter Benjamin's insight about language in his essay 'On Language As Such and the Languages of Man' (Benjamin 1996, pp. 62–74). Benjamin says 'There is no event or thing in either animate or inanimate nature that does not in some way partake of language, for it is in the *nature* of each one to communicate its mental contents' (p. 62, emphasis added). For Benjamin, language is not a tool to communicate messages between subjects, but a primary 'mediation' (p. 64): an immediacy interrupted by its own act of mediation. The interruption (i.e. the mediation of immediacy that *is* language) does not cause the communicative act to fail as one might expect, but precisely the opposite: it makes it possible and enables it. This failure opens language to the other, so that, in a sense, the other already has language (it is in its 'nature'), and is already able to speak. We can conclude from this the following: that things are not mute, self-enclosed non-beings, 'mere things' as Kant would have it, but beings already opened and capable of speaking back to 'man', the one who names them: 'if the lamp and the mountain and the fox

did not communicate themselves to man, how should he be able to name them?' (p. 64). Man has an originary involvement in the being of things, insofar as both share a common being-in-language as communicability. Furthermore this involvement is an immediate one, but an immediacy *already* mediated by language, already 'other'. See Chapter 9 for further discussion of Benjamin's concept of communicability.

20. As Manfred Frank points out, Kant's philosophy was exposed to its paradoxical foundations by the Jena Romantics, prompting Novalis to write: 'We *seek* everywhere the unconditioned (*das Unbedingte*), and *find* only things (Dinge)' (qtd. in Frank 2004, p. 50). In following Kant, early Romantic philosophy shifts from establishing unconditioned grounds to 'an infinite, open search for a foundation' (p. 51) and a '"presentation of the *unpresentable*"' (p. 53). These ideas pave the way for successive philosophical reflections up to contemporary times, for instance in Lyotard's theory of the sublime, as well as Heidegger's and Derrida's deconstructive accounts of the facticity of unconditioned being.

21. For instance, in the third critique, the *Critique of Judgment*, when Kant confronts the 'purposiveness' of natural organisms he does not abandon a mechanistic for an organicist view of nature, but shows how the function of the organism can be (needs to be) understood in a regulative rather than a determining way through the application of mechanistic principles. Kantian critique does not shift from a causal-mechanistic model in *The Critique of Reason* to an organicist one in the *Critique of Judgment*, but remains causal-mechanistic throughout.

22. In Part II, Division II of the *Critique of Judgment*, entitled 'Dialectic of Teleological Judgment', Kant settles the issue of how to deal with unaccountable things (at least in his own mind) by reaffirming his causal-mechanistic model as the only one capable of measuring up to the demands of critique: 'Rather, I am only pointing out that I *ought* always to *reflect* on these events and forms *in terms of the principle* of the mere mechanism of nature, and hence ought to investigate this principle as far as I can, because unless we presuppose it in our investigation [of nature] we can have no cognition of nature at all in the proper sense of the term' (Kant 1987, p. 268). And 'Reason is tremendously concerned not to abandon the mechanism nature [employs] in its products, and not to pass over it in explaining them, since without mechanism we cannot gain insight into the nature of things' (p. 295). Kant is saying that despite its teleological and purposeful nature, organic nature must be regulated by the laws of mechanical causality (see Breitenbach 2011, pp. 201–02).

4. Unground

1. See Grant (2006, p. 17) and Shaw (2010, p. 144) for the co-extensiveness of these works. Goudeli points out that the difference between Schelling's early *Naturphilosophie* and the middle period writing on freedom corresponds to a shift in his thinking from the transcendental conditions of absolute identity to the immanence of the absolute in material things (Goudeli 2002, p. 93). McGrath argues that there are significant divisions between the earlier period of the *Naturphilosophie* and the middle and later periods, but notes that 'what does remain consistent between the later and the early Schelling is the

refusal to follow the trajectory of early modernity and split spirit from nature' (McGrath 2012, p. 4). Lauer argues that these are all transitional works in Schelling's incomplete philosophical system that includes both *Naturphilosophie* and transcendental philosophy (Lauer 2010, p. 60). David L. Clark describes *The Ages of the World* and other texts of Schelling's middle period as 'rhetorically and conceptually hybrid texts that unwork German idealism from within' (Clark 2007, p. 169).

2. See Vater and Wood (2012, p. 11) for a discussion of Fichte's absolute subjective willing.

3. Fichte's ego philosophy was also attacked by the early German Romantics, contemporaries of Schelling, but with a different emphasis (Menninghaus 2002, pp. 33–34). See Lauer (2010, pp. 77–78) for Schelling's and Hegel's objections to Fichte's philosophy in relation to nature as 'unfreedom'.

4. See Letter 14 in Fichte and Schelling (2012). Schelling writes to Fichte in 1802 saying: 'The reason [for our differences] is that precisely this ideal-real I, which is *merely* objective but for this very reason simultaneously productive, is in this its productivity nothing other than *Nature*, of which the I of intellectual intuition or of self-consciousness is only the higher potency. I simply cannot imagine that in transcendental philosophy reality is just something found, nor something found in conformity with immanent laws of intelligence' (p. 44).

5. For Spinoza's distinction between *natura naturans* and *natura naturata*, see *Ethics I*, Prop 29, Scholium (Spinoza 1992, pp. 51–52). Lauer writes: 'as Schelling conceives the distinction, *natura naturans* is nature as acting and *natura naturata* is nature as produced' (Lauer 2010, p. 27).

6. Transimmanence means that nature and thought are transitively located in each other, as distinct from the immanence of nature in thought. For the distinction between transitive and intransitive in Schelling see Bowie (1993, p. 154).

7. Schelling discusses the 'third' as an 'eternal end' in *The Ages of the World* (Schelling 2000, p. 19). Schelling's concept of the third is similar to C.S. Peirce's concept of 'thirdness' in the logical relations of signs (Peirce 1991; see also Deleuze 1983, p. 197); Levinas employs the third in his concept of *illeity* as trace (Levinas 1996, pp. 62–63). Lacan identifies an unstated 'third locus' in interlocutions 'which is neither my speech nor my interlocuter' (Lacan 1996, p. 436). The Third derives ultimately from Plato's *Timaeus* and the place of *chora* as ungrounded beginning (see Sallis 1999, pp. 7–9).

8. Slajov Žižek discusses Schelling's pursuit of the unaccounted x in *The Indivisible Remainder* (Žižek 1996, pp. 51–52, et passim).

9. See Bowie (1993, pp. 65–66) and Frank (2004, p. 90 ff.). The ontological status of the copula draws us into long-standing problems in philosophical logic that cannot be fully addressed here (see Heidegger 1982, pp. 177–224).

10. Remembering requires an identity condition where A = A (absolute identity). But for Schelling A cannot equal itself without also being part of what it is not (A = B). Thus remembering is itself a forgetting of the x that both A = A and A = B share as their common being.

11. See Lacan, Seminar VII and his discussion of the thing as prehistoric (Lacan 1992). See also Lewis (2007, p. 47).

12. Although Schelling takes his lead from Spinoza's naturalism, here he rejects Spinoza's static model of nature and replaces it with a dynamic one. See Beiser (2007, p. 142) and Shaw (2010, p. 45).

13. In the *First Outline of a System of the Philosophy of Nature* Schelling outlines 'original heterogeneity' as one of the postulates of his *Naturphilosophie* (Schelling 2004, p. 10).
14. Beiser notes that Schelling draws from Kant's 'dynamic theory of nature' (Beiser 2003, p. 155).
15. As Merleau-Ponty has pointed out, in Schelling's idealist-materialism, 'light is a sort of concept that walks among appearances' (Merleau-Ponty 2003, p. 42).
16. Jean-Luc Nancy defines *partage* as 'being singular plural' (Nancy 2000).
17. Schelling's theory of dynamic atomism is an attempt to think ontological difference. See Schelling's *Bruno* (Schelling 1984, IV, pp. 235–36), and Beiser (2002, pp. 570–71). It draws on Plato's arguments for the immanence of being set out in the *Timaeus,* and prefigures the existential philosophy of Heidegger, Derrida's concept of *différance,* Deleuze's virtual philosophy and Jean-Luc Nancy's theory of sense as being-singular-plural. See Frank (1989, p. 263) for the connection between Schelling's theory of the Absolute and late twentieth-century-poststructuralist ideas of absolute difference. Schelling's ideas of immanent singularity also begin a kind of thinking beyond Newtonian physics and toward the world of subatomic particles of quantum physics (see Grant 2006, p. 69 et passim). But care should be taken in thinking along these lines, as quantum physics constructs a 'second nature purified of the otherness of sensuous nature' (Lauer 2010, p. 113). A materialist philosophy based on the construction of a 'second nature' mirroring an unreachable 'first nature' retreats into a transcendental position that maintains a strict methodological separation between nature 'in itself' and nature 'for us' and thus undermines Schelling's critical project, which is to think them together. For First and Second nature, see Chapter 2.
18. See *System of Transcendental Idealism* (Schelling 1978, pp. 211–12) and *The Ages of the World* (Schelling 2000, p. 44 ff.). I will take up the issue of the epochality of nature as being-as-becoming in Chapter 6.
19. The experience of chaos is not chaotic in the sense of unordered forces, but the stillness of forces felt in things as part of their 'unremitting urge to be' (Schelling 2000, p. 21).
20. See Matthews (2007, p. 5). The maxim can be found in Schelling's *Philosophy of Revelation.*
21. The term 'releasement' appears in *The Ages of the World*, well after Schelling had proposed and consequently abandoned his nature philosophy. Nature philosophy suffers from a tendency to collapse the human self into the will of the absolute, thereby wiping out the possibility of a wilful human freedom affirmed in specific contingent acts. However, the concept of releasement solves this problem by proposing the possibility of non-willing willing. See Davis (2007, p. 100 ff.) for an extensive discussion of the will and non-willing in Schelling's philosophy and Heidegger's appropriation of it.
22. Schelling's concept of the universal soul as a yearning expressed in the free self leads to a love of finite materiality as its source of freedom and self-experience: 'the soul does not hate the contracting force [of materiality] but rather loves this confinement as the only way that it can come to feel itself and as that which hands over the material and the, so to speak, means, which are the only way that the soul can come out' (Schelling 2000, p. 57). Schelling's philosophy of 'love of materiality' affirms negation: 'hence the soul does not want somehow to sublimate the negating force, neither in general nor as what precedes it. To the contrary, the soul demands and confirms the negating force and explicitly only wants to come out and

be visible in it so that consequently the soul, unfolding from the highest, is always enveloped and retained by the negating force as if by a receptacle' (pp. 57–58).

23. The unground is not groundlessness. Groundlessness refers to the mode of appearances of things without ground – the order of the simulacra. Groundlessness is an effect of the movement of grounding/ungrounding, and is not itself a ground. Schelling's concept of *Unground* prepares the way for Heidegger's concept of *ab-ground* in *Contributions to Philosophy* (Heidegger 1999, pp. 264–66).

24. Schelling calls this affirmation '*Nature as subject*' (Schelling 2004, p. 202).

25. '[T]he thunderbolt steers all things' (Heraclitus, Fragment 64, qtd. in Barnes 2001, p. 52).

26. Positive philosophy should not be confused with positivism. Positivism reduces all difference to the same that it then mistakes for the real; positivism tries to make the system equate with what it controls and enacts. On the other hand, positive philosophy is the affirmation of difference in the 'as such' or 'there is' of what it thinks about. While positivism has already determined what it thinks about in the calculations that it enacts, positive philosophy is always beginning in the thinking otherwise of possibilities seen in the finite event of what it thinks about.

27. This raises the problem of the beginning before the beginning, which Žižek claims is 'the crucial problem of German Idealism, [and where] Schelling's "materialist" contribution is best epitomized by his fundamental thesis according to which, to put it bluntly, *the true Beginning is not at the beginning*: there is something that precedes the Beginning itself – a rotary motion whose vicious cycle is broken, in a gesture analogous to the cutting of the Gordian knot, by the Beginning proper, that is, the primordial act of decision' (Žižek 1996, p. 13). The 'Beginning proper' does not begin prior to all other beginnings, but is itself ceaselessly beginning.

28. In *System of Transcendental Idealism*, Schelling proposes that self-becoming emerges in 'an infinite conflict in self-consciousness' (Schelling 1978, p. 50) acted out historically through epochal ruptures. See Chapter 6.

29. Deleuze and Guattari's nature philosophy, outlined in *A Thousand Plateaus: Capitalism and Schizophrenia* (1987, chapter 3), is influenced by Schelling's idea of volcanic becoming (Grant 2006, pp. 199–200). However, their work proposes a pre-critical vision of nature, thereby retreating into classicism, and deviates from a nature philosophy in the positive sense. Regarding Deleuze's work, Grant points out that Deleuze 'maintains the antithesis of nature and freedom [...] and therefore risks the elision of nature altogether' (p. 202).

30. These ideas relate to Plato's concept of *chora* – the place of the void – in the *Timaeus* (Sallis 1999, p. 114 ff. See this chapter, note 7).

31. Roland Barthes defines *signifiance* as the 'third meaning' of film: a stillness or void in the movement of film images (Barthes 1977, p. 65). *Signifiance* is the asignifying trait of the material 'becoming' of the film as the 'founding act of the filmic itself'. I take *signifiance* to be the mark of the possible found at the place of the void.

32. It is important to note that this beginning is not simply good, but the site of indecisiveness between good and evil (see Schelling 2006, p. 46). I take up this issue of good and evil in the following chapter.

5. Positive Freedom

1. Being a-part means being part of something but in the mode of a separation – as *partage*.

2. Schelling proposes 'the fact of freedom' (Schelling 2006, p. 9) as an immediate intuition of each individual that she is free. Freedom is itself the 'fact' that she is free, a fact that needs accounting for.

3. Ben Woodward's reading of Schelling and the possibility of an ecological ethics is apposite here. In light of Schelling's volcanic (i.e. dynamic) materialism and following a lead by Negarestani, Woodward argues that 'the ethical injunction necessary for ecology is the radical openness Negarestani links to the concept of affordance, balancing between actuality and potentiality in a world consisting only of moments. This absolute openness requires a relationship to pure externality, to an Other not as an anonymous but humanized otherness (a face) but a potentiality tied up with the uncertainties of humanity's abyssal freedom' (Woodward 2010, p. 87).

4. For sense see Chapter 2, note 3.

5. Following this theme Hans Jonas argues that the being of all organic life is freedom: 'if mind is prefigured in the organic from the beginning, then freedom is. And indeed our contention is that even metabolism, the basic level of all organic existence, exhibits it' (Jonas 1966, p 3).

6. The granting of freedom to things is to overcome the dead mechanism of the system of nature in both Spinoza and Kant, where things are reduced to either inert substances (Spinoza) or unknowable things in themselves (Kant).

7. Good and evil are not mutually privative (they do not cancel each other out) but share a common ground (an indivisible remainder) so that one is concealed in the other: 'Hence, good lies concealed in evil, albeit made unrecognizable by evil; likewise evil in good, albeit mastered by the good and brought to inactivity' (Schelling 2000, pp. 18–19). Evil is not the lack of good, but an insufficiency of the 'whole' of what is. To be good, evil is rendered insufficient, in the same way that to be sighted, blindness is rendered insufficient to the task of having to see. Being sighted and being blind compete for the sufficiency of the whole body. Insufficiency is resistive to what is the sufficiency of the whole. For sufficiency see Mitchell (2010, p. 105, note 7).

8. See Wirth (2003, p. 173) for a discussion of Schelling's theory of good and evil along these lines. Wirth notes a parallel between Schelling's theory of good and evil and the theory of health and disease proposed by Georges Canguilhem, whose ideas influenced Foucault, especially in his archaeological-genealogical analysis of medical discourse.

9. See Moss (2009) and Lemmens (2009) for a development of the ideas of 'detachment' as freedom in organic life. Moss and Lemmens draw on Hans Jonas's *The Phenomenon of Life: Toward a Philosophical Biology* (Jonas 1966) which argues for a return to Aristotle in order to think the interrelation of mind and nature in terms of a 'progressive freedom of action' (p. 2).

10. The seminal work on the distinction between positive and negative freedom is Isaiah Berlin's *Two Concepts of Liberty* (Berlin 1958). Put simply, in political thought, negative freedom leads to liberal ideas of individual freedom and rights, while positive freedom leads to communitarian-republican ideas of joint responsibility to common goals or ideals.

11. The concept of positive freedom avoids fatalism and quietism. Far from suggesting that we accept our fate in the determinism of the system, it indicates that we must decide responsibly with regard to all beings, in order to help bring about a change in the order of things, guided by principles of openness and potential fulfilment of being (*Bildung*). We must do this resistively, through the power we have to live life in reserve, even when obliged to live it for others. Positive freedom is a necessary heuristic for practical philosophy, that is, for any project of science organized by a 'regulative' principle that sets about changing the way things are.

12. Positive philosophy is not an alternative to negative philosophy but the positing of negative philosophy: 'the negative is itself positive since it posits the latter outside itself' (Schelling 2007, p. 197). Reflecting on his own philosophical development, Schelling says that the positive (i.e. the affirmation of a real existent as the basis of philosophical thought) can never be eliminated in negative (i.e. critical) philosophy – philosophy that begins from the negation of the real in order to secure purely rational grounds for thought; the positive must arise out of negation in negative philosophy's attempt to eliminate it in the name of pure reason (pp. 146–49).

13. In the second version of *The Ages of the World*, Schelling defines releasement (the freedom to be) as 'the *will that wills nothing*' (Schelling 1997, p. 132). In the third version, he discusses releasement as follows: 'And perhaps precisely that releasement (*Gelassenheit*) shows that something of the qualities of that primordial stuff still dwells within [things], of the stuff that is passive on the outside but on the inside is spirit and life' (Schelling 2000, p. 63). See also Chapter 4, section entitled 'The indivisible remainder' for further discussion of releasement and the will. Heidegger refers to Schelling's notion of 'released inwardness' (Heidegger 1985, p. 185) as a precursor to his own concept of *Gelassenheit* as 'letting be': 'to let beings be – does not refer to neglect and indifference but rather the opposite. To let be is to engage oneself with beings. On the other hand, to be sure, this is not to be understood only as mere management, preservation, tending, and planning of the beings in each case encountered or sought out. To let be – that is, to let beings be as the beings that they are – means to engage oneself with the open region and its openness into which every being comes to a stand, bringing that openness, as it were, along with itself' (Heidegger 1998, p. 144). For Schelling's concept of 'released inwardness' and its relation to Heidegger see Davis (2007, p. 118 et passim).

14. Hannah Arendt has argued that political freedom in pre-Christian thought was located in the 'I-can [as] an objective state of the body' (Arendt 1978, p. 19), enabling individuals to enter into relations with other individuals freely, without coercion. She differentiates this kind of freedom from the freedom associated with the 'I-will' that invokes the autonomy of the self and its drive to will itself into existence. Political freedom is the freedom of the 'I-can', not the 'I-will', the capacity to *be free* in open relations with others. The human-nature relation becomes positive when based on the I-can and not the I-will, thereby maintaining openness to the other. The I-can is 'the *will that wills nothing*' (Schelling 1997, p. 132) other than its own freedom, and hence freedom to be otherwise in open possibility.

15. Transitivity in art, for instance, occurs in contemporary environmental art practices that set out to actively change the relation between humans and nature in localized ways (Westin 2012).

230

16. Žižek thus continues the tradition of regarding Schelling's philosophy as an interesting yet flawed project, whose faults are rectified by Hegel in his dialectical rational system. But see Carew (2011). Carew argues that Žižek develops a position that is ultimately Schellingian.
17. Schelling's philosophy is positive from its very beginnings.
18. See Chapter 3 for the paradox of freedom in Kant. See also Crichtley (2012) for a discussion of Rousseau and the paradox of sovereignty (p. 21 ff.) as it plays out in terms of subjective freedom in the modern state.
19. The opening sentence is as follows: 'Philosophical investigations into the essence of human freedom can in part address the correct concept of freedom in so far as the *fact of freedom*, no matter how immediately the feeling of which is imprinted in every individual, lies in no way so fully on the surface that, in order merely to express it in words, an uncommon clarity and depth of mind would not be required' (Schelling 2006, p. 9, emphasis added). Schelling is saying here that the 'fact of freedom' is something more than the feeling that individuals have that they are free; a fact that requires a clear thinking of its connection to the system as a whole. Freedom, according to Schelling, is not the antithesis of the system, but its very basis. All systems are thus paradoxical at their core.
20. Žižek's construal of Schelling's free self here is closer to how he understands Kant's free self, which, in *The Parallax View*, he describes in the following terms: 'I am determined by causes (be it direct brute natural causes or motivations), and the space of freedom is not a magic gap in this first-level causal chain but my ability retroactively to choose/determine which causes will determine me. "Ethics", at its most elementary, stands for the courage to accept this responsibility' (Žižek 2006, p. 203). Žižek is suggesting that Schelling is simply following Kant in construing the free self in terms of 'my ability retroactively to choose/determine which causes will determine me'. See also Brockelman, who notes that Žižek's argument rejects the appeal to a self-immanent act of revolutionary openness in which the subject acts in the present on the basis of self-acknowledged freedom: 'Žižek can only save the revolutionary potential of the act by rejecting its immanence, the utopia of the present. The supposedly revolutionary desire to "live in the present" is, in fact, an unconscious subversion of the historical subject's revolutionary potential' (Brockelman 2008, p. 108). The issue here is really a question of the limits of the subject, and the possibility of a pre-subjective activity enacting freedom, which can only be recognized as such retroactively. The paradigm case for such an activity is art *praxis* (see following section). The *praxis* of art maintains and keeps openness open pre-subjectively.
21. This is a fall into an absolutely free openness 'where all support here fails' (Kant 1929, p. 513). See Chapter 3.
22. Schelling calls this an intellectual intuition, which is not an act of self-consciousness, but a pure act of thought thinking itself unconditionally (Frank 2004, p. 79). Such an act is necessary if thought is to be at all. Otherwise thought can only ever be thought of something and hence conditioned by what it thinks about, with no freedom to be. In his book on Schelling, Wirth defines intellectual intuition in the following terms: 'The intellectual intuition is not a way of somehow magically seeing what is *there*. Rather, it is the interruption of economies of presence by the insinuation within what is there of that which is not there' (Wirth 2003, p. 111). Intuition interrupts the economies of presence of identity formation

with an awareness of otherness as *there* by being not there. In his early essay 'On the Program of the Coming Philosophy', Walter Benjamin tried to think of intellectual intuition as a 'pure and systematic continuum of experience' (Benjamin 1996, p. 105) where knowledge is '*immediately* related in its continuous development' (p. 109). Benjamin was later to develop this idea of immediate intuition in terms of the 'flash' of the image of thought in thinking the absolute against the temporal horizon of time. Intellectual intuition is, as I will show in Chapter 7, related to *Augenblick*, or the 'blink of the eye' that sees otherwise in what is there to be seen; the glimpsing of the openness of otherness in the otherwise closed being of what is. To see in this way is to have one's existence affirmed as such; to be affirmed in the openness of 'free being'. Such an affirmation is only ever gained in the 'nothing' that awaits in the self's fall into absolute openness.

23. As testament to the absolute, the decision cannot be subjective. The difficulty here is in theorizing the decision as absolute without collapsing it back into a pre-critical concept of the Absolute, for example, a dogmatically theological concept of God, or some prevailing scientific idea such as natural selection. Walter Benjamin's essay 'Critique of Violence' (Benjamin 1996, pp. 236–52) is enlightening in this regard. Benjamin argues that the absolute decision involves 'divine violence' that breaks with mythic fate (the fate of the subject to be claimed by myth, by mythic violence of the law), and is thus an essentially free act. The absolute decision is the ultimate political act: the very event of the political. See also Derrida's discussion of the 'unconscious' decision in *Politics of Friendship*: 'the decisive or deciding moment of responsibility supposes a leap by which an act takes off, ceasing in that instant to follow the consequence of what is – that is, of that which can be determined by science or consciousness – and thereby *frees itself* (this is what is called freedom), by the act of its act, of what is therefore heterogeneous to it, that is knowledge. *In sum, a decision is unconscious* – insane as that may seem, it involves the unconscious and nevertheless remains responsible' (Derrida 1997, p. 69).

24. This raises the issue of an 'originary ethics' founded on an originary act of freedom. See Nancy's essay 'Originary Ethics' (Nancy 2003, pp. 172–95). Glossing Heidegger, Nancy writes: 'But what man is insofar he has to act is not a specific aspect of his being, but his very being itself' (p. 174).

25. For second nature see Lauer (2010, p. 113) and Chapter 4, note 17.

26. I take up the issue of the eternal decision in terms of Heidegger's concept of *Gelassenheit* or 'letting be' in Chapter 7. See also note 13, this chapter. Schürmann notes that in Heideggerian terms the eternal decision is revelatory or 'aletheiological' and 'necessarily non-human' (Schürmann 1990, p. 246–47). In following Heidegger, the eternal decision would need to be replaced by the epochal decision – the decisiveness that characterizes the split between different historical epochs of being.

27. In the second edition of *The Ages of the World*, Schelling writes: 'The decision that in some manner is truly to begin must not be brought back to consciousness; it must not be called back, because this would amount to being taken back. If, in making a decision, somebody retains the right to reexamine his choice, he will never make a beginning at all' (Schelling 1997, p. 182).

28. Breckman notes that for Schelling, God is 'pure will and free creativity' (Breckman 1999, p. 56). Here chance can be related to Plato's concept of 'errant cause' whereby for

something to come about, there must be the possibility of its being as such – its sheer contingency. The fact that something is, testifies to a necessity that it is contingently so, which is not a necessity of law, but of errancy, the possibility that this something could be otherwise. For a discussion of Plato's law of chance see Sallis (1999, p. 92). It follows that God must be bound up in such a possibility, as the openness of being as such – as the chance of being.

29. In *System of Transcendental Idealism*, Schelling distinguishes between two different artistic intuitions: one mechanical and the other what might be termed organic. In the former, the artist follows rules drawn from the schema (Schelling 1978, p. 136) so that the work of art is 'brought to completion' (p. 137) by following these rules. In the latter, the artist 'become[s] simultaneously conscious *for itself*, and unconscious' (p. 218), operating in a free but 'involuntary' way (p. 223), and following 'an unscrutable fate' (p. 223) by virtue of her being part of the 'dark unknown force' (p. 222) of organic becoming.

30. The quote is from Gilles Deleuze's *Francis Bacon: The Logic of Sensation* (Deleuze 2003). See note 3, p. 160 for a transcript of an interview with Bacon where the painter discusses the painting process in terms of decisiveness and risk.

31. Here Schelling anticipates the concept of *memoiré involontaire* proposed by Freud, Bergson Proust, and as developed by Benjamin in his essay 'On Some Motifs in Baudelaire' (Benjamin, 2003, pp. 313–55).

32. Whitehead calls the artist's brush stroke 'kinetic gesturing' (Whitehead 2003). However, Whitehead's analysis of artistic activity is not based on the deed of decisiveness; rather it invokes embodied sense, and as such remains within the terrain of the body that is recuperated as the site of aesthetic self-constitution. Ultimately, for Whitehead, the artwork is about artistic self-embodiment, and not with the openness of being as possibility. Whitehead uses the experience of art to think the embodiment of the artist as *autopoietic* activity, whereas what is needed is to allow the *poiesis* of the artwork to lead us into a thinking otherwise that makes possible new modes of being.

33. Generally, Schelling's philosophy of art does not point in the direction of a subjectivized aesthetics, but to an opening of being with nature to creative possibility in worlds not yet arrived – that is, not by anticipating their arrival in *techne*, but in letting them come, by unblocking technical and systemic closure into the same.

34. 'Everything passes in a flash of time, and this is the flash of time of painters' (Pierre Klossowski, qtd. in Wilson 2002, p. 19).

35. See Heidegger's comments on Schelling's concept of decisiveness in *Schelling's Treatise on the Essence of Human Freedom* (Heidegger 1985, pp. 154–56). Commenting on Schelling's concept of non-voluntaristic (i.e. non-willing) freedom, Shaw suggests that decisiveness involves the retroactive thought that 'I will have acted freely' (Shaw 2010, p. 31). I will discuss this retroactivity in terms of the future anterior tense in poetic acts in Chapter 8.

36. Derek Whitehead suggests that this space be called a space of '"unitary multiplicity," a poietical space wherein the artist, the work, and the receiver of such a work are brought forward in all the lineaments of their self-presentation' (Whitehead 2003).

37. Hegel writes: 'our present in its universal condition is not favourable to art [...] In all these respects art is, and remains for us, on the side of its highest destiny, a thing of the past'

(Hegel 1993, p. 13). For further discussion of Hegel and his argument concerning the inability of modern art to bear the truth of Being, see Chapter 7.

38. See Sallis, *The Verge of Philosophy*: 'whatever *is* is good precisely insofar as it *is*' (Sallis 2008a, p. 29). The good gives: 'It is in relation to this generosity – and not by bringing into play such modern concepts as value – that the goodness or excellence of things is to be understood [...] [For something] to be what it is – rather than being also other than what it is – is to be one and the same as itself. It is precisely this oneness that is bestowed by the good in its generosity' (p. 52, note 11).

6. Virtual Nature

1. The dividing of nature thus constitutes difference and hence the possibility of diacritical signification whereby things can be differentiated from one another according to their meaning. Divided nature enables signification, language and the law.

2. The turn to Spinoza has been encouraged through the writings of Deleuze (1990) and Deleuze and Guattari (1987). Their form of 'dynamic' Spinozism immanentizes material/ideational becoming as a floating 'plane of immanence', disconnected from and absorbing grounded nature. Timothy Morton's recent book *The Ecological Thought* (Morton 2010) shows strong evidence of this turn to dynamic Spinozism: the immanent plane becomes the thought of a 'mesh of interconnection' (p. 8). The thought acts as a transcendent-immanent possibility (a virtuality) that seeps through everything like a virus (p. 2). The major problem with this version of dynamic Spinozism is that there is no room for human freedom grounded in specific free acts; everything is reduced to an affect of the plane of immanence acting as a dynamized system of interconnected parts spiralling into infinity.

3. In a lengthy explication of Spinoza's philosophy in his book *Hegel or Spinoza*, Pierre Macherey, at one point, quotes Spinoza thus: 'Nature in its totality is a single Individual, whose parts, that is all the constituent bodies, vary in infinite ways, without changing the individual as a whole' (Spinoza, qtd. in Macherey 2011, p. 158). Macherey explains: 'To say that nature is always the same does not signify, then, that it is organized by a formal principle that constitutes it as a totality, but that it expresses itself completely through the sequence of its own determinations, to the exclusion of all external interventions' (p. 159). That is, Spinoza conceives of nature as a total system based on a universal mathematics with no excess (cf. Heidegger 1985, p. 34; Badiou 2005a, p. 120). There is no accommodation for a human self in some kind of special or free relation to nature (cf. Spinoza, *Ethics*, Part 3, Introduction; 1992, p. 102), a criticism levelled at Spinoza's system by both Schelling and Hegel (see Schelling 2006, pp. 19–21). Spinoza takes up a God-like position of all-knowing, which, Schelling argues, reduces the world to a mechanistic system of 'things' (p. 20). By way of contrast, Schelling's own position, adopting the full measure of critique post Kant, does not surrender its finitude with respect to the things it encounters and seeks to explain.

4. For globalism and the virtual, see Weber (2008, p. 33). Weber discusses Deleuze's philosophy of the virtual in terms of 'the global resolution of a problem' (p. 32), pointing to the '*living* organism' as the exemplary model of global integration. Jean-Luc Nancy develops a concept of

globalization that he defines as a disconnected, abstract process of global consolidation at the expense of contact with the finite world. He distinguishes globalization from *mondialisation* or world-forming, which is a finite-expanding process of connectivity, always in contact with itself and with the world which it helps create (Nancy 2007, pp. 27–28). These issues are dealt with more fully in Chapter 10.

5. Being a whole does not mean being complete and fully formed, but to be open in possibility. For instance, to be a whole person is to be *there* as open and enabled in possibility, and not to be closed into one way of being. A whole person is one who sees many aspects of herself as open and engaged with otherness. To be whole is not to be complete in oneself and hence closed to the world; rather, to be whole is to be incompletely so. A whole is thus an insufficient sufficiency as defined in the Chapter 5, note 7.

6. Schelling's concept of ecstatic time as a dynamic stretching of the 'now' – the in-between of the past and the future – prefigures Heidegger's description of *Dasein* (there-being) constituted through ecstatic time. See section 19 in Part 2, Chapter 1, *The Basic Problems of Phenomenology* (Heidegger 1982, p. 265). It also prefigures Benjamin's concept of extended space-time in technologically mediated contexts, and as proposed in his reading of Hölderlin's poetry. Samuel Weber identifies Benjamin's concept as 'a kind of *stretching*' (Weber 2008, p. 276). I take up the issue of stretched space-time in Benjamin in Chapter 9.

7. For ecocriticism based on paleontological eras, see for instance Chakrabarty (2009) and Dibley (2012).

8. This initial thought can be likened to Fichte's *Grundreflex* or fundamental reflex as the preconditioned 'I think' that necessarily accompanies any specific thinking about something (Fichte & Schelling 2012, p. 104; see also Vater & Wood 2012, p. 12).

9. There can be no more than three as these correspond to the absolute limit of time as becoming (past, present, future).

10. Schelling's triads also include inorganic, organic and universal nature and destiny, natural law and providence (Schelling 1978, pp. 211–12).

11. For recapitulation in Schelling's nature philosophy, see Grant (2006, p. 13). Schelling's dialectics is not an *entelechia* from materiality toward pure ideation, but a recapitulating movement of material-ideation as 'eternal beginning'.

12. The eternal beneficence of nature is not for the benefit of human being, but simply the 'it gives' of being itself. Human being must therefore be aligned with the 'it gives' of nature as being itself in order to benefit from it.

13. See Heidegger's essay, 'The Age of the World Picture' (Heidegger 1977, pp. 115–54): 'The world picture does not change from an earlier medieval one to the modern one, but rather the fact that the world becomes picture at all is what distinguishes the essence of the modern age [*der Neuzeit*]' (p. 130). In other words, dividing world-forming into distinct ages or epochs is a consequence of the modern practice of representation (the 'age of the world picture'). The epochs of the past are a product of a certain kind of thinking relative to the modern age.

14. The idea of a 'wheel of turns' is taken up by Derrida in his own critique of reason in *Rogues: Two Essays on Reason* (Derrida 2005, p. 6).

15. In Marxist theory of the human-nature relation, in a capitalist age the blockage comes from the forcing of the wage relation on otherwise free human being. Workers are blocked by the forced wage relation from realizing their 'free being' with nature as natural labour (see Chapter 1; see also Ryan 1984, p. 86).
16. The 'all or nothing' decisiveness of reason that Schelling proposes here can be applied to solve a vexing problem in evolutionary science that finds it difficult to account for the sudden emergence of a new order through gradual evolutionary change (for a discussion of this issue see Žižek 2006, p. 199).
17. Thus critique needs to begin from this stopped product, this stilled 'thing' in its ecstatic movement away from itself into otherness. In Schelling's later, theological writing he reiterates: 'in order to begin with that which just exists, in which nothing more is thought than just this existing – in order to see if I can get from it to the divinity' (qtd. in Bowie 1993, p. 145).
18. The age of providence is not any particular age, but always 'to come'. Modernity always imagines the future providentially as the fulfilment of promise already preparing itself in the present.
19. In Seminar VII of his seminars on the ethics of psychoanalysis, Lacan defines the Thing as a sublimation of the object (Lacan 1992, p. 112). The sublimated object is de-objectifed into an *Erscheinung*, or hallucinating image of otherness (p. 114). For further in *Erscheinung*, see notes 23 and 31 this chapter.
20. In effect the whole is an 'insufficient sufficiency' as it is always completing itself. See note 5 this chapter.
21. In *Clara*, Schelling outlines his philosophy of ideal immanence as distinct from ideal transcendence. He rejects the position that separates the ideal from material nature, and instead proposes that the ideal is always in a 'natural' (i.e. material) relation with nature (Schelling 2002, p. 5). Glimmering must be understood as an immanence of sense in the openness of possibility.
22. In *System of Transcendental Idealism*, Schelling writes: 'Nature, in its blind and mechanical purposiveness, admittedly represents to me an original identity of the conscious and unconscious activities, but [for all that,] it does not present this identity to me as one whose ultimate ground resides *in the self itself* [i.e. in self-reflection]. … An intuition must therefore be exhibitable in the intelligence [of nature] itself, whereby in *one and the same* appearance the self is at once conscious and unconscious *for itself*, and it is by means of such an intuition that we first bring forth the intelligence, as it were, entirely out of itself' (Schelling 1978, pp. 217–18).
23. Michael Rosen writes: 'As used by German Idealism, *Schein* is illusory only to the extent that our perception of an object in which *Schein* is manifest is somehow elusive or indefinite: although art is the realm of *Schein* this is not because art depicts a realm of objects and events that may not exist. *Schein*'s elusiveness is, rather, the index of the character of art as a kind of "occluded manifestation" of a higher reality' (Rosen 1996, p. 164). Hegel makes a distinction between *Schein* and *Erscheinung*. While *Schein* concerns the appearance of the 'essence' of the thing in itself, *Erscheinung* is the appearing of the essence itself, as the revelation of truth (see note 31).
24. For further discussion of Schelling's use of the concept of the symbol in his philosophy of art see Wirth (2003, pp. 146–51).

25. In the opening essay of *The Rhetoric of Romanticism* entitled 'Intentional Structure and Image', Paul de Man develops a reading of the symbolic image in Romantic poetry (here specifically Hölderlin's poem *Bread and Wine*) as 'the rediscovery of a permanent presence which has chosen to hide itself from us' (De Man 1984, p. 5). The poem enacts the possibility of an originary beginning (*poiesis*) forgotten in its own finitude in allegorical deconstitution (the forgetting of being). The Romantic symbol enacts a *remembering* of the forgetting of being as symbolic presentation, a 'painful' thought of the loss of full presence, which is nevertheless re-enacted in the symbolic image itself acting as a proxy for full presence. The epiphany triggered by the poem is accompanied by the realization of its impossibility.

26. The image as *Sinnbild* (symbolic, sensuously meaningful) is also a key part of Hölderlin's poetics. See Heidegger's analysis of Hölderlin's poetic hymn 'The Ister' (Heidegger 1996, p. 16).

27. Žižek claims that Hegel 'became Hegel' when he adopted Schelling's insight that the absolute was not outside the dialectical movement of self-reflection but precisely the very movement of self-reflection itself: 'Hegel "became Hegel" when he accepted that there is no Absolute *beyond* or *above* the reflexive oppositions and contradictions of the Finite – the Absolute is *nothing but* the movement of self-sublation of these finite determinations; it is not beyond reflection but is absolute reflection itself' (Žižek 1999, p. 95). However, for Schelling, the absolute as 'nothing but' the movement of self-sublation of finite determinations is itself positive, and not simply 'nothing'. That is, Schelling's insight is not that the absolute is nothing but absolute reflection; rather it is the 'nothing' that self-reflection requires in order to be the particular self-reflection that it is; the absolute includes both self-reflection *and* the 'more' or x that *must be*, but which has no being specifically assigned to it yet. See also Bowie (1993): 'Schelling reveals a fatal problem in Hegel's philosophy which has consequences for all subsequent philosophy [...] The basic issue is whether the aim of German idealism, the grounding of reason by itself, may not be a form of philosophical narcissism [as Hegel's philosophy suggests], in which reason admires its reflection in being without being able to give a validable account of its relationship to that reflection' (p. 128). And a few pages later, Bowie sums up Schelling's objections to this narcissism: 'Hegel fails to deal with the difficulty of how what is mediated can know itself to be identical with what is immediate without simply presupposing this identity. The fact is that the truth of being, which is supposed to be a *result*, would have already to be there at the beginning, thereby posing the question of how it could be known at all as itself (i.e. in the way I see myself, rather than a random object, in a reflection)' (p. 132).

28. Michael Lewis argues that '*any* notion of beings *as a whole* thinks that whole on the model of the *human being* and thus anthropomorphizes the whole' (Lewis 2007, p. 81). A subject can be taken as a 'whole' if its terms are exhausted in its efforts for self-completion, which is precisely the way Hegel understands the subject. There is an underlying closed system organicism in Hegel's thought of the subject (see Wilden 1980, pp. 127–28).

29. Wilden goes on to say that 'missing from it [Hegel's dialectical model] is the real and material context of "oppositions"' (Wilden 1980, p. 128). Wilden may, however, be confusing the 'real material context' with the phenomenal encounter with things. To invoke a 'real material context' is to slide away from the 'fact' of the x that must be in an encounter with things, into an empirical world already filled with 'objects'.

30. For further on dignity, see Chapter 1, note 15, and Chapter 10.

31. Hegel makes an important distinction between *Schein* and *Erscheinung*. Unlike *Schein* (appearance), *Erscheinung* (the appearing of appearance) opens the possibility of a world-beyond as the affirmation of meaning and the truth of experience. See Hegel 1977, p. 89. For the distinction between *Schein* and *Erscheinung*, see "Appearance, Illusion and Shining," in Inwood. See note 23 this chapter.

32. Lacan is asked by an interlocuter after the seminar 'Why do you speak to us about the Thing instead of simply speaking about mediation?' This is part of Lacan's reply: 'It is clear that we [i.e. Lacan himself] put the accent on the irreducible element [i.e. the x] in the instinct, on that which appears at the limit of a mediation and that reification is unable to encompass. But in encircling that something whose limits we explore, we are encircling the empty image [...] That Hegelian radicalism that was rashly attributed to me [...] should in no way be imputed to me. The whole dialectic of desire that I develop here [...] is sharply distinguished from such Hegelianism' (Lacan 1992, p. 134).

33. In Lacan's clinical work with psychosis, at the end of the sessions the psychotic person will hopefully see the delusion from which she is suffering for what it is and simply walk away. She is released from the delusion that is blocking her from being the person she can be. She lives on in full human and hence mythic connectivity, but without delusion.

7. Heidegger's Thing

1. Circumspective looking sees things either as ready-to-hand (*Zuhanden*) or as present-at-hand (*Vorhanden*). As ready-to-hand, things are seen in their usefulness as equipment for doing and making things. As present-at-hand, things are seen as particular objects, simply there to see (the way science 'atomises' things into calculable systems). Heidegger argues that readiness-to-hand and presence-at-hand are interrelated within a presupposed world. Thus, from Heidegger's perspective, Kant's reduction of things as 'objects' of transcendental analysis is itself a particular kind of 'use' of things within a presupposed world of mechanistic causation, where it remains undecidable whether 'readiness-to-hand is ontologically founded upon presence-at-hand' (Heidegger 1962, p. 101).

2. *Techne* does not mean simply technique for making things but a theoretical seeing-knowing: a look that knows what it sees in advance, as an idea (*eidos*) coming into being. The *techne* of a carpenter is not his practical skills at making a chair, but the bringing into being of the *eidos* of the chair he already 'has in mind'. *Techne* is a form of 'disclosive looking' (Rojcewicz 2006, p. 58).

3. Heidegger distinguishes between being and Being (with a capital B). The latter is presupposed by the fact that it can be said that there are beings: that something *is*. Being with a capital B cannot simply be another being (e.g. a proxy for God, divine presence, transcendent order, mysterious *plenum*, higher unity, etc.) but is both the possibility and limit of beings. Being is another name for the Absolute as employed by Schelling and in German Idealism. See also Introduction, note 7.

4. Heidegger notes that the system of efficient causality has 'changed once again. Causality now displays neither the character of the occasioning that brings forth nor the nature of the

causa efficiens [efficient cause], let alone that of *causa formalis* [formal cause]. It seems as though causality is shrinking into a reporting – a reporting challenged forth – of standing-reserves that must be guaranteed either simultaneously or in sequence' (Heidegger 1977, p. 23). Technology now orders nature in terms of the reporting of technical facts, leading to a 'deceptive illusion […] that modern technology is applied physical science' (p. 23).

5. See Chapters 2 and 5 for the distinction between first and second nature. Current developments in biotechnology lead to the conclusion that second nature science is already laying claim to first nature materiality (see Thacker 2007). See Chapter 10.

6. Nancy may have borrowed the term 'denatured' from Heidegger, who uses the term in his discussion of Hölderlin's poems 'Germany' and 'The Rhine' (Bate 2000, p. 256). For denaturing, see Chapter 1 and Chapter 10.

7. Heidegger's introduction to *Being and Time* begins as follows: 'this question [of Being] has today been forgotten' (Heidegger 1962, p. 21). This initial statement indicates the general positioning of Heidegger's critique in its earlier phase, which concerns the being to whom the question is addressed – human *Dasein* (there being). In his later philosophy, this position is reversed so the critique begins with the 'event' of Being itself (*Ereignis*). Heidegger's writings on technology belong to this later phase. See also Heidegger's 'Letter on "Humanism,"' (Heidegger 1998, p. 253).

8. This absence of any discussion of the function of art in relation to the technology in Brockelman's argument flies in the face of the essay's conclusions, which clearly invoke art as that which makes a decisive confrontation with technology while remaining 'akin' to it (Heidegger 1977, p. 35). We can only access the essence of technology through the realm of art, so Heidegger concludes. As Rojcewicz points out, the essay was originally a lecture delivered to a seminar arranged by the Bavarian Institute of Fine Arts in Munich with the explicit purpose of exploring the role of art in relation to technology (Rojcewicz 2006, p. 185).

9. Heidegger makes no distinction between artefacts and works of art, but this is in keeping with his more general point that artefacts are a form of artwork with respect to the particular *techne* that enables them to come forth and be seen in a particular way.

10. By saying that *poiesis* is not 'in itself' but in another, Heidegger does not mean that this being 'in another' is the goal or end point of *poiesis*; that is, he is not saying that the artist 'has' *poiesis* while the silver chalice does not. Rather, what he means is that both silver chalice and artist share *poiesis*, not as an overarching force or capacity, but as the possibility ('bursting open') that happens in their conjuncture. See Chapter 1, Section '*Poiesis*'.

11. In his essay 'The Event', Deleuze employs the term 'prehension' to describe the interconnectedness between things 'as something more than a connection or conjunction' (Deleuze 1993, p. 78). A prehension connects parts without a whole; that is, the parts 'carry' the whole as an incompletion. Thus each part contributes to the 'making whole' of that which it connects to, without this whole preceding the prehension.

12. Brockelman goes on to a completely misleading view of Heidegger's position on nature. Following Žižek's own criticisms of Heidegger (which is the topic of his book), he quotes approvingly Žižek's criticism of the concept of a natural equilibrium of nature found in his (i.e. Žižek's) *Looking Awry* (1992), a book published many years prior to Žižek's current critical work on Heidegger, when Žižek was still in sympathy with Heideggerian philosophy. In this

quote Žižek argues for the abandonment of the classical-mechanistic concept of nature as a homeostatic system in favour of a chaos theory concept of nature as stochastic process, so that nature 'is already in itself turbulent, imbalanced' (p. 38). However, in citing this passage, Brockelman imputes this classical-mechanical position to Heidegger. Nothing could be further from the truth. For Heidegger nature is not a homeostatic system obeying mechanistic principles, but that which 'stirs and strives' in encounters with things (Heidegger 1962, p. 100). Indeed for Heidegger, to see nature as a homeostatic system would be to see it as something present-at-hand through a circumspection reserved for scientific looking, so that its stirring and striving 'remains hidden'. Thus Brockelman attributes the wrong position to Heidegger. Žižek is not antithetical to Heidegger on this occasion but aligned with him. Brockelman then compounds the error by going on to argue that Heidegger's (now wrongly attributed) view of nature blinds us to 'another nature', the one Brockelman attributes to Žižek: 'the very view of nature implicit in Heidegger's "answer" to the technology question – the very "piety" carried in his "questioning" – blinds to us [sic] *another* nature' (p. 30). This other nature is concealed from us by the ecologists' adoption of the classical-mechanistic model supposedly encouraged by Heidegger's philosophy, which, so it is suggested by Brockelman, proposes a homeostatic model of nature. But this other 'turbulent' nature (Žižek) is in fact the same finite nature that 'stirs and strives' as described by Heidegger in Section 70 of *Being and Time*, already hidden from us when we 'see' nature as present-at-hand, as an objectified 'thing' in scientific terms, or as ready-to-hand equipment for use.

13. Heidegger's 'turn' in philosophy can be understood as a shift from an ahistorical account of human being in the early phase of his writings, characterized by the formal analysis of *Dasein* in *Being and Time*, to a concern for the historical (un)grounding of human being in technological enframing in the later phase. For Heidegger, philosophizing had become, in these later writings, a 'reflection on the situation and place of contemporary man, whose destiny is still but little experienced with respect to its truth' (Heidegger 1977, p. 54).

14. To make this distinction Heidegger uses a number of examples including the difference between pre-industrial and industrial modes of agriculture: 'The work of the peasant does not challenge the soil of the field. In the sowing of the grain it places the seed in the keeping of the forces of growth and watches over its increase. But meanwhile even cultivation of the field has come under the grip of another kind of setting-in-order, which *sets* upon nature' (Heidegger 1977, p. 15). *Techne* is used here by Heidegger to refer to the technology of pre-industrialized modes of harvesting of crops as a 'bringing-forth [...] grounded in revealing' (p. 12), but this also applies to modern technology: 'What is modern technology? It too is a revealing' (p. 14).

15. Mitchell points out that it is more accurate to translate *Ge-stell* as positioning rather than enframing: 'The spread of positionality is [...] not a framework that surrounds from without, but, in part, a process of conscription [*Gestellung*] that adopts and compels whatever it encounters into the order of standing reserve' (Mitchell 2012, p. xi).

16. The essay 'The Origin of the Work of Art' (1935–36) predates 'The Question Concerning Technology' (1949–55) by some twenty years (both essays began their life as lectures and were revised by Heidegger a number of times). The later essay places the question of the origin of art raised in the earlier essay within an expanded question of technology, and so the two can be read together as addressing the same question but in different modes. The volumes

published as *Poetry, Language, Thought* (1971) and *The Question Concerning Technology and Other Essays* (1977), contain a number of essays including the two mentioned above, that make up a body of work addressing the broader question of the relation of art, language and technology to the event of Being (*Ereignis*). I will refer to the essays in these volumes as a consistent philosophical writing addressing this broader question.

17. To say that something inanimate such as a work of art is capable of 'thinging' is not as unusual as it might seem. After all we routinely use the term 'influence' to describe the way books, art and other creative works can affect numerous people: a book is said to influence many people, explaining the way it 'gathers' them into its meaning.

18. Singular things are indeterminate. Kant proposes indeterminacy as the basis of reflective judgement of beautiful things (Kant 1987, p. 49).

19. Jacques Rancière argues that the aesthetic regime of modern art (and by this he means western art since the Romanticism of the late eighteenth century) asserts 'the absolute singularity of art, and, at the same time, destroys any pragmatic criterion for isolating this singularity' (Rancière 2004, p. 23). See also Vattimo (2008), who argues that Heidegger's ontology of art proposes that the artwork must be understood in terms of its 'absolute novelty' and in terms of 'the shock [*Stoss*] produced by the work [...] [which is] the fact that there is a work of art at all' (p. 68). Here shock is not to be reduced to a subjective state of inner emotions, nor to the marvellous wonder of art, but describes the mood (or attunement) of openness that happens in encounters with art as an event of opening a world. In its capacity to open up a world, the artwork 'is full of instituting force' (p. 69).

20. Heidegger's concept of *Gelassenheit* can be traced to both Nietzsche and Schelling. Frank Schalow points out that Heidegger's critique of Schelling (see Heidegger 1985) is a crucial moment in his philosophical development, as it marks the point at which Heidegger ceased thinking of freedom in terms of human *Dasein* as the ultimate good, and rather allowed him to think of freedom in terms of the co-existence of good and evil as absolute possibility (Schalow 1995, p. 368). It is at this point, so Schalow suggests, that Heidegger was able to throw off the vestiges of voluntarism (reducing freedom to a matter of the will), and propose freedom as space opened up in non-willing or *Gelassenheit*. For *Gelassenheit* (releasement) in Schelling see Chapter 4, p. 63 and note 21; Chapter 5, note 13.

21. Foltz mentions turning only once, as a 'turn away from the danger intrinsic to modern technology' (Foltz 1995, p. 105), but not as an operation within technology itself.

22. Twisting free is discussed by Heidegger in Volume 1 of his writings on Nietzsche (1979, pp. 201–02). Twisting free is not an overcoming that leaves nothing of what is overcome behind (it is not a Hegelian *Aufhebung*), but a turning out of and away that carries something of what it leaves behind with it. Heidegger also describes turning as a 'step back' (1969, p. 50) See Vattimo (1987, 2004, pp. 28–29) for a discussion of Heidegger's concept of *Verwindung* as twisting free from metaphysics: 'One lives metaphysics as the possibility for a change, the chance that it might twist in a direction that is not foreseen in its own nature' (1987, pp. 12–13). Twisting free is the Heideggerian source of Derrida's strategy of deconstruction.

23. 'But as a world opens itself the earth comes to rise up. It stands forth as that which bears all, as that which is sheltered in its own law and always wrapped up in itself. World demands its decisiveness and its measure and lets beings attain to the Open of their paths. Earth, bearing

and jutting, strives to keep itself closed and to entrust everything to its law. The conflict is not a rift (*Riss*) as a mere cleft is ripped open; rather it is the intimacy with which opponents belong to each other. This rift carries the opponents into the source of their unity by virtue of their common ground. It is the basic design, an outline sketch, that draws the basic features of the rise of the lighting of beings. This rift does not let opponents break apart; it brings the opposition of measure and boundary into their common outline' (Heidegger 1971, p. 63). The conflict between earth and world described here by Heidegger is drawn from Schelling's concept of *Unground* as the dialectical movement of indifferent Being in-between ground and existence (see Chapter 4). Sinclair claims that the concept of earth is Heidegger's 'discovery' (Sinclair 2006, p. 61); however it is clearly derived from Schelling's freedom essay and more generally from Schelling's anti-Hegelian dialectics. Heidegger's own critique of Schelling (Heidegger 1985) indicates a problem in Schelling's handling of the 'jointure of Being' – the disjunctive relation between ground and existence noted for instance in the above quote. Here is Heidegger's specific criticism: 'That is the difficulty which emerges more and more clearly in Schelling's later efforts with the whole of philosophy, the difficulty which proves to be an *impasse* (*Scheitern*). And this *impasse* is evident since the factors of the jointure of Being, ground and existence and their unity not only become less and less compatible, but are even driven so far apart that Schelling falls back into the rigidified tradition of Western thought without creatively transforming it' (Heidegger 1985, p. 161). Heidegger's response to the 'incompatibility' of ground and existence is to rework Schelling's argument so that the conflicting elements, renamed earth and world, are more clearly delineated in a finite sense, as an openness right at the place of disjuncture.

24. The term hypostasis is drawn from Aristotle's metaphysics and developed by the early Christian scholars to account for the existence of God's free person in the world: 'Thus God as person – as the hypostasis of the Father – makes the one divine substance to be that which it is: the one God [...] That is to say, the substance never exists in a "naked" state, that is, without hypostasis, without a "mode of existence"' (Zizioulas 1985, p. 41). In its religious usage, hypostasis is the substitution of material with divine substance in the singular person of God. In its quasi-religious usage, this substitution takes place in the absence of God. A thing is hypostasized if it is given a divine reality that is said to constitute its individuated being. In Levinas's philosophy, the face of the other is a hypostasized thing (Levinas 1996, p. 53).

25. This is how I understand Heidegger's phrase '*openness to the mystery*' (Heidegger 1966, p. 55). Mystery does not belong to another world, but to the otherworldliness (*unheimlich-ness*) of this world in its everydayness.

26. The same lack of innerness also applies to living things. A surgeon operating on a living human body simply reveals more things (organs, veins, etc.) openly arranged.

27. Schelling asks a similar question of natural things: the question is not what brings them together into a unity but what keeps them apart, what makes them singular in their relatedness to one another? (Schelling 2004, p. 19). The term for this keeping-apart is *partage*. See Chapter 4.

28. See Dreyfus and Kelly (2011, p. 116) for a discussion of divine innerness in the Christian understanding of truth. A hypostatic experience of nature, as Foltz suggests here, is one that experiences the divine presence 'indwelling' in things.

29. The use of the verb 'to thing' relates to original attunement (*Stimmung*): a primary orientation to being that opens things to possibilities of meaning, over and above their signifying function. As Vattimo suggests: 'things, in addition to having a function, possess an attuned valence (Vattimo 2008, p. 62). Original or 'affective' attunement is 'the opening moment of the world' (p. 66).

30. The void is not an empty abstraction of absolute nothingness; it does not negate being. Rather it is the in-between of being and not-being; we can 'tarry' in the void. Heidegger also uses the term the Open, borrowed from Rilke, to describe this openness of being. For the void as a positive see Chapter 2.

31. Heidegger's ontology is cosmic in scope, where cosmic is understood at the intersection of the finite and the infinite. The cosmic is the space opened up in-between the finite and the infinite. For cosmic in art see Vattimo (2008, p. 52). The cosmic reach of art relates to art's capacity to open worlds as part of *poietic*-cosmic becoming of everything, in the same way that pre-Socratic philosophy and art engaged directly with cosmic becoming.

32. Recapitulation is the event of 'enowning' (*Ereignis*): the turning-passing through of Being into openness: 'a turning, or rather *the* turning, which points out precisely the essential sway of being itself as the counter-resonating enowning' (Heidegger 1999, p. 184). Recapitulated meaning is always already ahead of *Dasein*; ahead of any attempt to claim it as one's own. Schelling's nature philosophy employs a concept of recapitulated meaning along similar lines (see Chapter 4).

33. For Heidegger, the step back is opposed to the lifting up of Hegelian *Aufhebung*: 'For Hegel, the conversation with the earlier history of philosophy has the character of *Aufhebung*, that is, the mediating concept in the sense of an absolute foundation [...] For us [i.e. Heidegger himself], the character of the conversation with the history of thinking is no longer *Aufhebung* (elevation), but the step back' (Heidegger 1969, p. 49).

34. In an age of consumption, technically produced objects are 'ersatz' objects; that is, objects 'already en route to replacement' (Mitchell 2010, p. 27).

35. Heidegger borrows the concept of the Open from the poet Rilke. The Open operates as an absolute concept, in the same way that the Absolute operates for German Idealist philosophy.

36. Heidegger's use of the term 'object' requires some consideration in relation to 'standing reserve'. In 'The Origin of the Work of Art', Heidegger says that we cannot get at the thingness of the art work by examining its context of references and intentions but must 'let it stand on its own for itself alone' (Heidegger 1971, p. 40). By this he does not mean that the artwork is an 'object' in the same way that science regards things as objects; rather its 'self-subsistence' – its object-like status as something present-at-hand and enduring – has something else about it, its 'work being' (p. 41): the work that the artwork does in bringing forth a world – its capacity to 'thing'. In proposing this concept of the artwork as a self-subsisting thing, Heidegger had yet to develop his concept of standing reserve – the mode of being of something on 'stand by' waiting to be called upon for ordering and use (Heidegger 1977, p. 17). Standing reserve 'no longer stands over against us as object' (p. 17). Standing reserve nevertheless can have an object-like look to it, not in terms of 'permanency, but the orderability and substitutability of objects' (p. 17, editor's note). Pieces of standing reserve

can be singularized as self-subsisting 'objects' and made to thing, for instance empty match boxes strung together in an art installation, as described by Lacan (see Chapter 6), or an old lamp from a previous technological era as described by Benjamin (see Chapter 9).

37. The ability of something to say yes and no at the same time with equal veracity requires that we grasp the time of this saying as open to all times: to the past, present, and future as absolutely possible. Heidegger's argument here has a precedent in Schelling's argument of the Yes and No of Being: 'As such it always remains that if one of them has being, then the other cannot have the *same* being. That is, it remains that both exclude each other with respect to time [...] For different times (a concept that, like many others, has gotten lost in modern philosophy) [...] are necessarily at the same time. Past time is not sublimated time. What has past certainly cannot be as something present, but it must be something past at the same time with the present. What is future is certainly not something that has being now, but it is a future being at the same time with the present. And it is equally inconsistent to think of past being, as well as future being, as utterly without being' (Schelling 2000, p. 76). Schelling's doctrine of time suggests that the 'moment' contains all of its possible tenses such that any given moment is an epochal opening, a beginning of possibility. The artwork opens up an absolute temporality epochally, in which Being begins in the absolute possibility of 'any-time-whatever'.

38. For a fuller definition of poetizing in relation to Heidegger's analysis of Hölderlin's poetry, see the following chapter.

39. John Sallis (2008) points out that Heidegger is responding to Hegel's announcement that art could no longer manifest truth in a direct sensible way (as Greek art was able to), thus announcing the end of art. Once truth surpasses sensible manifestation and takes on intelligibility, then art ceases to have an ontological bearing. However, Heidegger argues that Hegel's position relies on certain metaphysical ideas of truth in which the sensible and intelligible are united in the artform. Instead, Heidegger argues for a different kind of truth, one based on 'a new interpretation of the sensible' (Sallis 2008, p. 157): truth as openness or 'unconcealment' (p. 157), in the artwork itself: 'Setting truth into the artwork, setting it to work in the work so that it happens there – and only in such a setting – as truth, will not be a matter of setting something intelligible into a work that, simply by virtue of its sensible character, cannot measure up to that truth [i.e. it is not Hegel's position]. The truth that, in Hegel's phrase, obtains existence for itself in the artwork, will be a truth that – to reverse what Hegel says of postclassical art – is so akin and friendly to sense as to be capable of being sensibly presented' (p. 157). Heidegger counters Hegel's declaration that art can no longer bear truth, with a more 'originary' claim always already bearing truth in its singular work of sense opening to Being.

40. In the following chapter I show how Heidegger reverses his analysis by remythifying Hölderlin's poems in terms of the gathered being of a national type.

41. Derrida's comments on Heidegger's reading of Van Gogh's painting draw out a certain privileging of what Heidegger calls 'reliability' (1971, p. 34) or in Derrida's terms, 'preoriginary' contact with the earth – 'belonging [...] to the silent discourse of the earth' (Derrida 1987, p. 354). However, there is a necessary ambiguity throughout Heidegger's work about originary grounding especially in relation to technology. Derrida's comments

here that interpret Heidegger's reading of the shoes as belonging to the silent *discourse* of the earth equate discourse (*logos*) with poetic saying, but for Heidegger, following Hölderlin, poetic saying is the originary 'moment' of language as the naming of things. Poetic saying is the originary condition of discourse, and, as such, it cannot *be* discourse; rather it enables discourse to begin without being reduced to it.

42. This grounding/ungrounding of the thing in the painterly material is an important aspect of modern art from the early nineteenth century on. Yves-Alain Bois and Rosalind Krauss call this the *informe* or painterly 'slippage' (Bois and Krauss 1997, p. 15). The later landscape painting of J.M.W. Turner provides a good example of this slippage or unearthing of the 'idea' in the painterly gesture, for instance in the painting 'Rain, Steam and Speed' we see the vague outlines of a train approaching through swirling mist, releasing the 'forces of nature' as chaotic *informe*. The idea is not lying behind the painting but comes out at the viewer in a dissipation of sense. The image empties itself of form, plunging the viewer into a formless abyss. Turner's later landscapes effect a slippage that reaches beyond the limits of the cognitive-logical absolute of meaning and 'take[s] painting down a deserted path of no return that is indistinguishable from a final question' (Deleuze & Guattari 1994, p. 2).

43. It may be objected that by using ancient Greek art for many of his examples in 'The Work of Art' essay, Heidegger privileges the kind of artwork that things not in order to open up another world, but to maintain the openness of an already existing world. But this is to miss Heidegger's crucial point about the historicality of art, and the fact that western art develops through various epochs with different ways of revealing different types of worlds. Modern works of art, in their initial presentation to a public, may open up their world otherwise, but eventually this otherwiseness consolidates into familiar worldliness. At the time of their initial showing, Cezanne's still life paintings of apples precariously placed on proto-Cubist tabletops defying Newtonian physics may open up an entirely new world of postmodern visual and embodied experience in the latenineteenth century, but at some point, this world has been realized in routine ways, so that Cezanne's paintings cease to have any revolutionary effect and become absorbed into the fabric of the very world they helped open up, where they become, like the ancient Greek temple, sites that keep the world 'abidingly in force'.

44. If we follow Heidegger here, it is a mistake to reduce the creative art practices to a matter of circumspective looking, as if what counted was the capacity of an artist to follow any one of a number of possibilities seen in the anticipating *eidos* of a *techne*. Rather this circumspective looking must itself be inhabited by a counterwise seeing; a seeing that comes in the 'waiting' of the open encounter with things in letting them be: 'we should *do* nothing at all, but rather wait [...] the circle-of-vision is thus something open, which does not have its openness from the fact that we see into it' (Heidegger 2010, pp. 71–72).

45. In *Nietzsche*, Vol. 2, Heidegger describes the *Augenblick* as 'the image of time running forward and backward into eternity' (Heidegger 1984, p. 41). See also McNeill (1999, p. 220 ff.) for a discussion of Heidegger's reading of Nietzsche and the concept of *Augenblick*.

46. Heidegger describes this kind of seeing as 'the *beholding that watches over truth*' (Heidegger 1977, p. 165).

47. My reading of Heidegger's text differs somewhat from Derrida's in *Specters of Marx* (Derrida 1994, pp. 23–29). Derrida criticizes Heidegger for giving priority to 'gathering and to the

same […] over the disjunction implied by my address to the other' (p. 28). In other words, Derrida criticizes Heidegger for valorizing the unity of self-presence at the expense of the disjunctive forces within it that lead to openness and the possibilities of the otherwise. However, my reading indicates that Heidegger's concern is not to valorize self-presence, but to think from within it, in terms of the disjunctive forces (the force of *poiesis*) that Derrida says he disclaims. As Heidegger himself says, the 'fundamental trait of what is present […] is injustice' (Heidegger 2002, p. 266), where injustice is thought of in terms of primary disjuncture.

48. For Heidegger's discussions of *Gelassenheit* as releasement and letting be, see 'On the Essence of Truth' (Heidegger 1998, pp. 144–45) and *Country Path Conversations* (Heidegger 2010, pp. 70–80). *Gelassenheit* involves a fundamental freedom to be in the otherwise of open possibility, and as such retains elements of Kantian critique. See also discussions of *Gelassenheit* as releasement in Schelling's philosophy, in Chapters 4 and 5. See also note 20 this chapter.

49. For a discussion of *Gelassenheit* and non-willing in Heidegger see Davis (2007, pp. 15–17 et. passim.)

50. Derrida notes that justice concerns the turning (the 'eternal recurrence') of being in which the other returns to inhabit the same: 'in this logic of the turn or round, of the other turn or round, of the other time, thus of the other, of the *alter* in general' (2005, pp. 30-31). Besides its importance for Derrida's and Heidegger's account of ontological justice, the theme of ontological turning is also prominent in Schelling's account of freedom and the epochal becoming of Being (the 'wheel of nature'). See Chapter 6.

51. This figuration can be understood as technical slippage or *informe*. See Mules (2006).

52. For a presentation of an open democratic space prefigured by artwork see Philip Armstrong's analysis of the 'space of exposure' revealed in photographs taken of the resistance to capitalism at the 2000 G20 meeting in Seattle (Armstrong 2009). See also Mules (2010a).

8. Poetics: Benjamin and Celan

1. Myth is an originating moment that reconciles human being and nature, thereby justifying what is in terms of essential meaning. See Chapter 6.

2. See also Žižek's criticism of Heidegger's reading of Hölderlin's poetry, leading to a reinscription of technology into the 'organic state-community' (Žižek 2006, p. 277).

3. '[T]here is no such thing as either man or nature now, only a process that produces the one within the other and couples machines together' (Deleuze and Guattari 1983, p. 2).

4. Samuel Weber traces the use of the term *Dichten* or 'poeticizing' in aesthetics to Kant's *Critique of Judgment* (Weber 1996, p. 22). For Kant, *Dichten* is the power to 'sustain free play' of the imagination (Kant 1987, p. 244). *Dichten* sustains the subject suspended in the free play of the imagination when confronted with indeterminate things. Thus *Dichten* becomes a key term in thinking about the possibilities of a self in non-determined, non-conceptual openness.

5. Weber notes that the addition of the word 'others' (*anderer*) extends the 'life' of the poem to a virtual determinacy as a '*looking away from, rather than a looking toward*' (Weber 2008, p. 18). This looking away is a flight from rather than a facing toward the event of Being.

6. A reading of Heidegger's analysis of *Dasein*'s relation to the Other in *Being and Time* (Part 1, Sect. 4, no. 26) provides an illuminating counterpoint to Benjamin's strategy here. Heidegger says that *Dasein* (the possibility of human there-being) must first be thought from an encounter with everyday things already assigned to others as 'a world which is always mine too in advance' (Heidegger 1962, p. 154). That is, *Dasein* cannot 'be' unless this being is thought in terms of the otherness of things as appropriable to it. Compare this with Benjamin's account of otherness as an addition '– and others' – in his reading of Hölderlin's poem, which begins not with *Dasein*'s dilemma in having to individuate its own being from the 'they' that one already is, but with a movement of the poetized that enables a co-existence of *Dasein* in otherness through the same transitive movement, in terms of an inappropriable open possibility.

7. The theme of gathered being is developed in *Being and Time* (Part 2, Sect. 5, no. 75), the section entitled 'Dasein's Historicality, and World History' where Heidegger analyses *Dasein*'s 'authentic historicality' in terms of Being-towards-death as destiny. In relation to the 'question of the "connectedness" of life', Heidegger has this to say: 'the question [...] asks [...] in which of its own kinds of Being *Dasein loses itself in such a manner that it must, as it were, only subsequently pull itself together out of its dispersal, and think up for itself a unity in which that "together" is embraced*' (Heidegger 1962, p. 442). *Dasein* must 'pull itself together' out of its 'dispersal' or 'thrownness' in the indifferent 'they'.

8. Roland Barthes's theory of myth is apposite here. In his essay 'Myth Today' in *Mythologies*, Barthes identifies myth as a gesture of racial inclusion in which the colonized are incorporated into the myth of a naturalized empire at the expense of their specific historical struggle with the colonizers (Barthes 1973, pp. 109–59). His well-known analysis of a photograph of a young black soldier saluting the French flag on the cover of *Paris-Match* (pp. 116–31) suggests that the mythic work of the image here in including the 'black' man under the 'white' French flag is equivalent to Heidegger's strategy, in his reading of Hölderlin, of including the non-white women as part of the white German folk.

9. However, this charge needs to be seen in the full light of Heidegger's elucidations and poetizing of Hölderlin's poetry, as discussed in the previous chapter. It is not the case that Heidegger simply has no understanding of what is specifically poetic about Hölderlin's poetry; rather, having exposed its radical implications, he fails to follow through on them and instead retreats into myth.

10. In an earlier publication, Lacoue-Labarthe has identified the political ramifications of this retreat into mythic origins as symptomatic of a nationalism based on the historical destiny of the German people as inheritors of the 'Greek beginning' (Lacoue-Labarthe 1990, pp. 55–56). Shaw notes that Schelling's philosophy of art also appeals to a Greek beginning that 'was an ideological projection of German social relations onto those of ancient Greece' with dangerous political consequences (Shaw 2010, pp. 85–86).

11. Truth here is the truth of the exception, where the singularity of the artwork affirms being otherwise: an absolute affirmation of being-as-other, and hence as pure possibility or chance.

12. As already noted, Heidegger also uses the term 'poetized' (*Dichtung*) in his readings of Hölderlin (see previous chapter).

13. In his essay 'Myth Today', Barthes argues that the function of modern poetry is the reverse of myth, but notes that in its difference from myth, poetry 'surrenders to it [myth] bound hand and foot' (Barthes 1973, p. 134). However, this would not be the case for demythifying poetry, that is, poetry that begins within myth in order to demythify myth. Barthes further notes that there is only one type of non-mythic language: the language of transitive action, where the words said relate to a 'doing' that transforms the world, as distinct from intransitive action where the words said relate to a mediation through images: 'There is therefore one language which is not mythical, it is the language of man as a producer' (p. 146). However, as I have argued, this too is mythical insofar as man's labour is understood as natural labour: as the labour of nature, where the 'doing' of man is undertaken in terms of human freedom or amelioration toward a natural state of 'free being'. There can be no non-mythic language, not even the direct language of transitive action. This leaves us with only one option: to deconstruct the mythic foundations of language itself (through ontological critique), not in order to propose a non-mythic language, but to free us in demythified connectivity. This is the task of poetizing.

14. For 'vague abyss' see Hölderlin's poem 'Hyperion's Song of Fate' (Hölderlin 1998, p. 27).

15. For Benjamin's links with *Frühromantik* see Löwy 1985.

16. Here we can see a connection with Schelling's idea of affirmative negation in the beginning as proposed in *The Ages of the World*. For Schelling, beginnings withdraw (negate) being but then need to overcome this negation in order to be (Schelling 2000, pp. 16–17). A beginning must therefore be a de-instituting of its being in order to overcome itself and become anew 'otherwise', but by still retaining its essential being, its connection to the absolute and hence to mythic oneness. This means that for Schelling we live in the beginnings of a demythified world that is in want of new myths.

17. Benjamin's deconstruction of Hölderlin's poem is part of his broader project to allegorize the symbolic imperative of German Romantic and Idealist poetics. As 'other-speaking', allegories are movements of figuration operating in the ruins of subjective experience opened to absolute possibility. Here we can think in terms of Benjamin's theory of allegory, found mainly in *The Origin of German Tragic Drama* (Benjamin 1998), but spread more generally throughout his writings. These issues are taken up more fully in the following chapter.

18. Lifedeath is the condition of nature proposed in the nature philosophies of German Romantics and Idealists, described by David Krell as 'the fatal imbrication in nature of birthing and dying' (Krell 1998, p. 2). For instance, in his Freedom essay, Schelling writes of 'the sadness [mourning] that clings to all finite life … [and] the veil of dejection that is spread over all nature, the deep indestructible melancholy of all life' (Schelling 2006, pp. 62–63). The term 'life death' is used by Jacques Derrida in his deconstruction of the logic of the 'beyond' in Freud's *Beyond the Pleasure Principle* in his book *The Postcard: from Socrates to Freud and Beyond* (Derrida 1987, p. 259).

19. For Heidegger, death as an absolute limit is appropriated by *Dasein* in the necessity of 'having to be': 'Death is a possibility-of-Being which Dasein itself has to take over in every case' (Heidegger 1962, p. 294).

20. The issue here can be illuminated through Derrida's reading of Levinas's philosophy in his essay 'Violence and Metaphysics' (Derrida 1978, pp. 79–153). Derrida counters Levinas's criticisms of Heidegger's ontology (Levinas 1969, p. 45 ff.) by revealing a residual ontological

dimension to Levinas's own ethics that operates in terms of the authority of the other and a certain 'messianic eschatology' (Derrida 1978, p. 83). Defending primary ontology against Levinas's attacks on it, Derrida writes: 'Not only is the thought of Being not ethical violence [as Levinas claims], but it seems that no ethics – in Levinas's sense – can be opened without it. Thought – or at least the pre-comprehension of Being – *conditions* (in its own fashion, which excludes every ontic conditionality: principles causes, premises etc.) the *recognition* of the existent (for example, someone, existent *as* other, *as* self, etc.). It conditions the *respect* for the other *as what it is*: other' (pp. 137–38). That is, Derrida shows that Levinas's ethics is itself dependent on an ontological dimension that it disavows. The issue then, is not one of overcoming ontology – the 'question of being' – with an equally originary ethics as does Levinas, but of proposing an ontology that is sufficiently attentive to the issue of being-with, such that it does not retreat into an individuation incapable of 'respect for the other *as what it is*: other'. Such an ontology will then be enabling for an ethics to live up to the requirement that the other be allowed to 'be itself'. Celan's poetry leads in this direction.

21. Eskin's position becomes clear in the following quote, which suggests that Celan's objection to Heidegger is his ontologizing of language: 'Heidegger's impersonal, ontologized language, Celan writes, is "a language, not for you and not for me"' (Eskin 2000, p. 151). But the quoted words 'not for you and not for me' are uttered by a voice in Celan's prose essay 'Conversation in the Mountain', and need to be read more carefully in terms of the context of the essay's argument. As I demonstrate in this chapter, the argument of 'Conversation in the Mountain' can be read as affirming the ontological originariness of language, as the 'speaking' or voice of nature. By reading the speech here as simply representing Celan's own view on ontological language, Eskin overlooks the very poetizing of the writing in the essay itself, which requires that we read the dialogue as already inhabited by a third voice speaking through it.

22. Derrida's use of the term 'the third' here has overtones of Levinas's 'third' (*illeity*) as the 'whole enormity, the whole inordinateness, the whole infinity of the absolutely Other, which eludes treatment by ontology' (Levinas 1996, p. 61). I take Derrida's use of this term to refer to a more limiting sense of the third as otherness as an 'enabling' possibility, sensed 'right at' the openness enacted in the singular poetic event. For further discussion of the third, see Chapter 4, note 7.

23. In fact, Celan's poems are dialogues in which the 'you' is absent; that is, they are dialogues in which one of the voices speaks to an absent other, not as if the other were present, but in the structured impossibility of the other's presence. They are 'the communication of the incommunicable singularity/community' (Nancy 1991, p. 76). In his 'Meridian' speech Celan says that 'the poem intends another, needs this other, needs an opposite. It goes toward it, bespeaks it'. But then, a little later: 'Whenever we speak with things in this way we also dwell on the question of their where-from and where-to, an "open" question "without resolution", a question which points towards open, empty free spaces – we have ventured far out. The poem also searches for this place' (Celan 2005, pp. 164–65).

24. The future anterior tense is also important in Schelling's ideas of retroactive freedom (see Chapter 5, and Shaw (2010, p. 143).

25. The aorist tense concerns an ontological relation to time and death. In his discussion of the peculiar temporality of looking at photographs of people who have since died, Roland

Barthes suggests that this ontological dimension is 'an anterior future of which death is the stake' (Barthes 1993, p. 96). See chapter 10, note 28.

26. For *énoncé* and *énonciation* see Benveniste (1971).

27. Quoted from Bate (2000, translation by Michael Hamburger, pp. 269–70), also published in Lacoue-Labarthe (1999, pp. 5–6). Another translation consulted is by Pierre Joris (Celan 2005, pp. 122–23).

28. Felstiner says that the line 'looks back to the 1930s' (Felstiner 1995, p. 246), locating the question in terms of its historical context and the autobiographical details of Celan's life. In his study of Celan's poetry, Lacaou-Labarthe provides no detailed analysis of the poem's structure, but makes general comments about the language in relation to a poetic speaking after Auschwitz. With reference to the lines written in Heidegger's book, he interprets the poem as saying that Celan 'no longer knows who signed before him' (Lacaou-Labarthe 1999, p. 38). Bate also presumes that the voice asking the question belongs unproblematically to Celan, although he conjectures 'the name written in the book would have been "Celan", not his inherited surname "Ancel"' (Bate 2000, p. 271).

29. I am indebted to Colin Shingleton for advice regarding the syntax of this translation in relation to the original in German.

30. Felstiner notes that the words (translated into English) were 'Into the hut-book, looking at the well-star, with a hope for a coming word in the heart. On 25 July 1967 Paul Celan' (Felstiner 1995, p. 244).

31. See Heidegger (1962, pp. 67–68).

32. This possibility is reinforced by some factual information. According to Felstiner, the poem originally had another line inserted so that it read:

> for a thinker's
> (un-
> delayed coming)
> word
> in the heart.

The 'un-delayed coming', a clear reference to Celan's 'hope' for an apology from Heidegger, was taken out of the poem later by Celan when the apology was not offered (Felstiner 1995, p. 247). The hyphenating and splitting of the word 'undelayed' into separate lines anticipates the non-response and foretells the event. The poem's initial hope of reparation – whose non-delivery is foreshadowed by the discontinuous syntax – is fully suspended in a redrafting that nevertheless continues to retain its openness and hope.

33. Eskin discusses the possible meanings of this altogether or 'wholly Other', citing various sources including Buber's rejection of the onto-theological notion of the divine, and proposes a linguistic basis where 'the wholly Other is always already diachronically engaged, that, hence, a (mystical) union with the wholly Other is impossible [...]. Insofar as it is linguistically-diachronically engaged, further-more, the wholly Other reveals itself as a dialogic sense-position, as an absolutely other interlocutor rather than a putatively supreme ontological entity' (Eskin 2000, p. 155, note 104). My view is that the wholly

other is an absolute limit in speaking, a 'sense-position', as Eskin suggests, but one defined not simply by potential dialogue with others, but by its absolute status; by its possibilities as such.

34. Felstiner reads the speaking in 'Conversation in the Mountains' as a conversation between the two Jewish cousins without a third voice speaking through it (Felstiner 1995, pp. 139–45). His reading is concerned with what the conversation tells us about certain facts of Jewish culture and language.

35. In *Brod Und Wein* (*Bread and Wine*) Hölderlin writes of the blindness of humans to nature's gifts: 'blind he remains, unaware./First he must suffer; but now he names his most treasured possession,/Now for it words like flowers leaping alive he must find' (Hölderlin 1998, p. 155).

36. The essay borrows heavily from Büchner's novella *Lenz*, in which a young man, Lenz, goes on a journey to the mountains where he experiences a sense of overwhelming oneness with nature that sends him mad. Lenz is trapped in a lifedeath existence that he must live yet cannot endure (Büchner 1993).

37. Stones feature elsewhere in Celan's poems. 'Radix, Matrix' opens with the following lines: 'Like one speaks to the stone, like/ you,/to me from the abyss' (Celan 2005, p. 83). Speaking to the stone is like speaking to you from the abyss. The dense muteness of the stone signifies the abyss of the earth that one speaks to as the 'nothing of night', echoing Schelling's concept of the nature as indifferent *Unground*, which absorbs the 'you' and the 'me' into it.

38. For the distinction between speaking (saying) and talking, see Chapter 2.

9. Benjamin: Collapsing Nature

1. The collapse in Being can be likened to Schelling's postulate of a recapitulating 'original heterogeneity' (Schelling 2004, p. 10). In *Being and Time* Heidegger considers Being in terms of 'falling': 'falling as [...] an absorption in Being-with-one-another' (Heidegger 1962, pp. 219–220). However, falling is not a collapse in Being itself, but a condition of *Dasein* in its wanting to be. In *The End of Philosophy*, Heidegger writes of a 'collapse of the world characterized by metaphysics' (Heidegger 1973, p. 86), but not a collapse in Being. For Heidegger, Being always retains the sense of enduring in open possibility.

2. The essay from which this passage is drawn is the second version of 'The Work of Art in the Age of Its Reproducibility'.

3. Invoking a similar scene John Sallis writes: 'the imaginative engagement by which vision actively, freely, playfully, traces the outline of the mountain can be enlivened by a certain aesthetic sensitivity to the varying curvature of the line [...]. Even as your vision enfolds the figure taken up in imagination, you will also no doubt be drawn to the scene in such a way that *the distance across which you would have observed it gives way to an affective proximity*' (Sallis 2008, p. 2, emphasis added). The experience described is one of 'transfiguring of sense' (p. 4) or transitivity. Sallis points out that such experience 'requires that one forgo operations of signification' (p. 2).

4. The 'auratic mode of existence is never entirely severed from its ritual function' (Benjamin 2002, p. 105). Through ritual, aura fuses human being and nature into myth.

5. In Lecture 1 of the Freiberg lectures, Heidegger proposes the impending [*Gegen-wart*] as 'what waits toward us [*uns entgegenwartet*], waits for whether and how we expose ourselves to it, or contrarily, close ourselves off from it' (Heidegger 2012, p. 79).

6. Compare this 'letting go' of the seer into the seeing with Heidegger's thrownness of *Dasein* into the world (Heidegger 1962, p. 174). Although *Dasein* is always thrown and 'falling' into the world of the indifferent 'they' (p. 223), there is a sense that it is already across it in 'anticipatory disclosure' (p. 307). *Dasein* casts a net in order to retrieve itself from being thrown in the 'they'. *Dasein* reaches into the world in order to extract itself out of it.

7. Jean-Luc Nancy's idea of a subjectless politics is apposite here. A subjectless politics 'define[s] a space without return to the identical [...] [and is] [...] not without authority or decision-making power – but without a self that reaps, in the end, the benefits of its action' (Nancy 2007, p. 106). For speaking in a subjectless voice see Chapters 2 and 8.

8. Bate's argument is the obverse of Marx's analysis of the restoration of the human to natural 'free being'. For Marx the return to nature comes through a dialectical *Aufhebung* of capitalism into a post-capitalist worker utopia, whereas for Bate, the return is a restitution to a state of nature *before* the fall into capital.

9. The motif of the lightning flash as originary appearing of the cosmos (the unconditioned) begins with Fragment 64 of Heraclites: 'the thunderbolt steers all things' (Barnes 2001, p. 52). Schelling employs the lightning motif in *The Ages of the World*: 'one can think that everything occurred just as if in a lightning flash' (Schelling 2000, p. 77). Benjamin's theory of the dialectical image of time experienced as an auratic 'flash' in V of 'On the Concept of History' (Benjamin 2003, p. 390) resonates with these ideas, as well as with the concept of *Erscheinung* in German Romanticism and Idealism (see Chapter 6).

10. First and second technologies are equivalent to the mythic and allegorical phases of Schelling's ages of the world. First technology fuses human being in a totalized first nature, while second technology undoes first nature through dialectical 'play'.

11. Play is an important concept in German Classicism and Romanticism. For Schiller, the 'play impulse' was a significant element in *Bildung*, or the education of the human being through aesthetic attunement with nature (Schiller 2004, p. 74). See Chapter 2, note 5.

12. This other nature echoes Heidegger's identification of another nature already at work in systems of production, releasing things from their equipmental mode of being (see Chapter 7).

13. Jonathan Beller argues that in the field of contemporary cinema, 'imaginal functions are today imbricated in perception itself' (Beller 2006, p. 1) and 'Perception is increasingly bound to production' (p. 3). That is, human 'nature' – the perception-affect regime of the human senses – is increasingly becoming interconnected to the apparatus of cinema itself, leading to an illusion of natural plenitude played out in the 'body' of the cinematic audience.

14. See Gasché (1986) for an 'open matrix' (p. 147) of 'structurally nontotalizable arrangements of heterogeneous elements' (p. 100).

15. In IX of the 'On the Concept of History', Benjamin describes history in terms of the 'Angelus Novus' looking backward while being swept forward by the storm of progress, looking down on the wreckage of the past piling up before him that he is powerless to restore (Benjamin 2003, p. 392).

16. Schelling also suggests that the symbol can be reversed by allegory, but warns that such reversals are a denial of the necessity of the symbolic connectedness to 'absolute indifference' as the '*first element*' (Schelling 1989, pp. 47–48).

17. In *Mimesis: The Representation of Reality in Western Literature*, Erich Auerbach notes that 'the basic impulse of the Homeric style [is to] represent phenomena in a fully externalized form, visible and palpable in all their parts, and completely fixed in their spatial and temporal relations' (Auerbach 2003, p. 6). The audience members hear the events unfold as a perpetually present foreground, without 'background' mediation through a psychologized character or narrator: 'the Homeric style knows only a foreground, only a uniformly illuminated, uniformly objective present' (p. 7).

18. This allegorical way of seeing is further developed in Malick's more recent film *The Tree of Life* (2011) that presents a collapse in the way of seeing of the film itself. This collapsed way of seeing opens out possibilities of otherness in and through the event depicted (the life of a family in mid-twentieth-century-America affected by the death of a son), triggering meditations on human existence answered by the film's *poietic* revelations of nature (see Mules 2013).

19. For discussion of the 'indifference' of nature in *The Thin Red Line*, see Crichtley (2002), and Sinnerbrink (2006). Sinnerbrink reads the film in terms of Heideggerian revelation of Being, making a case for film as 'cinematic *poiesis*'.

20. For instance, the film depicts scenes of an idyllic life that the soldiers might have with the local villagers as symbolic of a unified human-nature relation (the film begins with two of the soldiers absconding to spend time with them), but this life is denied as the battle commences and the soldiers' interaction taints the villagers' lives with conflict and hostility (one of the absconding soldiers returns later to find the villagers hostile to each other and suspicious of him). In another set of images, another of the soldiers flashes back to highly romanticized scenes with his unfaithful wife. Any 'symbolic' reading of the film will need to account for the poetizing movement – the film's stance with respect to what it says – simultaneously offering and withdrawing symbolic transcendence.

21. Lorraine Connelly-Northey's work was exhibited at the Queensland Art Gallery in 2006 as part of the Xstrata Coal Emerging Indigenous Art Awards. I became acquainted with her work there, and had a lengthy conversation with her about her method of manipulating found material, and the places where she found the material.

22. See Woods (2006, p. 10) for Connelly-Northey's wire bowls as koolimans – traditional bowls in Australian Aboriginal culture. The artist's spelling (kooliman) varies from conventional spelling (coolamon).

23. In Australian Aboriginal culture, country is the original relation with the land: a 'being-with' nature lived out as care for the earth that provides connectedness to all things. See Rose (1996, p. 7); Mules 2008.

24. See Mitchell (2010, pp. 58–61), for a discussion of the bas-relief as support.

10. Nancy: Renaturing and Bio Art

1. See Deleuze and Guattari (1983, p. 2).
2. The UN Convention on Biodiversity defines biotechnology as 'any technological application that uses biological systems, living organisms, or derivatives thereof, to make or modify products or processes for specific use' (*United Nations Convention on Biological Diversity* 1993) (http://www.cbd.int/convention/articles/default.shtml?a=cbd-02). Biotechnological engineering is the employment of engineering (i.e. mechanistic) principles to the production of (organic) bio life.
3. Nancy describes this withdrawal as an 'exhaustion' (Nancy 2007, p. 82). Elsewhere Nancy refers to this withdrawal in terms of sense: 'the world *no longer has* a sense, but it *is* sense' (Nancy 1997, p. 8). The world no longer draws from another world (i.e. a transcendent order of the divine) in order to mean anything; rather in its 'exhaustion' of meaning, it becomes its own sense; it produces its own meaning.
4. Catts and Zurr's artwork was the central focus for a symposium entitled 'The Art and Science of Synthetic Biology: Critical and Creative Perspectives on "New Life"', funded by a University of Queensland-University of Western Australia Bilateral Research Collaboration and presented by the Centre for the History of European Discourses, University of Queensland, Brisbane, Thursday 22 November 2012. The chapter has been enriched by discussions with Catts as well as other participants at the symposium, including Elizabeth Stephens and Greg Hainge.
5. This is, of course, not to underestimate the considerable differences between Schelling's and Foucault's philosophical positions. Foucault's genealogical-archaeological reading of the 'becoming' of western rationality owes a major debt to Nietzsche's writings on historical enactment as *Ursprung* – the origin as a violent irruption of difference within the order of the same (Foucault 1977). But, as I have demonstrated in this present work, Schelling's writings on *Ursprung* (see Chapter 4) prefigure Nietzsche's and in some respects go beyond Nietzsche's subjectification of the will to power, toward a theory of releasement, much closer to Foucault's own understanding of power as a productive principle working within and against disciplinary systems and institutions.
6. See also Chapter 1, section entitled 'Myth'.
7. Ecotechnology describes the elision of nature by the allegiance between technology and the economy – the presentation of economic and technological relations and processes as if they were naturally ordered and produced. The prefix 'eco' is derived from the Greek *oikos*, meaning home or dwelling place. An 'eco'-technology is something that, amongst other things, tells us that we are at home (that we dwell) in economic-technological-natural interconnectivity.
8. For instance the localized technique of propagating cultivar plants (e.g. local varieties of indigenous trees and bushes) through grafting, requiring a careful splicing and binding of individual plants by a skilled person with precise knowledge of local conditions. Grafting involves a manual technique requiring the careful handling of seeds and cuttings at odds with the abstract processes of industrial production. Larger scale grafting and propagating of seeds by NGOs based on environmentalist principles occurs in many places throughout the

world, for instance by the Organization for the Rehabilitation of the Environment (ORE) in Haiti enabling local farmers to make a living while respecting and repairing the environment severely damaged by natural disasters and deforestation (http://www.oreworld.org/index. htm). The Wollami Pine Recovery Plan put in place by the New South Wales Government aims to propagate the recently discovered Wollemi pine tree to save it from extinction (NSW Government 1987). The plan requires harvesting of seedlings from a unique local site with care for the environment (9.9).

9. See Shiva (2012). The multinational company Monsanto has a monopolistic grip on the production and distribution of genetically modified seeds throughout the world, indebting farmers and governments alike to its technological formats and commercial imperatives.

10. The Indian artist Sharmila Samant has produced art installations that bear witness to these disappearing worlds in rural India. For instance the installation entitled 'Against the Grain' is composed of hundreds of handcrafted cobras clustered together on sticks. The cobras are made of grain and bamboo, and were crafted in collaboration with farm workers whose livelihoods have been threatened by the use of genetically modified rice grain. See interview with the artist at http://www.au.timeout.com/sydney/art/features/3006/sharmila-samant-against-the-grain. See also Bandari (2012).

11. A person is not the same as a subject. In his reading of Patočka's *Heretical Essays in the Philosophy of History*, Derrida writes 'the individualism of technological civilization relies precisely on a misunderstanding of the unique self. It is an individualism relating to a *role* and not a *person*' (Derrida 1995, p. 36). For Patočka, in Derrida's reading, the person cannot be reduced to a role, but always remains a 'mystery' (p. 37), or, in other words, a reserve that resists subjectification and the 'force' of objectification.

12. For dignity as standing on one's feet see Chapter 1, p. 24 and note 15.

13. The 'ear mouse' was made by grafting living tissue onto the back of a mouse (see Kac 2007, p. 7).

14. A distinction needs to be made between tissue and genetic engineering. Tissue engineering involves cellular intervention of living tissue, whereas genetic engineering involves manipulation of the 'code' of living forms. Indeed, as Catts and Zurr argue, 'biological art that deals with other nongenetic forms of manipulation [eg. tissue engineering and stem cell research] can be used as a way to counterbalance the view of life as determined solely by the DNA code. This is done by presenting the complexity of life and its interdependent relations with the environment; the development of living or semi-living entities is affected and effecting its surrounding rather than a "coded programme" imposed on the environment' (Catts & Zurr 2008, p. 129). Catts and Zurr's own artworks involve tissue engineering and stem cell research to maintain contact with 'visceral sentient life' (p. 129) and counter the reduction of bio life to abstract forms through genetic engineering.

15. See also Catts & Zurr (2012) for further discussion of their art project as a critique of genetic engineering in relation to nature, the environment and the take-over of biology by engineering imperatives.

16. For mimicry as play see Gregory Bateson's essay 'A Theory of Play and Fantasy' in *Steps to an Ecology of Mind* (Bateson 1972, pp. 177–93). Catts and Zurr understand their artwork in

terms of irony as 'an artistic and philosophical response to technological determinism' (Catts & Zurr 2008, p. 131). Ironic play makes their semi-living creations speak otherwise to the technology that 'determines' or limits them in what they are, as products of biotechnological engineering.

17. To state a norm is to employ another norm by which the statement gains its validity. Thus all stated norms imply an unstated norm to support them. An unstated norm is an empty signifier (see Chapter 2) held forth to gather an audience in common meaning and identity. Unstated norms are not universal or essential, but diacritically related to the gathering. A gathering is not possible without a norm, but once the norm is stated, the gathering is threatened with dispute, dispersal and differentiation. The issue is not whether the unstated norm is 'good' or 'bad' but that it be there in order that a gathering might take place. For instance the norm that 'one should obey the king' may imply an unstated norm that 'kings rule by divine right'. If the unstated norm were to be stated, then this too would invoke a further unstated norm such as 'all societies should be ruled by kings' and hence promote dissent within the community with the arrival of alternative views and meanings. The unstated norm rules out the 'unthinkable' in the stated norm – for instance that a society might be ruled not by kings but by their own citizens. Unstated norms require that the 'subject' of language remain as an unconscious achievement always in excess of an 'I' or self-conscious ego (see Lacan 1996, p. 421).

18. The artists claim that their artwork also presents the audience with a solution to some of the ethical problems of exploiting living animals as a food source. Their artwork duplicates the kind of experimental work in synthetic food production undertaken by biotechnological engineering. If such synthetic food production were to take place on a mass production scale, then 'the killing and suffering of animals destined for food consumption will be reduced. Furthermore, ecological and economical problems associated with the food industry can be reduced dramatically. However, by making our food a new class of object/being – a semi-living – we risk making the semi-living the new class for exploitation' (Catts & Zurr 2007, p. 243). Thus their project is not entirely critical of the burgeoning industry of synthetic food production, but involves a collaboration with it. However, the collaboration stops short of outright duplication, and is founded on an ethics of care for the singularity of their own creation to ensure any 'exploitation' of the cells and living tissue used in the artwork does not reduplicate the mass consumption practices of the food industry and the consumers of its products, nor the objectifying practices of the science upon which it is based.

19. The ear mouse could thus be seen as a chimera: a hybrid creature that warns of the dangers of 'messing' with nature (for chimera see Andrieu 2007).

20. Having stated the unstated norm, I have, of course, exposed it to another unstated norm, in a potential cascade of norms. For a discussion of the problem of cascading norms see Glabb and Engelkamp (2011).

21. Alba is the name of a rabbit genetically modified with the GFP gene found in jelly fish so that it glows green when placed under a blue light. Alba is (was) part of a living artwork 'GFP Bunny' (see Kac 2007, pp. 165–66).

22. For the problem of force in worker-capital relations see Ryan 1984, p. 86 (see also Chapter 5, note 14). A forced thing becomes subject to the power of the ecotechnology.

23. Her collaborative artwork with Catts involves an ethically motivated 'killing ritual' where audiences are invited to touch their semi-living creations, thereby infecting them with fungi and bacteria that inevitably kills them (Catts & Zurr 2007, p. 239). A meditation on the paradox of touch as an impossible contact can be found throughout Jean-Luc Nancy's work. See for instance the essay 'Corpus' (Nancy 1993, pp. 189–207).

24. Thus Kac's bio art, despite its currency in new life technologies, belongs to the modern paradigm of autonomous art.

25. Kac argues that his art prompts society to 'ask how it will prepare itself to welcome new citizens who will be, themselves, clones and transgenics' (in Osthoff 2009, p. 5), as if these new citizens were an addition to the existing citizenry with similar rights and capacities. However, it is more likely that these new 'subjects' of the biotechnological age will not be citizens but slaves in online and offline master/slave relations, constituting a compliant non-human proletariat obedient to management protocols. These relations will be entirely coordinated by the guiding imperatives of the algorithm, serving the interests of the owners of the software and patents by which the human subjects who use them gain their identity. There will be no simple welcoming here, but the renewed struggle for a just work-life relation underway since industrialization, extended to include the proletarianized work of non-human life.

26. The claim for the autonomy of art can be understood in terms of a *poietic* 'moment' in the becoming of nature that enables something to 'be'. This moment is inhabitable by humans as their free being, but at a cost, as it occurs in-between two threats: the indifference of nature's becoming, and the claims of the nature-machine that nature has now become.

27. The same cannot be said of Catts and Zurr's artworks, which maintain a resolutely ironized stance within and against the technology they inhabit. Their work is not demiurgic and remythifying, but deconstructive and demythifying.

28. Barthes's example is a photograph of a condemned man, Lewis Payne, found guilty of an attempted assassination of the US Secretary of State in 1865. The pathos of this photograph is triggered by a doubled temporality in which we feel ourselves to be in the presence of a living person, but one whose life has been violently cut short by state execution. Barthes's own caption to this photograph reads: 'he is dead and he is going to die' (Barthes 1993, p. 95) suggesting that photographic images of this kind involve a peculiar aoristic grammar, in which the continuity of the past into the present is made possible by its reverse: the discontinuity of the past and the present through the intervention of death. Barthes sees this in terms of 'an anterior future of which death is the stake' (p. 96). The past and the present are united, but only under condition that what the spectator risks is death itself, as an inevitability that nevertheless might be overcome in the play of life and death that the photograph invokes. See also Chapter 8, note 25.

29. Piccinini's creatures are 'abjects'. Julia Kristeva defines the abject as follows: 'the abject is not an ob-ject facing me, which I name or imagine. Nor is it an ob-jest, an otherness ceaselessly fleeing in a systematic quest of desire. What is abject is not my correlative, which, providing me with someone or something else as support, would allow me to be more or less detached and autonomous. The abject has only one quality of the object – that of being opposed to the *I*. If the object, however, through its opposition, settles me within the fragile texture

of a desire for meaning, which, as a matter of fact, makes me ceaselessly and infinitely homologous to it, what is *abject*, on the contrary, the jettisoned object, is radically excluded and draws me toward the place where meaning collapses' (Kristeva 1982, pp. 1–2.). My analysis of Piccini's artwork *Nectar* confirms this abject state of the creature – as a thing rejected for its abhorrence yet 'fascinates desire' (p. 1), drawing the viewer toward 'the place where meaning collapses'. However in many of Piccinini's other works, where her creatures take on a more familiar humanoid form, they cross the threshold of abjection to become anthropocentric projections of human desire for self-identity in the other.

30. *Nectar* 2012: Silicone, fibreglass, human hair, refrigerator, Edition of 6, displayed at Heidi Gallery, Melbourne. Viewed 13 October 2012. In conversation with the artist, she revealed to me that it was important that the fridge be old and well worn. The fridge was by no means the latest model and displayed signs of wear and rust. My use of the term 'blob' to describe the organic figure featured in this work is derived from Catts and Zurr's use of this term to describe semi-living organisms produced in science laboratories (Catts & Zurr 2007, p. 232).

31. Heidegger's concept of ruinance (*Ruinanz*) found in his early work (*Phenomenological Interpretations of Aristotle*) indicates a movement in the collapsed nothingness of an essential lack that life *is* in its factical affirmation of its own possibility (see Raffoul 2008, pp. 77–81). Technological ruinance is technological life discovering that it can exist otherwise in the ruins of technological obsolescence.

32. See Jean-Luc Nancy, 'Shattered Love' for love as exposed being: 'to joy is not to be satisfied – it is to be filled, overflowed' (Nancy 1991, p. 106).

Conclusion: Towards Ecopoetics

1. For Foucault, power relations are always enacted as part of a technical productivity, as techniques of power (Foucault 1980, pp. 141–42).

2. Heidegger argues that the age of the world picture is not a picture of the world, but 'the world conceived and grasped as picture' (Heidegger, 1977, p. 129). A world picture is the world picturing itself through decisions about 'representedness' (p. 130).

Index